ARTS OF DYING

ARTS OF DYING

Literature and Finitude in Medieval England

D. VANCE SMITH

THE UNIVERSITY OF CHICAGO PRESS

CHICAGO AND LONDON

The University of Chicago Press, Chicago 60637
The University of Chicago Press, Ltd., London
© 2020 by The University of Chicago
Published 2020

29 28 27 26 25 24 23 22 21 20   1 2 3 4 5

ISBN-13: 978-0-226-64085-3 (cloth)
ISBN-13: 978-0-226-64099-0 (paper)
ISBN-13: 978-0-226-64104-1 (e-book)
DOI: https://doi.org/10.7208/chicago/9780226641041.001.0001

The University of Chicago Press gratefully acknowledges the generous support of Princeton University toward the publication of this book.

Library of Congress Cataloging-in-Publication Data

Names: Smith, D. Vance, 1963– author.
Title: Arts of dying : literature and finitude in medieval England / D. Vance Smith.
Description: Chicago : University of Chicago Press, 2020. | Includes index.
Identifiers: LCCN 2019024354 | ISBN 9780226640853 (cloth) |
    ISBN 9780226640990 (paperback) | ISBN 9780226641041 (ebook)
Subjects: LCSH: English literature—Middle English, 1100–1500—History and
    criticism. | Death in literature.
Classification: LCC PR275.D43 S65 2019 | DDC 820.9/3548—dc23
LC record available at https://lccn.loc.gov/2019024354

It took me a long time to realize that the intense despair and the intervals of exhilaration and clarity that both propelled me through this project and kept me from finishing it were not caused by these texts. I didn't realize that I wouldn't master these moods by mastering the problems in these texts. It's partly because of them that I discovered that I was suffering from bipolar disorder, a condition that these texts certainly didn't alleviate. They almost brought me to an end several times. Fortune, hap, grace may have kept me alive; but the efficient cause was finding a smart therapist and a good psychiatrist (in my case, Dr. Marilyn Lyga and Dr. David Nathan, respectively). If I were to rewrite *La roman de la rose*, Reason would be Marilyn Lyga helping the dreamer see that everything isn't actually about despair ("met l'amor en nonchaloir, / Qui te fait vivre et non valoir"). I dedicate this book to her for helping me through my struggle, and to all mental health workers (including my wonderful and patient wife, Lucia), who work daily simply to keep people alive.

A very eminent colleague of mine here at Princeton committed suicide this spring, six years and one day after I first tried to. If work and reputation could save you, he might still be alive. I'm writing all of this because I hope that it will make it easier for other scholars to write things like this, or—which is much more important—to let your concern for your life outweigh your concern for your work and career. Literary critics, historians, and philosophers are trained to think about the self; but we aren't necessarily capable of thinking about our own selves very well. As Scripture says in *Piers Plowman*, "multi multa sciunt et seipsos nesciunt." If you are in this situation, find someone who can help you know yourself: a professional therapist. Any possible stigma in seeking help, or even in letting your "secret" be known, is vastly preferable to death. If you are someone who has any kind of administrative power, please work as hard as you can to erase this stigma, or even the perception that there is one.

Trenton, New Jersey
National Mental Health Month 2019

what we talk about when we talk about death is really dying. The distinction between these two is important. For the Middle Ages, death has two properties: it is a nullity about which nothing can be said, and yet it is also resolved. There is not much doubt that a soul lives on, nor that death is ultimately a state preferable to life. But dying lies in between life and death, and I want to examine what happens when writers suspend that moment as long as possible in order to think it through without resorting to a priori, exterior information about what happens after death. This exercise allows for speculation where there might otherwise have been dogma. Precisely because one is not following a template, or an order of narration that one already knows, the readiness for death—one's own condition of dying—pursues an intrinsic logic that does not arrive at a conclusion or a demonstration: one does not know one's own ending until one is outside of it altogether.

This condition is one that dying shares with literature. By literature I mean something akin to the formalist notion of a discourse that is self-contained and follows its own, organic or structurally inevitable, set of rules. It, too, is never definitive, never arrives at a unified meaning that can be transposed to some other, more useful, register.[3] But I do not mean that the logic of dying and of literature does not reflect the world: indeed, it is profoundly *about* it—about what it means, what it is for, what it could be. But dying and literature both point toward a messianic moment at which they do not arrive, and which might provide the answer. In that sense, dying and literature are profoundly *not* about the world, or we would already be in a world with answers, and there would be no need for dying or for literature.

The question is, how do we think what we cannot otherwise think? We suspend our knowledge that the condition we impose is impossible—that there be dying without death, literature without the possibility of saying things otherwise—and acknowledge that this is already the logic of dying and literature. The literature of dying is about making sense of the insensible, about what lies beyond experience. This does not mean that the literature of dying is not inflected by funerary and memorial practices; indeed, it can be one of those very practices itself. But I do mean that it is unconstrained by the demand for utility: it does not need to enact or facilitate a particular burial, nor to respond to just one death. And its purposive form is not necessarily directed toward action—certainly not as clearly as "purely" didactic literature is. What are we supposed to do, for instance, after finishing Chaucer's *Book of the Duchess*? I am not insisting on a split between pleasure and instruction, or an absolute one between the literary and the didactic; what I am considering is the potential for some writing about death to turn self-consciously to the resources of linguistic and literary theory to express—or to attempt to express—the aporia of dying. Because its focus is directed elsewhere than the pragmatic and bodily facts of dying and death, this writing imagines, indeed enacts, a work that goes on beyond the moment of death—not the work of eternity, but the work of dying that is still to come and that ultimately will, in the imaginary of the text, never arrive.

The literature of dying in the English Middle Ages occupies itself with three moments: dying as the emergence of the soul, dying as the entrance into a crypt, and dying as the dispersal into an archive. To an extent, each of those moments appears whenever the subject is dying, but more particularly this book will argue that the three moments of dying are fundamental orientations toward death that are culturally influenced and are also moments of history. Each of these moments of dying, that is, appears predominant at different historical periods, and I will suggest some reasons why this is so. This is not a merely historicist reflex. It is part of my contention that dying is also about the world. I do not want to argue, either, that each of these is an historically necessary form, or that particular conditions of social relations are reflected or obscured in the ideology of death and dying.[4] What I want to focus on is the way in which literature itself finds the forms with which it represents death problematic because it lacks a language to describe it. I am not, therefore, writing a history of how people conceptualized death, or the various ways in which it might be represented. My interest is in looking at how literature goes about the problem of describing dying. In recognizing that death presents a problem for the resources of representation that seems intractable, literature both marks its failure and the continuing desire to formulate a language adequate to what no one can fully describe. Literature tries, more simply, to outlive death, to provide some kind of continuity, or an assurance of it, when it most fully marks finitude.

There are many other works that could be added to what I study here, but I have particularly concentrated on some in which the problem of death becomes the problem of a work's finitude. That is, I am looking at moments at which the enigmatic nature of death and the uncertain nature of literature correspond. The problem of how to imagine anything beyond mortal finitude is the same as the problem of how to validate or authenticate that very question. What is it about a certain kind of writing or art that presumes to do what other forms of representation seem to be unable to do? Its exceptionality is twofold: it suggests that it is a way to think of death that we would not otherwise have, and it does this by circling back to the question of what form or mode would be the exception that marks its success. If a certain style were sufficient to move beyond finitude, then that style, or its mark, would be the answer to death (if there is a single question). It would be life itself. But we do not have an infinite language, a discourse for infinitude, and the promise that we can discover one in *this* language is exactly what makes it exceptional—especially to itself. This final gesture of futility is what makes it possible to imagine that we can indeed speak beyond finitude: we recognize more fully the finitude that we wish to leave behind in language.

This is more or less what Theodor Adorno called late style. It is the very impossibility of thinking about being dead that characterizes and fractures late style: it is what one can say about termination while continuing to say it. One of the most interesting readers of Adorno's thinking about the work of the dying artist, Edward Said, died before he finished his last book, published posthumously as *On Late Style*.[5] It is impossible to read it without being aware of how pervasively Said's knowledge of the imminence of his own death structures the book, nor of how aware Said is that this awareness defines his writing as his own late style. "I come finally to the last great problematic," he says near the beginning, meaning we are arriving, on page 6, at the third important topic of a list. But this is also a self-portrayal, a problematic that is chosen "for obvious personal reasons." These reasons apply also to the artists he discusses, who are implicitly aware of the end of their lives and begin to work in a "new idiom." This idiom itself is troublesome, characterized by tensions, irresolutions, and contradictions: the phenomenon of ending is written in a great problematic style.

For Said, as the personal aside suggests, that style intertwines endings and subjectivity. Knowing that the end of the subject is near marks a precise dimension of subjectivity that is produced by its articulation: what makes style late is the incommensurability of the knowledge of the subject's imminent termination and the unresolved, interminable quality of that articulation. This is not the same as reading a work as an expression of the biographical details of death or dying. It suggests, in fact, the refusal of the individual to relinquish subjectivity, to allow dying to become the mere form of a sensible and perfect death. Thus Said describes Beethoven as inhabiting the "late works as a lamenting personality, then [seeming] to leave the work or phrases in it incomplete" (11). The drama of the subject's death is obscured, unfulfilled, by the suspension of the work in which termination is both greater and less than the possibility of ending: irresolution is the effect of an ending that points forward and beyond. For Said, the drama of the subject provides a trace of coherence in late style: it voices lamentation, but it also violates our expectation of what the subject of that lamentation would do. We expect Beethoven's late work to have "serenity

and maturity," qualities that we attribute to it as a condition of our knowledge of Beethoven's biography, but we do not find it. The cost of continuing
to hear a biographical lament in the work, however, is a certain reification
of the work, a delicate stability but a stability nonetheless. Here Said re-
solves a question that for him remains unanswered in Adorno's own work
on Beethoven: what it is, exactly, in the end, that holds the work together.
One of the characteristics of late style would seem to be that it does not
answer this question. Indeed, Said says, "*naming* the unity, or giving it a
specific identity, would then reduce its catastrophic force" (12). Yet this is
more or less what Said does when he describes the features of late style that
pose the problem of unity: irresolution and curtailment are not "ornamental" but in fact "constitutive" of the work itself (12). To specify how the
interruptions and breakages of late style work is to replace at least some of
its catastrophic force with the work of formal constitution, and to continue
to narrate the subject's movement toward death.

Tracking subjectivity's registration of death demands a complex, if not
contradictory, series of acknowledgments. Not the least of these contradictions is that it is subjectivity, not dying or death, that becomes the subject
of this operation. In late style, subjectivity is produced and simultaneously
distanced from us in at least three orders of reference—analogy, encryption,
and (possibly a twofold) negation: it is "*like* a cipher" that communicates
"only through the blank spaces from which it has disengaged itself" (emphasis mine).[6] Yet Adorno is not really interested in outlining an elaborate
epistemological or ontological structure. This whole complex movement
can be reduced to a gesture, and an "irascible" one at that. And it *is* a movement: it continues to take leave and to communicate. It is not the expression
of a death already given, but of the eventuality of death. More succinctly,
late style is not death, but dying itself.

But I would like to expand this formulation. Much of what Adorno says
about late style applies also to his much more general category of art. More
generally, art operates *as* late style, as the movement toward death; in some
sense, art comes to being only in the proximity, and as an effect, of death.
In *Aesthetic Theory* Adorno describes the fragmentariness of late style as
the "breaking through of form by spirit," by which he seems to mean the
supersession of finitude by the infinite (what could be described as the possibility of the duration of a work) and the abandonment of the definition
of the bounds of finitude themselves: late style can never be equivalent
to death itself.[7] Its infinitude comes in part from its perpetual approach to
what it cannot replace, which is nothing less than the threat of universal replacement, the death of the sensuous. This, in short, is what Adorno refers

to as the breaking through of spirit, which, in a telling phrase, he calls the "fatal corrective" of all art.[8] Elsewhere he compares the spirit of a work to a haunting, making more explicit the double sense of *Geist* as both spirit and ghost.[9] The figure of haunting itself suggests a work that is unterminated, lingering, as yet unfulfilled. The belated, the late, quality of a work's spirit is also troubled by its failure to complete its beginning, to have become spirit, to have achieved the death that endorses its existence. Indeed, says Adorno, spirit in an artwork as such does not exist, but is "something in a process of development and formation."[10] It is the account of what never arrives in the work—the end that authorizes both the completion of the work and the final existence of the spirit. Instead, the spirit is continually emerging, not so much in a style that is "late" because of its proximity to death, as in a style that is the process of dying itself.

For the most part, dying in the Middle Ages was not the ultimate expression of the irreplaceability of the individual subject, what is peculiar to one, "one's ownmost," as Heidegger calls it—what no other can take on for you. It was literally scripted, an internalized protocol rather than an artifact of subjectivity. But if it was an internalized protocol, it was internalized not by the dying subject but by those who observed the process. The signs of death, a catalog stretching back as far as Galen and Hippocrates, was originally meant for the use of physicians making a diagnosis and included processes that the patient clearly did not consciously perform, such as the making of urine or milk, or could not observe, such as the uninterrupted sleep of an old man.[11] In moral treatises and sermons, these signs became a formalized trope that symptomatized not the subjective insistence of death, but the methodical disappearance of the life of the patient. This is a technical, indeed medically precise, account of dying. But it ends in death, and a death that is emphatically terminated and complete: "þi body nath bot a clout" because "þi soule is went out."[12] The direct address underscores the fact that the second person has become a null function, a deictic marker for what is no longer there. We do not follow the self into the realm of the spirit, and the possibility of spiritual continuity is explicitly evacuated from the poem's oontology: after the body is "i-loken" in the earth, the "soule al clene is for-ȝeten."[13] The poem's denial of transcendence is so complete that it forecloses even the kind of spirituality that would make it what Adorno would recognize as a work of art. All that remains is to negate it as a work altogether, to undertake whatever will impart the existence of a spirit that the poem does not have. The poem describes a finitude so constrained that all we can do is try to remember our own souls, to cultivate mere dread without the consolatory work of penance. It teaches responsibility without suggesting a possible response, didacticism without a lesson to be put into action. It is, I would argue, a pure expression of didactic structure, the reduction of a set of phenomena to a single point. That this point may disappear from the poem altogether might make it more interesting than a typical didactic poem. But what I want to emphasize is the coincidence of the failure of spirit, the forgetting of the soul, and the treatment of death as a final termination, beyond which nothing can be said.

Didacticism returns us to the world with the knowledge of our finitude sharpened. But it does so at the cost of the soul's entanglement in language, because it fails to remind us that language exists to call us to something that is not there. To be precise: something that is not there yet, because language does not represent just the loss of presence. It represents something beyond the finitude of the mere sign: the very loss of presence that assures us that language is not bound by finitude. This seems to be precisely the consolation that a late-medieval innovation in the English liturgy offered. In many churches the priest would recite the opening of the Gospel of John at the end of the service, after the office of the mass. Even a requiem mass would have ended with the first fourteen verses of John.[14] Neither the formal conclusion of the office nor completely outside of it, the Gospel answers the finality of the office, its song of finitude, with a hymn to the infinitude of language, and its eternal commencement: "In the beginning was the Word. . . ."

PART I

Soul

CHAPTER ONE

Out of Death, Art of Dying

The readiness is all.
—Hamlet

The spirit of Caesar troubled both Brutus and, apparently, Clark Kent's editor: "Great Caesar's ghost!" he used to exclaim. But in the Middle Ages Caesar was robbed of his afterlife. He became the stock example of a conundrum of language and metaphysics: how can you say "Caesar is dead" without attributing being to him—that is, without also saying that he *is*? Some very rigorous logicians argued that even the fact of his death didn't exist, and they sometimes got so worked up that they called anyone who thought otherwise "insane": you could be called insane if you actually said that he was dead. At least, that was what the maverick philosopher Roger Bacon said about his fellow English philosopher Richard Rufus of Cornwall and his "stupid" followers, who claimed that you *could* say that someone was dead at all.[1] For Bacon and many others, Caesar was neither dead, strictly speaking, nor was he simply not alive. He was not Caesar anymore, just as he was no longer a man, "just as a past essence is not an essence."[2] Strictly speaking, you couldn't call the past essence that was Caesar by its name anymore. That essence didn't still exist: its name signified nothing.

The derision of the "Doctor Mirabilis" didn't change the way we talk about the dead, because we still talk about them. There have been some excellent books about the medieval dead in the past twenty years—by Michael Camille, Paul Binski, and Robert Pogue Harrison, among others.[3] This book does not argue that people did not speak about the dead in the Middle Ages, just that careful and thoughtful writers recognized the impossibility at the heart of the attempt. In their works, the problem became a part of what makes these works literary: unlike logic, speculative theology, or pastoral instruction, the literary mode places imagination, style, and form on an equal footing with philosophical questions. It is because the problem of what we mean by death is fundamentally a problem of designation that the distinctive qualities of literature—metaphor, trope, allegory, riddle— allow the problem to be posed and worked through imaginatively.[4] More precisely, this literature treats the formal problems of its own language as a way to represent both the difficulties of speaking of death and the possibility of really saying something. Its worry about its own utility, and about its difference from other discourses, other ways of potentially speaking, makes the forms and the terms it uses also a kind of self-justification. But this self-justification, this close examination and exploration of the particular language it uses, is not merely a self-absorbed concern with distinctions of genre. It is also the way in which this literature justifies itself as a language that can say the unsayable. Literature doesn't have to worry about truth claims, and it knows quite well how to talk about nonexistent things. Death is the greatest of these, and the enigmatic, stylized language of dying is how literature names it.

And so a necessary circularity characterizes representations of death: when it seems to appear, its absence of being calls into question the means by which it is supposedly represented. The possibility of death turns back on the limits of representation. If death represents a threat it is not the annihilation of representation—that is, it cannot threaten not to be represented— but the collapse of its finitude. What people in the Middle Ages feared in representations of death was not total nullity but the profusion of its signs, the absence of the limits that characterize and define the decorum of being: *ratio*, order, categories, and predicates. The problem with representing death is not strictly that we *can't* see it, but that it deranges the senses that give order to the world. It inflicts an excess of intuition, not an absence of it. It overwhelms the finite capacities of the mind, yet it also gives order to the world.

One of the best examples of this paradox is an illustration (fig. 1) that accompanies a poem known as *Death's Warning*, by the fifteenth-century poet John Lydgate.[5] The illustration is partly about saying too much—about the excess of language that results when one attempts to represent something beyond language. Apart from a skeleton that dominates (and violates) the frame, the most striking feature of the illustration is the repetition of the word *death* in the background—nineteen times in all. But death has not yet actually arrived: Death is approaching the dying person while bells are ringing to call everyone in the vicinity to prayer—a call that John Donne refers to in his famous line about the bell tolling.[6]

and hys mourtbe be sput fro
synnefe aufwer.

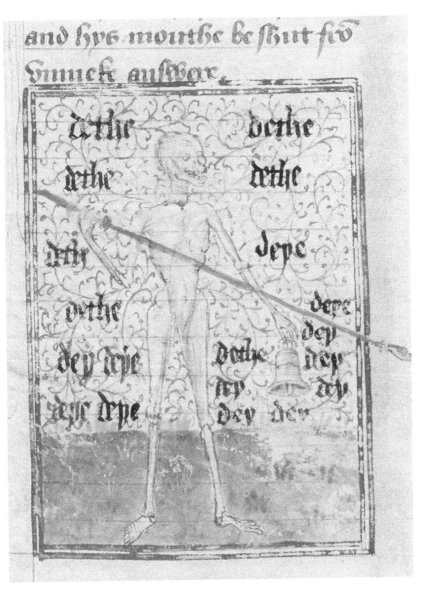

Fig. 1. Death and its terms. Illustration for John Lydgate, *Death's Warning*
(fifteenth century). MS Douce 322, fol. 19v. Photograph: The Bodleian
Libraries, University of Oxford.

Nevertheless, Death is the purported subject of the illustration; its real subject is, to be precise, the term *death*, which is no more the real thing than the term is the sound that the tolling bell makes. Michael Camille sees in this slippage of categories a synesthetic appeal to the senses, an acknowledgment of the universality of death.[7] But I see in it something less definitive: the reduction of what should be a universal fear to a mere orthographic anxiety. The various spellings of the word *death* in the background indicate a worry not over the nature of death as a concept, the "inmost possibility of being," as Heidegger called it, but the word *death*, written with a *th*, with a thorn (þ), with or without a final *e*—precisely the accidentals that many editors are trained to disregard. It's as if death's bell is making sure that the referent is clear, that no one will miss it because it is marked with the wrong rubric. You will still see it whether you think *death* should have a final *e* or not. These idiosyncratic differences of inscription, which are of course noted and observed by a single scribe here, are an orthographic version of the common fifteenth-century trope—death comes for all, rich and poor alike. Even the grade of the script signals this message: it becomes more current, faster, more crowded, and more informal as it moves down the page toward the bottom. By the bottom of the illustration what started as *textualis* is *anglicana formata*, the hand used in most Middle English manuscripts. The prestige of the hand diminishes as it draws away from the Latinate hand to the vernacular: most of the letters written with the native-form thorn are written informally (with one or two exceptions, higher up the page). No writing is immune from death, and—even more chillingly— Death knows all of its inscribed forms. The problem here is not that death is elusive, but that it is too present. Embodied, pictorial, legible, aural, it spills over the usual distinction between the work of a scribe and the work of an illustrator. Yet the scribe is also punctilious about capturing death's orthographical alternatives, which suggests that the response to the derangement that death brings could also involve scrupulous attempts to register the various epiphenomena of its presence. Death is threatening not because it is mysterious and enigmatic, but because it appears in every guise that we can imagine. This response, which I argue appears most frequently in the fifteenth century, is characteristic of what I will describe as the archival response to death, which shapes and motivates much of the literature of the fifteenth century.

As I will argue, one of the distinctive features of post-1348 English literature is its obscuring of what might otherwise be the perfect topic for a didactic sermon for the most didactic of preachers: the unprecedented catastrophe of the Black Death. There is surprisingly little moralizing about its causes outside of chronicles that describe its arrival. Rather than using the Death (as it was called) as a perfectly obvious exemplum of mortality, post-1348 texts tend to treat the Death—and indeed death generally—as an unrepresentable, unfathomable mystery. Death is only obliquely glimpsed *in enigmate*, its challenge to categories of being locked away in language, in the recurring image of the crypt—both a literal and figurative cryptitude.[8] All four poems by the *Pearl* poet, for example, are arguably suffused with the symptomatic language of plague, yet they do not mention the Black Death directly.[9] The catastrophe that death brought through plague and famine in the fourteenth century is most frequently described by its witnesses as something beyond comprehension.[10]

If death in the fourteenth century could have been assigned a category, it would seem to be that of the traumatic experience.[11] But even the meager consolation of knowing how to categorize it was not available, logically speaking, to those devastated by the widespread death around them: death is, at most, a privation, and certainly not a category, because that would predicate being of it. There is not, and there probably cannot be, direct evidence for a connection between the existential terror of death in the fourteenth century and the medieval academic project of trying to understand how to speak of it. Nevertheless, death represented a problem of reference that was one of the most-discussed topics of late Scholasticism, and the paradoxical exposure of the fear of nothingness is the price it paid for the sustained interest in logical and dispassionate ways of talking about the limits of existence.

For the later Middle Ages, the most important development in the technology of describing the seemingly indescribable occurred toward the end of the twelfth century. A precise science of terms, called either the *logica moderna* or terminist logic, based on the wider dissemination and study of Aristotle's so-called *Organon* (made up of his *Prior* and *Posterior Analytics*, the *Categories*, *Topics*, and *On Interpretation*) began to supplant the *logica vetus*, the old logic, and with this new science began to introduce a more complex understanding of the relationship between language and motion—or, put not so differently, between language and the cessation of motion.[12] In my *Book of the Incipit*, I wrote about one way in which treatises on *incipit* and *desinit* shaped the thinking about the relation between inception in physics and in language.[13] In this book I will be writing about the equally complex relationship between physical cessation and language—in a word, the nature of termination in all its senses. I will discuss the discourse of finitude shaped in our times by the work of, above all, Martin Heidegger, Maurice Blanchot, and Gillian Rose, but also by the incomparable work on limitation in late medieval Oxford.

In the first half of the fourteenth century, a group of thinkers at Oxford University using the resources of terminist logic analyzed a vast array of phenomena, from theological grace to fire to modal auxiliaries, in terms of the Aristotelian physics of motion. This group, which included such important thinkers as Thomas Bradwardine, Walter Burley, William Heytesbury, Richard Swineshead, and Richard Kilvington, was distinguished by its close ties. Most of them were both members of Merton College, Oxford, and of the household of the great humanist Richard de Bury, the author of *Philobiblon*. Some of them, like Thomas Bradwardine, who was the archbishop of Canterbury for a year before he died of the Black Death, became influential well beyond the walls of the university. The ubiquity of their work in terminist logic, and its wide applicability, meant that the framing of questions and the positing of solutions in terminist logic influenced the representation of even the most private, grave, and earthly subjects as the moralized circles of life in psalters.

In the psalter made for Robert de Lisle around 1308, for example, surprising citations of this Scholastic tradition occur. The early fourteenth-century de Lisle Psalter uses a wheel (fig. 2) with roundels to depicts the different stages of life, from infancy to youth to old age to decrepitude.[14] The figures in each roundel draw upon conventional representations, although the iconographic citations are unusually diverse and wide-ranging, and the mottos in each were probably composed specifically for this psalter. The legend that appears in the roundel at four o'clock, in which the person is "given over to infirmity," says merely, "I begin not to be" (*incipio deesse*)—a seemingly straightforward description of what is in fact happening.

Yet the language of the wheel, and of a Latin poem on the degradation of age that accompanies it, echoes the sophisticated scholarly tradition of analyzing beginnings and endings. This literature ultimately resulted in independent treatises on *incipit* and *desinit*, which concern the question of whether there is an instant in which something no longer exists, or exists for the first time. The distinction between death itself and the movement that leads to it—dying—is clearly important in the poem and illustration, and it ends with that final distinction: the last two stages of life are *moriens* and *mortuus*—dying and dead, respectively. Death is easily recognized by physical and corporeal signs: it is merely "food for worms, a smell in no way pleasing."[15] But the signs of dying are far more abstract and inferential. *Moriens* is not a statement of a condition, but an attempt to define exactly what dying is. More precisely, it is an attempt to define, literally, a term: "*Terminus* est in quo mundum moriendo relinquo." Superficially, this phrase suggests either intractable circularity or infinite regress: the definition of dying is a term that is defined by dying.

Fig. 2. "I begin not to be." The Wheel of the Ten Ages of Man, from the Psalter of
Robert de Lisle (early fourteenth century). MS Arundel 83, fol. 126v. Photograph:
© The British Library Board / Robana / Art Resource, New York.

Lying beneath this apparent tautology is the rigor and complexity of a
long Scholastic tradition beginning with Albertus Magnus. In his commentary on Aristotle's *Physics*, Albertus systematically opposes Aristotle's belief that created motion is eternal by arguing that every motion has a limit
(*terminus*) by which it is defined, and beyond which it no longer exists. He
rejects what he refers to as the sophistic belief that limits mark something
beyond themselves: "in nullo autem quod in mundo est, finis potest esse
suae terminationis."[16] The terminus, for Albertus, must be *in* the world. In
several senses, too, it marks the end of the world: the world is finite, and
the end of life is the end of our world. It is clear that Albertus is talking

about death here, for in the very beginning of his independent treatise *De morte et vita* he defines death as precisely this limit: because "nulla virtus rei generatae movet per tempus infinitum," movement must end, and its ending is death: "hic terminus est mors naturalis."[17] In dying we relinquish the world: that is the terminus.

The extent to which the designation of a final instant of motion remains important well outside the domain of academic physics is demonstrated by Ranulph Higden in his handbook on preaching. Commenting on the biblical verse John 16:28, "relinquo mundum et vado ad patrem" (which underlies the de Lisle poem's expression "mundum . . . relinquo"), he claims that in expounding it three motions are required, and the first is the *terminus ad quo*, which is "relinquo mundum."[18]

At the end of the thirteenth and the beginning of the fourteenth centuries, then, the problem of death was analyzed as the physical problem of dying, and Aristotle's *Libri naturales* inspired much of the thinking about how to represent its difficulties. But in the course of the fourteenth century the problem of death became more overtly a problem not for physics only, but also for the philosophy of language.

I do not mean to suggest that death did not became a problem of language until the fourteenth century—rather, that this was when the problem became most fully a preoccupation of philosophies of language. As far back as Boethius, the question of what to call a dead body raised a kind of aporia. In his *Consolation of Philosophy*, written in the short time he knew he had left before his own death, Boethius confronted the possibility that he would, after death, come to nothing. As Lady Philosophy says in it, once he becomes a cadaver he can no longer be called a man: "you may call a cadaver a dead man, but cannot call it simply a man. . . . For a thing is which maintains its place in nature and acts in accord with its nature. Whatever fails to do this loses the existence which is proper to its nature."[19] In the ostensibly Stoic context of the *Consolation*, this moment could be written off as a moral dismissal of the significance of the body and the individual. Not only will Boethius cease to be a man, but, more precisely, he will cease to be the thing that had being that was Boethius.

This existential quality is essential to the definition of "man" throughout the Middle Ages—that is, a thing that has being. For that reason, Lady Philosophy's proposal of a term that would adequately describe what remains of Boethius after death lacks the very philosophical rigor that the problem usually demands. She appears to resort to *rhetorica*, using a term that evokes repugnance, rather than to *dialectica*, whose analysis would evoke radical uncertainty. The question of what to call a dead person is not really a taxonomic one, whether to use the term corpse, cadaver, or body; it is a referential one, a problem not of classification but of the very adequacy of language. How does a term deal with the radical absence of what it designates? The problem is not that a person becomes something else in death, but that the very thing that constitutes what that person *is*—his or her being—is no longer there. What remains? Aristotle's answer—in effect, nothing—had the effect of making the description of the dead a confrontation with privation in the abstract, and of leaving the problem in the realm of language. As Aristotle says, after death a man's hand is no longer really a hand because it no longer fulfills the work (*ergon*) for which it is intended; and a dead man is a man "in name only."[20]

So how is it that we can continue to talk about, I don't know, Aristotle? Aristotle's own example in *On Interpretation* is telling: he uses the example of Homer, of whom we can continue to say "he is a poet" because we refer not to his existential condition as a man, but to the survival of his work in language. As the historian of the philosophy of language L. M. de Rijk puts it, when we talk about a poet whose works no longer exist, "one says 'He was a poet,' rather than 'He is a poet.' "[21] The only form of survival, then, would seem to be a survival of and in language. Our encounter with the dead suffered its linguistic turn at almost the very beginning of Western philosophy.

The question of how to refer to someone who was dead became, in the later Middle Ages, one of the central problems in theories of reference. If Socrates is dead, then how does a proposition such as "Socrates is the Philosopher" make any sense, since Socrates no longer has the existence proper to his nature? And if all that remains of Socrates is his body, how then can we talk about it, as a thing whose definition is nonbeing? For Scholastic philosophers, these questions struck at the very heart of the assumption that language could say anything about phenomena that were not immediately apprehensible or true at the time we speak of them.

An answer first articulated by Peter Abelard suggests that the problem is only an apparent one: when we talk about the existence of a dead person, we are speaking figuratively, not logically. The corpse, the referent of the sentence "a man is dead," is only similar, or analogous, to a living man.[22] Abelard's objection lasted until at least 1300, when the Parisian grammatical theorist Radulphus Brito used it to save the integrity of modistic theories of signification: the original imposition of the term *man* in the phrase "dead man" appears here only "improperly," as a "similitudinary signification," or as what William Ockham will later call "figurative custom." It does not have any "real" referential or logical meaning.[23] Other attempts to save the

modistic theory of signification in the face of death included the argument
that "dead man" *did* mean something real, because when the term *man* was
first used (as modistic grammarians would say, first imposed), it included
the sense of "corpse" or "cadaver" as one of its potential meanings, a "second signification."[24] But this solution did not account for the transition between life and death; it simply toggled between the two, without being able
to describe what dying was.

As Richard Kilvington, an early member of the Oxford Calculators—
the extraordinary group who argued that everything can be measured and
quantified—argues, death can never be a predicate of the human; it is false
to say that a man "*is* dead" (*est mortuus*), false to say that being can be a
predicate of nonbeing. We can talk only about the duration of dying itself:
homo moritur, homo moriebatur.[25] *Dead* means the privation of life, its
logical opposite, and to apply it to a person—to refer to a "dead man"—says
Aquinas, is as nonsensical as describing an irrational, inanimate body that
is also a rational, animate body.[26] It's not possible to say what we mean
when we use the term *dead*. Indeed, Abelard argued several hundred years
earlier that "simul enim moriens est et homo, sed non simul mortuus et
homo" (*man* and *dying* belong together, but not *man* and *dead*).[27] Death
takes us out of time and beyond language. Only *dying* can be linguistically
analyzed, because it is still a movement toward something, an aspect of the
unfolding of time.

The problem of what to call a body after its death is difficult enough,
but the problem of how to describe that duration of dying was also an old
problem. One of the earliest, and certainly most eloquent, attempts to spell
out why it is so difficult to talk not just about death but about dying is Augustine's, in the thirteenth book of his *City of God*. What do we call those
who are at the ends of their lives, but not yet dead? It is difficult to explain
(*explicare difficile est*):

> On the one hand, no one can be called dying, if a man cannot be dying
> and living at the same time; and as long as the soul is in the body, we
> cannot deny that he is living. On the other hand, if the man who is ap-
> proaching death be rather called dying, I know not who is living.[28]

For Augustine, this is no idle linguistic play. It signals a deeply disconcert-
ing problem, one that we recognize along with the knowledge that we are
mortal. Living is to "move ceaselessly toward death" from the moment of
birth. Rather than think of our lives as an ever-increasing measure of time,
it might be more appropriate to think of our lives as the increase of the

I will argue in this book, to chart this difficulty in vernacular language is to chart the ongoing fascination of a language with its limits, with its terms in both senses of the word: what it can say about our relation to the infinite—precisely what lies beyond language, the denotation of a finite speaking—and what it can say about *how* it does or does not speak about our finitude. All of this would seem to be easy with a soul, but as I will show in the next chapter, there were conditions placed on what the soul could say, and when it could say it.

Yet the conditions that permit such a language to be used negate its very usefulness. For several hundred years, roughly between the writing in the late tenth century of the first poem that this book studies and the Fourth Lateran Council in 1215, the literary soul speaks only after death, and its speech describes what the body should and should not have done while it was alive. Because the body can no longer act, and because both body and soul are already doomed, the language that the soul uses is beside the point. The purpose of dwelling on this moment, and on the impotence of the soul after death, is of course monitory: to encourage those of us who still have conjoined souls and bodies to do what the soul advises, in order to remove the eventual occasion for our own soul's speech, which it presumably cannot yet make. The soul in these early poems is both in its primal clarity, perfected by its separation from the body, and terminated, able to put into language what it wished it could all its life, but also unable to give itself the meaning for which it longed. In one sense, it is the longing for a language for what we do not yet know that creates the conditions for the soul's ability to speak.

The very act of speaking brings the spirit into being; it either presupposes it or makes it necessary. As the philosopher Gillian Rose summarizes Hegel's argument about speech and spirit: "We cannot speak without spirit, without, that is, taking up a relation to the relation, to the ensouling of things when they become meaning. When we speak of death, which is the demarcation between physical nature and signification, we take up a relation to the relation of body and soul, their salvation or damnation."[47] The hope that we can say something meaningful about death, then, is also the sign of an extreme confidence in the life-giving properties of language, in their ability to put death in its place *and* to move beyond it. This confidence was the target of much of Derrida's early career, in which he assailed both the privileging of speech over writing and that of presence over absence. My interest here is not in weighing the consequences of Derrida's arguments, but only in pointing out that precisely this confidence in the ability of language to overcome finitude animated much of the literature of death and

dying in the Middle Ages, as did the desire for that special property somehow locked up in language, buried within it, to be called forth.

The beginning of the literary history in this book, however, lies with
the emergence of a consciousness of futurity—with, that is, the emergence
of the soul after death; and that is very decidedly not an experience of hope.
Early debates in English between the body and the soul share a common
quirk: only after death can the soul speak. There are a number of reasons
that this might happen: the soul is trapped in the prison of the body; the
soul cannot participate in the stir of matter; the soul is really speaking to us,
not to the dead body. Yet none of these answers is satisfactory. Why would
the limits of imagination stop just there? If we can imagine what the soul
might say after death, why could we not imagine what the soul might say
in life? What does its muteness signify? Why is it only death that gives the
soul language? I will argue that it is because what the soul talks about is
finitude after it is over, the extended actions of the body in time.

In the fifteenth century, as we will see in later chapters, death might
have been imagined as an archive, but the consuming problem of death five
hundred years earlier was that the soul had no language to speak about the
only thing that mattered to it—its future. Yet it does speak about the past,
and this impossible speech act—its ability to say, in effect, "I am dead" (and,
conversely, its inability to say "I am" while alive)—is the tenuous possibility that language and the soul are equivalent in some way, even if it is only
in the soul's ability to talk about the impossible. But the relation between
language and soul is a negative one: these poems exist only because of the
impossibility that they describe: that language is freed after the finitude
that gives birth to it can no longer be avoided. These poems, then, are not
ultimately about a semiotic impossibility, but about the impossibility of an
absolute state of death. Even the damned soul has to speak. The next two
chapters will discuss the conditions under which the soul may speak after
death in several Anglo-Saxon and early Middle English poems that follow
in the next two chapters, we will see how the soul that is silent when all
things are possible finds its voice only when it can no longer do anything.

CHAPTER TWO

The Old English Grammar of the Soul

Gewite seo sawul ut, ne maeg se muð clypian, þeah ðe he gynige . . .
—Aelfric, Sermon for Shrove Sunday

In these next two chapters I will be examining some English poems written between the late tenth century and the early thirteenth century. They
fall on either side of the shadow supposedly cast on English writing by the
Norman Conquest of 1066.[1] This penumbra has made it difficult for traditional literary history to tell the difference between the somber topic of
individual death and dying and the allegory that is the shade itself: an historical catastrophe that silences language altogether.[2] In discussing closely
related texts that span this supposed gulf, I will be trying to separate the
philosophical content of these poems about dying from the allegorical burden that scholars have placed on them. They speak to us, I will argue, about
the continuing struggle to come to terms with death, with one's ownmost
fate, rather than with nostalgia over a time that is long dead. But in order
to read the "interminable work" of these poems closely, I will first show
how we must step out of the shadow of history that has determined how we
read them.

Because *The Wanderer*, *The Seafarer*, and *The Dream of the Rood* are
taught so frequently in introductory undergraduate classes, Old English is
often treated as a literature thoroughly suffused with sorrow and death. If
this is an accurate perception, it is not because there is a recognizable form
of mourning in Old English poetry. The term often used to describe these
poems, *elegy*, is problematic for several reasons. It was not a term used in
Old English, and so whatever we call such poems it cannot really be elegy. In
Latin literature, elegy was likely to be associated with either the verse form
(a couplet made up of a hexameter and a pentameter), or with the somewhat

generically mixed Augustan elegy. Attempts to define a distinctive genre of elegy in Old English thus must focus on the content of the poems, not their shape. It is therefore intellectual history, not literary history, that identifies the boundary markers of Old English elegy—whatever we can call it.

But it is not clear why we need to call it anything that assimilates it to our own experiences of forms of mourning, nor is it clear why so much Old English poetry is mournful. Its "melancholy regret for departed glories" has been explained as anything from "a compound of Teutonic melancholia and Christian utilization of the *ubi sunt* motif" to "a mourning over some lost temporality."[3] Its causes and its objectives as a body of literature might be indeterminate, but scholars have almost universally interpreted the reappearance of the elegiac mode in early Middle English as a mourning for the lost object of Old English poetry itself.

Until recently, we have read poems about regret and loss written after the Norman invasion as meditations on the end of an indigenous literature, a literature that is reanimated by these few defiant assertions of survival.[4] The elegiac strain within Old English poetry became, when picked up again in a reconstituted literary English, the elegiac recognition of Old English culture itself precisely through its evident absence.[5] As Seth Lerer memorably put it, such poems "inhume Anglo-Saxon England," partly because the survival of these poems themselves was so precarious.[6] The most spectacular example is the Beowulf manuscript, which was almost destroyed in the Ashburnham House fire of 1731, and whose singed margins have been crumbling away since then. Other poems are written in margins or on pages that became the binding of other books, were lost altogether, or were heavily damaged by water, rats, and scholars. The three fragments of the poem *Solomon and Saturn* exemplify every one of these fates except the second. It is almost as if archival history has determined that Old English poetry should be remembered chiefly for its histories of manuscript destruction and survival and has arranged that the poems that do survive are profoundly engaged with the theme of historical destruction and survival. With few exceptions, it is a body of literature oriented toward the grave, an obsession that has been difficult not to understand as some kind of historical melancholy. Even the exceptions have been treated as little more than the "débris of an old literature," replaying the tropes and genres of late Old English.[7] The besetting morbidity of much of this literature is easily read as a set of reflections on the relation between the death of a metonymic personal body and the death of larger bodies of knowledge and practice. Yet a literature of endings simply raises questions about the adequacy and finality of the endings it reflects. As Thomas Hahn says of the last entry in the *Peterborough*

Chronicle in 1154, "This last burst of history writing . . . has, ironically, frequently been identified as one of the first examples of eME."[8] This literature of ending would not have the leisure to become a literature in the first place unless the historical forms it represents still persist, especially when it is, as it seems to be with early Middle English, a literature about the ending of literature. In this chapter and the next I will examine what it means for a speaker of early Middle English to look back at Old English as a language that needed as much formal study as Latin to understand.

I will argue, however, that this early Middle English literature is interested not in the fact of the silencing of Old English as much as it is in the paradoxical conditions of ending under which language is articulated. A copy of Aelfric's grammar and his *Colloquies* made by the same person who wrote—or copied out—one of the most extensive poems about dying in early Middle English (which I will examine in the next chapter) shows us how the poem's elegiac mode is not actually motivated by the "death" of Old English, or by historical loss, but by the unresolved endings that are a problem of the literature itself, the way in which literature is coterminous with dying. In an almost literal sense, in much Old English poetry the grave becomes not a place of silence and rest, but a theater of speech animated by a soul freed from the body.

In a philosophical, rather than a merely historical, sense, all literature, as Maurice Blanchot argued somewhat enigmatically in his landmark 1948 essay "Literature and the Right to Death," *"begins* with the *end."*[9] This end is more or less the death that language brings about: when we designate something, or even form an idea about it, it takes on a different order of existence; it is no longer the thing itself, but the word or the concept that names it. Blanchot's essay imagines that literature deals with both the relation between things and their designation, between their life as existing things and their death in orders of representation. Literature, in other words, looks both back toward the hecatomb of things and ahead toward a kind of freedom from the finitude of names, a death that liberates as opposed to one that constrains and merely cancels possibility: "The language of literature is a search for this moment which precedes literature."[10] It is an analytic of finitude, a means of understanding how the search for terms, for the precise and permanent naming of things, can be such an unending and infinite enterprise, the play of pure possibility. In its representation of the death that is immanent in language, as Blanchot says, "literature is language turning into ambiguity."[11]

That is why so much of the writing about mourning in the texts I am discussing here is so literary. This writing concerns not just the disappearance from the world of a specific language and literature, but the way in which disappearances of language (forgetting, stuttering, babbling) prefigure our own disappearance from the world. Indeed, the association of language and body—the assumption that language must involve the body, in speech, hearing, and sight—short-circuits the recognition that language is fundamentally a mental phenomenon, what Augustine called the stirring of the mind. In other words, bodies relay only what has already just occurred in the mind. The body is, in that sense, the corpse of language: the remnant, even the memorial, of something that has already taken place.

What happens, then, when a text literalizes this somewhat abstract state of affairs? When there is speech without a body, what form does it take? How, and why, is it possible? These questions are at the heart of two Old English poems, one found in the Exeter Book and the other in the Vercelli Book. They are very similar, although the Vercelli Book version is longer and includes an additional passage spoken by a redeemed soul.[12] In both of them, however, *only the soul* speaks. With one exception, however, every other Body and Soul poem I have found not only allows the body to speak, but takes the shape of a debate between the two.[13] The exception is a poem, *The Soul's Address to the Body*, that I will discuss in the next chapter. It is an early Middle English poem, but the sole manuscript is in the hand of a single scholar in post-Conquest England who took a profound and almost lifelong interest in Old English.

Although the relation between three poems imagining language after death and the historical death of one language in particular may seem to be an historical accident, it is an accident that helps to highlight an underlying theme in all three poems. All three are about regret. The soul does not mourn not its fate in the afterlife; rather, it regrets the body's obsession with its own satisfaction, its "sin-lusts," its gluttonous consumption of wine and food, its love of boasting about its own magnificence. What is slightly unexpected, however, is that in all three poems the soul taunts the body not just about its destruction, but about its *inability to speak* any longer: it cannot answer the soul, and indeed the soul punished the body *with* speech: the soul returns every night to stain the body (*wemman*—to disfigure, to reproach, to pollute, to profane) with words,[14] as the body once did to it (64). In the early Middle English *Soul's Address to the Body*, the soul berates the dead body for not using its mouth to bewail its sins (*neode*) and for not praying for mercy while there still was time.[15] Now the body is silent and about to be taken away from the living, its tongue locked in its mouth forever.

The soul's lament that the body did not save itself through speech suggests that the distinction between the body and the soul is not a Manichaean one in which matter is simply evil. But neither would a purely *bodily* action have saved the body: it is the *vox* that matters, which, according to Boethius, signifies the passions of the mind (*in anima passionum notae*).[16] Unrealized until it strikes the air, the *vox* is the substantial means by which the body speaks on behalf of the soul, or whatever it is that causes language to happen. The slippage suggested by Boethius's word *anima*, which I have translated here as both "mind" and "soul," is, I think, precisely the point.[17] It is only in its silence that the body ultimately becomes ensouled, releasing the voice that existed in it only *in potentia*. Another way of saying this is that the self after death is finally articulate about its *whole* life—both its spiritual component and its final condition.

Yet this is a special kind of articulation, one that takes place after precisely the elements that constitute speech have ceased to work together. In a well-known passage on the dimension of the soul, Augustine compares the division of a word into its constituent letters to the departure of the soul from a mangled body.[18] The word suffers a "kind of death" and loses its *significatio* altogether. But meaning itself is not destroyed—only its bodily signifier, which is sound. Meaning survives, because it is the "soul of the sound" (*significationem eius quasi anima soni est*) and cannot be divided any more than the soul can.[19]

But in another sense, the meaning of a word is understood by the very process of dividing it up. That, after all, is the fundamental procedure of grammar, which begins with the study of the orthography and phonetics of *litteras*, without which words cannot be understood. The *divisio* of the sound of a word into its letters—what Aelfric in his grammar says is "todaeled" when one begins grammatical analysis—is the first step to grasping the soul of a word.[20] As we have seen, however, this mangling of a word is its death, just as the mangling of a body is its death. Which of these procedures, then, is really an *apocalypsis*, a final uncovering of meaning? The answer, I think, is that they are both necessary to grasping it. The death of a word frees its meaning, and the death of the body frees its soul. In a double sense, then, death does not really happen: the disintegration of the body is actually the revelation of a life that can neither disintegrate nor be terminated. Even the damned soul, says Aelfric, will persist, although it will be dead to all joy.[21]

I would like to argue here that the paradoxical state of the soul of meaning, that it is enabled by a death that nevertheless never arrives, is precisely what makes literary texts such fertile ground for exploring the condition of the soul. Poems about the soul speaking after death are profoundly concerned with endings that have yet to be enacted, but that can be glimpsed at every turn. I would like to explore this idea further by turning to a discussion of a kind of literary writing that is marked by a simultaneous recognition of the patterns of its own history and the awareness that they will acquire their full significance only when they are finished.

Aelfric's own curriculum for the training of students for the priesthood begins with an extensive Latin grammar and proceeds to the *Colloquies*, which utilized a series of worldly occupations to increase students' mastery of Latin. As they took the steps that led to the priesthood or a monastic profession, in other words, they were translating themselves into the world—into the *saeculum*, not out of it. This is not entirely surprising, for the creation of priests who could exercise their pastoral duties intelligently was as important—at least according to Aelfric's schema—as the ability to read the Bible and its commentaries. Latin became the means by which the priest acted as a mediator who speaks the language of *sacra scriptura* and can name in it the people he sees around him.

Aelfric seems to have intended these texts to be used in a sequence, moving from the grammar, which is written in English although it uses Latin examples, to the *Colloquies*, which are written entirely in Latin. The grammar has both an English and a Latin preface, which, as the student moves through Aelfric's language curriculum, should become equally intelligible, until the student is able to move on to read Aelfric's cycle of Latin sermons. These texts are clearly intended to initiate Old English students into a wider literate community, into the lifelong practice of an international language. More important, however, they are intended to reverse the decline of Latin itself, to prevent its premature death. The English preface to the *Grammar* warns that without a book like Aelfric's, sacred learning will disappear, just as it did among the English until Dunstan and Aethelwold made learning an important part of the monastic life.[22] Aelfric's Latin preface is full of the language of youth, of inception, of futurity: this book is for tender youths, who can plant Priscian and Donatus in either language now, until they achieve a "more perfect study" (*perfectiora . . . studia*). Beginning to learn Latin with English is only incidental, a contingency that leads to the terminus at which every educated person in Europe will arrive: the complete expression of terms in Latin. Aelfric's grammar is no country for old men: it will be, as he says, better suited to unknowing youth (*inscientibus puerulis, non senibus, aptandum fore*).[23] This equation of fluency and knowledge with age, only implicit in the Latin preface, becomes, when it is made more explicit, one of the themes of the English preface.

If the inception of language is located in youth, then it is also bound by time, even defined by and against it. One of the corollaries of Aelfric's insistence that elementary grammar is the work of youth is not just that language and life are equitable, but that the right use of language is equivalent to right living, like the Roman equation of *prosa* with literary and ethical rectitude.[24] Even more than that: anyone who knows Latin and doesn't instruct others deserves be bound and thrown into outer darkness, like the servant in the parable from Matthew who buried his master's "pund" rather than give it to others to multiply it; he was "gebunden and geworpen into þeostrum" (2).[25] In Aelfric's English preface, translation is a way to death, a way of dying in language rather than outside it, in the shadows of a senile and interminable despair.

More generally, in the literate world beyond this particular preface, the work of reading is represented as an encounter both with the illumination of the mind and also with an obscurity equally entailed in it, even lying at its core. And this obscurity threatens the foundations of knowledge not because it's the opposite of a lucid, programmatic declaration of monastic learning, but because it establishes the utter limits of knowledge, the terms beyond which knowledge can have nothing to say. It's literally an apocalyptic threat to knowledge because it will ultimately open to us the discomfiting perspective that knowledge actually has no limits, but only because the object of knowledge is infinite, disturbingly unknowable. In one of the homilies he wrote after completing his grammar and glossary, Aelfric retells a vision that Bede writes about in his *Historia ecclesiastica* concerning a man named Drihthelm, who returned to life after having died and seen both heaven and hell. Drihthelm first finds himself in "the penal place" (*witnungstow*), whose length is almost infinite (*fornean . . . ungeendod*), before coming to hell itself, a place so filled with shadows or darkness (*þeostorfulre stowe . . . mid þiccum þeostrum oferþeaht*) that he can no longer see. That it's not simply dark but a place that undoes the senses (remember that Hegel said that the senses begin in darkness), that makes the conditions of sight impossible, is suggested by the paradox that Milton and William Golding later made famous: hell is filled with "sweartes fyres," black flames, darkness visible.[26] It's a place of such confusion and uncertainty that even the angel accompanying Drihthelm, it turns out, has to leave him standing in the midst of the darkness in order to find out what Drihthelm's "faer," his immediate destination and his ultimate destiny, would be. Halted but not terminated, unable to find rest: that is the destiny of the souls in hell, who are endlessly caught up in the flames, only to sink down into the abyss again. But that's almost our situation, too: at least, we're much like Drihthelm, unable to know what the end really is, how the story turns out. Yet knowing that we don't know might be enough to transform us, to act

toward an end we can't yet see, but one that we hope we anticipate clearly
by negating the senses. That is half the point of Aelfric's sermon: that Drihthelm never found anything in life as disturbing as the condition in which
he found himself in the vision, and that nothing in his subsequent solitary
life set apart even from the other brothers in his monastery was as privative
as that moment in the midst of shadows. The other half of Aelfric's point, of
course, is that only the life that ends in good works can see Christ or be seen
by him (*Christes gesihðe*), an act of illumination that dispels the shadows
of our lives.

Dwelling in these shadows, Aelfric seems to suggest, is not unlike the
condition of living, of which reading and writing are an especially intensified
form. Drihthelm is allowed to return to his body as long as he pledges to
right (*gerihtlaecan*) his deeds and habits. That's also the pledge Aelfric ex-
tracts from his own scribes, asking them to "gerihte wel" what they need to,
so that the text doesn't fall away in its afterlife into unintelligible shadow.
But there's also clearly a powerful attraction in Aelfric's work, and in much
Old English writing, as Seth Lerer has pointed out, to what lies hidden,
dyrne—to, as we have seen, the shadow, the *thystro*, that lies within the
text.[27] The Exeter Book riddle whose answer is the bookworm refers to the
"þeof in þystro," the thief lurking in the darknesses of a book, who could
also be a reader, especially the reader of the riddle who remains in the dark,
who doesn't get the riddle.[28]

Falling away into shadows is the condition of the riddle, a condition
that lays us before the unknowable answer, the unknown terminus, to all
riddles, which is to say before the one riddle: the nature of death. But this
is still something we need to think about, even if we have to contemplate
what we are afraid is unthinkable, or figuratively and literally too deep to
understand. The injunction that begins the Old English *Body and Soul* says,
"It is necessary for each person to come to terms himself with . . . how deep
[it will be] when death comes" (Huru ðaes behofaþ haeleþa aughwylc / þaet
he his sawle sið sylfa bewitite, / hu þaet bið deoplic þonne se deað cymeð
[Anderson, *Two Literary Riddles in the Exeter Book*, lines 1–3]; *deoplic* is
a word that connotes something profound, grave in both senses, unplumbable). The separation of the body and soul is the inception of a riddle, the
beginning of an interrogation that does not always arrive at an answer.

My point here is that death in late Old English poetry above all poses a
question, not that the Soul and Body poem in the Exeter Book is necessarily
the inception of a larger "riddlic" complex.[29] What ties the riddles and their
outlying poems together is the question of how the bodies of things continue
to accumulate meaning or to act, not a narrower determination of generic

form. In each riddle, it's precisely a terminist preoccupation that motivates the list of qualities and attributes, the word that collates all of the distinctive, peculiar descriptions of the riddle: that is, as Porphyry writes, "Individual is said of one particular alone. Socrates is said to be individual, and this white [thing], and this approaching [person], and son of Sophroniscus, if Socrates be his only son. Such things are said to be individuals, since each of them consists of properties whose collection will never be the same in another."[30] Part of the pleasure of riddles is in the acts of collation and disjunction, the process of deciding what properties make something uniquely different, that is, distinctive enough to name. They are also read for their usefulness in demonstrating forms of versification and facility of composition (cf. Aldhelm's preface to the *Aenigmata*)—that is, for their cogency in learning *grammatica* and *rhetorica* (*aenigmata* are, after all, *figura*). But they can also be read as demonstrations of the ontological analysis of terms. Porphyry's *Isagoge* and Aristotle's *Categories* and *Peri hermeneias* laid the foundation for the analysis of syllogistic terms. They gave the dialectician the analytical forms for the definition of the signifying properties, the scope of the terrain covered, of words used dialectically.[31] The most important, at least the initial, group of words in the approach to *dialectica* was nouns, because they show most clearly, without the added complication of time that the verb brings with it, how a word is related to a thing.

Alcuin's dialogue on dialectic calls the *Isagoge* the *introductio* because it brings into our understanding (*sensum nostrum . . . introducit*) the property of a thing by the division of common things.[32] That is, we understand the nature of a thing by analyzing it into one of five categories: genus, species, *differentia, accidens,* and *proprium*. The first two are familiar to us in Linnaean classification: the *Rosa eglentaria*, for example, is the eglantine or sweetbriar rose. The *differentia* are the distinguishing features of a thing— say, what distinguishes one species of rose from another. The *accidens* is whatever happens to (*accidit*) or slips away from something—without the "corruption," or destruction, of a substance. The fifth category, *proprium*, is whatever can be added to a species that will distinguish it absolutely from every other member of its common class of species (such as a horse's *quinnitas*, or a human's laughter). Boethius's commentary on the *Isagoge* defines all of these distinctions of what came to be called "predicables" in terms of a descending apparatus of differentiation:

> A *genus* is that which is predicated in respect of what-ness of many things different in species. A *species* is that which is predicated in respect of what-ness of many things not different in species. A *differentia* is that

which is predicated substantially and in respect of quality of many things different in species. A *property* is that which is predicated of one species only in respect of quality and not substantially. An *accident* is that which is predicated in respect of quality and not substantially of many things different in species.[33]

We can see this branching procedure in operation in a gloss to the first of Aldhelm's famous collection of riddles, known as the *Aenigmata*. The gloss, which explains the subject of the riddle, "earth," begins with several etymologizing glosses for the word *terra* but points out that "properly . . . terra [is designated by] its distinction, difference, from sand."[34] Two features of this gloss suggest that it is motivated by an interest in the definition, as opposed to the mere description, of a term as set out in the pursuit of dialectic. The word *proprie* signals a turn to a more rigorous set of criteria, and the very distinction the gloss makes is one of *differentia*, distinguishing one species of the genus *tellus* from another.[35] This interest in placing the terms of the riddles in relation to the schema of division into genus and species continues through the manuscript. A gloss in the second riddle, for example, says that the word *oak* is used as a "species pro genere pro omnibus lignis."[36] And a riddle about magnets, which a gloss on the title says is "genus lapidis," also says that the "adamante cypris" is "adamans genus lapidis in cipro."[37] Both the construction and the solution of riddles involve precisely the same work we undertake in naming anything: that is, either the work of description or that of definition. In either case, Boethius says, what we do is name by dividing, which he demonstrates by dividing "division" itself into three kinds: the division of genus into species, of ambiguous words into two meanings, and a whole into parts. This last kind of division occurs when we "resolve" (*resoluimus*) something into the things of which it is composed, as when we say that the human is made up of body and soul.[38]

One reason that souls begin to speak after death is that they have undergone something like this process of division: they now, finally, have names. The later Middle Ages had a number of forms for memorializing the names of the dead: necrologies, bede rolls, chantry chapels, and epitaphs. Some of these pay particular attention to the name of the deceased. Beginning around the eighth century, prompted by the Cluniac reforms, mortuary rolls inscribed with the names of monks who had died were circulated to the various houses of the order for inclusion in prayers for the souls of the dead. Many, if not most, of these monks became more famous in death than they had been in life, their names published in places they may never have visited.[39] Especially for the more elevated monastics, the name on such rolls was the focus of meditation and exposition. Several entries on the mortuary roll made around 1230 for Lucy, the Countess of Oxford and prioress of Henningham, expound on the aptness of her name for someone who imparted the knowledge of light (scientia lucis).[40] The name of the dead is what remains present to us in the absence of the body, but also what calls into being the work of imagining and representing a continuity that will be faithful to the name, to what emerges once its parts are dissolved. As Hegel puts it in the introduction to his Phenomenology, "The activity of dissolution [Scheiden, also "dividing"] is the power and work of the Understanding, the most astonishing and mightiest of powers," because it is "the tremendous power of the negative . . . of Death."[41] At least one of the Exeter riddles represents death as precisely the work of a division that generates terms—that makes it possible, if not necessary, to talk about what makes up a self.

Ic wat indryhtne   æþelum deorne
giest in geardum,   þam se grimma ne mæg
hungor sceððan   ne se hata þurst,
yldo ne adle.   Gif him arlice
esne þenað,   se þe agan sceal
on þam siðfate,   hy gesunde æt ham
findað witode him   wiste ond blisse,
cnosles unrim,   care, gif se esne
his hlaforde   hyreð yfle,
frean on fore.   Ne wile forht wesan
broþor oþrum.   Him þæt bam sceðeð,
þonne hy from bearme   begen hweorfað
anre magan ellorfuse, moddor ond sweostor.
Mon, se þe wille,
cyþe cynewordum   hu se cuma hatte,
eðþa se esne,   þe ic her ymb sprice.

[I've heard tell of a noble guest;
man entertains him. He's not prey
to hunger pangs or burning thirst;
age and illness are unknown to him.
If the servant tends him well, satisfies
this guest who must go on a journey,
both will be happy in their home,
live in prosperity, surrounded
by a family; but there'll be sorrow

if the servant neglects his lordly guest,
his ruler on the journey. Think of them
as brothers, fearless of each other.
When they depart, together desert
one kinswoman (their mother and sister),
both suffer hurt. Let him who can
put names to the pair I describe—
the guest, then his servant, the host.][42]

The last words tell us explicitly, in case we missed the point, that the whole passage is constructed as a circumlocution, literally as a speaking around (*ymb sprice*) what cannot yet be called, invoked, named (*hatte*), or described precisely. To "cyþe cynewordum" means to make known something like "fitting words," dignified words: the prefix *cyne-* usually means royal, kingly, but that sense doesn't quite fit, especially if it's the soul that is lordly, not the body. That might be a pedantic quibble, but it makes more sense if we were to think of *cynewordum* as something like "words of kind," words that fit both their subjects and that form a suitable and admirable concord. That is, the words are also genus words (*cyn* is glossed often as "genus" in Old English glossaries), words that indicate the generic commonality of the two separated objects.

This long disquisition allows me to discuss a second reason that the soul speaks only after death. The act of separating the soul from the body, I have argued, actually begins a kind of ordering and classification, one characteristic of logic, grammar, and natural science. In the Exeter Body and Soul poem the soul says that it could not wait, while it was alive, to be "daeled" from the body, using the word that Aelfric does for *divisio*. But the body itself is subjected to further division after its separation from the soul: it does not rot, but instead is pulled apart by worms, who principally attack its head—but in particular his tongue, which is pulled apart into ten pieces, rendering it (so to speak) even more incapable of speech.

Why would the poem emphasize the partition of the tongue—and not the corruption of the body—if not to imagine a kind of speech that is completely disembodied? In doing so, it imagines speech that exists *because* of disarticulation, the systematic taking apart of the body that makes speech. It is obvious that the body cannot speak because it is dead. But the poem nevertheless makes the partition of the tongue the *causa efficiens* for the body's inability to speak with its own soul. It enacts the process by which speech is made, according to Priscian. It is assembled, put together, from parts that make up a whole. In speech, he says, the various parts are like the members of a body, and its life, its soul, is its meaning.

But it is not as simple as that: the soul of speech is not necessarily immanent in an utterance. Priscian is careful to insist that the soul of speech only comes to life when an utterance is grasped in someone else's understanding. The speech of the soul in these Old English poems, in other words, is merely a dramatization of what happens every time we speak. Our language ensouls not ourselves, but the other—whoever hears and understands. The soul of the other completes what the speaker's body cannot. The meaning of the Body and Soul poems, in other words, is in the understanding we bring to it, an understanding that animates our recognition that we can still choose life.

Among the many other problems that death brings with it is what to call the work it leaves behind. That is a problem particularly because we can only make sense of that work in language; the only recourse we have is to use words that will somehow fit what is difficult, if not impossible, to talk about. The deep ("deop[lic]") that confronts us at the beginning of the Exeter and Vercelli Soul and Body poem, that is, at the end of a life, is not something that we can forget, something we do our best to turn away from. At the moment we read this, we discover that we know already that we have to come to know more: to know the journey, the depth, out of which we will come, the profundity from which we speak but do not know. The soul of every person who died was accompanied by these words at burial, but had already heard them, in the psalm *De profundis* said every day in the Office of the Dead: "Out of the depths, O Lord, have I cried to thee."[43] As Porphyry suggests, however, that abyss is also precisely how all beings become unique "properties whose collection will never be the same in another."[44] That work of collection, as we have seen, proceeds by disjunction, analysis, difference. We can only discover the work of a life by its disjunction, by undoing its unique collection of properties, the body and soul that emerge at the beginning of the end, as the next lines of the Body and Soul poem recognize: when death comes and "asundrað þa sibbe   þa þe aer somud waeron, / lic ond sawle" (4–5). The double movement of assembling and sundering echoes in, and to some extent is visible only in, language, in the collation of the sounds of antithetical motions, "asundrað" and "somud."

The work of *grammatica*, of what Aelfric calls "staefcraeft," the beginning of the craft of books is, as he says, the key that unlocks the "andgit," the "perfectiora . . . studia," that will keep us from being cast into the outer darkness, but it's also the obligation laid on us that threatens us with that fate. We keep those shadows at bay by learning what casts them, by learning not just what separates day from night, dry land from sea, but everything from everything else. It is a way of proceeding haunted by the final separation of body from soul, because if it *is* true that for the purpose of description everything can be divided into a collection of its own unique properties, then there must be an ontological difference between all things, too, and not least between the two selves that make us up. That may be one reason that Aelfric's glossary culminates in a series of terms for the dead body, for kinds of sin, for juridical and theological condemnation, and for the violent termination of life.[45] But if so, that is the result of Aelfric's *modus procedendi*, a mode he derives, of course, from the procedure of all grammars. Following Priscian, Aelfric divides the "partes orationis" of Latin grammar into eight parts, which he calls "daelas" (8), and the rest of the grammar is largely structured by these eight divisions. The end of the grammar recapitulates the total study of the *grammaticus* by analyzing it into thirty parts ("todal" [289]), including the primary eight, which include matters from *notae* and orthography to tropes, *figurae*, and *historia*. Parts 14 through 30 rest on distinctions themselves, on the ways in which each of them is a kind of partition from another. Especially instructive is part 20, on *differentia*, which shows us that this work of analysis is not merely heuristic, a temporary division that makes it easier to remember the components of language, but a real and ontological division between things. *Differentia* is the "todal betwux twam þingum" (293) that are. But his grammar begins by analyzing language into its smallest unanalyzable part, the "laesta dael," called the "staef," or *littera*: "we todaelað þa boc to cwydum and / syþþan ða cwydas to daelum, eft ða daelas to staefgefegum and syðð þa staefgefegu to stafum: þonne beoð ða stafas untodaeledlice; forþan ðe nan staef ne byð naht, gif he gaeð on twa" (4–5). Unlike Donatus, the source here, however, Aelfric doesn't use letters as the index of meaning. For an English speaker, the question of what *stafas* means, precisely, makes the question of whether the *littera* really is the termination of language, its inmost term, a complicated one. It is possible, and probably likely, that Aelfric and his audience thought at this moment that *bocstafas* and *litterae* were equivalent terms.

But at other moments we know that English speakers living in the late Old English period continued to be troubled by the enigmatic, even cryptic, nature of the written word in English. The word *stafas* carries with it the history of the material text in England: it indicates the staff or stick on which runic texts were written, and perhaps even the sticklike aspect of runic letters. But *stafas* also connoted something like the heterogeneous, even talismanic, force that runic letters represented late into the Old English period. It is clear that writers have runic letters in mind when they use the term *runstafas*,[46] but that doesn't necessarily mean that *bocstafas* couldn't possess the same complexity, or that the two kinds of *stafas* always represented different relations to writing and, more generally, language. The poetic dialogue between Solomon and Saturn not only calls the rune for *R* the "best of bookstaves" (*bocstafa brego*), but it also spells out the Pater Noster acrostically with runes, a prayer that the poem says every warrior should "singan" when he takes out his sword.[47] The power of that prayer, by implication, is at least partly derived from its inscription, indeed, its encoding, in runes within the poem; but the poem also represents the warrior who prays it as writing not just with but on his sword, in a series of appositive clauses that subordinate even learned, Latinate kinds of writing to the complex, atavistic force of runic writing: "He writes on his weapon a lot of fatal marks [*nota*], he engraves on his sword baleful bookstaves" (awrite he on his wæpne   wællnota heap, / bealwe bocstafas,   bill forscrife / meces mæro).[48] Like Grendel's sword, such a sword would inscribe its own history as it proceeds. But it also offers the fantasy of an object that is its own language, that proceeds by both doing and meaning—unlike Heidegger's hammer, which we cannot both use and think about.[49] And it collapses together the formal *notae* of academic reading, the *bocstafas*—letters that, as Aelfric says, cannot be "todaeled" further, but here appear as they cut apart body and soul of enemies: writing and epigraphic inscription.[50]

At least in the *Excerptiones de Prisciano* on which Aelfric based his grammar, the letter is an irreducible element that, because of its unity, stands for, and indeed grounds, lucidity, if not meaning itself. For Donatus, anything that cannot be written is meaningless (*vox confusa*). But Aelfric defines a meaningful utterance as one that carries meaning, as opposed to one that doesn't. He gives two examples that help us out of the circularity of his definition: the opening of the *Aeneid* is meaningful, but the bellowing of cattle and the neighing of horses aren't. Implicit in this distinction is the theory of the physics of sound that readers of Chaucer's *House of Fame* will be familiar with: sound, *vox*, is the striking of the air so that a voice carries to the ear of the listener. Unlike Donatus, Aelfric almost literally traces out this process: as "arma virumque cano" is sounded, it strikes a listener with a new life and is reborn as "ic herige þa waepnu and ðone wer," a reanimation of the opening of Latin epic in the form of the English alliterative line (4). At least part of the reason Aelfric doesn't include Donatus's more graphicentric definition of the voice is that writing seems to be reserved for Latin. Or, more precisely, that Latin, unlike English, can be approached only in writing. What Aelfric calls Latin speech (*ladenspraece*) throughout the grammar is an encounter with a cryptic utterance, a speech that must be opened (*geopenaþ*) as if it were a crypt in order to be understood, held, apprehended, fully. But it is cryptic not just because it is not easily understood, a mere riddle with a solution; it is cryptic also because its very structure is, as the figure of opening a language, a speech, suggests, difficult to conceive. It suggests, indeed, the interminable relation between speech and writing. The speech, the *ladenspraece*, that is reanimated in the study of grammar is the way to fuller understanding—a way to "ledenboca andgit"—but a way that can only be inscribed, not spoken. The elements, the parts, of grammar that lead to the opening of the book of learned wisdom are the written *stafas* of a represented, not a voiced, language: a language dead in the most elementary sense with which Priscian and Aelfric define a language—as a voice. Grammatica is the "staefcraeft" that "geopenaþ and gehylt ledenspraece, and nan man naefþ ledenboca andgit befullon, buton he þone craeft cunne" (289). Unless the soul can speak, unless understanding comes alive, *grammatica* is only a memorial practice, holding what is otherwise forgotten, bringing what is otherwise without a voice to our senses. Yet, even when we care for it, it is a language that comes to us out of its own dying away.

CHAPTER THREE

The Tremulous Soul:
The *Worcester Fragments*

Tremens factus sum ego, et timeo.
—Versicle from Third Nocturne of the Office of the Dead

This chapter will focus on late Old English written in the hand of someone now known only as "The Tremulous Hand of Worcester," who
also wrote (or copied) a later version of a Body and Soul poem. The numerous entries in his distinctive, shaking hand in manuscripts in the Worcester Cathedral library record his long interest in learning and understanding
Old English at the moment it was becoming old. But rather than suggest
that we can read his interest as a metonymy of the disappearance of Old
English after the Norman invasion, I want to emphasize that the Tremulous Hand's interest in these texts is distinctively personal and literary, not
world-historical or even Anglo-historical.

It might be better characterized as an interest in the phenomenon of late
style that I discussed earlier. Subsequent chapters in this book that discuss
self-consciously literary writers such as John Lydgate, Thomas Hoccleve,
and John Audelay will show how extensively, and how imaginatively, their
late style encompasses the ambiguity of wanting to complete something,
yet also wishing to continue it. These tensions are certainly there in the
work of the Tremulous Hand. One difference with these later poets, however, is that the Tremulous Hand's late style is both less self-conscious and
more diffuse and scattered. He tells us nothing about himself, nothing about
his preoccupations or the relevance of the texts to his consciousness of mortality. Yet the particular juxtaposition of his restorative work in Aelfric's
grammar with his interest in poems about dying amounts to a late style.
Even if the notion that grammar is what we do in order to keep the death of
language alive, interminable, were not implicit in Aelfric's grammar, what

follows it in the Tremulous Hand's manuscript makes it explicit. On the same folio as the end of the grammar, the Tremulous Hand copied (or possibly wrote) a poem called *St. Bede's Lament*. It was probably composed in the second half of the twelfth century and therefore would have traditionally been considered an obviously Old English poem.

St. Bede's Lament is often read as a lament over the death of Old English, or at least of the cultural knowledge lodged in it.[1] Yet this poem (and a small number written at about the same time) also represents the continued vitality of English.[2] These poems are in early Middle English, not quite the Tremulous Hand's own language—they seem to be a little older than his—but not Old English.[3] They embody a literature interested in the past; but they use a language that affirms its own place as the continuation, or the fulfillment, of a past language. Their theme, however, is rupture and discontinuity. The linguistic vitality of the poems, in other words, belies their elegiac content in the same way that the soul's ability to speak belies the poem's conceit that it is too late to change anything.[4] To the Tremulous Hand's contemporaries, these poems would have had an archaic flavor that poignantly underscored their concern with the degeneration of the world, of bodies, of learning. As Seth Lerer observes of this and the slightly older poem *Durham*, the poets' interests in the pastness of the world of Old English learning and devotion "inhume Anglo-Saxon England."[5] Many of these "transitional" early Middle English poems share a fascination with "the structure of burial, with the architecture of death, whether it be the grave itself, the reliquaries of the saints, the churches that house their bones, or the unshaped earth that conceals the body."[6] *Durham* and *St. Bede's Lament* were written about the same time, and the latter is not just an elegy for learning, but a cryptic poem: it is interested in the past not just as the object of undirected nostalgia, but precisely because the past is something that becomes difficult for us to understand, even to endure, something from which we also have to protect ourselves.

After the anxiety about the ways in which learning is always an engagement with the unknowable and the forgotten, it is surprising if not reassuring to find an act of heroic hermeneutics in *St. Bede's Lament*, an embracing of the mystery and darkness that surround the passage of texts. Both Bede and Aelfric (who is named six lines after the end of his glossary) are memorable for their translations ("boc [a]wende"), which, the poem says, brought learning to the "Englisc leoden" (3).[7] It makes sense that a poem in English would focus on the legacy that both writers left in English, or at least the legacy that the poet thought they had left. Most of the rest of the poem is a catalog of bishops from the Old English period who, the poem claims, were important because they continued the pastoral and scholarly work of Bede and Aelfric in their vernacular: "þeos laerden ure leodan on Englisc" (16). The very language of the poem seems to attest to the endurance, if not the extension into vernacular literature, of that legacy. But the tradition the poem commemorates is less obvious than it seems. Three of the bishops, Burinus, Paulinus, and Aidan, are not English at all. Indeed, Aelfric's life of St. Oswald recounts how it was Oswald who had to translate Aidan's preaching because he knew Irish (scyttyse) and Aidan could not yet turn his speech "to norðhymbriscum gereorde" quickly enough.[8] Bede's accounts of Paulinus and Birinus only implicitly indicate that they spoke English, although both of them are noted for the power of their teaching and, in the case of Paulinus, the ability to decode dreams.[9] It is not as difficult to see why many of the other names are on the list: Aldhelm, as we have already seen, wrote a number of important texts, and Aethelwold initiated an important liturgical and scholarly revival at Winchester, the most famous remnant of which is his beautiful *Benedictional*.

In Bede's *Historia ecclesiastica*, John of Beverly is praised for doing what Bede does in the *Lament*: making difficult texts easier to understand. Bede writes an even more concrete account of how John of Beverly instructed in English, even to the extent of giving the language, indeed, the gift of language, to a man unable to speak:

> "Pronounce some word," said he; "say yea," which, in the language of the Angles is the word of affirming and consenting, that is, yes. The youth's tongue was immediately loosed, and he said what he was ordered. The bishop, then pronouncing the names of the letters, directed him to say A; he did so, and afterwards B, which he also did. When he had named all the letters after the bishop, the latter proceeded to put syllables and words to him, which being also repeated by him, he commanded him to utter whole sentences, and he did it.[10]

The curriculum John follows is precisely that of Priscian, moving from the *littera* or *staef* through syllables to words and sentences. A figure such as John certainly belongs on a list of heroes of the vernacular, but, like the other figures I have discussed, he belongs precisely because he animates the language by bringing it into accord with the tradition of Latinate grammar. To the extent that Latin is already implicit in the propagation of English, to the extent that it is represented in English historiography as little more than a calque of English, the poem laments a fate that is entailed in the very work it describes. The form of learning, we read, that was bequeathed by those bishops has now been forgotten: "Nu is þeo leore foreleten,   and þet folc is forloren" (17). But the poem quite specifically does not say that all learning is lost: what replaces it is what "oþre leodon" teach the people (18)—that is, Normans are now teaching us in Latin. The ending of the poem does represent the termination of English as an enduring language. We are now thrown into the language of Jerome and of God: "Nu saieþ ure Drihten þus,   *Sicut aquila prouocat pullos suos / ad uolandum.   Et super eos uolitat.* / This beoþ Godes word   to worlde asende, / þet we sceolden faeir feþ   festen to Him" (20–23). The work of Bede and Aelfric is quite undone, and mere Latin is loosed upon the world. In a poem that equates literacy with Englishness, and thus inverts the traditional definition of a literate person as one who understands Latin, its termination in Latin traces the poem's own declination of terms adequate to describe that very decline. Englishness brings us necessarily to terms with Latin.

It is a part of the power of the poem not to point out explicitly what has to remain unthought in English: if we encounter the word of God in Latin, there must be, indeed, something adequate and sufficient in Latin. In other words, now only in Latin can we think about the relation between humans and God. The very verse quoted here presents us with a God hovering over us, ensuring that we rise, but rise in Latin. That relation is something to which we must, quite literally, habituate ourselves: when the passage from Deuteronomy containing that verse is sung, the congregation is required to rise. The verse is part of what the breviary calls the Canticle of Moses, the last discourse of Moses to the Israelites, which was recited or sung every Saturday at Lauds and on the Monday after the first Sunday of Advent.[11] Its regularity and solemnity suggest why the poem ends by reminding us of an obligation in and, unexpectedly, to Latin itself: this is now, as the poem says, "Godes word." Indeed, the Canticle, which is treated by the breviary as a prefiguration of the Incarnation, is structurally a series of metaphors of the relation between humans and the divine word: it will fall like dew or rain, it is like an eagle, it is a rock. The poem's citation of a passage that celebrates the adaptability of the word, its ability to conform to various demands of the natural world, is thus a deep indictment of the capacity of the very human language of Old English, of its inability to become a nurturing or sustaining word. The work of translation represented by Bede and Aelfric, who "turned" books into English, is not only undone by historical forgetting, but by the telos of the poem, which terminates in a turn to Latin, even where there once existed an English book with these words (in Aelfric's translation, "Swa earn his briddas spænð to flihte & ofer hi flicerað, swa he tobrædde his feðeru & nam eower cynryn & bær on his eaxlum"). The impossible predicament we find ourselves in at the end of the poem is nothing less than the dying of language—its becoming history, our own bid to speak in a language that must always be other than our own.

The main subject of the Canticle of Moses is the historical forgetfulness of the Israelites in exile, in a land that now is given over to foreign practices, "to new gods that came newly up" that their "fathers feared not." And the predicament of the Israelites, who Moses says "are a nation void of counsel, neither is there any understanding in them," is like that of the English now, as the poem's allusion to this verse of the Canticle makes clear: "Nu is theo leore forleten, and thet folc is forloren." What has been forgotten in English must be remembered in Latin in order to recall, even to describe, the forlorn condition of a language moving into oblivion.

The poem is a canny document of the persistence of English as a language trying to remain sacralized. Although there was only one Anglo-Saxon bishop remaining after the Conquest, Wulfstan of Worcester, he put into place a number of initiatives to preserve the role of the traditional English church. In general, as Susan Rifkin says, Wulfstan's cathedral preserved a large number of pre-Conquest liturgical forms and scribal practices that lasted after his death, "as if Wulfstan's place as bishop upheld insular practice in these threads of the community's life."[12] Along with the deeply traditional monastery at Evesham, Wulfstan was responsible for the increasing presence of English saints on calendars at the two institutions.[13] Shortly after 1079 he had the body of St. Oswald translated, partly to assert against the incursions of the archbishop of Canterbury, Thomas I, the long history of the rights of the cathedral church that Oswald had founded.[14]

If the Normans did not exactly bring "new gods" with them, they did bring a hagiographic repertoire that largely neglected traditional English saints, and Wulfstan not only helped to preserve the legacy of these saints, but also demonstrated to Norman bishops now concerned with establishing the rights of their new dioceses the utility of local and national hagiographic knowledges.[15] As a consequence, a number of new saints' lives, translations, and initiatives to register and confirm the legacies of these saints appeared in the twelfth century, including William of Malmesbury's lives of Dunstan and Aldhelm, his translation of the English version of Wulfstan's life, and Henry of Huntingdon's *History of the English*, which includes an entire book devoted to English saints.[16] The list of saints in *St. Bede's Lament* is a late example of just this kind of archival establishment, and, as might be expected in a list written in Worcester, where Wulfstan's observation of the

daily observance of the Office of the Dead and his concern for the security
of the cemetery continued well after his death, it is organized around the
places where these saints are buried.[17]

Such a list has a great deal to do with twelfth- and early thirteenth-
century interests in the Anglo-Saxon past, especially at such places as
Worcester and Winchester, where the relics and bodies of the saints vener-
ated there also represented both the foundation and the continuity of ecclesiastical and scholarly tradition. Local calendars included such local figures
routinely, and in the form of obits and necrologies they often listed large
numbers of the dead, whether saintly or not. The litany of the saints, the
penultimate portion of the Office of the Dead (although it could be used on
other occasions, such as ordination), often included a large number of local
saints. Several of these litanies—most notably in Wulfstan's own so-called
Portiforium—include most of the names in *St. Bede's Lament*.[18] Where they
appear as part of the Office of the Dead, a litany containing English saints
would have been a daily reminder of the great cloud of witnesses to the life
to come and also of the more local habitations of their earthly remains.
But although litanies of the saints are often divided into categories—angels,
patriarchs, prophets, Holy Innocents, martyrs, confessors, monks, and her-
mits—they do not usually include the places with which the saints are associated, whether in life or death.

A more likely generic model is related to the litany and organized not
around the calendar or the type of saint, but according to the resting places
of saints. According to David Rollason, this kind of list is most common
in Italy in the Middle Ages, and it is possible, he suggests, that the Old English fascination with Rome contributed to its adoption in England.[19] But
the English lists are significantly different from the Roman ones: most of
the saints in English lists are English saints, and few of the Roman saints
appear. This list, like the short one in *St. Bede's Lament*, is thus a territorial
assertion of mortuary rights, an attempt to make England a place of death—
not just a place where people have died, but a place made important because
of the continuing presence of the bodies in those places. It is a list structured by the termination of a life, however saintly, that comes to an end.
More important, it is a list that gives to that place the peculiar property of
work that extends beyond death, what Blanchot would call a step beyond
it.[20] A place thus represents—or contains—a termination, but also interminable work, a labor that cannot be contained because it outstrips its place:
why else would we bother to know just where it is that other saints are buried? It represents a necrological knowledge that is not just a knowledge of
ourselves as beings that stretch out of history into the future, indeed out of

time, but of ourselves as beings whose work can continue precisely because it is circumscribed, contained, and laid to rest.

This is the other reason that souls speak only after language has left the body. As we have seen, the analysis that makes it possible to say something of anything involves separation above all, an analysis that makes it into a discrete—that is, no longer functioning and organic—object. Names come from the division of selves into things. Perhaps that's why the poem that follows *St. Bede's Lament* begins with an account of creation that at first seems to echo that common trope of Old English poetic writing, but moves toward not an expression of the continuity of creator and creation, but the painful disintegration, almost the derangement, of the order of things in the uniting of soul and body. In *The Soul's Address to the Body*, the birth of the human is accompanied, actually marked ("bodeþ"), by mourning: "þaer biþ sor idol / þet bodeþ þet bearn þonne hit iboren biþ" (there is a sorry separation / that that child announces when it is born [A 5–6]).[21] Human speech begins with that first cry, a cry full already of the knowledge of being and cessation, predicated on the separation of the elements that first make speech possible—the body and the soul. As this poem intimates in a number of ways, this separation is a termination in the richest sense: it is the completion of the self, its death the instant that marks the end, the fulfillment, of being, and the breaking up of the self into its constituent parts that enables us to know what made up the complex of being, to name ourselves precisely because we stand outside ourselves.

Perhaps to say anything about the self is to destroy it, to begin to take it apart, to acknowledge its terminated being, whether now or at the end of time. As this line suggests, we cannot come into the world without the knowledge of separation, the knowledge that we are, in terms of medieval cosmology, exiled from our true, original country. As Hegel might put it, we can come into the world only to the degree that we know we must leave it, that we are finite yet knowing beings. To be more precise, Hegel would probably say that we are finite because we are knowing beings: spirit (*Geist*) "is the movement which is cognition—the transforming of that *in-itself* into that which is *for itself*, of Substance into Subject, of the object of *consciousness* into an object of *self-consciousness*, i.e. into an object that is just as much superseded, or into the *Notion*. The movement is the circle that returns into itself, the circle that presupposes its beginning and reaches it only at the end."[22]

What is so remarkable about the sadly fragmented opening of this poem is that it begins with an account of beginning, and one that does not attempt to write a brief account of historical time so much as it cannily acknowledges

the very implication of the end in the beginning, the necessity of thinking about all kinds of termini in thinking about the ending of things, the
discourse of finitude. Indeed, the fifth line of the poem is poised between
the two antithetical poles of this movement of becoming, the gathering
together of a life that is made up only to be dispersed and fragmented: "Soft-
liche he [that is, God] heo isomnede,   ac þaer biþ sor idol / þet bodeþ þet
bearn   þonne hit iboren biþ" (Tenderly he gathered them together, but
there is a sorrowful parting which that child laments when it is born [A
5–6]).[23] That is, the collecting together of soul and body is itself an acknowledgment, a knowing, of their separation from the beginning. But it is also
a *legein* in that other sense, an initial gathering together of the knowledge
of the predicament of dying in language, or into the dying of language, the
delimitation of the terms whose constituent parts make up the gathering-
together of our speech. The "bode" of the newborn child is already the
grammar of dying, already the lament over the dissolution into parts, the
"sori idol" that ends the process. Like Aelfric's grammar, which demonstrates that we move into language by crumbling it into its mere atomies,
its "daela," this poem's opening reiterates the "dael" that terminates life
in two end-stopped lines, as if to say that partition is unavoidable even if it
comes in slightly different forms (*idol/idaelen*): "þet sori idol: / þet soule
schal of licame   sorliche idaelen" (that sorry separation: that soul shall
separate from body with sorrow [A 8–9]). As we saw in the previous chapter,
in Aelfric's grammar that word *idaelen* is pregnant with the action of division, partition, definition, and irreducibility and indeed represents its mode
of proceeding, just as it seems to represent the mode of living and dying in
St. Bede's Lament.

   The moment of death recapitulates this complex relation between the beginning and ending of a life, the two termini that designate it. Beginning with
an act of perhaps mere description, the foreboding of death, life ends with a
knowledge that makes its initial speech act more pointed, really a designation of a precise and completed span of time, a term in the temporal sense:

Þonne biþ þet soulehus   seoruhliche bereaued
at also muchele wunne   þe þerinne wunede;
þus biþ þaes bearnes   bodunge ifulled:
þeo moder greoneþ   and þet bearn woaneþ.
So biþ þeo burdtid   mid balewen imenged,
So biþ eft þe feorsiþ   mid seoruwen al bewunden.
þonne þe licame and þe sowle   soriliche todaeleþ:
þonne biþ þet wraecche life   iended al mid sori siþ. (A 22–29)

[Then is that soul-house   deprived sorrowfully
in this way of much happiness   which dwelled within it;
thus is the child's   foreboding fulfilled:
the mother groans   and that child mourns.
Thus is the time of birth   mingled with pain,
Thus is the going forth   wound around with sorrow.
Then the body and the soul   part sorrowfully:
Then is that wretched life   ended with a thoroughly sorrowful time.]

That final word, *siþ*, means a number of things in this poem: fate, fortune, occasion, departure, and above all time, a time that is now quantified, known—rendered as a term—because it is terminated. Precisely because it means something like "terminated time," it designates what is most compelling, what most demands a response from us, at the instant of death. It is only at this moment, after all, that the soul can finally speak.

But just why is it that this voice can only now speak? It has had the desire to do so for its entire life, and only now can it address the body, and only in a discourse comprised entirely of memories. Why does death give it a voice that it didn't have in life? Partly because this voice, and every voice, is composed of memory. For Hegel, the stopping of air in the utterance of consonants, for example, prefigures death and gives the voice its structure, the halting discourse of the *pneuma* whose pure sound is interrupted by consonants, what he calls the "true and proper arrestation of mere resonation."[24] Elsewhere he dislocates the voice from the mere sensousness of experience and indeed describes voice as the figure, the experience, of ideality, which in Hegel is also the experience of death: "In voice, sense returns to inwardness and is negative self or desire—the feeling of its insubstantial nature as mere space, whereas the senses are saturated, filled space."[25] Conversely, as this poem seems to say, in death sense returns to inwardness, to what Augustine called the *homo interior*, the part of the self "envoluped," as Chaucer's Pardoner puts it, in sin, sensuality, and sensuousness. That envelope of exteriority is opened only after death, that inner self finally present to the world.

The soul is immanent in the body, but it is only disclosed in death, only able to talk when it is too late, when the body cannot give utterance to the desires that make it impossible for the soul to speak. More precisely, they are desires that the soul can only witness, desires for which it has only a responsibility rooted in utter passivity. We would ordinarily think of this as a lack of responsibility precisely because the soul doesn't seem to be a moral agent just at the moments that matter most. But that responsibility is rooted in its knowledge of the effects of moral action, the obligations of actions and decisions that are no less real and no less necessary because the soul knows but does not desire them. Or the soul might desire them but is powerless to act on that desire because the human will is not lodged in it. The soul is passive but knowing, unshakable in the rectitude of its desires but powerless to act on them.[26]

The soul's discourse is determined by what has been said, by the speech of the living body even, or especially, in its falling silent, because that silence is the index and expression of its passivity, its refusal to say what should have been said in life. The second half of the poem is more or less structured as a series of strophes in which the soul accuses the body of a series of failures of speech. Toward the end of the poem, these failures take the form of an anaphora, a more formal declaration of what hasn't been said before: "noldest þu mid þine muþe bimaenen þine neode" (you would not bemoan your need with your mouth [F 5]); "noldest þu mid muþe bidden me none miltsunge" (you would not ask for some forgiveness for me with your mouth [F 15]). The soul confronts the body not just with its lack of volition, but with its lack of the desire to speak, whether to recount and to bemoan its own sin or to petition for forgiveness. Part of this insistence on the physicality of utterance may be due to the poem's interest in orality. Judgment will come from the "muþe" of God (E 46): a recurrent metonymy of death is that the tongue lies still in a mouth that is itself a grave (G 15). This interest suggests that the poem imagines that the world the body and soul inhabit is above all a speech community. Because this body, it seems, has uttered less-than-charitable things in its life, its silence is an occasion for gladness among those who suffered its speech as insult and reproach (*teone*):

> Þeo men beoþ þe bliþre, þe arisen aer wiþ þe,
> þet þin muþ is betuned, þu þeo teone ut lettest
> þe heom sore grulde, þet ham gros þe aȝan,
> deaþ hine haueþ bituned, and þene teone aleid. (C 16–19)

[The men who arose against you before will be the happier, that your mouth is shut; you let out insult that grieved them sorely, that frightened them against you; death has closed it, and ceased the insult.]

We could here alter the old ethnographic claim that the rites of death are more for the living than for the dead to the observation that silence is more for the living than for the dead. Silence signifies, for the living community, assent, or at least the absence of the *agon* that disturbs consent, and the articulation, quite literally, of community. From the perspective of the body, of course, it is not so much death as the inability to speak that has cut it off (*afursed*, driven it away) from human society:

Nu þu bist afursed   from alle þine freonden,
nu is þiin muþ forscutted   for deaþ hine haueþ fordutted. (E 37–38)

[Now you are removed from all your friends, now is your mouth completely shut, for death has stopped it up.]

That internal rhyme in the last line is an intermittent feature of the poem. It appears at its most extended in two fragments, where the words *siþ* and *lif* are the rhymes and indicate, as I suggested earlier, the ways in which life can be represented as a span, a distance, a time, a term. In this line, the rhymes themselves echo the terminating of speech, the repeating dull thud of a dental preterite that sounds like the obstruction with which this line ends—"fordutted." Underlying this formal recurrence is the problem of how to understand just what relations are, or can be, established at this moment. What likenesses might still remain between the body and soul? What genus do they belong to, if not each to a separate genus? The scattering and dissolution that the poem traces seems to call each element of the self back to its constituent kinds, to reveal exactly what they have actually been all along, the body hardening like the clay to which it is "ikunde" (A.32).

The body implicitly seems to have believed that as long as it was capable of speech it could stay alive, that to be a *zoon politikon* was also to be a *zoon logon*. Human speech defers death, keeps it at bay. As such, the body is a good-enough but unwitting Hegelian, too, because its mastery of and in speech is predicated against death. It believes, as the soul points out, that speech is possible precisely because there is no end to it, that as long as one can talk one stays alive: interminable speech is placed against, supposited by, the end that is death.

Þu wendest þet þin ende   nefre ne cumin scolde;
to longe þolede deaþ þe   þet he nolde nimen þe,
for efre þu areredst sake [stirred up lawsuits]   and unseihte were,
and ic was wiþinnen þe   biclused swuþe fule.
Þu were wedlowe and monsware . . . [violator of an agreement and a
   perjurer]. (D 43–47)

[You believed that your end would never come; too long death tolerated
you and did not take you; you always stirred up strife and were quarrel-
some, and I was shut up within you most foully. You were a betrayer and
a perjurer.]

The body is obviously not enough of a Hegelian to know that its speaking
without end is what Hegel would have called a bad infinity, a deferral of the
principle that defines and completes a movement rather than an indeter-
minable, that is to say, transcendent, movement. The body cannot be anything more than a perverter of language, a violator of precisely what it says,
because to stabilize language in that way would be to bring it to an end, to
bring being to an end.

Yet one cannot die silently. One can't hope to redeem oneself merely
by withdrawing from the pathology of speaking compulsively to stay alive.
One has to speak in the right way, to say the right things. What is left un-
said is also what would bring this life to terms with itself: the sins that en-
velop the soul, trapped and mute in a welter of perjuries and forswearings,
bound by chains of signification. What we are—more precisely, what we have
failed to become—needs to be uttered to make ourselves determined beings.
We need to speak what makes us fail, what will obliterate us if it remains
undetermined. That is, we must, as those who have sought salvation have,
indict ourselves. Sinful men, the soul says, ought to

> bimaeneþ hore misdeden   and seoþþen miltse onfoþ,
> þurh soþne scrift   siþieþ to criste,
> seggeþ hore sunnen   and hire soule helpeþ. (F 9–11)

[bemoan their misdeeds and afterwards receive forgiveness, through true
shrift travel to Christ, reveal their sins and help their souls.]

In a period before the Fourth Lateran Council of 1215 enjoined yearly confession on all Christians, this meant that confession was usually an act undertaken at the point of death, that is, when one knew one's life was coming
to an end. Speaking one's sins was a final act, a termination of life.

Speaking sin is the final act in which the body has any volition. And it
is possibly the last moment at which the soul's volition is anything more
than an infinitely deferred potential, the desire to act without the capacity
to act. Throughout the poem the soul remains something like the body's
ideal, a form to which it should conform itself without the body's complete
awareness of it. Although the entire poem except for the first fragment con-

sists of the soul speaking to the body, and although the body is utterly silent throughout the poem, the shape of the discourse, its ideal form, is determined by the body. The soul doesn't speak on its own initiative; death doesn't free it from the body so much as confront it with the determinations that the body has already made, and that now shape the capacity of the soul to speak. It is, to return to the discussion that began this chapter, in every sense a late style.

Almost everything it says is voiced as a regret for the actions and inactions that the body has committed: "woa wrohtest þu me" (you worked me woe), begins the soul, and proceeds to list a series of what we could call null sets, the things the body accumulated that are now vanished and meaningless: pride, money, clothes, gold vessels, relatives to sit beside the sick and dying body. And yet the soul's articulation of the body's failures, which could be a mere recitation of proscriptions and taboos, amounts to a kind of decorum, a conversion into the work of literature of the evanescent and eminently reversible work of the body.

In this poem we discover only in death what we should have known all along—to be more precise, what we should have heard all along: the music of intercession, the sung masses for the souls of those who know that their bodies are merely the lodging of their more permanent if silent selves. But these selves are drawn out by a music that redeems. Only in death do we hear that we should have heard music all along, and this poem relates to us what we should know before it's too late: that this music itself is the discourse of death, the relating of the knowledge that is inseparable from the work of the poem. It is not only a poem that is founded on the work that the scribe himself presumably undertakes regularly in praying for the souls of both living and departed brothers or laypeople in and around Worcester, but one that celebrates, even apotheosizes, the work of learning. Learning is imagined here as a joyful, literally redemptive practice, recuperating not merely the past but also, and more important, the dead:

Noldest þu makien lufe wiþ ilaerede men,
ʒiuen ham of þine gode þet heo þe fore beden.
Heo mihten mid salmsonge þine sunne acwenchen,
mid hore messe þine misdeden fore biddaen; . . . (B 20–23)

[You did not want to make praises [or practice charity][27] with learned men,
To give them some of your goods so that they would pray for you.
They might have subdued your sin,
With their Mass prayed for your misdeeds.]

In isolation, this quotation refers in an almost sly, squinting way to the economies that sustain a monastic community in the twelfth century, the interpenetrating economies of petition in which pecuniary and spiritual interests, lay and clerical modes of devotion, coincide. There is obviously a petitionary element here, a degree of pecuniary self-interest. But it is also a serious statement of the function of learning for a scribe who values learning deeply, and whose exercise of it is an act of recuperation and a form of salvation. The literal sense of "making"—a *poeisis* of the body and the community—probably extends the petitionary mode outward to the rest of the poem, suggesting that its making is an aspect of the real petitionary work we all should perform, the fashioning of a discourse of the soul before its moment to speak can arrive, the moment when it is precisely too late.

Yet the poem *is* set at the moment when it is too late, at the moment when the conditions for a music of the soul have become visible, but also when the connection of language to the world is coming untethered. The list of null sets that begins the soul's discourse actually uses the formal register of the *ubi sunt* trope: "Hwar is nu . . ." and its variants repeated five times in eight lines (B 4–11). As grisly as the subject of the soul's speech often is—it includes concrete and particular descriptions of what will happen to the body once it is in the grave—it still has a certain elegant formality. The soul repeatedly uses such figures as prosopopoeia (A.11, D.44, E.38, F.16), amplificatio (F.20–33), elaborate chiasmus (B.44–45, C.48–49, F.12–13, F.21–22), zeugma (D.12–14, F.8–11), polyptoton (B.7, E.43, F.48), and, of course, anaphora, as in the "Hwar is nu . . ." passage.[28] But perhaps his characteristic figure, because it is one that also represents his whole mode of speaking, is *antitheton*, or *contrapositio*, technically a figure of thought rather than of speech, in which a succeeding clause asserts the opposite of the preceding one: "þu were þeow   of þines weolan" (you were the servant of your goods [B 32]). Augustine says that this figure of speech gives an utterance beauty, not least because it imitates the way in which the opposition of contraries gives a certain eloquence to the composition of history itself, making it, in the words of Marcus Dods's translation, "as it were an exquisite poem set off with antitheses."[29]

It is antitheton that makes the exquisitely subtle ontological balance of this poem possible. The speaker is, after all, a soul that has not achieved its terminus, and that never will experience the full enjoyment of being. And the topic, the topos, the place, of the soul's discourse is a body in the midst of annulment, not yet entirely gone but rapidly disappearing (bones "daeled," etc.). The poem is, in other words, an expression of the terms of being at a moment in which the self turns to nonbeing: the very objects and events by which the body-self defined its being are now emptied, and emptied ontologically by the soul's very analysis of them.

The reason for this turn is, of course, that so much of the soul's discourse has to focus on the body's negations, on the privations that come into being when the body dies. This particular line, for instance, describes three kinds of privation: of an ethics of utility, of the knowledge of the real nature of the relation between person and wealth—of subject and object—and, of course, of the privation of these goods altogether by this point: "Luþerliche eart þu forloren from al þet þu lufedest" (You are wickedly removed from everything that you loved [35]), the soul continues. A great deal of what the soul says, then, is made up of the naming of things that no longer exist, or at least no longer exist in a relation to the body. Yet the very beauty of the soul's awareness of these things means that they still exert a kind of pull on it, which is to say, on us. The death that comes to the body is not exactly a negation of things in the simple sense, their obliteration and disappearance altogether. It is more like the kind of negation that Hegel describes in his account of how we come to understand the world through a succession of sensory experiences that we leave behind, a negation, as he says, that "cancels and preserves."[30]

Another way of putting this is that the soul has become an archivist. Its mode of antitheton is one sign of that: it is the way in which the polymorphous pleasures of the body in life are registered in death, according to a formal system of registration of which the body remained unwitting. But then the body's unwittingness was always the problem. It never seemed to know what was right before it, what could have been taken into the mind with the senses. What the soul tells the body in its own vernacular, "þu were þeow þines weolan," was always there to know, as the soul says, "on boken" (30). And what is in books is often better than what we experience, or what we ourselves can describe. The soul cites a far better, more elegant, example, of *antitheton* than it comes up with itself: "qui custodit diuitias seruus est diuitiis" (31). It fits the soul's mode of address even better than its own version does, too, with the reversal of the logical subject and predicate (*diuitias*) more explicit, even marked by their position as the final alliterating stresses in the A and B verses. Knowledge is formed by something beyond or prior to the self. In many ways the soul's place in death is that of the body's in life. It stands before the body as the body stood before its experiences, seeing what the body should have seen before: the power of the archive to bring us to terms with ourselves:

Ne heold ic þine eiȝen opene   þeo hwule ic þe inne was?
Hwi noldest þu lefen   þa þu hi iseiȝe,
Hu þine fordfaederes   ferden biforen þe?
Nu heo wunieþ on eorþe,   wurmes ham habbeþ todaeled,
Iscend hore sorhfulle bones   þe þeo sunne wrohten. (D 21–25)

[Did I not hold your eyes open when I was within you?
Why would you not believe when you saw it,
How your forefathers before you ended up?
Now they dwell in earth, worms have dismembered them,
Ruined their sorrowful bones with which they wrought sin.]

The body should have been urged on to nullify its relation with what would become its archive (or crypt?): its malicious speech, its merely and infinitely inert body. Yet they are still there, and somehow as readers we are meant to experience their persistence as a part of the meaning of the poem.

We are meant, I think, to experience in this poem a work of negation, precisely and literally something that preserves and cancels. The mouth is preserved, as we are told over and over, but it is shut up with a key, stopped up with clay, silenced forever. It is incapable of confession, an act that the soul berates the body at some length for never practicing. But, in a mordant quotation from Psalm 119 (118 in the Vulgate), the soul points out that it will never again be the *spiritus* that expresses its longing for God: "os meum aperui, et attraxi ipsum." The rest of the verse explains that "I" do this because I long for the commandments of the Lord. But the body did not open its lips in life to express that, and now it never will. The verse now means something completely different: it describes, as the soul goes on to say, the body drawing the soul to it at the moment of conception or birth. But rather than function as a metaphor for panting, breathing earnestly, for God, the verse suggests the capture of the soul in the prison of the body: you "drew me to thee," says the soul. The death of the unrepentant body, silent before God, now draws the soul to it once more as it sinks to the earth, in a death that horribly recalls and cancels the original drawing together of body and soul when the self was created.

The beginning of the poem makes it clear that this body drawing—really dragging—the soul is itself being drawn to the earth. After death the body continues to change, growing cold and stiff after it is laid on the floor:

He coldeþ also clei—hit is him ikunde.
Mon hine met mid one ȝerde and þa molde seoþþen

Ne mot he of þaere molde habben nammore
þonne þet rihte imet rihtliche taecheþ.
þonne liþ þe cleiclot colde on þen flore. (A.32–36)

[He cools like the clay, to which he is akin.
Someone measures him and then the earth with a rod
Nor can he have any more of the earth
Than, justly measured, pertains to him.
Then the clayclot lies cold on the floor.]

Dying is here a process that terminates in the body's return to the earth. That return is marked by the body's susceptibility to the processes of nature, by its powerlessness to prevent its natural coldness from returning to it. Its dying involves the reassertion of a logic of identity that it has repressed: its essential affinity—"ikunde"—with the earth that is its starting and ending point. From this point on, that logic of identity governs the treatment of the body. Measuring it so that its grave is no bigger than it needs to be reinforces the equivalence of these two forms of matter: the earth and the body are equal in quantity and, by extension, in quality: the body can't take any more earth because it is now itself inert earth. The underlying point is not so much to show how the labor of gravedigging is apportioned—that is, how the grave is measured out—but to show that the measurement of the body and the earth is, in the end, a meaningless exercise, a demonstration of the equivalence of the two before they become, quite literally, the same thing: a body that is finally just a "cleiclot" on the floor.

It is surprising, after the uncompromising logic of the body's becoming earth, that near the end of the poem the soul tells us something quite different about that logic of identification. In the fourth fragment, in fact, the soul tells the body in the grave that it is *unlike* the earth:

Nes hit þe nowiht icunde   þet þu icoren hit hefdest;
nes hit icunde þe more   þen þine cunne biuoren þe. (D 19–20)

[Nor is what you have chosen more suitable for you because you have chosen it; and it is not more suitable for you than for your ancestors before you.]

Earlier, the merging of body and earth was as inevitable and as expected as the measuring out of its portion of earth suggests, as necessary as the metrical beat of those lines made of "molde" and clay. At some level, the work of the poem and the work of nature are equivalent, and what the narrator or poet seems to take for granted at that stage is that the language used to describe the process of dying and the event itself will converge in the reinscription of conventional observations about the signs of dying.

But in this dissolution of the body and the earth, not only does the poem, in the voice of the soul, contradict that very set of what seemed to be biologically determinate tropes; it negates the very terms it established for the relation of self and earth, the language of classification and genre that imply the voice of established custom and ontology. I argued earlier that the work of classification and genre begin in death, and the very order under which the body seemingly falls to the earth is itself subject to the dissolution to which the body is subjected. In other words, the identity of body and earth is established as a result of their fundamental non-identity: we know that we're not "really" earth, but we act, or ought to act, as if we really are. That non-identity tends to be enacted in such mortuary poems as a kind of phenomenological horror holding that knowledge at bay while not entirely negating it. Here the soul describes a more profound form of forgetting, in which what seems to be a normative ethical stance toward the fate of the body is itself, surprisingly, represented as a willful oblivion. Not only has the body not acted authentically as a mere extension of earth; it really shouldn't have, anyway, because from the perspective of ethics that wouldn't have been its authentic fulfillment. To be earth is not to become earth, but to overcome it. The body's fate as a mere "cleiclot," it turns out, was a choice, an expression of a freedom it didn't quite know it had. And it's also the choice of the poem: to inscribe the conventional physics of dying, rather than another form of dying that would allow for transcendence, a body out of the earth, an experience of the negative. What is earlier "kunde," natural, alike, is precisely its negation from the perspective of the soul, the work of the self that continues, and that uses a language of emptied terms. In the next chapter we will see that the desperate reiteration of words (and in the case of the next poem, the reiteration of the word *earth*) to describe what happens at the instant of death not only does not console; it empties meaning altogether.

PART II

Crypt

CHAPTER FOUR

Unearthly Earth:
Mortuary Lyric

The earth does not move.
—Edmund Husserl

Memento, quaeso, quod sicut lutum feceris me, et in pulverem reduces me.
—Third Lesson, First Nocturne of the Office of the Dead

I have been arguing that the literature of dying concerns the almost desperate desire to write about death, but that it also, reluctantly, admits the impossibility of doing it adequately—or even doing it at all. At least part of any attempt to write about death involves the metonymic problem of writing itself: it cannot embody what it is about. Derrida famously named this problem *différance*: writing motions us toward the objects it denotes but cannot take us all the way there. In the case of death, writing stands at two stages of remove from what it is telling us about: we cannot enter death through writing because we are left at its limits, which border on, but do not touch, the real world. In death the real world is substantially changed—it is no longer there—and if writing could somehow get beyond its own horizon, we would still have to find a way of entering something that denies our existence. In this chapter I will be discussing a poem that uses a single word obsessively to try to break beyond these limits. It shows us exactly why we cannot write about death: the more we try to approach its ground, the more tangled we get in the approach itself.

The poem is only four lines long, and its brevity is a significant part of its power and meaning. There are two reasons it is often overlooked in studies of the Middle English lyric: it is the shortest version of a trope— earth returning to earth—that is the subject of much longer (and probably related) poems. Hilda Murray's Early English Text Society edition includes

twenty-four Middle English versions of the poem in manuscripts stretching
into the seventeenth century, and she records a version of it on a tombstone
from as late as 1837.[1] Her edition encourages readings of the four-line poem
as the embryo of better-developed poems, a primitive example of a tradition
more fully worked out in later decades and centuries. The other reason this
short poem has been overlooked is that it is part of the large and complex
anthology of poems that include the Harley Lyrics—one of the most substantial and important collections of lyric poems in the early fourteenth century.
Among them are many oft-cited poems: *Alysoun, Song of the Husband-
man,* and *Lenten ys come with loue to toun.*[2] In such compelling company,
this shortest of Harley Lyrics seems too taciturn to draw us away from the
longer and apparently more complex poems in the anthology. But, as I will
argue in this chapter, its terseness is a fundamental part of its meaning: it
embodies a meditation on death and dying far more complex and profound
than we find in many much longer poems.

> Erþe toc of erþe erþe wyþ woh;
> Erþe oþer erþe to the erþe droh;
> Erþe leyde erþe in erþene þroh;
> Þo hevede erþe of erþe erþe ynoh.

> [Earth took of earth earth with woe;
> Earth drew other earth to the earth;
> Earth laid other earth in an earthen chest;
> Then earth had of earth enough earth.]

In this poem, the word *erthe* signifies the ultimate, final ground of our being. But this very finality also makes it something like a nonsense word, so
self-contradictory that its meaning is virtually impossible to disentangle.

Underlying the confusion that besets this word is the metamorphosis that
death involves, a metamorphosis that, in a sense, does not take place. After
death, bodies remain the same earth of which they are made in life, but
they also become abject, *un*earthly things. At the moment of death they are
separated from their own earth, which they have just become. They are dirt,
not earth. But the difference between them is purely one that we make ourselves. As Mary Douglas and Julia Kristeva have argued, the presence of dirt
says much more about the way we organize ourselves and our places in the
world than it does about the essence of dirt.[3] For Douglas, especially, dirt
threatens the order of symbolic purity because it contaminates the place
where it appears. That place is what creates dirt in the first place. Drawing

symbolic boundaries requires us to imagine that they delimit certain regions and constrict limitless space into places of interdiction and permission. That is, a place is something that can be violated by bringing into it matter that we believe does not belong there.

Speaking about the irony that British farmers were willing to pay exorbitantly to import Peruvian guano to fertilize their fields, when fertilizer could be found abundantly in any English town, the nineteenth-century British parliamentarian Lord Palmerston first defined dirt as "nothing but a thing in a wrong place."[4] For most of our lives the avoidance of dirt means staying away from the wrong places or objects, or not moving things where they do not belong. But in death, I would argue, the body becomes a thing out of place simply because of its obdurate refusal to change the place it occupies, which is another way of saying that it becomes horrible when it becomes implacably and unalterably a thing of mere matter. A body is no longer a thing with intelligence, spirit, or soul; it is simply there. Paradoxically, what Aristotle said makes it a body—the faculty of motion—is what allows it to commit impure and taboo acts in life. But the very absence of the faculty of motion in death makes the body a thing out of place, wherever that place happens to be. The body's denial of transcendence in death makes it merely continuous with other matter, and that is precisely why death is seen, especially in early Middle English, as the horror of the body or, more specifically, the profound disturbance of place. The dead man's friends in the Worcester Fragment *Soul's Address* cannot wait to get his body out of the house, away from them: "Now they think it all too long that you lie near them, before you be taken to where you will be buried" (Nu ham þuncheth alto long þat thu ham neih list / aer þu beo ibrouht þaer þu be grafen scalt).[5] The horror of death, represented this way, is that matter no longer belongs with itself.

To separate ourselves from the earth even while we are made of it is a problem that haunts the literary, if not the philosophical, imagination in the Middle Ages. The resurrection of the body raised the question of how bodies with a claim to the same particles of matter could be reconstituted fully, or in what way the body could be transformed if it is composed of its original form and material.[6] A full account of the debate would be a monument to the sustained attempt to make sense out of the earth once death and the possibility of resurrection enter into it, and it might or might not resolve the problem.

Bonaventure, for one, argues that making sense of the earth is impossible from the outset. Earth is a problem of language, not of physics or material science, because it is an elemental substance, yet in its elemental state does not yet have the form of earth: it is not dirt, soil, the globe, the body.

The elemental earth underpins all of those earths. But if the element is not the same as what we call earth, what do we then call it? When we call the element "earth," we are merely using the name that it eventually acquires when its forms are imposed on it, turning it into recognizable and intelligible matter. To talk about elemental earth is impossible, says Bonaventure, and any attempt to do so results in babbling (*balbutiendo*).[7]

In the hands of some writers, *earth* is a loquacious discoverer of synonyms. The question about earth that Pippin asks in a Latin dialogue that Alcuin wrote is both a precursor of the "Erthe" poem and its semantic opposite. Rather than crowd the world into the single signifier "earth," Alcuin finds in it a treasury of signifiers: "What is earth? The mother of the growing, the nurse of the living, the storehouse of life, the devourer of all things."[8] But in reminding us that earth is a devourer, and mentioning it last, Alcuin hints at the ultimate collapse that is described by earth poems' reduction of almost everything we can imagine into a single term. Alcuin saves the notion of annihilation for last, having built up a treasury of statements of the ways in which *earth* is itself a storehouse of the multiple forms of generation. This final, contradictory notion—earth as the devourer of all things—paradoxically completes the series, yet undoes it at the same time. The devouring that follows generation and sustenance clings to its opposites just as earth clings to everything we know. Underlying this mode of composition and reading is a more fundamental ontological security about the relation between word and thing, a conviction that words signify because of an originary imposition of material sense on the word or phrase. The example, in fact, that Isidore of Seville gives in his famous encyclopedia *Etymologiae* for etymologies that come *ex origine* is the twin physical and morphological origin of the word *homo*: man comes from earth, "homo . . . ex humo."[9] In Isidore, this isomorphism is a point of embarkation, the first branch of the many that will eventually become the whole tree of life. But by the fourteenth century the synecdoche of *earth* was more likely to suggest the ultimate decoupling of all linguistic distinctions in the face of death.

The paradoxical lesson of the return of all things, however ornate and sumptuous, to dust was thematized in fourteenth-century memorial brasses between the early 1320s, when a London funerary brassmaker offered a French version of it,[10] and as late as 1367, when a brass was made for John, the Third Lord Cobham, who died in 1408 (fig. 3).[11] The legend around the edges of the brass is a paraphrase of Genesis 3:19: "De terre fu fait // e fourme * et en Terre et a terre suy retourne * Iohan de Cobham. . . ." It differs from the inscriptions on the brasses belonging to his father and brother (which may have been made in the same workshop): those petition the reader to pray for the soul of the person. This one, however, takes a Bible verse and stretches it to the verge of vernacular poetry. The additional "et fourme" is hardly a qualifier critical for the sense of the sentence, but it produces two nearly octosyllabic lines, with a near-rhyme on "fourme" and "retourne." The division of this sentence into two lines is highlighted by the engraver, who put a small quatrefoil between them, as well as before the first word and following the word *retourne*, framing these lines as a discrete unit. Read as a unit, these lines enact visually what they concern: the return of the body to the dust of the ground. The lines start at the top left corner, above the head of the figure on the brass, and continue down the right-hand side to the feet, ending in the lower corner with the name "Iohan de Cobham." The process of reading the inscription draws the eye down the body, just as rhetorical manuals say to do in *effictio*, to the feet planted on the earth.

John Cobham's brass is the most visible form of the dark engine that pushes these poems forward, the paradox of trying to represent the comprehensive experience of a collapse that undermines the distinctions that make representation possible. The central conceit is that everything in the poem, as in the world, is reduced to a single element; but the more things the poem names in this reduction, the more it impeaches its critique of naming. It decouples itself, in other words, from its most interesting feature: the poem's production of its form out of sameness and repetition, rather than difference and relation (the joining together of heterogeneous elements by sonic association). And this is where the poem's aesthetic principle is also its most important lesson: the more one violates the stark purity of the form with adulterating nouns, the further away from our experience moves its essential demonstration that form is the collapse of possibility, that it is merely the vestige of what we imagine we say about something we cannot actually experience.

Another poem written around the same time uses precisely the opposite strategy. Rather than show how earth negates language, it attempts to encompass, even to transcend, the earth with its languages. I say "languages" because it is a remarkable trilingual poem, written in Latin, Anglo-Norman, and Middle English. It probably isn't possible to determine, on internal evidence alone, in which language the poem was originally written, because each version exploits the logic and resources of its language differently, and each version amounts to a different poem.[12]

Found on the back (dorse) of a roll recording the statutes to depose Edward II's friend Piers Gaveston and other "evil counselors," none of the poems is recorded elsewhere, and Hilda Murray found few correspondences between any of them and subsequent earth poems.[13] Like all versions later

Fig. 3. Formed of earth, bounded by *terre*. Brass for John, 3rd Lord Cobham (ca. 1367). Church of St. Mary Magdalene, Cobham, Kent. Author's photograph.

than the one I will discuss at length, these poems either make their moral explicit ("of erþ þou were makid and mon þou art ilich") or break character to address the reader directly.[14] In the trilingual version, the French poem addresses us, reminding us that we are taken from earth and will return to it ("O tu cheytiue tere de tere, remembrez / Vous estes pris de tere & tere deuendrez").[15] The Latin poems ends with a direct address to earth: "O tu terre domine! terre miserere."[16] Other versions use *vesta, humus, tumulum, ops, mundum,* and *fatum,* among other synonyms, where the English parallel uses only *erthe.*[17] In examples like this, the loss of the play on a single term that is central to the whole conceit of the poem may indicate that the Latin is a translation of the English.

The two poems in Latin and French have a profusion of things other than earth that act upon earth: angels, blood, *terminus, tubus, corpora, gloria* (Latin); and *Ruyne,* medicine, temptations, *frelete humeyne,* king, Jesus, God (French). By contrast, the extraneous nouns in the English poem are only *assize, Helle,* and *Louerd.* Even in this extended version, the English poem makes us feel as if we are caught claustrophobically in the web of one noun.[18]

The four-line "Erthe" poem is part of a booklet in one of the most important anthologies of early fourteenth-century French and English poetry, British Library Harley 2253. A collection of the Middle English lyrics in Harley 2253 was published by G. L. Brook in 1948 and for a long time was one of the standard texts for teaching Middle English lyrics. We know a lot about the manuscript—that it was written about 1340, that it has connections with Franciscan texts, scribes, and houses, that we can even name other manuscripts written by the same scribe—thanks to the extraordinary efforts of Carter Revard, who scoured local records offices for several decades; but we do not know anything more about this particular poem.[19] It is probably older than the manuscript, because several of its linguistic features are earlier than the manuscript (the rhyme in *oh* involves a back vowel that had moved further forward by the 1320s–1330s, and a velar fricative that had disappeared as a terminal feature). So what can we tell about the poem from the manuscript, since there is nothing else to go on, and the poem itself tells us so little? What we *can* do is look at how and where the poem appears in the big anthology of texts in Harley 2253, to see what was read along with it then, and whether the distinction I have made between a work of art and a merely didactic piece might be recognizable to the poem's readers. Is it, in other words, a poem about death or a poem about dying?

The booklet in which the poem appears itself is certainly an anthology of the literature of death and dying, no matter what the distinction between them might be. The booklet begins with a Latin prose account of the death

of St. Ethelbert, the king of the East Angles, who dreams about the "dissolution of his body" before he is martyred.[20] The second narrative is *Quant
voy le revenue d'hyver*, a poem describing the domestic cycle of the great
household against the repetition of the seasons, a formal device familiar from
the great stanza of *Sir Gawain and the Green Knight* describing the year that
elapses between the visit of the Green Knight and Gawain's setting out. The
next two poems concern the eschatology of death—in other words, the work
of dying: one is *The Harrowing of Hell*, a poem that examines the complex
interminability of the death of Christ in a debate between Christ and Satan.
The other is a "Debate between the Body and the Soul" (beginning "Hon
an þester stude I stod an luitel strif to here"),[21] which recasts the preceding debate as a dispute between body and soul and ends where *Harrowing*
does, with the banishment of Satan "bouten hende doun in helle grounde"
(104). This debate places in the foreground the problem of temporality and
finitude: the body has "liued to longe" (21), and all the soul can do now is
lament about a time that is definitively concluded ("Ful sore mai I mene
þenne þat ilke wile" [8]). The poem ends with a summary of the signs that
will mark the seven days before of the end of the world itself, a list that appears in the minor subgenre of poems on the signs of doomsday. Its connection between the end of individual lives, the end of the world, and the unending condition of the afterlife condenses in a single work the interlacing
concern of the booklet as a whole with the semantic, physical, and metaphysical extent of termination.

The "Debate" poem's interest in kinds of ending remains close to a tax-
onomy, however. The traces of the several genres from which it borrows are
still visible. The most obvious and extensive is the signs-of-doomsday list,
but at least twice the poem moves into the *ubi sunt* mode, and its depreca-
tion of the body's acts while alive borrows from romance and satire. The
possibility of contemporary citationality in a poem about dying is explored
much more directly and fully in three of the five remaining poems in the
booklet. Two center on recent executions that followed baronial revolts in
the second half of the thirteenth century—the *Song of Lewes* and the *Execution of Simon de Montfort*. Political death, the judicial termination of life,
moves even closer to the contemporary moment in the next poem, an account of the execution of Simon Fraser in 1306, which took place no more
than two or three decades before Harley 2253 was compiled.

All three of these poems about political dying suggest that judicial termination is anything but final. Although the subject put to death might not
literally become a revenant, the death they recount is still *dying*. A poem
such as the *Execution of Simon de Montfort* shows us how medieval au-

thors worry over what terms, what kinds of language, best describe the complex memorializations that a death like Montfort's demands. The poem calls its language a "dure langage," partly because its topic is the "dure mort" of Montfort. In the background one can sense the kind of advice offered in rhetorical manuals such as Geoffrey of Vinsauf's *Poetria nova*: that one should use words and figures appropriate for particular occasions.[22] But this poem doesn't pull out the rhetorical stops—anaphora, apostrophe—that such manuals encourage. It simply suggests that there's something difficult about, in, or around the language it *should* be using—it is "dure." Death in that poem, in other words, is an ontological and a political problem, not a problem that implicates from the beginning the language used to describe it, a language that is "dure" only because death itself is "dure."

Even so, in its philosophically modest way this poem concerns, as the "Erthe" poem does, the interminable nature of death. It's a death hardened against us, enigmatic from the start, and sealed off from our experience. There is still something unrequited about this particular death, a kind of work that goes on, and which informs this particular work, the hardened language of repetition. It is not only a "dure mort" that recurs in each chorus, but an experience of mourning represented as universal yet irresolvable precisely because it is not particular and individual. It is not I who lament over de Montfort but everyone, which is to say no one in particular. This lament, which begins as a personal and effective one, motivated by the poet's heart and tears ("Mon cuer le voit / . . . Tut en ploraunt" [My heart, all in tears, wills it; 1–4]), is, by the chorus, merely the trace of its own passage: "Molt enplorra *la terre*" (The land greatly bewailed it). What is repeated is not this lament, but the lament that has already terminated: this hard death has already been "molt enplorra," fully mourned by the end of the poem, which has already turned us to the earth again and again, the earth that, it turns out, is what had lamented death all along.

The bad infinity of this lament is, in fact, the formal expression of the paradox of political continuity with which the poem begins, the dismemberment of baronial bodies that allows the salvation of "Engleterre" (12). Thus, the poem's chorus echoes the collapse of a certain political determination—the failure of the baronial revolt—but also the failure of a determination of a more important kind, the determination that marks off all earth from the earth that is uniquely and obdurately "Engleterre," the earth that is England.

Two very short texts, one Anglo-Norman and one Latin, immediately precede the "Erthe" poem. Taken together, they make up what Susanna Fein has described as a "trilingual meditation on mortality," sandwiched between the accounts of the deaths of the two Simons.[23] The eight-line Anglo-Norman

poem, *Charnel amour est folie!*, urges us to avoid carnal love ultimately because it doesn't make good use of time: "Qe velt amer sagement / Eschywe
ce quar breve vie / Ne lesse durer longement" (2–4). The problem is not that
carnal love will lead to spiritual death or deprive one of the beatific life, but
that it doesn't last long—it is a "brief delit," and its brevity simply doesn't
outweigh the torment "sanz fyn" after death. The poem's form echoes the
balance and judgement that it is about: line 7's "brief delit" echoes line 3's
"breve vie" (they're also linked by the *-ie* rhyme) and line 8's "santz fyn
dure" echoes line 4's "Ne . . . durer longement" (linked by the rhyme *longement* [4]/*le torment* [8], drawing the poem's lesson out aurally across its
length). There's a certain elegance, almost wit, in the poem's structure. But
its first words hint at the more disturbing mordant wit that structures the
"Erthe" poem: "amour charnel," carnal love, also suggests the kind of love
that leads to the charnel house, the chapel where disinterred bones are
stacked together for permanent preservation.

The Latin distich right after this poem restates, more compactly, the ab-
surdity of balancing time against eternity: "Momentaneum est quod delec-
tat, / Set eternum quod cruciat." "Moment" and "eternity" rhyme, but so
badly that their juxtaposition just suggests how badly they fit together; what
really belong together are delight and torture. It's difficult to misconstrue or
misunderstand this couplet, which explains its frequent use in sermons.[24] It
is an almost pure expression of didactic discourse, teaching with the merest
modicum of delight. As befits a sermon, its point is clear and unambiguous;
but it begs to be fleshed out with an exemplum or two. Its precision and clarity, indeed, set off the "Erthe" poem's ambiguities even more starkly: we move
from the semantically sharp Latin terms *momentaneum* and *eternum* to the
murkiness of Middle English *erthe*.

The "Erthe" poem asks us to think of a number of different registers even
apart from the liturgical and biblical merely to unravel its meaning. "Taking" earth, in the first line suggests birth or even conception, the assumption
of matter by the form of the soul or the intellect; the curse placed on Adam,
which required him to till the soil "in sorrow" in order to sustain his life; and
the incarnation, in which God takes on the earthly substance of the human.
The shape, the narrative, of the poem as a whole depends on a similarly
diverse range of discourses, which determine the meaning of the poem. It
spells out part of the burial service (from Job 10: "as clay thou madest me,
and into dust thou wilt bring me again," from the first nocturne); the explanation that God gives Adam for the curse on him (Gen. 3:19: "dust thou
art, and unto dust shalt thou return"); the whole life of Christ, in which the
"other earth" of his persecutors drives him into the "earthen place," and in

his bodily ascension leaves the earth behind; the principle of medieval gravity, in which everything, as Chaucer's eagle in *The House of Fame* says, is
ruled by "kindely enclynyng," the attraction of every kind of matter to its
appropriate place; the logic of possession, in which we only acquire things
"with wo," take them out of circulation ("erthene throh" echoes the play of
the two senses and functions of coffers and chests in the late Middle Ages,
to store wealth and to contain corpses), drive ourselves to our deaths in their
pursuit, and finally end up with nothing—that is, in the fine understatement
of the final line, with "ynoh."[25] And, finally, the poem is also about its own
inevitable termination: "thou hast of erthe erthe erthe inough" means that
we have had too much of the word *earth*.

Reminding us that we are formed "de Terre," the quatrain couches the
question of our being, and its termination, in terms of form: is our form the
form of the earth, the form that the earth takes? If so, then what form does
earth take to accommodate—literally form itself to—our earth? The haunting brilliance and morbid wit of this poem abides in its presentation of
"erthe" as a formal problem: the conventional rituals that mark transitions
into and out of life are usurped by their forms of enactment. The lines evac-
uate terms we have heard often, but perhaps have not thought about often.
The verse turns to, turns up, turns over "erthe," not just as the subject of
our thought, but as the end of thought, the end of the subject: Adam (named
for earth) is less than what he was because of the curse of earth; Job is reduced to mere earth. Earth is the end, and centuries before Wallace Stevens
the quatrain imagines the end of imagination. Earth, as substance, is independent of time and all-encompassing. It is both subject and predicate. "Erthe"
taking "erthe" from "erthe" is at once severely restrictive (we are only always "erthe" after all), and astoundingly capacious ("erthe" is everything).

The repeated use of the word *earth* stages both a repression and the return of the repressed: we tend to notice the formal likenesses of each repetition of the word, to experience first the chilling sameness of the term that
suggests death in all of its leveling force, and only then to start to work out
how each occurrence is an index to a different phenomenon. What might
be the consolation—that earth enfolds everything, that it literally grounds
us—turns out to open onto the empty space of thought. Like a revenant, the
word asks us to look at the world around us differently, to think about why
we see a repetition where there is really only fatal difference. I think that
the later version of the poem, with the two-line address to the reader, points
out what constitutes this fatal difference: the lag between oneself and one's
death. If it is untrue that what we are as separate beings is constituted by
the essential sameness of our deaths, or at least (which is all we can know)

the essential sameness of the terms by which we live, then life is something more than just the return of the same. There is a sense in which life is a meaningful, sensible term. This might be what Augustine referred to, in his discussion of the wake of the first death in the world, the murder of Abel by Cain, as the capacity to distinguish rightly. Yet distinction itself is the fatal impulse: Abel makes the right distinction and dies; Cain makes the wrong distinction and ends another's life. Cain's sin is "not distinguishing rightly," and so his life is marked *by* distinction, by a physical sign, by a life lived under certain terms, by the emergence of civilization. In short, Cain's is marked as a life, just as the only term possible for life in this poem is the capacity to distinguish, which undoes the very terms by which the poem defines the terms of life.

The act of distinguishing stirs up a further problem. If we rescue the meaning of the poem by distinguishing rightly what each occurrence of the word *erthe* signifies, then we have to deny that it is the same term in each case. In the strictest sense, each occurrence is a different word. When the poem is read aloud (or even read silently) the term *erthe* becomes a *vox*, an utterance that has its own unique situation in time and space, a materiality that cannot be uprooted. No matter can inhabit two spaces at once. In that sense, the "Erthe" poem should be, theoretically at least, utterly intelligible once it is read aloud, since its meaning unfolds as each word is anchored to a specific utterance.[26] Once each term is uttered, it is distinguished absolutely from every other. The tangle of iterations that at first appears baffling is straightened out, each knot undone in turn. So far this ideal resolution to the problem of the poem accords with logical procedure as well: in a syllogism, for instance, which uses three terms twice each, the same utterance, as Walter Burley summarized the argument, cannot be pronounced twice.[27] Yet it must remain true that the *term* meant by the utterance can be repeated, or a syllogism would not work.[28]

Similarly, the "Erthe" poem's meaning depends upon both the obvious identity of the occurrences of the word *erthe* and the possibility of differences among them. We know that the poem is about "erthe," in other words, but might not know yet how, precisely: it is suspended between the semantic permissiveness of logic and the strict and literal jealousy of grammar. Part of the lesson of the poem's form, then, is that we cannot easily attach together the various instances of finitude, yet they all amount to the same thing. It might be possible to discern the meaning of the iterations of *erthe* in the abstract, but the poem's difficulty unfurls as one turns to each instance of the word, and the terms are fixed in time. No ordinary audience could pinpoint the meanings of each utterance as they appear one after the other: if the poem was ever uttered aloud, it was also not fully understood. If it is *vox* (in the abstract) that guarantees meaning, it is also *vox* (as a speech act) that undoes it: a voice must be singular and yet somehow universal.[29]

The repetition of the word *earth* involves a further difficulty for separating its sense. I have discussed already how much of a problem it had been ever since Aristotle to refer to a state of nonbeing. The problem is compounded in this poem by its use of the same term to refer to states of being and nonbeing; the problem behind the word is that not just of recovering fine shades of meaning, but of making sense of two meanings, each of which implies the annihilation of the other. On the one hand, *erthe* refers to the quickening of flesh that took place in the incarnation ("erthe toc of erthe"), but on the other, it refers to the reversion of humans to mere materiality ("erthe in erthene throh"), to their nonbeing. In that sense, *erthe* has the "antithetical sense of a primal word,"[30] a word that refers to two meanings that could not be tenable together in the physical world, just as "cleave" means both to "cut apart" and "join together." But the antithetical sense of *earth* is just the most obvious manifestation of a problem that underpinned all references to nonbeing. For Roger Bacon, terms that refer to states of nonbeing are necessarily "equivocal" (*De signis*) and can acquire sense only when they are linked with temporal verbs (an action that he, and other philosophers of language, called "ampliation"). In other words, nonbeing can be designated only by referring ever more precisely to moments, or a moment, of being—the very work of the verbs *toc, droh, layde,* and *hevede,* which are the elements of the poem that tether each use of the word to a specific sense. Perhaps the most obvious paradox of the poem, apart from the contradiction within the word itself, is that it depends upon repeated actions to make its ultimate point that earth is a quiescent, inactive substance that contains, if it contains anything, only nonbeing.

To be (if one can say that at all) mere earth is to have the senses dulled, inseparable from the thing perceived, to forget the senses of the body—there is nothing separate to sense—to forget the senses of the words that are rooted in the material; there are no distinctions to be made in the merely material. In that sense, one confirms one's own state of being by parsing the different senses of the term *earth,* making distinctions that ultimately tell us that we are not—rather, are not yet—indistinguishable from nonbeing. But once we do that fully, the word *erthe* flashes into multiple points of being, and the stifling sameness that haunts it does not exist, at least for the moment in which we understand the meanings of *earth.* But the originary repetition of the poem, the earth returning to the earth, forces us back continually into the recognition that our ownmost possibility, indeed potential, is to become

what we were, to become something that can no longer become. Even as the
poem suggests that we move toward our own unique and peculiar points of
disappearance, its address to us as individuals is undermined by the very
didactic imperative that we are supposed to incorporate in our lives: we
face death, and our choices ought to be informed by the recognition that
our lives could become terminated works at any moment. We can see more
clearly how this happens by looking at the stanza's ending in the slightly
different version of the poem in Harley 913.

> Of erth thou were makid, and mon thou art ilich;
> In on erth awaked the pore and the riche.[31]

In death we become universal, but also empty of social and temporal par-
ticularity. This poem intensifies this loss by speaking to us, by pointing us
out deictically: "Of erth *thou* were makid. . . ." But the address here is far
from intimate: "thou art ilich," that is, you might as well be anyone else.
These last two lines move toward a *moralitas*, even a solution, that the
Harley poem rigorously forecloses. In longer versions, the remaining stanzas, like all of the later, different versions of the poem, unriddle what lies so
compactly and enigmatically in the Harley poem. This radical disambigu-
ation in the body of the poem, as a part of the poem itself, belongs to the
larger development in the terms of Middle English literature this book will
be tracing. But the unspooling of the first stanza by a couplet of fourteeners
in this poem suggests that the later history of the poem continues in the
general direction of a solution to the problem.

    This is especially clear in a version copied around 1440, in the Lincoln
Thornton manuscript, which ends with the rubric "Mors soluit omnia."[32]
This is often translated as "death undoes everything," but perhaps a more
pointed rendition for our purposes is "death solves everything," like the
gamesmaster of Ingmar Bergman's film *The Seventh Seal*. This sense of the
word *solvit* is echoed in the juxtaposition of the "Erthe" poem in Harley
913 with a group of riddles in Latin, which suggests that the poem itself
belongs to the genre of the riddle.[33] The riddles in Harley 913, too, point
back to the complexity of death and reference in the poem. Some of these
riddles are well-known, and they work along similar lines: most are cryp-
tograms, riddles that substitute letters, words, or phrases for other letters
and words. One riddle, for example, describes the shapes of the letters to be
inscribed: the answer to "Prima triangula, post tripidem, post pone rotun-
dum" is "Amo."[34] Others refer punningly to vocalizations and tend to be

multilingual, crossing back and forth from Latin into French and English: "ego," for example, stands for the letter *g*, or *je* in French; "apis" stands for the letter *b*, or *bee* in English. As Andrew Galloway says of these riddles in particular, they produce "a kind of intricate and playful trilingualism like that in some of the poems in London, British Library, Harley 2253."[35] But where the "Erthe" poem relentlessly mines a single word for its multiplicity of meanings, these riddles range across the lexicons of other languages in order to make sense of what is implicit in them.

But these riddles suggest more than an ecumenical interest in the play among the three languages of medieval England. Many of them hint that they engage specifically philosophical interests in theories of language and reference—and especially in the ways terminist logic helps to resolve the riddles of Latin and the vernacular. Several riddle collections include short treatises that implicate this academic interest in theories of reference, such as the one known as the *Secreta* from the first part of the fourteenth century, or the enigmatic, cryptic prophecies of John of Bridlington, which are glossed by a friar named Erghome, who wrote a preface about the ten modes of occultation that Bridlington used to write his riddles. Erghome's sixth kind of occultation, for example, involves obscuring an English name in a Latin phrase, so that according to the "communem modum loquendi non intelligitur" (common mode of speech it is not understandable): by the exposition "istorum terminorum, *carus vicus*, significatur istud nomen, *Derby*" (of the terms *carus vicus* the name *Derby* is revealed).[36] Here, as in other examples, the gloss invariably analyzes not words, but specifically terms. It is clear that the work of occultation, or at least of unriddling it, is influenced not only by terminist logic, with its focus on the terms that make up meaningful sentences, but specifically by the theory of supposition. One kind of riddle, formed by dropping a letter or prefix, is analyzed as a term that has diverse acceptations. That is, the term can supposit in several ways in a sentence. This doesn't mean that it has diverse references, but that it is treated within the sentence in diverse ways. The example sentence in Erghome's prologue is the following: "Si quis habet taurum, caput amputat, inde fit aurum." Taking the head off the bull means not decapitating the animal, but taking the first letter of *taurum*, which leaves *aurum*. As the prologue explains, the riddle works because the "terminus, *taurum*, non accipitur pro animali," but is accepted only for "isto termino, *aurum*." That is, the term *taurum* is treated, the prologue says, materially, according to what terminist logic calls material supposition, the self-referential treatment of a term. This is a kind of acceptation that appears in the final line of "Erthe toc of erthe." But another kind of acceptation analyzed by Erghome explains the *modus tractandi* of the poem more generally. This kind, what we now would class under the heading of ambiguity or ambivalence, is called *aperta aequivocatione*. When the terminus *cancer* is used ("ponitur"), he says, it can signify a fish of the sea, a sign of the heavens, and the king of Scotland. Open equivocation is indeed perhaps the best description of the way the "Erthe" poem works, with an equivocation so open that it uses virtually no other terms. This kind of occultation of all the others is defined in terms most directly indebted to the theory of supposition: it occurs when "aliquod nomen ponitur ad supponendum pro pluribus et ignoratur pro quo supponit" (One noun is posited/placed [*ponitur*] suppositing for many and it is not known for what it supposits).

The questions innate to terminism had already made the genre of the sophism one of the most popular in Scholastic literature and helped to make its riddling form one of the expressions, and provocations, of philosophical wonder. In England, especially, *sophismata* were used as more than mere teaching exercises: they advanced the theories of terminist logic, which sought to refine the ways in which terms could be understood. That is, it tried to explain not what terms meant in isolation, but how understanding comes about through the particular functions that terms take in sentences. Unlike the modal logic that was dominant at the University of Paris, which sought to link together the parts of sentences and the parts of the world, terminist logic at Oxford concentrated on the particular claims that a sentence made. It explained how the supposition of a sentence, the claims it intended to make, could be recovered by its audience, and how terms could be used by a writer or speaker to convey just the sense he intended.

Work on supposition had long identified the difficulties in using the word *homo* to stand for being, and it could be so difficult to use it to refer to dying and death that the qualifications necessary to make it clear would be cumbersome. The word itself often underwent theoretical and hypothetical grammatical transformation under the pressure of the drive to correct fallacies and untangle *sophisma*. A *summa* on the *Sophistocorum Elenchorum* shows how the word can be subjected to a grammar that we can only call virtual in the fullest sense of the word to solve the problem of imponderable nonbeing:

Homo est in sepulcro
Sed omnis homo est animal rationale
Ergo animal rationale est in sepulcro.

Sophisma est secundum figuram dictionis, quia interpretatus sum genitivum casum nominativum. Cum enim dico: "homo est in sepulcro,"
idest pars hominis, et ita "homo" genitivi casus est ibi secundum intel-
lectum. Sed cum assumo "omnis homo est animal rationale," ibi accipitur "homo" pro nominativo. Et ideo non sequitur, quia interpretatus
sum genitivum nominativum.

[A man/the man is in the sepulcher.
But every man is a rational animal.
Therefore a rational animal is in the sepulcher.

This sophisma works according to the figure, or the fallacy, of dictio,
because the genitive is interpreted as the nominative. When I say "a man
is in the sepulcher," I mean a part of the man, and therefore "man" is
in the genitive case there according to understanding. But when I assert
that "every man is a rational animal," there "man" is taken, accepted,
for the nominative.][37]

The sophism can be solved, that is, made intelligible, by reading each occurrence of the word *homo* in a different way: in the first instance, it means the
part of a human that is the body; in the second, it means the entire human,
including especially the faculty of reason. So the sophism does not assert
what it impossible, that a dead human is the entire human—and more particularly, it does not assert that a dead human *is*: the term for the human in
the sepulcher does not supposit for being.

Like a sophism, the "Erthe" poem asks its readers to make sense of terms
that seemingly supposit for being when (a) they either supposit for nonbeing also, or (b) nonbeing cannot be supposited of anything in the first place.
The only way to make logical sense of the poem in these terms is to understand *earth* as functioning differently in each case. In the line "erthe leyde
erthe in erthene throh," for instance, the first "erthe" refers to the live human or humans burying the second "erthe," a dead human, in the ground.
As our *Summa* logician would say, the first "erthe" is understood as genitive, the second as nominative, and the third (now an adjective) as dative or
nominative—and that is where the poem becomes difficult to understand
or resolve (as the *Summa* would say, "non sequitur"). It does not seem to
depend on valid syllogistic connections between the terms and may indeed
be a true sophism along the lines of "homo est in sepulcro." The line, if not
the entire poem, is constructed by the "figure of diction" in an even more

rhetorically implicated sense than the syllogism is. Earth is both the container and the thing contained, the part and the whole.

The poem suggests the deep phenomenological provocation that we cannot know, or indeed experience, what supposits for death, not because it is singular but because it makes itself known in too many ways. Even where a "thow" appears, even where we find a distinct supposition, as in the two-line Harley 913 addition, we find that it—we—are "mon ilich"; we find only similitude where we had thought to find finitude. To paraphrase Freud (not to mention the book of Ruth and *Sir Orfeo*), where "thow" was, there shall we be: where we begin to think for ourselves, we find ourselves thinking of being and nonbeing in general.[38] That is partly what Heidegger meant in a reading of a fragment by Parmenides, which says that thinking and being are "the same." Pointing out that "the same" is the grammatical subject of that sentence (that is, it reads something like "the same are thinking and being"), Heidegger argues that merely uttering the sentence doesn't exhaust its meaning, because (to use the terms of medieval logic) its supposition would merely be distributive or determinative, not discrete.[39] To demonstrate the truth of the proposition would require a continuous thinking of it: we could never specify what particular thing "the same" is, because that would be to disambiguate thinking and being—that is, to demonstrate their *dis*similitude in their reduction to a common term. Thinking the link between the two is also to terminate it, to engage in the act of bringing thinking, that is, being, to its terminus—to bring thinking to nonbeing.

We become earth, and we come from it. How can we think of it any differently than as a terminus that is unthinkable precisely because it points beyond both thinking and being, and does it simultaneously, in the strong, suffocating power of the term *earth* itself? It's perhaps this very sameness, the repetition without difference, that the poem deliberately terminates in both senses of the word in its final line: "Tho hevede erthe of erthe erthe ynoh." The "ynoh" here is also a "too-much," a litotes that signals the infinitation of discourse and describes what happens in this final line: a hypermetric line, ruined by the very repetition that had been a formal principle until then, an earth alliterating on the three of four stresses that make up the Middle English alliterative line and ruined by the poem's own primary term, ruined by earth.

That final line moves us from the mortal return that the rest of the poem tells us makes up our lives, the endless coming-to-be and passing-away of matter, to a discourse of finitude. It's initiated by the deixis of the first word, the temporal adverb *tho*, which points to a specific moment, a moment outside of the flux of the rest of the poem. It's then, at that time, that earth can be enough, or can have enough, only then when it comes to rest—that is, only when earth dies and is bounded by and in earth. This deixis again seems to point insistently at the location of irrepressible morbidity. But the very boundedness of what had been, in the first three lines, unbounded, certain to return, points us toward a more affirmative, even transcendent understanding of earthly termination.

The poem shows that this very burden is what tells us we are living, that we have enough of this burden. Merely to have enough of the earth is not, finally, to *be* the earth: recall Freud's maxim "I have it, that is, I am not it."[40] Being spoken to like this at the end of the poem is a reminder that the poem is in fact wrong, a reminder that the termination of life is not the same as life, that earth and being are separate categories. But to say that we "have" the earth, in the context of this poem, is to realize eventually that having is a litotes: having earth is ultimately to be possessed by it. In the terms of the poem, we have "enough" of earth simply because it is too much for us to bear, too much for us to possess at all without becoming it. Our possession *of* it is a possession *by* it, a kinder way of saying that we have enough of it because it already has us in our entirety, that it has us, as we prefer to think of it, too much.

The poem produces this effect of occultation not by hiding its terms, but by keeping them in plain sight. Nothing could be more immediate to us than earth, of whose substance we are made and against which we define ourselves—that is, define our lives precisely as the difference from the earth that we know we will become. This might sound vaguely Heideggerian, another version of the authenticity that death brings us. And it is. The earth is not just a covering keeping us from seeing what lies underneath us, but the very substance against which our senses and understanding founder because it is so much already the substance of our thinking about ourselves as individuals who define our very being as our ability to keep something from ourselves: our own nonbeing, which we imagine as radically unthinkable. As Heidegger argues, we understand most fully what the earth is when we understand, experience, it as "that which is by nature undisclosable, that which shrinks from every disclosure and incessantly keeps itself closed up."[41] Heidegger's predecessor Edmund Husserl put it more vividly: "The Earth, as Ur-Arche, does not move."[42] It is the beginning, but it stands outside the movement that it begins. That qualification seems to leave us with nothing more than an earth, a life, that is radically terminable: the substance we turn to at the end of thought, only to discover that it has the name of ineffability, the name of interminable death. But—and this is what this particular poem shows us so brilliantly—the earth is only the figure of the undisclosable because it appears before us: because we can perceive it, make something of it, because we can treat it as a work, even if it is never completed.

If there is drama in the poem, it is the drama of misrecognition. What at first seems simple becomes almost unthinkably complex: a poem composed almost entirely of one of the most primal, concrete words imaginable dissolves into intractable abstractions. But this drama unfolds only when and if we think about it. In several of his poems Chaucer turns this abstract work of understanding into the very logic of their central drama. Two of these, *The Book of the Duchess* and "The Pardoner's Tale," are structured around the inability of central characters to comprehend the full meaning of the terms *death* and *dead*. We are probably meant to think of these characters as venal, stupid, or self-absorbed. But what they fail to understand about death is also something that very few of the living themselves seem to have grasped: it is a catastrophe beyond understanding.

"Alway deynge and be not ded": *The Book of the Duchess* and "The Pardoner's Tale"

> Pestilence is in fact very common, but we find it hard to believe in a pestilence when it descends upon us.
>
> —Albert Camus, *The Plague*

I

It is not really fair to call the Man in Black from Chaucer's *The Book of the Duchess* venal, stupid, or self-serving. There is something elemental, even existential, about his plaints, even couched as they are in second-generation French courtly tropes. "[I] am sorwe," he says, "and sorwe is y" (597), an elegant chiasmus that is also a self-defining allegory. Allegory, as every medieval and classical scholar knows, is speaking otherwise; but the Man in Black articulates a fantasy of absolute self-identity. If what he says is an allegory, it is an allegory of something that cannot be allegorized. It is his sorrow over a death that is stubbornly intractable: he "is Alwey deynge," he says, but never actually dead. For him, death is the cessation not just of sorrow but of all the complaining that sorrow speaks through him. Death is conceptually unbound—indeed, not a concept at all, something that is absolute and annihilating: he longs for the "pure deth" (583). Purity here is probably the opposite of a quintessence, the distillation of something to its essential quality. As Kant defines it, purity is something like radical indeterminacy, the freedom from the obligation to be something. Purity, as he puts it, does not have a *Bestimmung*—a vocation, destiny, or determination—but neither does it have a voice, a *Stimme*. The Man in Black speaks of a pure death, but in speaking of it he renders it anything but pure: he imagines it in various roles, but they are also roles that death almost immediately undoes. Death is like a creator, whom "deth hath *mad* al naked"; but an enjambment at the end of that line ends the sentence with a death that an-nihilates: death has made him "naked / Of al the blysse" (577-8). Death, like a chivalric adversary, is his "foo," yet it is also arbitrary and coquettish, like a timid deer: "whan I folwe hyt, hit wol flee" (585).

The revelation at the end of the poem that all of this is really "herte-huntyng" suggests that no matter what the Man in Black says about death, he is actually thinking about either hunting or love. But part of what rings true about the Man in Black's orientation to death is precisely the way in which he has to speak about death in other terms. He cannot help but ap-proach death through love—at least, through love's conventions in the plaint and ballade. And yet the Man in Black wants to express something that we cannot seem to relate to about death—something that the Old Man of "The Pardoner's Tale" will also express—something that is nevertheless the one fundamental truth about death. In seeking death (especially a "pure" one), both figures will continue to fall into language and being: "Alway deynge and be not ded."

The Man in Black articulates a series of moving and elegant scenarios and metaphors that borrow heavily from the courtly literature of late medi-eval France. These speeches serve as evidence that English poets were extraor-dinarily attuned, if not oriented, to this literature, and they show, through a patchwork of allusion, how profoundly Chaucer had assimilated the work of, in particular, Guillaume de Machaut and Jean Froissart. In this early poem, at least, Chaucer's English poetry clearly echoes French poetry—tonally, thematically, and often verbatim.[1] Its general sources are clear. But Chaucer introduces a twofold mystery into the poem: why he so thoroughly obscures those sources, and why the main action of his poem—those speeches—should be so difficult for the narrator to understand. Both of these features may be a symptom of Chaucer's meditation on his burgeoning English po-etic project. They might also be an in-joke for those who had read Machaut and Froissart. But, as I will argue in this chapter, they are also the trace of the difficulty of writing about the topic of death in the first place. One of the poem's jokes—or one of its horrors—is that its many courtly tropes would be entirely intelligible if they were about love; because they are about death, they are inscrutable and befuddling.

The mystery at the heart of *The Book of the Duchess* is why the narrator doesn't understand the elegant but hardly opaque metaphors that its central character, the Man in Black, uses. At least three times the Man in Black constructs an elaborate and elegant metaphor about the death of his wife, only to have the narrator ask him what he means. This obtuseness is one of the most-studied aspects of the poem and is usually seen as a forerunner to the ironically naive narrators of Chaucer's later works, most famously of *The Canterbury Tales*. What I want to suggest, however, is that in one sense the narrator understands all too well what the real topic of the plaint is. He is actually a clear-eyed observer of death: he cannot understand it because it can't be put into language, and the gap between what he ought to know and what he is capable of knowing represents the gap between the impulse to narrate death and our ability to understand it.

The narrator's inability to grasp this straightforward statement stems from his apparent desire to read an amorous story into the fact of death. His attention turned to the superficial metaphors of courtly play that the Man in Black uses, the narrator repeatedly encrypts the bald truth of death with what he hears as mere courtly discourse: "What los ys that?" he asks the Man in Black, "Nyl she not love yow? Ys hyt soo? / Or have ye oght doon amys, / That she hath left yow?" (1139–42).[2] At times the narrator mistakes a metaphor taken from chess for the death the Man in Black has suffered: "ther is no man alyve her," he says, "Wolde for a fers make this woo!" (740–41). It is this cryptic play that shields from the narrator the ultimate knowledge that the Man in Black finally states baldly: "She is deed." The verbal and semiotic range of the Man in Black's discourse creates, at least for the narrator, a crypt that shields him from the morbid truth with a carapace of courtly figuration. That this is not merely a misprision of the etiquette and language of the court is reinforced by an otherwise unaccountable play on the name Blanche. The poem translates it as "good fair White," more than a mere calque of her name.[3] Chaucer's French sources for the passages in which the name White appears actually use the proper name of the Man in Black's beloved: Blanche, as an adjective meaning "white." The name White, then, involves a double encryption, of the proper name *and* of its uncanny coincidence in a language and text that Chaucer encrypts by translating it. To have preserved the name Blanche in his translation would have been to create an archive of amorous, courtly discourse, showing immediately how much of Machaut and Guillaume de Deguileville lay behind the Man in Black's supposedly singular experience. In obscuring his extensive sources, Chaucer in effect seals off what might have been an archive, the legacy of late medieval French poetry, and turns it into a crypt.

The dreamer's inital "melancolye / And drede" (23–24) has attracted a lot of critical speculation. He has suffered it for eight years, a sickness that has been interpreted as unrequited love, among other things.[4] But it's likely that the eight years signals an enigma that we would not have been able to unravel unless we were part of Chaucer's close circle of friends and readers. The eight years is another kind of crypt, marking something that happened

in life but that the death of Chaucer and his friends now leaves us with a content we can never know. It suggests the underlying pattern of *The Book of
the Duchess*, a series of references, phrased in courtly diction, to the death
that the dreamer cannot grasp at the level of narrative. Part of the pleasure—if that is what it is—of reading *The Book of the Duchess* comes from
watching the narrator fail to grasp what we think of as obvious, and what
he finally gets in a flash of demotic insight: "'She ys ded!' 'Nay!' 'Yis, be my
trouthe!'" (1309).

The entire French tradition, in other words, has failed to communicate
the poem's main point to its own dreamer. He understands the Man in
Black's elegant and elliptical courtly tropes only when the Man in Black resorts to desperate and pungent English. I think this is more than just a
bleakly comic moment that dramatizes the dreamer's obtuseness, his failure
because of a lack of wit or education to follow what the Man in Black says.
It might be true that the dreamer is too stupid or ignorant to understand
elliptical courtly discourse. But we the readers (more or less) understand it,
and I think we understand by it something more than references to the
death of the Duchess, Blanche. The very analogies and metaphors the Man
in Black draws to refer to the death of Blanche also universalize her death,
extending it into the depths of history, legend, and myth, with references
to the fall of Troy. The paradox of *The Book of the Duchess* is that this universal history of death makes no sense to the dreamer—what is it, exactly,
that you have lost again? he asks repeatedly, as if unable to acknowledge
the Man in Black's clear desire to make his grief universal, world-historical.
The dreamer understands neither the philosophical importance of the Man
in Black's complaint nor its kernel of grief. He doesn't technically affirm
that he understands the Man in Black's eventual exasperated statement of
Blanche's death; he denies it: "Nay!" That single word is a metonymy of
Chaucer's early English poetry: a disavowal of what comes before it—but a
disavowal, as Freud pointed out, is really a deeply felt affirmation.

The word "nay" also signals a confusion: revelation comes in the form
of a refusal. That very point is the crux of the Man in Black's history of how
he wooed Blanche. He is unable, he says, to "countrefete" what she said to
him, but the "grete / Of hir answere" was the single word "Nay!" (1241–
43). This is the only word that Blanche speaks (if one can call it that, since
it's a summary of what she says and is relayed by the Man in Black) in the
poem.[5] It signifies, just as the dreamer's "nay" does, the revelation of what
seems to be the truth. Yet that "nay," in both cases, is the final step in a long
and exhaustive discursive chain, whether of wooing or of mourning. Rather

than denying their complexity, the word "nay" contains the echo of all the previous failures of communication and understanding. It restates, far more succinctly, the confusion with which the poem begins: the wandering melancholy in which everything seems "alike"; the dreamer has "felynge in nothyng" and is as if "a mased thyng." The antecedent of "mased thyng," however, is not clear: it could be something the dreamer *might* have feeling in, but then the feeling would be opaque or inaccessible—since it is "mased"—which is to say that it is not really a feeling; or the antecedent could be the "I" of the dreamer, who is stunned. If the latter, then the syncope of the subject of "mased thyng" makes the point literally: the self is lost in a maze of language.

The maze of language here is more than syntactical. It is also literary: the meandering, aimless thoughts of the dreamer are, in a literal sense, not the dreamer's, nor Chaucer's, but Machaut's and Froissart's. The poem's first line and a half are a translation of the first line and a half of Froissart's *Le paradys d'amour*: "I have gret wonder, be this lyght / How that I lyve" (1–2); "Je suis de moi en grant mervelle / Comment tant vifs" (1–2). As Ardis Butterfield puts it, the opening "I" of *The Book of the Duchess* is a translation of Froissart's "I," and this in part explains the nature of the "veiled, gagged, or simply, loudly, silent" "I" of the poem.[6]

Put differently, the "I" of the poem experiences itself as cryptic, a mystery to itself. Its unexplained insomnia makes it unable to restrain its random thoughts, which in turn leaves it unable to focus on anything else. This is, at first, similar to the predicament that Machaut describes, except for three crucial differences: first, Machaut says that that kind of thinking happened when he was younger, in a state of relative innocence; secondly, it doesn't seem pathological, just frivolous; and thirdly, there was always an exception to it. Just as it is for Chaucer, everything seems all the same to him—"Tout m'estoit un" (51)—*except that it actually isn't*: he "always inclined / [his] heart and all [his] thought / Toward [his] lady" (52–54).[7] The butterfly-like thoughts of Machaut seem random, but they actually have a goal. Chaucer turns this delicate, maybe effete, indirection into genuine perplexity, melancholy, and disorientation: "Suche fantasies ben in myn hede / So I not what is best to doo" (28–29). It is as if the self in *The Book of the Duchess* is trapped in Machaut's four brief lines about his fleeting works and his varying thoughts, sealed off from the love that occupies the rest of Machaut's text.

If anything unites the digressive and literarily heterogeneous first part of *The Book of the Duchess*, it is this self's discomfort and preoccupation

with his place. He is restless, even when in bed, and sits up to read the story
of Ceyx and Alcyone. He famously leaves out the ending, in which the love
that Ceyx and Alcyone have for each other transforms them into birds after
Ceyx's death. Indeed, the end of his story is abrupt and bleak: Alcyone simply dies on the third day after hearing of that Ceyx has died. There may be
no better evidence of the dreamer's profound befuddlement than his complete lack of interest in this pathetic and somewhat affecting ending. Instead, he fastens on the possibility that the god Morpheus in the story might
grant *him* sleep and imagines repaying him with a sumptuous bedroom,
which he describes in great and concrete detail (there actually couldn't be
a better gift for the god of sleep). Yet, he says in passing, he doesn't know
where the god's cave is. There's a comic disjunction between, on the one
hand, the "cloth of Reynes" (255) and the "fine blak satyn doutremer" (253)
that Chaucer wants to give Morpheus and, on the other, the reminder that
it's all destined to be put in a cave "as derk / As helle-pit" (170–71).

The poem's beginning has trouble getting beyond the bedroom. That
trouble might in fact be what prompts the dream itself to begin in a bedroom, the "solution to the problem enacted or propounded by a dream to the
problem which gave rise to it," as A. C. Spearing puts it.[8] The dream, after
all, begins with the dreamer waking up in a bedroom—a singularly strange
one, but a bedroom just the same. The birds on its roof sing so loudly that
the whole chamber rings with the sound; the entire Troy story is "wrought"
on the windows which are somehow also "cleer"; all of the nearly 22,000
lines of *The Romance of the Rose*, as well as its "glose," are painted "with
colors fyne" (in other words, not *written*) on the walls; and, finally, the
dreamer leaves the chamber on a horse that has apparently been there the
whole time. The "impossibles" of the chamber, as I will argue later, point to
a deeper, and nononeiric, dislocation. For the moment, though, I just want
to draw attention to the ways in which the site of the bedroom has studi-
ously omitted love or sex.

The bedroom becomes more a studio for reading and historical reflection,
a place for reflecting on far larger and further-flung events than a poet or
dreamer thinking delicate thoughts about his beloved. It is a place in which, I
would argue, the earlier "mased thyng" appears as the arena of literary and
cultural history itself. "Arena" is not quite the right word, of course, because
this is a bedroom; but the difficulty in finding the right term to describe
it paradoxically makes its nature clearer. It is both intimate and vast, near
and yet far, composed of narratives that defy or contradict their own media.
It is "mased" as much as is the dreamer while he is awake, which is not surprising, since it is in many senses a chamber of his mind. As such, it is a

smaller, less abstract version of a kind of labyrinth that underlies the narrative of *The Book of the Duchess* itself, a narrative that twists and winds its way around discursive dead ends, cryptic references, and, most profoundly, distances that collapse the exotic and the mortal together.

The paradoxical withdrawal within oneself in order to contemplate the universals that normatively apply to everyone explains the strange architecture of memory in *The Book of the Duchess*. In both of his primary models for the poem, *Le jugement du roy de Behaingne* and *Le jugement du roy de Navarre*, the dreamer finds himself in the relatively public part of an "enclosed, aristocratic space."[9] But in *The Book of the Duchess*, the dreamer finds himself in his bed, "al naked," and joins a courtly group (the hunting party of "th'emperour Octovyen") only after he leaves his chamber. The heart of the poem, the complaint of the Man in Black, does not begin until the dreamer has latched onto the hunt for a while and then followed a random little whelp into a wood, where he finds the Man in Black sitting. In contrast with Machaut's poems, *The Book of the Duchess* begins with an extraordinary itinerary of actions, texts, and places, and the central plaint is linked far less closely to the regularity of an art of rule, or even usual mnemonic practice. The dreamer's arbitrary adventures suggest precisely the "wandering" that makes memory impossible, and its turn to cryptic practice—its negation of puns, the narrator's obtuseness—lodges the recuperation of the unimaginable somewhere in the work of literature.

The dream begins with the light streaming through windows that portray "hooly al the story of Troye" (326). The claim for the comprehensive scope of the "story" is overdetermined, however, considering that the poem almost succeeds in omitting entirely the crucial point of the Trojan story: its destruction and its foundational status in the civilization of Western Europe. The fall of Troy is a double action much like the action of memory itself: a death that engenders life. The whole "story" emerges, just like the death of Blanche, only gradually and reluctantly. The repression of the destruction of Troy in *The Book of the Duchess* suggests that Troy stands for the repressed origin of memory, or for a horror, such as plague, that has a foundational status but must nevertheless be repressed by the *distancia* of inadequate memory. The dream itself, that is, begins by evoking a place that, for Western European historiography, instigates precisely what Michel de Certeau calls "mortuary circulation." It is entirely appropriate that a poem that is itself a commemoration should begin at the origin of Western secular memory by suggesting a plenitude of narrative ("hooly al the story"), yet suppressing it.[10] Troy, in other words, is the location of the necessary failure of memory. The anticathectic impulse in *The Book of the Duchess*

that links complete recall to death is strong: the dreamer's failure to understand that the Man in Black's wife is dead after he has been told about it
twice parallels the deferred acknowledgment of the outcome of the Trojan
story. Only when Troy is mentioned the third time, in the Man in Black's
description of his wooing of Blanche, does the poem admit anything like the
"woo" that Cassandra experienced when she "bewayled the destruccioun of
Troye" (1247–48). The Man in Black's amatory discourse is in fact entangled
in the dynamics of elegy. His utterly conventional dilemma in confronting
Blanche for the first time is peculiarly pathologized in what follows (the
section before Cassandra's lament):

> I most have told hir or be ded.
> I not wel how that I began . . .
> I trowe hyt was in the dismal,
> That was the ten woundes of Egipte. (1202–7)

The only explicit acknowledgment of plague in a poem memorializing a
woman who probably died of the plague comes just at a point where its
principal character experiences a failure of memory, and precisely where
he articulates a conjunction between the repressive character of memory
and the imaginary location of an origin in a time of plague. "I not wel how
that I began," says the Man in Black; "I trowe hyt was in the dismal / That
was the ten woundes [Lat. *plagas*] of Egipte." In a tangle of cryptic reference, the Man in Black somehow locates his initial love for Blanche in the
arrival of plague *and* in Egypt. The *plagas* of Egypt are a wound that will
not heal: love, for the Man in Black, will forever begin with annihilation.
Even when he recounts his initial wooing of Blanche, his language is so
shot through with mortality that we have to decide whether his appropriation of the tropes of *fin amor* is so mindless that he evacuates his discourse
of meaning altogether, or whether it is all too pregnant with meaning. He
speaks to her the first time (in the "ten woundes of Egipte") with "sorwe"
and "with woundes dede," and with an urgency that he claims is a matter of life and death: "I most have told her or be ded." He speaks, he says,
although he thought he shouldn't, "mawgree my hed" (1201), a pun that
Chaucer uses at the beginning of "The Wife of Bath's Tale" to collocate
virginity, capital crime, and entreaty. The Man in Black speaks despite himself, speaks perhaps without even knowing what to say. He says, "I not wel
how that I began" (1203)—he knows nothing about what he said, except
that he can locate it in the traumatic moment of the "woundes of Egipte."
That moment he can well understand. What cannot be understood well is

precisely the material of the poem that both characters are uttering: *The Book of the Duchess* is full of moments in which both characters are befuddled by discourse. At the beginning of the poem the narrator says that his head is so full of "fantasies" that he "not what is best to doo" (30). Not knowing how to talk about what one is in fact talking about is an admission that recurs multiple times in the poem. In a sense, the poem begins by acknowledging that it does not know how to begin, and proceeds by not allowing that narrator to know how to end. The Man in Black's courtly discourse continues only as long as the narrator does not know what it means. As Kathryn Lynch puts it, the poem depends upon both "understanding and misunderstanding."[11] I would argue that misunderstanding betokens something deeper: the *inability* to understand because of something that lies buried and unknowable.

The very activity of memorializing Blanche dramatizes the problematic structure of memory, the entailment of an *ars oblivionis* in an *ars memorativa*. The Man in Black's comparison of Blanche to the "fenix of Arabie" (982), for instance, makes her a figure that embodies this very doubleness of memory, of the "mortuary circulation" that depends upon the Castor and Pollux–like complementarity of life and death. The Man in Black's attempt to memorialize Blanche involves other erasures of her presence. She seems, indeed, necessarily entailed in that erasure. The Man in Black's configuration of his own memory prior to the inscription of Blanche in it still acknowledges her presence and figures proleptically the obliteration that memorialization engenders. The inscription of the craft of love in his memory, he says, was particularly enduring because it was the first impression on his mind:

> I was therto most able,
> As a whit wal or a table,
> For hit ys redy to cacche and take
> Al that men wil theryn make,
> Whethir so men wil portreye or peynte . . . (779–83)

The conventional figure of the memory as a blank slate or a tablet of unmarked wax is modulated by the memory of Blanche. She is remembered as an aspect of the technology of memory itself: it is difficult not to read the "whit wal" of the Man in Black's memory as a canting reference to the figure the poem refers to just a few lines later (948) as "goode fair White" herself. Indeed, the passage in Machaut's *Remède de fortune* from which Chaucer borrows at this point refers to the "table blanche" of the state of innocence.[12] The English transliteration occludes, rather than calls attention to, Blanche's intrusion into this important mnemonic moment. Her presence signals both the initiation of the poem's memorializing enterprise and its corollary forgetting. Although the Man in Black insists that he "nyl foryete hir," Blanche seems to stand for the ability of the memory to reconfigure the places that it presides over, and on which it depends, to accept new inscriptions that obscure the traces of original inscriptions.

The spectral name of Blanche, in other words, embodies the kind of work Chaucer did and did not do when he borrowed swathes of Machaut's and Froissart's poetry for the poem. The borrowing is so extensive that Chaucer's poem almost amounts to a mashup or a *cento*, a text made up only of lines from other poems (primarily from Virgil in late Roman antiquity).[13] The "malencolie" and disturbance that the narrator mentions in the poem's prologue owes a great deal to the "malencolie" that Machaut describes at length in his prologue to *Le jugement du roy de Navarre*.[14] Most of Machaut's prologue, as I have suggested, is taken up with a list of the things that have made him melancholy: the structure of the prologue is a catalog of those very causes. By contrast, Chaucer is vague and cryptic about his illness, saying little more than that he has had it for eight years, that he is afraid he will die of it, and that only a now-inaccessible "physicien" can heal him. Chaucer's diffidence, delicacy, or discretion about his condition almost comically deflates the wide range and specific detail of Machaut's prologue. But the most striking difference, one that it is hard to imagine is not deliberate, is what Chaucer leaves out. The most basic premise of Machaut's catalog is that the poet has shut himself up in a room to escape the plague. As with the term *blanche*, Chaucer neglects an obvious parallel—almost a synchronicity—between his poem and those of Machaut and Froissart. Machaut's vivid fear of the plague is diminished to a few cryptic references scattered throughout *The Book of the Duchess*.

Yet what Chaucer shows in his poem is that it is the deferral of knowledge that keeps us listening. Sometimes we do not want the answer, and all the pleasure lies in not knowing. In that sense, *The Book of the Duchess* demonstrates the cryptic nature of all literature, which consoles by allowing us to experience the deferral of its truth. Conversely, the moments of revelation and termination in the poem are extraordinarily taciturn. The poem ends with the abrupt declaration "This was my sweven; now hit ys doon" (1334), which sounds more like a scribal colophon than a poetic conclusion. This sudden ending is cryptic: it poses a problem precisely while it closes the poem. Yet it does *not* close the poem, for the final lines imagine a possible future in which this poem will be written "be process of tyme . . .

in ryme," or simply record what the dreamer planned to do in the past, which is now done. In the end, we do not know precisely when or where being "doon" is located (1331–32).

Similarly, the poem's most taciturn declaration (and its most demotic moment) comes just when the Man in Black resorts to a simple declarative sentence: "'She ys ded!' 'Nay!' 'Yis, be my trouthe!'" (1309). Those are in fact the Man in Black's final words: he stops discoursing on his wife's death just when he asserts the truth. This moment suggests that the assertion of the truth of death is also the final act, an act that terminates the "herte-huntyng," which, it turns out, had been going on around the two men all along in a highly metaphorical, cryptic register. In that sense, the Man in Black's last words are an elegant conclusion to a discourse that conceals while it reveals. But the dreamer's immediate response to the revelation of death is his inarticulate "Nay!": a blurt of sound, a demotic interjection ("nay!" and "yey"). Death itself cannot sustain poetry; it is its deferral, or rather its immanence, its approach, that makes poetry possible. The poem collapses once death is named; its structure is, quite literally, the convergence with death, or—which is the same thing—the dilation of the meeting with it.

But there are two more sounds that shape the ending of the poem. The first is the "strake" that signals the end of the hunt, which we have by now almost certainly forgotten about, the hunt that already belongs in some strange spatially and temporally dislocated world where the emperor Octavian chases a "hert" in a late medieval, presumably English, countryside. This blowing of the horn is not what precisely brings the hunt to an end: it is actually something that is said in the final exchange between the Man in Black and the dreamer: "with that word" the hunters "gan to strake forth" (1311–12). It's impossible to tell just what that "word" is: "dead," "los," "routhe," "nay," "yis," or the entire exchange. But the point is that the hunt ends in, or with, that conversation: the final apprehension of death (the dreamer's, that Blanche is dead) brings the hunt to an end. But it isn't certain that the hunt has obtained its objective; it is just done "For that tyme" (1313).[15]

The parallel structure of the hunt and the dreamer's questioning of the Man in Black is not nearly as clear, of course, as the parallel scenes of seduction and hunting in *Sir Gawain and the Green Knight*. But the end of *The Book of the Duchess* deploys a pun to make this latent connection clear: it is not just the hunt that is done, it is the *herte*-hunting. What is over, then, is the background hunt for a deer, but also the hunt for the "heart," which includes the dreamer's search for what is in—or what is lost in—the Man in Black's heart; the metonymic heart that is the Man in Black's beloved; and, finally, the search through the places, the topoi, of the Man in Black's memory, a faculty that in medieval psychology was seated in the heart.[16] Indeed, the hunt itself may be a figure for the very work of memorializing that the Man in Black has been doing throughout. As Thomas Aquinas says, "When we recollect we are hunting."[17]

Not only is the heart cryptic, but it is unclear at this point whether it has been located at all. If it's the complete recognition of death that ends the hunt, then the heart is cryptic in that material sense as well: it hides a death that can never fully be captured. It is easy to get the impression that the hunt has ended conclusively, because the poem ends precipitously and with a kind of earnest finality that links together the end of the hunt and the end of the dream: "al was doon . . . This was my sweven; now hit ys doon" (1312 and 1324). Generations of readers have found this ending troubling, perhaps none more vociferously than F. J. Furnivall, who said that Chaucer should be "ashamed of himself for this most lame and impotent conclusion."[18] Furnivall's reaction implies that the poem is *not* done, that Chaucer didn't manage to conclude whatever he needed to in order to conclude the poem. Furnivall is actually quoting Desdemona's response to Iago ("O most lame and impotent conclusion!") after Iago has "demonstrated" that even the most supreme virtues leave a woman able only to "suckle fools" (act 2, scene 1).[19] Whether he was aware of it or not, Furnivall implies that the ending of *The Book of the Duchess* is not incompetent—rather, indeed, that it is devious and deliberate. It somehow accomplishes the opposite of what it seems overtly to be doing; it provokes questions precisely because it hurries to hush them up. If Furnivall had lived later, he might have called the ending of the poem overdetermined.

The poem's closing allusions to Chaucer's patron, John of Gaunt—the thinly disguised model for the Man in Black—do not necessarily tie up the loose ends. It is entirely likely that the name of "good faire White" would have been sufficient to let us know whose grief the poem is about. But the "long castel . . . Be Seynt Johan, on a riche hil" signals that the Man in Black is John the "Lancastrian" going to his palace in Richmond (1318–19). The cryptic reference is much like the kind of authorial signature that medieval poets often use, but in this case it identifies the real-world protagonist of the poem. It does not, however, explain anything about the strange silences, misapprehensions, and disturbing memories of the body of the poem—it doesn't, in other words, really conclude the poem. The name of Gaunt is, in the end, little more than a cryptic container for the heart that remains undiscovered and unrequited.

If there is any ending to the poem's hunt for the heart, any possibility of moving beyond the condition of "Alway deynge and be not ded," it lies beyond the poem.[20] The noise that brings the dream to an end by waking the dreamer up is the noise of a different memorial order, a regime that is directed against precisely the impasses and griefs of secular memory: the bell in the castle that strikes "houres twelve" announces the final canonical hour of the day (1323). The offices said during the day depend upon and reinforce the work of memory in multiple ways. Most participants need to commit to memory the numerous prayers, hymns, versicles, and psalms that make up the offices. Deeper, more contemplative involvement in the offices draws on the techniques of association learned from the art of memory, so that texts associated with the office readings can be meditated upon, as well. The offices were also themselves acts of memorial: one pastoral manual says that the hours are said "in memory of the passion of Christ."[21] The hours also memorialized and commemorated people and events that shaped particular communities. The liturgies of the saints, for instance, recall the actions of locally important individuals, a repeated recollection that reinstates and reinforces a communal religious identity. Indeed, as Cecilia Gaposckhin points out, the word *memoria* came to mean precisely the citation of a saint in a liturgy.[22] So the bell that rings the twelfth hour at the end of *The Book of the Duchess* announces the intrusion of a regime of memory that depends upon repetition rather than forgetting; but, more important, it suggests a regime that is able to contemplate historical death directly and somehow translate it into meaning.

What meaning might lie in the Man in Black's grief isn't immediately obvious, partly because the poem doesn't actually move into the regime of prayer and contemplation. Indeed, this is the point at which the poem effectively ends—and that, I think, is the point here. The problem of termination, as we've seen, haunts the reception of the poem; but the poem's interruption *by* the canonical hours gestures toward the very concern with termination that characterizes this particular canonical hour.

The twelfth hour marks the end of the day, and, as such, it throws the metaphorical night of death over the end of the poem. The two final offices of the day, vespers and compline, were often held together in late medieval England; they were essentially meditations on dying, calling attention to the analogy between the hours of the day and the stages of life—evening quite clearly being the final stage. But "evening" is ambiguous: do the services mark the end of the day or the beginning of the night? Analogically, vespers is paired with the final stage of life—that is, the last moment of living, when, in both the service and in daily life, we dwell on the final limit of our mortality ("decrepitam ducimus ad memoriam").[23] "Compline" in Latin is *completorium* or *completa*, so named because it marks the completion of the day. Its liturgy, however, does not precisely celebrate completion: it uses the occasion of the end of the day to pray for a completion that is still to come. Its opening benediction asks for a quiet night, but also, and a bit more unexpectedly, a *finem perfectum*, a perfect end. As we will see, it anticipates a recurrent anxiety in early fifteenth-century writing: how to end a work not just well, but well enough that it says something about the ending of life itself. The phrase *finem perfectum* itself appears in decidedly secular contexts, such as commentaries on Aristotle's *Metaphysics* and related texts. Thomas Aquinas says that something is perfect when it achieves a perfect end, a formulation that he seems to have derived from Averroes.[24] Whether or not the phrase in the liturgy of compline has anything to do with the Aristotelian causes, it indicates a concern with endings in general, not just with the termination of a single life. The last half line of *The Book of the Duchess* could be a literal translation of it: "This was my sweven; *now hit ys doon*" (1334). This is the very end of the poem; "hyt ys doon" is a literal translation, a calque, of *perfectum*, a word that means not just "perfect," but also "achieved," "carried out," "finished." This prayer for completion occurs just as the dreamer awakes and hastens to complete his own work.

The hymn for compline represents completion more abstractly, even apocalyptically. It asks for protection during the night, but its opening, "Te ante lucis terminum," represents the coming night as the termination of light. Night is the unmaking of the world, the termination of the light that marked the very beginning of creation. The next line of the hymn, indeed, addresses the "Rerum Creator." On a less cosmic scale, the hymn could be said to refer back to the mental agitations that begin *The Book of the Duchess*, summed up in the dreamer's lament that "Suche fantasies ben in myn hede / So I not what is best to doo" (28–29). The second stanza asks for the removal of "somnia / Et noctium phantasmata" (dreams and the phantasms of the night). In one sense, what is happening at the end of the poem is precisely the removal of the dream, the precipitation of the dreamer into his own world by the very bells of vespers or compline.[25] But the verse also, belatedly and arguably too late, announces a more straightforward and less inflammatory response to those disturbing and immobilizing fantasies than does the strange version of the story of Ceyx and Alcyone at the poem's beginning. It suggests a version of dying that opens not onto the unplumbable depths of memory—and literature—but that is willing to accept night and death as the phenomena of a well-regulated and orderly ritual of living.

II

But is death as cryptic as it is in *The Book of the Duchess* because it is embedded in the arcane, privileged discourse of French courtly poetry? Is it cryptic because the poem in which it appears is, well, cryptic? Later in his career Chaucer wrote a poem that seems almost to answer that question directly: "The Pardoner's Tale," in which death—and not just any death: *the* Death, the Black Plague—is framed by a sermon, a discourse designed to be clear and intelligible. Yet the tale's Three Revelers, who set out on a quest for death, find it only because they do not really know what they are looking for, despite the tale's many clear instructions about what it is.

It is partly because the Revelers represent an effort to encounter death as lucidly as possible that they misunderstand it. It cannot be designated; it can only be encountered in the body. The Three Revelers in the tale die because they fail to understand that the death they want to confront—indeed, to kill—is abstract. It is really nowhere. The common interpretation of this debacle is essentially the one that D. W. Robertson articulated well over half a century ago: that the Revelers die because they fail to read spiritually (that is, allegorically) what is patently an allegory.[26] They die because they understand death in a literal and bodily sense. But, I would argue, they also do not understand that literal and bodily sense fully enough: they assume that death has a body but fail to anticipate that the body death has will be their own—the only body it could possibly have. The Revelers continue to think abstractly, not literally: they fail to see that death is not the other, it is the ownmost.

Near the beginning of the tale, the Revelers miss the obvious, ominous warning that death is near. A bell is being rung to accompany a corpse to its burial; the dead man, a boy tells them, was "an old felawe" of theirs. The Revelers do not seem at all interested in finding out which of their friends has just died, perhaps because they are distracted by the boy's account of how death has taken all the people in the country, at least "a thousand" from "this pestilence." The scale and spectacle of these manifestations of death in the boy's account encourage them to forget the intimacy of the death of a close friend.

The boy's speech is a virtual encyclopedia of the late medieval iconography of death:

> . . . a privee theef men clepeth Deeth,
> That in this contree al the peple sleeth,
> And with his spere he smoot his herte atwo,

And wente his wey withouten wordes mo.
He hath a thousand slayn this pestilence.
And, maister, er ye come in his presence,
Me thynketh that it were necessarie
For to be war of swich an adversarie. (675–82)

Death holds a spear (as in fig. 1). And Death is a thief and a leveler (kill-ing "al the peple," rich and poor alike), toward whom the only possible re-sponse is care (in every sense of the word—what Heidegger calls the *Sorge* of being-toward-death): we can only "be war" of it, as the third dead king in the de Lisle Psalter also warns. Less obvious, although lurking just beneath the surface, is precisely the kind of death that became so consequential in the fourteenth century that it became a name in its own right—*the* Death. That is clearly what the boy describes ("He hath a thousand slain this pes-tilence") and what the Taverner elaborates on further ("he hath slayn this yeer, / Henne over a mile, withinne a greet village, / Bothe man and wom-man, child, and hyne, and page" [686–88]). The Taverner's belief that Death now has his "habitacioun" there is either mordant or as unwitting as the Revelers' belief that Death is a person. In either case, however, Death's hab-itation in a village suggests two things about the response to the plague: it is here to stay, and its relation to us cannot be fully explained or understood.

The tale says nothing further about the plague and its unfathomable hor-ror, but one of its central characters embodies and literalizes what the Rev-elers refuse to recognize about death: that their quest for it, on their terms, will be, in every sense of the word, interminable. The next figure they en-counter is the Old Man who cannot die. He wanders the earth (as far as "Ynde") looking for someone who "wolde chaunge his youthe" for the Old Man's "age," but unsuccessfully: death, he says, "wol nat han my lyf" (722–27). Not surprisingly, many readers of the poem have suggested that the Old Man is an allegory of death, who demonstrates the fatuousness of the Three Revelers' declaration that "Deeth shal be deed" (710)—if he is death, of course, he cannot be dead, too; that is, he cannot *be* dead, because he can-not be at all.

This reading raises a number of questions about how to predicate any-thing of death, about how to say anything about it. Of course death will not "have" the Old Man's life, because possession implies being as a predicate, which death does not have. Indeed, death cannot "have" anything at all; death is the absence of the capacity to possess. Yet it's not any clearer why, if the Old Man is death, he would be continually dying. As I've suggested, dying is the closest we can ever come to "being dead," precisely because it is *not* death. The miraculous logic of death is, as the *De miseria conditionis humane* (translated by Chaucer at some point, and written by the man who would help to place penitence at the center of the Christian life, Lotario dei Signo, the future Pope Innocent III) says, the more you live, the closer you are to death. Indeed, the *De miseria* suggests that the only way we can represent death to ourselves is to somehow capture it in life, in which case we would be doomed never to die. In the context of the treatise, that means never becoming subject to what lies beyond death. Lotario is noticeably silent about the kinds of enjoyment and bliss that await the righteous, partly because his is a work that urges a *contemptus mundi*. But it's also silent about eternal life, because it depends upon a resolution to life that is final and complete. The treatise's primary images of suffering are drawn not primarily from an afterlife of hellish pain and torment, but from a life that never ends, a life that just keeps on going. The consequence of not despising the world enough is to remain caught within it, never to comprehend its termination—that is, never to be able to imagine anything other than its nontranscendence. That, says the *De miseria*, is the source of punishment, the "indeficencia tormentorum": "death will be undying . . . They shall seek death and not find it, and they shall desire to die, and death shall fly from them" (erit mors immortalis . . . querent homines mortem et non invenient eam, et desiderabunt mori, et fugiet mors ab illis).[27] I'm dwelling on this passage from the *De miseria* because it accentuates the strange yet rigorously logical phenomenology of the Old Man in "The Pardoner's Tale": to be able to talk about death is also to be incapable of death, but not of dying. Otherwise we would have nothing to say about it.

This is partly why so many dying people in Chaucer have so much to say. I am thinking about all of those lovers who experience love as a death that has not yet come—as an imagined experience, that is, that can never actually *be* experienced. "I nam but deed" is the continual complaint of lovers and those deprived of love in Chaucer—of Ceys (who really is dead, although he doesn't technically say this himself), the Man in Black, Arcite, Alison in "The Miller's Tale," Symkyn's wife in "The Reeve's Tale," the Sultan in "The Man of Law's Tale," and the Knight in "The Wife of Bath's Tale." We tend to read this claim "I nam but deed" as a hyperbolic complaint, part of the conventional language of the French and Provençal plaint: "suffering this way is almost like being dead, or it's the next thing to death." But as I've been arguing, this is also what we have to say when we want to talk about death: the only thing I could say about me is that the next stage would be death.

In a sense, the Old Man's predicament is a thought experiment: what would it be like if we lived this life forever? What would it be like to be free of finitude? "The Pardoner's Tale" imagines that the "problem" of finitude has been suspended for him, yet he continues to long for it. Chaucer might be signaling that the Old Man is longing for the wrong kind of thing, that his desire itself is not an allegory or a correlative of St. Paul's old man of sin (i.e., longing for transitory goods is really longing to die). But the Old Man is experiencing a horrible realization: that the removal of finitude is not the same thing as dwelling in infinity. His infinity is created by refusing him finitude—death—and situates him in the intolerable paradox of longing for finitude for eternity, to be "*Alway* deynge and be not ded." That is what it is like to be immune from death, to experience the avoidal of finitude but to be absolutely aware (and desirous) of it at the same time.

What we talk about when we talk about death is its propinquity, its presence just outside of our view, often in ways that we do not fully understand or that address the less ratiocinative parts of our faculties. In the book of Job it comes to Elphaz as a terrifying nightmare that makes the hair on his arms stand up.[28] What is close to death seems to be terror, and terror awakened by a particularly powerful imaginative capacity. The unsought proximity of death is both the theme and a structure of Lotario's *De miseria*. In the section titled "De vicinitate mortis," he sums up pithily the responsibility we have and should have toward death because of its unexpectedness, its immanence in all human affairs, and its imminence in all plans we attempt: "Time passes, and death approaches. 'A thousand years in the eyes of a dying man are as yesterday, which is past.' For the future is always being born, the present is always dying, and whatever is past is utterly dead" (Tempus preterit, et mors appropinquat. 'Mille anni ante oculos morientis sicut dies hesterna, que preterit.' Semper enim futura nascuntur, semper presencia moriuntur, et quicquit est preteritum totum est mortuum).[29] There is something strangely consoling, even distracting, about the rhetorical force of Lotario's beautiful language: "It is better to die for life than to live for death, because mortal life is nothing but a living death" (Melius est mori vite quam vivere morti, quia nichil est vita mortalis nisi mors vivens).[30] Death and life are an elegant chiasmus, and if nothing else we will have the pleasure of knowing that one can say something beautiful about death. Yet there remains something disturbing, of course, in what Lotario calls this "mirabile," even though, and because, the relation between the two violates the rules of representation and physics: "by as much as it increases it also decreases, because the more life advances the more it comes near to death" (quanto plus crescit tanto magis descrecit, quia quanto plus vita procedit tanto magis ad mortem accedit).[31]

As if this section ends too neatly, Lothario next writes a section on the terror of dreams. While this sudden shift may exhibit something like the cinematic shock of the image, I would argue that it continues the project of the preceding section, acknowledging the subterranean ways in which death works, ways that exceed the capacity of rhetoric or the work of *recte loquendi*: "Even though what dreamers dream are not actually sad or frightening or troublesome, still dreamers are actually sad, frightened, and troubled, so much so in fact that in sleeping they sometimes cry and on waking are often perturbed" (Et licet non sint in veritate tristia vel terribilia seu laboriosa que sompniant somniantes, tamen in veritate tristantur, terrentur, et fatigantur, in tantum ut et dormientes aliquando lacrimentur et evigilantes sepissime conturbentur).[32] It is difficult to understand dream fictions as anything like innocent suspensions of quotidian laws of causality and authority, as the occasions for the exercise of fictionality, after having read these two sections of the *De miseria*. The propinquity of sleep and death is disturbing, but so is the rephrasing of the approach to death as a kind of dream, and indeed dreams as another, equally disturbing, recognition of the ubiquity of the impossible logic of death.

Death is an unpurposive object, a purely aesthetic artifact that appears when it no longer has the utility that is anticipated for it. Within the narrative of the Pardoner's exemplum, the Revelers' quest for death appears simple-minded, oblivious not just to the nuances but also to the largest ontological principles of death, which we know to be present in a sense the Revelers do not. They imagine death as a physical presence, as an agent of destruction that can be encountered without being destroyed: "Deeth shal be deed." We seem to be able to make the distinction between being and allegory that they cannot; we know that death cannot be predicated of anything, even of death, because it is a state of unbeing that stands outside of any predicate. And indeed the Revelers discover death only when they no longer seek it, once they find gold and no longer care about death. Death, in other words, appears only when it cannot appear, only when it is no longer pressed into the service of precisely the kind of moralizing exemplum that the Pardoner's sermon turns out to enfold. When the typology of death disappears from the Revelers' horizon of expectation, then real death becomes possible.

One cannot find death without forgetting about it. That is also the truth of the exemplum: death arrives when one no longer cares about it, when the desire to overcome it, no matter how misplaced or ironized, is replaced by a desire for something else, indeed by desire itself. The beautiful possibility represented by the gold displaces the schematic and tropic nature of the death sought by the Revelers. Only then do they find death, misdirected toward it by the allure of the gold, which they, though not the Old Man, fail to see as death. But that is why they find death. Pure death resists representation; it lacks the predicate of being and cannot be something other than what it is, because it is not anything at all. The knowledge that we and the Old Man share—that gold is death because it will bring death about— is not the knowledge that the Revelers have, because they know that death is a phenomenon with particular attributes. Caught in discursive death by its schemes and tropes, they begin to seem a little like the death that they seek, becoming thieves who work "ful prively."[33] Yet a further irony of the exemplum is that the Revelers' initial orientation toward death is also true, at the level of typology, which is part of the universe of exemplary representation: death *will* be dead in the homiletic world of which this tale offers itself as an example.

The advice that the boy offers in the tavern participates in the scheme of the *artes moriendi*, if it is not in fact their very foundation. To be aware of death is to have to confront finitude. What does it mean, after all, to "be war" of death? Does it mean to watch out for it and so avoid it, and in avoiding it evade finitude for the moment? Or does it mean to be perfectly aware that everything we do will be constrained by finitude, so the very ethics of dying demands that we be aware of the finitude that emerges whenever we do anything, the death that haunts our every action? The Three Revelers take the admonition to beware of death with the kind of literal acceptation that "The Pardoner's Tale" is partly about—a *vetus homo* of sin appearing as an old man—and go off seeking death. But if the advice about death relayed from the boy's "dame" is normative in any sense, if it really is advice about how to confront finitude, then no one in that opening scene of the poem's exemplum seems to understand what death really is.

Yet it's the most catastrophic and massive aspect of death that suggests that no one here is really "war" of death. The boy's evocation of death during "this pestilence" is just a way of marking a moment in time—that is, the time when a thousand people were killed by a figure who can actually only be known by the death of thousands. The boy's personified Death is really the trace of death, its memorial. It is not death itself, or even its agent. It is the scant consolation that presents itself when we get too close to unimaginable death.

The Revelers die because they misunderstand the relation between death and representation, the possibility that death is anything at all, although they also die because they discover something that comes to mean everything to them. Death is what resists representation, yet it is also the lure of representation itself, the bedazzlement that endows something with the significance of life and death: the gold that leads the Revelers to kill each other. Death, in other words, is manifest when it is no longer purposive. The truth of death is there in the tale but is, strictly speaking, exorbitant to the exemplum. The Revelers' quest for death is meant to be comic or ironic, the dramatization of carnal reading, of the inability to recognize allegorical personification: a death by literalization.

Yet, as I have been arguing, the Revelers die also because they fail to read literally, carnally, enough. Death is none of the things that the Revelers believe it to be, because death is within them, or is part of the complex of disordinate desires for which they have no real regard. But the truth of the tale is also that death is all of those things: it is a thief that comes in the night, it is catastrophic and massive annihilation, it is something that can be dead, although it acquires these predicates beyond the Revelers' horizon of expectation, and indeed beyond the horizon of the exemplum's *moralitas*. Death's predicates are exorbitant to the exemplum: it cannot be any of those things for the Revelers, or they would be able to recognize its oblique, allegorical presence elsewhere. If they understood what it really meant to say that "Deeth shal be deed," they would also understand that death does not take forms, that the very putting to death of death is the exceptional death of Christ, a death that is actually life, and that is recalled in just this way at the Easter vigil in the antiphon "O mors ero mors tua," taken from Hosea 13:14.[34] There is a sense in which death enters into representation at such moments, but only because death is in the process of being robbed of its predicates once and for all. Death only means something when it is really implicated in life—when it really is no longer purposive.

A more protracted demonstration of the exorbitant death that comes to mean something only when death is annulled is the youngest Reveler's purchase of a poison so potent that no more than a piece of it the size of a grain of wheat is needed to kill someone ("That he ne shal his lif anon forlete" [863–64]). As H. Marshall Leicester points out, the reference is to John 12:24: ("unless a grain of wheat falls into the earth and dies, it remains alone; but if it dies, it bears much fruit. He who loves his life loses it"), a passage that is commonly read to refer to the Eucharist.[35] Within the logic of the exemplum, the poison is simply an agent of death, another possible form that the Reveler overlooks in his neglect of the original quest for death. He has found it and almost recognizes it, and the annulment of that form of death gives this moment its ironic kick. But that typological overlay only works if death is similarly annulled by whatever audience the Pardoner imagines to be attuned to allusions that do not advance the point of the exemplum.

Indeed, for this allusion to work at all, we have to annul the death that the poison represents: it cannot both be poison and the Eucharist, any more than the poisoning deaths of the other two Revelers represent the death that bears much fruit. We recognize the allegory but suspend it; it becomes a possible death that does not appear within the frame of the exemplum. Just as the Revelers do, we deny the allegorical quality of death in order to sustain a real encounter with it, to witness death rather than merely to find it.

Death really "is" none of the things that the boy and the Taverner claim it is. We can only believe it to be those things if death is not in fact cryptic, the figure of what we have to be aware of without being able to name it, for naming it is beside the point. Indeed, the exemplum rigorously avoids using the copula of being and death: in the child's account of what has happened, he does not say that Death "is" a "privee thief," but that men "call" this thief Death; Death doesn't use words, so it is hard to say what he "is"; he "is" not the pestilence, but he acts during it. If such a massive visitation of death on the world as the plague cannot bring us before death, if Death's "habitacioun," to use the word that the Taverner does, is not really in a nearby village, it is outside it. And because its "habitacioun" is also nowhere, because we can only speak of death allegorically, it is also everywhere, hidden in its own phenomena.

In Chaucer's "Knight's Tale," Theseus sounds as if he has sorted out the philosophical knottiness of death. Although he lives in a pagan world, he seems to know more about death than the Revelers do, even though they live in the epoch of late medieval Christianity. Yet their willingness to admit that they don't know quite what it is makes Theseus's philosophical confidence seem in retrospect misplaced, and his ostentatious and spectacular attempts to master it almost willful denials of its implacable mystery. Saturn, the lord of chaos, has an orbit that exceeds even Theseus's.

CHAPTER SIX

Dying and the Tragedy of Occupation: "The Knight's Tale"

Eventually we have to put a term to the interminable. We do not co-habit with the dead for fear of seeing *here* collapse into the unfathomable *nowhere*.
—Maurice Blanchot

The death of Arcite at the end of "The Knight's Tale" is one of the most extensive and physiologically accurate—in medieval terms—descriptions of dying in Middle English. After being pitched from his horse, Arcite is carried into Theseus's palace, where the animal spirit eventually fails to expel the venom in the blood from "thilke vertu cleped natural," and he succumbs to the corrupted blood in his lungs and heart.[1] As the Knight says, somewhat grandiosely, "Al is tobrosten thilke regioun, / Nature hath now no dominacioun" (I.2757–58), rhyming somewhat abstract words as the discipline of physic gives up the specific domain of Arcite's lungs, heart, and "every lacerte in his brest" (I.2753). Like Theseus in his tale, the Knight controls and dominates the spaces before him, aware that his tale is a "large feeld" and announcing that he will "telle forthe as I bigan" (I.1354), apologizing for his brevity in lengthy *occupationes* and *praeteritiones*.[2] He is in no doubt about where to take the body once nature loses its domination: "Go bere the man to chirche!" he says, anticipating the obsequies and rituals of death that we saw in "The Pardoner's Tale." He knows where a dead or dying body goes. Yet he refuses to name the region where Arcite finds himself after death, because it is, at least in part, unknowable: "ther, / As I cam nevere, I kan nat tellen where" (I.2809–10). This moment, in fact, signals the poem's general discomfort with talking about the state of death.

The place of the soul is unknowable because the body does not belong there, and as long as the Knight insists that eschatological knowledge be founded on experiential, corporeal knowledge, he will refuse a place for the soul—indeed, as his change to the plural pronoun just after this moment suggests, a place for all souls. I refer to his refusal because the knowledge is lodged in this discourse, although he painstakingly argues that it does not exist in any "register," nor does he wish to recite the opinions of those that do, in fact, "writen wher they dwelle" (I.2812, 2814). All that matters is the state of the body, which is now cold. It is precisely at this point of the *Teseida* that Boccaccio spells out in some detail the passage of Arcita's soul to the inner surface of the eighth sphere before going to the place allotted for him by Mercury, a passage Chaucer uses later to describe the journey of Troilus's soul.[3] The Knight rejects the very "register" that shows precisely the relation between Arcite's soul and his death. In refusing to sustain the relation between the archive and the soul, or in denying the soul by also denying the archive, the Knight refuses to acknowledge the relation between the body and its ensoulment, refusing to take up what Gillian Rose calls a "relation to the relation."[4] The conspicuous silence over Arcite's soul is perhaps the most obvious and startling of the changes that Chaucer makes to the *Teseida*, and the most obvious sign that the tale is not interested in, or cannot talk about, the condition of the soul in death. It deliberately rejects the answer that lies on the newest shelf in the poem's archive (or, in medieval terms, among the top documents in the chest).

This annulment of the archive also characterizes the Knight's interruption of the Monk's recitation of a string of tragedies.[5] His initial objection, that they simply weigh too heavily on the audience, addresses on the one hand the formal disarray and agglutinative quality of "The Monk's Tale"—it lacks proportion and ratio: "namoore of this! / That ye han seyd is right ynough, ywis, / And muchel moore." (VII.2767–69). On the other hand, in acknowledging the plenitude of "The Monk's Tale" he also assesses it according to its adequation to the truth of things—it is "right ynough . . . And muchel moore," accurate enough in some ways to be more than sufficient on its own terms. In its medieval context, what tragedy is accurate about is the necessity of the care of the soul, the necessity of recognizing the inevitable loss of everything except the soul and its relation to God.[6]

In repudiating the excess of tragedy, the Knight also repudiates the relationality of the soul, which appears to him as the paradoxically weighty mode of tragedy itself, insistently and blindly seeking out other catastrophes to relate, and to which to stand in relation. Rather than admit the strength of this repeated anecdotal evidence of the necessity for the care of the soul, the Knight obliterates its most important moral lesson: that this collapse is necessary and ubiquitous. He simply reverses the course of the narrative, turning adversity back into prosperity: "it is a gret disese," he says; "Whereas men han been in greet welthe and ese, / To heeren of hire sodeyn fal, alas! / And the contrarie is joye and greet solas, / As whan a man hath been in povre estaat, / And clymbeth up and wexeth fortunat, / And there abideth in prosperitee" (VII.2771–77). Yet the Knight does not actually say that this condition, this mode, exists. It is simply the "contrarie" of the trajectory of tragedy—its negation, which may or may not be real. His posing of a phantasmatic alternative leaves the soul after tragedy merely in a place of "gret disese."

The great irony of the tale the Knight tells is that it repeatedly finds itself at sites of great unease because of its failure to enlist this phantasmatic alternative to tragedy. Theseus's discomfort over hearing about the fall of Theban nobles ultimately leads him to leave a pile of their bodies outside Thebes's walls; Arcite fails to apply to himself his caution that we know not what we do; Theseus's speech about the First Mover fails to account for the work of Saturn and is derailed by his own championing of honor in the face of death, which offers the only consolation for a life cut short. Yet this consolation fails to address the condition of death itself. The subject of Theseus's speech is finitude: the oak that dies, the stone that erodes, the river that dries up, the towns that rise and fall. These are all aspects of the phenomenon of generation and corruption, which dictates that things survive only to the degree that they are succeeded by others and are "nat eterne" (I.3015). This happens because everything we see is a part derived from a whole that is "parfit" and "stable" (I.3009). Each part is imperfect and corruptible because it lacks the perfection of being whole, and part of its imperfection is that it takes its origin from some other thing. Only Jupiter, the cause of all things, possesses this wholeness. Everything else, as Theseus says, "moot dye" (I.3034), especially men and woman, who die in one of "termes two"—youth or age (I.3028). Death is otherwise indiscriminate, taking kings and pages, sailors, sleepers, field workers.

Theseus does not make clear why these two terms are so important, however much they sound like a truism: he leaves a negligible but evident difference between them. At this point Boccaccio's *Teseida* adds a line about the detriment of living to old age, to "oscura vecchiezza piena d'infiniti guai."[7] One one hand, Theseus's speech omits even the hint of infinitude, however full of woe it may be. On the other, the omission makes the alternative of living to old age simply one of the two "termes," a term that itself is dispassionate and neutral. The minimal difference between dying humans, then, is simply the term in which they die, and that difference will become the foundation of Theseus's argument that Arcite's death should be celebrated: the honor that a man dies with is at its height when he is young and will only pall with age. Of the two ways of dying, in youth or in age, Theseus says that the first, in which a "man hath moost honour" (I.3047), should actually be a cause for rejoicing: "gladdere oghte his freend been of his deeth, / Than whan his name apalled is for age" (I.3053–53). And in urging this joy on the Athenians, Theseus echoes the metaphysics of the beginning of his speech, which is borrowed from Boethius's *Consolation of Philosophy*: "I rede that we make of sorwes two / O parfit joye, lastynge everemo" (I.3071–72).[8]

In what follows, I will be looking at several such borrowings from the *Consolation*, mostly on the part of Theseus. It is my argument that Theseus is fundamentally a misreader of the *Consolation* in a particular way. Just as the Knight's borrowings from Statius's *Thebaid* do, the echoes of a previous text resituate and often make ironic what might otherwise be unproblematic enthymemes. This is not exactly the haunting of Chaucer's text, but it is a structural reflection of the tale's recurring definition of finitude as the state of inescapable consequence—in other words, of the return of the repressed. Finitude is the continually dawning recognition that the future is bound because we are bound by the past: "Right as ther dyed nevere man . . . That he ne lyvede in erthe in some degree, / Right so ther lyvede never man . . . In al this world, that som tyme he ne deyde" (I.2843–46). These lines are in fact an instance of the tale's complex reinscribing of Statius's *Thebaid*: they are a comic reduction of Adrastus's attempt to console the Argives at Opheltes's funeral, a series of bromides about death followed by the possible consolation of momentary exceptions to it with observations about fate and destiny ("nunc fata recensens / resque hominum duras et inexorabile pensum, / nunc aliam prolem mansuraque numine dextro / pignora" [VI.47–50]).[9]

In bringing parts together to form a perfect whole, Theseus is undoing the work of corruption and the fundamental ontology of nature, because parts, which have beginnings, cannot form the whole as Lady Philosophy defines it. And he does it in the search for perfect joy, precisely the experience that this section of the *Consolation* says can only be found with God. This is the phantasmatic alternative to tragedy. It is not just that death should be the occasion of joy, but that joy is simply the difference between two kinds of death.

Theseus's forgetting of the place of the soul is the most abstract of his efforts to organize place. He starts "The Knight's Tale" outside the gates of Athens as the conqueror of the Amazonian "regne of femenye, / That whi-

lom was ycleped Scythia" (I.866–67) and is diverted by the pleas of the Theban women to clear the space in front of Thebes of its dead and unburied
men. Earlier, as his device of the minotaur on his pennon suggests, he had
mastered the labyrinth at Minos by unraveling its unintelligible space with
the help of Ariadne's thread, putting an end to the long tradition of sacri-
ficing Athenian men and women there. For these reasons he might be described as a master of death, attacking it in its various guises: as a cruel ty-
rant who desecrates the bodies of his enemies, as a bestial devourer of the
young, and as the labyrinth itself, that fatal and unintelligible place. Yet
although Theseus arrests particular *forms* of death, the tale is structured by
repeated confrontations with the *problem* of death.

Theseus's device of the minotaur, half man, half bull, reminds us that
the bodily self remains unruly and bound not only to its bestial nature, but
also to its mortality: in the *Inferno*, the minotaur's fate is to suffer death
throes for eternity.[10] Lying between life and death outside the walls of Thebes,
Arcite and Palamon, too, belong to neither. They are found "nat fully
quyk ne fully deed" (I.1015), brought out of the heap of the dead as no more
than bare lives, caught in the moment of dying. That bestial self that insists
on dying is emblematic of Theseus's activities, whether in conquering or in
memorializing those he conquers. He leaves behind a field of bodies when
he conquers Thebes; he displaces even the gods when he prepares a space for
Arcite's funeral. The forgetting of imperatives follows in the wake of bodies: to undertake the care of the dead, to revere immortal selves. The hybrid
body is also an emblem of oblivion, a kind of fatal conjunction of principles
that annul one another or fall together in death, as the soul and body could
be said do to at conception or birth. At least this is how Boethius imagines
that union—as a form of death that brings forgetting with it: "I loste my
memorie be the contagious conjunccioun of the body with the soule," he
says, and "eftsones afterward, whan Y lost it confounded by the charge and
be the burdene of my sorwe."[11] Loss and forgetting follow from the union of
body and soul and from the recognition that they will not always be united,
that the body lacks something that the soul craves—or that the soul lacks
something that the body craves. Such is the predicament of Arcite, whose
transformative sorrow over having to leave Emelye behind in Athens alters
the nature of his body, so that "lene he wex and drye as is a shaft; / His eyen
holwe and grisly to biholde, / His hewe fallow and pale as ashen colde"
(I.1362–64). Love, or the supposed loss of it, turns his body into a signifier
of death, and the "humour malencolik" dominates his appearance (I.1375).[12]
But he is also dying through a derangement of place, the necessity of being

in Thebes rather than Athens. This sense of dislocation is not necessarily prompted by geopolitical or even erotic considerations: Arcite's notion of place has already been subjected to an array of metaphorical and literal transformations.

The most apparently oppressive of these is the prison in which Palamoun and Arcite are confined for a number of years.[13] The poem's understanding of just what a prison means broadens to include the world external to the prison—everything, in fact, that is *not* a prison (1224); it includes Arcite's freedom to go "wher that hym liste over al" (1207), to hell (1226), and to the "prisoun of this lyf" (3061). Arcite and Palamoun are kept in places that are increasingly straitened, moving from a "tour" (1056) to a "dongeoun" (1057) to a "chambre" at the top of the tower (1065). The real restriction, however, does not come until Arcite finds himself free in the larger, vaguer prison of the world. In this space that, for him, has no location because Emelye cannot be placed in it, he embodies the dilation and divagation that is characteristic of someone unable fully to remember.[14] He is free to go wherever he wishes but is unable to see Emelye. His prison is a notional one, exerting its influence precisely where his memory operates: the greater his awareness of Emelye, the greater the knowledge that his mind and the world fail to correspond. The prison he is in exerts its discipline in the smallest places of the mind, but precisely where place has the most important function—in the faculty of imagination, the "celle fantastik" (I.1376). If the very word *celle* conjures up the prison he has forsaken, it is not because the word was used in such a way in the fourteenth century—it was not, except to describe monastic dwellings or storerooms—but because we, and Arcite, have been cultivated to think of the cell of memory as the disciplinary space of repetition, of habit and ethics. His inability to repeat the scene of gazing at Emelye in her own place of confinement in the enclosed garden juxtaposed with the tower makes his memory as diffuse and nonspecific as the indifferent world he now sees as the space of imprisonment. He has become a melancholic, in other words, subject to a "manye, / Engendred of humour malencolik / Biforen, in his celle fantastik / And shortly, turned was al up so doun / Bothe habit and eek disposicioun / Of hym" (I.1374–79). Melancholy, the symptom of mnemonic failure, is not exactly oblivion, because it carries with it an awareness of both place and space. But it prevents one from making the crucial distinctions between the two, abdicating the tasks vital to memory of "habit" and "disposicioun," the orderly, sequential address of things to places.

The Knight's later reception of the Monk's string of tragedies, a reception that is similarly turned "up so doun," longing for joy and solace where there is none, could also be characterized as a melancholic response. In its refusal to apply the explicit lesson the Monk announces at the beginning—"Lat no man truste on blynd prosperitee" (VII.1997)—it exemplifies a kind of generic oblivion, the unwillingness to see beyond the overwhelming presence of catastrophe to the normative conditions of possession. This unwillingness characterizes the tale he tells as well and is embodied in one of Arcite's significant speeches. Yet this tale is scarcely free of the cycle of tragedy.

"The Knight's Tale" replays the trajectory of tragedy a number of times: as the recovery from the initial "adversitee" of Arcite and Palamoun (which would seem to suggest the trajectory of comedy, although the poem actually begins with their fall from "prosperitee" as Theban princes), as Arcite's adversity at being exiled, as Arcite's recovery of prosperity at the Athenian court, and as the ultimate adversity of his own death. As Egeus suggests, there is something reversible about these categories in the first place: "this worldes transmutacioun" (2839) causes things to "chaunge bothe up and doun" (2840), with "joye after wo, and wo after gladnesse" (2841). Although the world he lives in is certainly unstable, that itself is one of the defining features of tragedy, as is the very trajectory with which he sums up this "transmutacioun": the arrival of "wo" after "gladnesse." Arcite's own canny, but momentary, knowledge of his own oblivion, a canniness not invalidated in the least because he expresses it in universal terms, contemplates a tragedy that is frequently entailed even in the very action of avoiding it:

> Som man desireth for to han richesse,
> That cause is of his mordre or greet siknesse;
> And som man wolde out of his prisoun fayn,
> That in his hous is of his meynee slayn.
> Infinite harmes been in this mateere.
> We witen nat what thing we preyen heere;
> We faren as he that dronke is as a mous.
> A dronke man woot wel he hath an hous,
> But he noot which the righte wey is thider,
> And to a dronke man the wey is slider.
> And certes, in this world so faren we;
> We seeken faste after felicitee,
> But we goon wrong ful often, trewely. (I.1255–67)

And Arcite immediately proceeds to go wrong by expressing the sincerest conviction that his bliss would be total if only he could escape from prison. He is not, ultimately, slain in his "hous," but the return to a murderous domestic space imagined in this meditation on the disasters of desire and epistemology is a concise account of tragedy in both the Chaucerian sense, as the passage from prosperity to adversity, and in the Boethian sense, as a trivial but fatal mistaking of economic goods for the *summum bonum*. It also anticipates Horatio's severe account of tragedy at the end of *Hamlet*, which consists of a similar mistaking: "purposes mistook / Fall'n on th' inventors' heads" (act 5, scene 2, lines 385–86). The comedy of "The Knight's Tale" consists in our even cannier knowledge of its events, recognizing that Arcite immediately puts into play exactly the machinery of tragedy that he warns against. That knowledge also is an uncanny knowledge, since we know that it is his desires that condemn him, and that his achievement of victory is ephemeral and fatal. What is even more disturbing, we know that the places in which the poem's main characters seek refuge are haunted by death, and by a death that is peculiarly self-inflicted. Despite Theseus's pretensions to master space, constructing a mile-wide tournament list that represents the world, "ful of degrees" (I.1890), for instance, he leaves an extraordinary wake of death and disorder behind him.

Not only is Theseus a "conqueror" of diffuse places, but he also exhibits a compulsion to order places, to prevent them from collapsing into spaces of panic. This compulsion is hinted at from the beginning of the tale. His confrontation with the Theban women arrayed before him outside the gates of Athens provokes a brief but thematically complex exchange. He asks a question of them much like the one the dreamer asks the Man in Black in *The Book of the Duchess*: why are you, he asks, "clothed thus in blak"? (I.911). Of course, he first attributes to them his paranoid assumption that they are jealous of his "honour," asking also a question much like the one the Three Revelers ask of the Old Man in "The Pardoner's Tale": "who hath yow mysboden or offended? / And telleth me if it may been amended" (I.909–10). The answer he does not hear, which echoes through the rest of the tale, is that the offense is that of an unpropitiated death, inflicting an injury ("mysbode") that is also a false summons ("bodian," to announce), a turning of fascination and horror from the unthinkable to the very figure of tyranny, Creon (I.941), who fully embodies the horror he has provoked, "fulfild with ire and iniquitee" (I.940). It is this dangerous plenitude that turns Theseus from his own course, to do what the work of mourning must do: confront death in its habitation, in its materiality and presence. But the appeal of the Theban women also turns to the objects that this deadly plenitude displaces, the topics of aristocratic enjoyment themselves, which death threatens to overwhelm. Using the very language of Fortune's vicissitude, to which the Knight later proves himself to be exquisitely sensitive, they remind him that death threatens not only the Theban state, but the state of everything: if this can happen to us, they say, who (as Theseus thinks, echoing the Knight's wistful opening of the tale) "whilom weren of so gret estaat" (I.956), then "noon estaat assureth to be weel" (I.926).

The Theban women are immediately provoked, of course, by the horrific place that has emerged outside their walls, which now demands work directed precisely at death: the pile of bodies Creon has left unburied in a field outside the city, "on an heep ydrawe" (I.944). It is at this juncture that Theseus first unveils his peculiarly ambiguous banner with the sign of the minotaur, or at least when it is first described. Theseus's work of propitiation outside Thebes will add an important dimension of ambiguity to his banner, that of the *limen* between life and death, figured in the bodies of Arcite and Palamoun, "nat fully quyke, ne fully dede" (I.1015). This phrase is a concise account of all of Theseus's subsequent attempts at mastery, which repeat in various forms the primitive founding of Thebes in an act of destruction, itself repeated in the chthonic emergence of Palamon and Arcite in the manner of their ancestors, the *terrigenae* springing forth from the field Cadmus sowed with the teeth of the serpent he has slain.

After essentially obliterating Thebes (I.990), Theseus restores the bones of their men to the women and makes camp for the night in the same field. This act of repetition is not just a function of military economy—it is cheaper and easier to rest where you fight—it is also part of an eerie economy that is traced in virtually all of Theseus's actions. He has installed himself in a place outside Thebes that is becoming increasingly familiar, and he has also produced what is becoming increasingly familiar in that place: a pile of dead bodies, "a taas of bodyes dede" (I.1005) that "pilours" ransack through the night, stripping the bodies of their armor and clothing. Theseus turns out to be virtually like Creon, leaving a pile of unmourned, abandoned bodies in the same field. But he may also be worse than Creon, for the pile he leaves is described only (and three times, at that) as a "taas" (I.1005, 1009, 1020), a word that elsewhere is used to describe a pile of bodies, a pile of coins, and (most often) a hayrick.[15] Theseus leaves in his wake a deeply ironic legacy, but one that also reproduces one of the most banal figurations of death in the Middle Ages: death as a harvest.

His morbid economy at Thebes shows that a death he cannot get rid of, Death itself, is both a facet of his production of spectacle and wealth and an exorbitant presence. All of his subsequent attempts in Athens to install the kind of order that he believes he has installed at Thebes, righting the wrongs of death, repeat this inability to foreclose the production of death, to dispense with, to manage, or to use up its very exorbitance. Theseus ensures that each of the Theban confrontations at Athens take place in increasingly displaced symbolic modes, or rather in the form of increasingly symbolic displacements. Theseus first finds the rivals Palamon and Arcite knee-deep in their own blood (I.1660), then agrees to wield the summary judgment of death that they both demand (I.1715–47), only to accede to the women's requests to spare their lives (I.1763–1844) and to resume the conflict in the form of a tournament, and then to decree on the day of the tournament that it will take a symbolic form, a nonlethal contest (I.2543–57). In the course of Theseus's assertion of symbolic power and efficacy, the copious and literal blood that covered the ground in the grove is elutriated of its corporeality, becoming the sign of an abstract nobility that must be preserved. He does not now consider the death he was willing to inflict on the individual bodies earlier; rather, he worries about safeguarding the dynastic capital of the two Thebans in this almost purely symbolic economy, an economy in which nothing can really be consumed or destroyed. This is why he warns against the "destruccioun / To gentil blood" that might occur in an actual conflict (I.2538–39). As Lee Patterson remarks, this work of symbolization is also the project of the Knight's narrative: it is meant "to record the disarming of an aboriginal Theban ferocity by Athenian civilization, the replacement of a regressive Theban ferocity by Athenian civilization [, a narrative intended] as an allegory of the progress of chivalry, a secular fraternity that imposes order first upon itself—the Order of Chivalry—and then upon an unruly world."[16]

Theseus's impositions fail not only because they exemplify, as Patterson argues, the immanent failures of chivalric practice, but because they do not address death directly, continuing to make the mistakes of displacement and metonymic misdirection that we see in the initial scenes of the poem. That is, each of Theseus's attempts to manage the violence of Palamon and Arcite, to convert it by exemplary assertions of the Athenian Symbolic, is established in the place of the destruction it is attempting to annul by positive example. These symbolic assertions, however, work more like the secondary inscriptions Freud describes as the procedure of memory, beneath which the very topics that this inscription should consign to oblivion show through as in a palimpsest.[17] The lists that Theseus orders built are an extraordinary concealment of symbolic overdetermination: imagined as a supermundane object—"swich a noble theatre . . . I dare wel seyen in this world ther nas" (I.1885–86), says the narrator—it is also a theatrical space, a civic enclosure a mile around, it is "walled with stoon, and dyched al with-oute" (I.1888), the figure of writing, of the very "ars-metrike" (I.1898) being enacted in this narration, and, above and including all of these, an attempt to displace space itself: "swich a place / Was noon in erthe, as in so litel space" (I.1895–96). Within its circumference are three temples dedicated to Mars, Venus, and Diana containing images of the mythic and allegorical history of each. These images reiterate the overcrowding of the lists them-selves "as in so litel space," with the Knight claiming that Venus's temple, for instance, contains "all the circumstaunces / Of love" (I.1932–33) and "mo than I kan make of mencioun" (I.1935). They function, in short, as an archive of the *res gestae* of the gods, and their comprehensiveness is an index of the power of the gods themselves.[18] The actions of the gods are described in terms of their archival reach: "Noghte was foryeten by the in-fortune of Marte" (I.2021). It is perhaps because of the extensive catalog of death and catastrophe in Mars's temple that the Knight describes it as built "in memorie" of him (I.1906). His temple is a vast archive of the vari-ous deaths he has visited on humans, and even a memorial of the god's own impossible death. Mars's temple contains what is largely a catalog of horrific deaths—accidental, arbitrary, purposive, massive, appalling because no eti-ology is known, not even that of plague: "A thousand slayn, and nat of qualm ystorve" (I.2014), as if a thousand deaths from the plague would be a form of consolation in its own right. The comprehensiveness of Theseus's project, his mastery of the space of the lists (in both senses of the word), meets its vanishing point in the temples of the gods. The denial of mas-sive death at the hands of plague diverts us from one of the larger horrors lurking in the space beyond this theatre: that of plague itself. The reference to plague, "qualm," here is an echo, and the ambivalent disavowal, of the most explicit citation of plague in the main body of The Canterbury Tales, in the Death of "The Pardoner's Tale," who "hath a thousand sleyn this pestilence" (VI.679). The mathematics of catastrophe demand that plague (personified as Death) counter the deficit it incurs at the hand of Mars—the thousand deaths that it does *not* cause—by slaying a thousand later in The Canterbury Tales (later in both its narrative order and its compositional his-tory, as if Chaucer remembers, for several years ("The Pardoner's Tale" was written some twenty years after "The Knight's Tale"), and across hundreds of lines, that death's debt must be paid.

The shadow of death falls, too, across the artificial conjunction of plan-ets constructed by Theseus. The larger space outside the theater, above the world, had already witnessed a conjunction that caused death by plague to irrupt into the world. John of Reading attributed the third great outbreak

of plague in 1369, which immediately preceded Chaucer's composition of
"The Knight's Tale," to the inauspicious conjunction in 1356 of the male
planets mentioned in "The Knight's Tale": Mars, Jupiter, and Saturn.[19] The
first, and most horrific, outbreak of plague had already long been blamed
on the same conjunction, most extensively by the Paris medical faculty in
1348, citing Pseudo-Aristotle's work on the elements and their causes: "he
says that mortality of races and the depopulation of kingdoms occur at the
conjunction of Saturn and Jupiter, for great events then arise, their nature
depending on the trigon at which their conjunction occurs."[20] In his *Judi-
cio solis*, Simon de Covino points out that *all* of the planets were in conjunction with Saturn in 1345, and that, just as in "The Knight's Tale," "a
great dispute arose between Jupiter and Saturn over the human race."[21] The
moon, Diana, was also seen to have had an important effect on the events
engendered by this conjunction. An eclipse of the moon occurred two days
before the conjunction,[22] which, Geoffrey de Meaux ingeniously argues, accounts for the time that elapsed between the conjunction and the first appearance of the plague. "It is known to all astronomers that the duration of
obscurity of the lunar eclipse when there was the conjunction of the three
superior planets (Saturn, Jupiter, and Mars) determines the time its effect
will last, according to Ptolemy: for as many months as there were hours
of darkness . . . when it occurs with something else, such as a conjunction of Saturn and Jupiter, the duration of its effect will be proportionately
lengthened."[23]

I am not arguing that Theseus's tournament lists reflect precisely this
cosmological conjunction. In fact, I am arguing that it consigns cosmological space to a kind of oblivion, configuring instead the place within its walls,
triangulated by the three temples, as a kind of contagious conjunction. Like
Boethius's virulent bodily forgetting, the conjunctions urged by Theseus in
his spectacular place of order—and the meeting of the gods themselves—
blot out knowledge of translunary space. We find out only near the end
that the most powerful of all the gods in the poem is one who is apparently
unknown to everyone in it: Saturn, who, we have already seen, is the dominant god and the activator of plague. As he says, in the only description of
a god in this tale that is neither ventriloquized (Theseus, with Jupiter) nor
ekphrastic (Venus, Mars, Diana): "My lookyng is the fader of pestilence"
(2469). "Lookyng" is a close translation of the astronomical terms *aspectus*
and *vultus*, but it does do some damage to the usual sense of the word—and
indeed this damaged reading must be entertained if one is to make sense of
the verb "looking." It looks like a verbal gerund, because that is the sense
we would ordinarily make of it, and it is the normative construction for

Chaucer: Saturn looks. But to attribute to it the sense it has in astronomy, one must think of "My lookyng" as a passive gerundive phrase with unexpressed objective and subjective complements: "The occasion of my being looked at by people." Doing this is a Saturnian exercise: it makes sense only when missing figures that turn out to govern the action are made manifest. The meaning of the sentence, that is, demands a cryptic reading, the deciphering of a puzzle where one did not at first seem to exist. Simply *looking* requires one to think about the relation of bodies to each other in the cosmos, to become disoriented by the orientation unfathomable of the space between Saturn and us.

Saturn's palaetiology of plague depends, in fact, on the possibility of unrestrained space, a space not regulated by the usual rules of grammaticality and observational knowledge. Saturn's orbit is a space that cannot be conquered even by Theseus, only in part because Theseus knows nothing about the extent of Saturn's influence: "My cours, that hath so wyde for to turne, / Hat moore power than woot any man" (I.2454–55). His orbit both exceeds and is unknown to human capacities of representation, his only obvious work to confound attempts to organize earthly space: His, he says, is the "ruyne of the hye halles, / The fallynge of the tours and of the walles" (I.2463–64).

The sublunary manifestation of Saturn's work is the work of tragedy, which we have already seen consists in tracing the devastating turns of Fortune, of, in the literal sense, "adversitee," a turning against. In referring to his orbit as a "cours," however, Saturn specifically links his capacity for destruction to the scene of the tournament, where the word refers to the arts of horsemanship and ritualized encounter. And Saturnian discourse reminds us of the impossibility of Theseus's project to render the scene of death merely symbolic and archival. "No longer shal the turneiyinge laste," says Theseus as the last of his injunctions (I.2557), oblivious to Saturn's ineluctable, ineffable "cours, that hath so wyde for to *turne.*"

The arresting of "turneiyinge" would have echoed the devastations of war and plague beyond the scope of this chapter. For one thing, royal governments throughout the fourteenth century worked strenuously to manage the extent and form of tournaments, which provided both a forum for knights to train for war and a locus in which antiroyal power could organize itself.[24] Tournaments, too, were often seen as a social pathology, one that allowed the worst excesses of display and violence. They could even be imagined as a cause of physical pathology—especially the plague. As Rosemary Horrox points out, Henry Knighton's account of the plague is immediately preceded by an account of the sexual licentiousness, frivolous dress, and economic waste at tournaments, as if to suggest a causal link.[25] The chronicle of Meaux Abbey makes the link more direct: "In the year before the pestilence came to dominate England, the nobility of England held tournaments and hastiludes in various cities and towns throughout the realm. . . . But scarcely any married woman attended with her own husband, but had instead been chosen by some other man, who used her to satisfy his sexual urges."[26] John of Reading recounts that, at the start of the second pestilence in 1361, two armies of tourneying knights phantasmatically appeared "in level, abandoned places" (in locis planis, desertis) in England and France—an eerie realization of the ways imputed social etiologies come to fill imaginary places, or even the places vacated by plague itself.[27] Theseus's failure to manage the eventual outcome of the tournament, his failure to prevent a death that intrudes from beyond the law he imposes on it, reveals to us the impossibility of obliterating adversity altogether with the tactics of displacement and transfer, especially because the conqueror of the labyrinth ought to remember that troping, turning, is a dangerous strategy. Even Dedalus, the builder of those turning passages, "vixque ipse reverti / ad limen potuit."[28]

We could see the Knight in similar terms, as we do when he interrupts the Monk's story, as the architect of a subversion of the course of tragedy, deflecting it into prosperity when it seems least likely to do so, and even as illogical and deluded. But he does tell us at the start that he has a big job ahead of him, "a large feeld to ere" (I.886). His appropriation of an ancient metaphor for writing should not surprise us, given the rich repertoire of such figures in his description of Theseus's lists. But it does seem a strange figure for a knight to use, even in the context of a story about a brutal, bloody, uncivilized city founded by a man violently tearing up a field. What may be significant here is the Knight's interest in narrating a turn from adversity; the figure of plowing offers itself as a diversion, a doubling back on its own tracks, a turning that is also the act of narration itself. The *versus*,[29] the verses, that the Knight uses to achieve his project turn it aside from the story's own potential as tragedy, almost as "adversitee" emerges at the very inception of the poem. The large domain of his narrative is never quite fully extirpated of adversity, never quite free of the traces of death. Theseus's city is adjoined throughout by the disturbing, chthonic space of both contest and burial. Theseus himself can only be consoled over Arcite's death by Egeus's information that we all die, subject to "this worldes transmutacioun" (I.2839). He lives in a world, like the bodies of Palamon and Arcite, "nat fully quyke, ne fully dede," that is not quite the *stabilitas* imagined by the places of memory nor the wholly unintelligible real of the space of death and Saturn.

The heterogeneous place that is Theseus's body, and the double-formed body that is his own device, recall another sense we can associate with panic space. In Plato's *Cratylus*, Socrates explicates the double nature of Pan, half goat and half man, as an embodiment of the relation between truth and untruth, or, more precisely, as just the relation of the *versus* we have seen in "The Knight's Tale": "speech signifies all things [literally, *pan*], and is always turning them round and round, and has two forms, true and false." For that reason Pan is the embodiment of the convertibility of speech, being rough below and smooth above.[30] It is not surprising that Pan's top half is associated with truth and the divine form of the gods, while the bestial bottom half is associated with roughness and untruth. What is surprising is Socrates' coupling of roughness and untruth with the specific form of tragedy: "falsehood dwells below among common men, is rough and like the tragic goat; for tales and falsehoods are most at home there, in the tragic life."[31] Greek tragedy, in other words, configures human bestiality and untruth as its very topic, and in this sense is conditioned by the same logic that we see in medieval tragedy: ambiguity, repression, return, reversibility, and adversity itself—in short, what we have come to imagine as the topic of tragedy. Both forms of tragedy abhor the possibility of disorder, and the pathetic dimension of tragedy consists in human attempts to forestall it.

In fact, the very fate of the grove outside Athens is tragic: Chaucer's putatively immediate source, Boccaccio's *Teseida*, imagines the forest not simply as a site of regressive *religio* nor primitive thearchy but, Vincent Di-Marco says, "as a symbol of peace, security, and permanence through natural change."[32] Boccaccio's own source for the passage, Lucan's *De civili bello*, represents the forest outside Athens as a primally violent place of disturbance, a place of dishabitation from time immemorial that was also a place of death and of "savage rites, the altars . . . heaped with hideous offerings, and every tree was sprinkled with human gore."[33] It is a site of prohibition so powerful that the forest gods themselves had not found a home there, including Pan, already disinhabited from the forest that Theseus's drive to civilize will eventually eradicate as a possible inhabited place altogether; he, along with the forest gods, will no longer have a home and will be driven out by the Athenian rites of death. Theseus wishes to construct an archive out of the suffering of the Athenians and the Thebans, but he leaves encrypted space behind him. The gods are disinherited, roaming through the space left by destroyed woods. In placing his archive in the same spot where so much of the action of "The Knight's Tale" occurs, Theseus disinherits the Athenian past, disenchanting one of the most crucial spaces of memory in the tale. The drive to order the world disorders it, a process governed not by Theseus or the First Mover, but by the tumultuous and cryptic god Saturn, the only god not to appear in the Athenian archive.

Why should Theseus not acknowledge this cosmology? His speech on the First Mover is sometimes read as an unwitting and misplaced attribution of power to the wrong god, and his faith that love binds all things a phantasmatic optimism. "Greet was th' effect," he says, and "heigh was his entente" (I.2889). Referring the duration of things to the intention of Jupiter, Theseus argues that their passing away fulfills the destiny the god established for them. Not only do things fulfill an allotted span, but they fulfill the telos suggested by their causes when they do so, converting into their "proper welle / From which it is dirryved" (I.3037–38). Eventually all things will conform to the intention of the First Mover, even if they do not seem immediately to do so. But Theseus's argument here covers over a contradiction. It is precisely because things do not seem to fulfill their ends that they are converted into their "proper welle"; passing away, corruption, is the means by which this happens. Their ends are fulfilled when they seem not to have been fulfilled; the true condition of a thing is the cause that gives it being, yet that cause is revealed in the instant of nonbeing. Rather than a vision of generative, decorous love, Theseus's cosmogony is predicated on the annihilation of things:

> Considereth eek how that the harde stoon
> Under oure feet, on which we trede and goon,
> Yet wasteth it as it lyth by the weye.
> The brode river somtyme wexeth dreye;
> The grete tounes se we wane and wende.
> Thanne may ye se that al this thing hath ende. (I.3021–26)

It is a vision not unsuitable to the Saturnian worldview. Indeed, all of the examples that Theseus gives of this final converting concern ruin and catastrophe, whether of trees, towns, pages, or kings.

What Theseus's speech covers over is precisely its lack of consolation, its recognition that the conversion of things to their "proper welle" is just another alibi for a death that encroaches everywhere.[34] Building to an acceptance of what Theseus calls the "necessitee" of death, the speech turns crucially on just what kind of necessity Theseus has in mind, the necessity of Arcite's death in general or the necessity of his death by a particular accident. The examples he uses, of the passing away of things, seem to endorse a general conclusion about the nature of mortality. That is precisely what illustrates simple necessity in the *Consolation of Philosophy*: that "alle men ben mortal or dedly"—death is a predicate of the human.[35] Yet Theseus has in mind more than a straightforward existential assertion: he seems to mean that death is the only predicate of the human. Not only do we die, but we are human *because* we die. Yet what in Boethius is an example of the logical entailment of "mortal" in "human" becomes in Theseus the ontic mortality of all things, which defines them. By "necessitee," then, he seems to mean a much more pervasive and fundamental kind of death than the kind Boethius talks about; where he seems to be talking initially about the haphazard death of Arcite, which is an example of a conditional necessity, he turns out to intuit something like the catastrophic death that is represented by Saturn in "The Knight's Tale." The "necessitee" of which he makes a "vertu" implies the passive acceptance of mortality, rather than an orientation toward it, a mode of being toward death.

This urging of a "vertu" characterizes Theseus's drive to order, evident throughout the poem. Yet it also reveals his Saturnian side, the impulse that destroys precisely by trying to conserve: Arcite's death is the result not of execution, but of his imprisonment by Theseus; of Theseus's love for Perotheus, who intercedes on Arcite's behalf;[36] of Theseus's decision to hold a tournament; and even of Theseus's prohibition of sharp points to prevent "destruccioun of gentil blood." The conditional necessity that is Arcite's death comes about through conditions added by Theseus, who in relation to Arcite's death has assumed an essential passivity in the face of order, which opens onto its ruination. That is no "vertu" at all, and the Knight leaves open the possibility that what Theseus is making is not an embrace of necessity but the fabrication of a concept. Part of what is made, after all, when Theseus builds the tournament lists is the concept of Theseus as a builder of structures that carry a considerable conceptual weight, "fulfilled of degrees," charged with an *ars poetica*, housing three gods. His totalizing poetics is its own object, a sign of the encompassing purpose of the Thesean concept. It does not come without considerable corollary damage, however, and in terminating the habitation of the gods themselves in his attempt to give Arcite a conceptually fitting funeral, Theseus demonstrates how, in the words of Alexandre Kojève, the concept can be the murder of the thing. Another way of putting this is to say that Theseus offers no real alternative to the death that irrupts in his kingdom: the consolation that his speech offers is that there will always be a need for consolation. To "maken vertu of necessitee" (I.3042) is to fabricate a concept where death itself is the thing to be confronted, and all but to acknowledge that this concept takes the place of what is necessary. That, indeed, is Theseus's response, valorizing a "fame" that its progenitor can never possess as the compensation for death, a gesture that Falstaff devastatingly parodies in *Henry V*, or attempting to "make of sorwes two / O parfit joye, lastynge evermo" before they "departen from this place" (I.3070–72).

But neither Falstaff nor Theseus fully acknowledges the presence of death within his own kingdom, the necessity beyond the power of any being that transforms all corruptible things. In *Mourning Becomes the Law*, Gillian Rose offers a vociferous defense of the real necessity in the face of death—acknowledging that one's "will, action, reflection and passivity have consequences for others and for oneself which may not be anticipated and can never be completely anticipated; which *comes to learn* its unintended complicity in the use and abuse of power; and hence to redraw, *again and again*, the measures, the bonding and boundaries between me and me, subject and subjectivity, singular and individual."[37] What Theseus leaves spectacularly out of his speech, if we understand him as a kind of *compilator* of the Boethian passages that make it up, is the real nature of necessary death. It includes the contemplation of mere mortality, the necessity that entails us in death without justifying it as spectacular or catastrophic. To extricate a philosophy of capitulation from the acknowledgment of death might seem compatible with Lady Philosophy's ultimate advice in the *Consolation*. But there is an important difference. The *Consolation* affirms a general cosmological order, not a personal and microcosmic one. The universe is bound together by love, but loving something cannot bind us to it. Nor can our love for something endorse its existence, even if what we love is ourselves. The first extended lesson that Boethius learns is that our subjection to finitude means that we cannot produce permanent order or stability; we can only, and ultimately, discern it.

Theseus's cosmological speech extends the underlying irony of "The Knight's Tale," which begins with the Knight's own protestations of narrative enfeeblement ("wayke ben the oxen in my plogh") and ends with Theseus's transformation into a maker so powerful that he not only ties the loose ends of narrative together but transforms what is most resistant to change—"necessitee" itself—into the human capacity for virtue. He is powerful, but in the end Theseus still remains at the point of Boethius's initial failure of perception: he continues to desire to make the world instead of merely but ethically—and correctly—perceiving it.[38] That subtle form of denial is actually the shape of *occupatio* or *praeteritio*, which occurs twice at the end. The naming of something by eschewing it is precisely what Theseus does with "necessitee." Fatal necessity is imagined as something other than mere finitude. It is the source of "virtue," the engine for spectacle—yet a spectacle that is simultaneously the catastrophe that deprives Athens of its ancient *cultus*. The disinhabiting of the gods suggests a disturbance of the promise of life beyond, or outside of, death; it exposes the rickety framework of divinization that has created the gods, and consequently the extent, and even the possibility, of immortality. If the gods can be devastated by earthly ruination, then their divine immortality is not something beyond the reach of finitude. That the position of the immortals can be compromised by the earthly home that mortals give them suggests the ultimate inability of Athenian religiosity to rid itself of the problem of euhemerism, the notion that the gods are, finally and primarily, the narrative products of a human longing for the divine and the infinite. The infinitude of the gods depends, however, upon the actions of the Athenian polity, and it is ultimately Athenian finitude that shapes, and compromises, the Athenian form of immortality. The gods dwell *in* finitude, and their actions and reactions are subject to the contingencies of time. This is a problem that underlies the embarrassment of conflicting divine promises at the heart of "The Knight's Tale," the mutually conflicting assurances that Mars, Venus, and Diana give to Arcite, Palamon, and Emelye. That the conflict can be worked out only by means of a destruction sanctioned by the most powerful and remote god—the one furthest from the aspirations of the humans in the tale—suggests not that the Knight's theology is founded on cynical anarchy, but that the actions of gods are no less contingent—bound by finitude—than are the actions of humans.

The catastrophe inflicted on the gods by the destruction of the sacred grove is described precisely as a disinheritance. That very mortal misfortune is a strange calamity to befall gods, who virtually by definition ought to be immune from the strokes of fortune. Even if they were the subjects of the lesser god Fortuna, it is hard to imagine how one can be a god but still depend for one's "habitacioun" on a particular place on the earth. Although the grove is sacred to the Athenians, the very possibility that the gods can be alienated from their land suggests not that the gods lack *dominium* in the world, but that they might not be gods in the first place. Disinheritance, after all, is predicated on the inevitability of death and the severing of mortal ties to property: the very concept of inheritance demands that there be a horizon beyond which possession cannot continue: it demands that there be mortality. Indeed, the poem ends with the irrepressible return of death to the very space that had been set aside to make a sacred immortality possible: the space of ritual sacrifice is the space of Arcite's wounding and burial, and the space that is now divested of its original association with immortality. But all of this is to say that the poem ultimately recognizes that immortality is the result of a mandate whose source of power is the in-eradicable condition of mortality itself, of the Athenian desire to transcend what they recognize as their inevitable, mortal limits.

The degree to which this desire for transcendence suffuses the poem's ending can be gauged by the tendency of the poem's readers themselves to read Theseus's speech as an unproblematic endorsement of Philosophy's vision of infinite justice, in which everything is connected by a fair chain of love to Jupiter/God, the infinite source of justice.[39] One of the ironies of this speech, however, is that it itself is embedded in a section of the tale that consists of entangled and doubled-backed narratives, a negative and formal image of what Theseus is attempting to endorse. Much of the speech itself is a straightforward translation of Teseo's speech in the *Teseida*, with minor rhetorical *amplificatio* and embellishment: the speech itself, *strictu sensu*, leads back in an orderly textual inheritance to the principles of book 2, metrum 8 of the *Consolatio*. But the events surrounding it come from Chaucer's disturbing source for what he doesn't take from Boccaccio's *Il Teseida*: the *Thebaid* of Statius, the bloody and tumultuous epic of vio-lence and disrupted succession that recounts the civil war of Thebes.[40]

The *Thebaid* furnishes the epigraph for the entire "Knight's Tale," *iamque domos patrias*, whose very placement becomes metonymic of the dynamics of the poem, the additional turn (*iamque*) of an action we have not yet seen from the source of the poem from which this one is largely drawn. And it is a line that returns us to an ancestral house, opening onto a poem that begins with Theseus on the verge of returning home, yet thwarted by news of the Theban war. The entire pattern of the passage with Theseus's speech could be said to be the pattern of interrupted inheritance, of the thwarted return to origins. The preparation for Arcite's funeral is one of Chaucer's most extreme deviations from Boccaccio, taken mostly from the preparation for the funeral rites for Opheltes, Lycurgus's infant son, in the *Thebaid*. The overwhelming tone of that passage is one of inconsolability. Adrastus gives a speech much like Egeus's in "The Knight's Tale," laying out the pros that balance out the cons of mortality, but Adrastus's speech is interrupted by the resurgence of Argive mourning ("nondum orsis modus, et lamenta redibant" [VI.50]). Not much later, Amphiaraus has to urge the Argives to stop their lamenting, which is an omen of still more disaster to come (VI.221–23).

The corpse at the center of the funeral is the very embodiment of thwarted inheritance; it is that of Lycurgus's son, who will never inherit

Argos, and whom Amphiaraus renames Archemorus, a name that signifies the onset of finitude, the beginning (*arche*) of death.[41] The origin of the description of Arcite's funeral in that of Opheltes devastatingly undercuts Theseus's desire to match the ritual magnitude of the occasion with the ostensible magnificence of Arcite's death, and especially his tendentious argument that Arcite's sudden death is timely because it will reinforce the honor of his name. Even his syntax suggests that this argument is tacked on to, rather than proven by, the meditation on finitude that Theseus is delivering: "Thanne is it best, *as for a worthy fame,* / To dyen whan that he is best of name" (I.3055–56, my emphasis). Fame is a bonus, an unsought good, that works best when its recipient is no longer there to enjoy it. The roots of this scene in Opheltes' funeral underscore the speciousness of Theseus's argument for the virtue of fame here: Statius heightens its pathos by extensively contrasting the magnificent scale of the rites with the puny body and lack of accomplishment of the child, whose body is borne to the bier "as though" (*ceu*) it had the weight of an immense warrior (VI.68–69). Eurydice, Opheltes' mother, refers to the whole exercise as "worthless rites" (*inania . . . iusta* [VI.168–69]). Unlike Chaucer, or even the Knight, Statius makes clear his cynicism about the form of consolation that this rite offers: it is merely "empty and barren fame [that] aids the grieving" (cassa tamen sterilisque dolentes /fama iuuat [VI.70–71]). But Chaucer heightens the impression of futility in the passage by blurring the order of the events. In Statius, the gifts of the Argives are laid on the bier, while at the same time and "in another place" (*parte alia*) ancient woods are razed to furnish the fuel for the pyre (VI.84–117). In "The Knight's Tale," the destruction of the grove seems to be part of the sequence of the funeral, and—in the *ordo narrandi* at least—follows a description of Emelye with "fyr in honde, as was that tyme the gyse, / To do the office of funeral servyse" (I.2911–12), and in the same place where the destruction has apparently taken place. Like the lamenting that follows, and interrupts, Adrastus's attempt at consolation in the *Thebaid*, destruction and lament keep breaking out, just as this scene in "The Knight's Tale" keeps jumping back to its own prehistory—as if that has never terminated. Above all, however, the passage that describes the destruction of the grove and the gods themselves running "up and doun" bears a peculiar rhetorical distinction: it is the longest sentence in Chaucer, and it is also an extended *occupatio* or *praeteritio*, a way of (not) telling a story while another story is waiting to unfold—in this case, (not) telling the story of the destruction of the grove outside of Athens, which is a way of (not) telling the story of Opheltes' funeral, all while we wait for the story of *la nozze d'Emilia* finally to unfold.

This figure of *occupatio/praeteritio* is the greatest expression of narrative ambivalence, indeed of the way in which stories themselves both have being and do not. The prominence of this particular *occupatio/praeteritio*, I would argue, calls attention to the structural and thematic importance of its mechanisms throughout the tale. The Knight's characteristic tic, is, of course the *occupatio/praeteritio*, which he first uses seventeen lines into the tale to tell us how much of the prehistory of the opening he is not going to narrate: "How wonnen was the regne of femenye . . . the grete battaile for the nones . . . how asseged was Ypolita . . . the feste that was at hir weddyng . . . the tempest at hir hoom-comynge" (I.877–84). In a poem that so deliberately links narrative with the subjugation of space, it is striking that *occupatio/praeteritio* is imagined as little more than an incursion or interruption. From the perspective of the *occupatio*, indeed, the poem's underlying drive is toward singularity and compression. In much of the tale, the Knight's use of *occupatio/praeteritio* is marked by the word *poynte*, a word that connotes narrative matter, the sharp end of a sword, and the center of a circle. Theseus's command to fight without sharp weapons prohibits the "point bitynge" of the short sword, a metonym of the vacuousness of the tournament, in which the mechanisms of war have no larger point, either, and are thus rhetorically an extended *occupatio/praeteritio*. The Knight twice uses the word *point* as a term for the burden, the *matiere*, of the narrative, to signal the end of an *occupatio/praeteritio*, first after (not) describing the feast when Palamon and Arcite return to Athens for the tournament, and next at the end of the long *occupatio/praeteritio* on the funeral of Arcite. Read strictly, the figure of a narrative point calls into question the relevance of *most* of the narrative: it suggests the fulfillment or termination of a narrative—something like a *moralitas*—or the one important, outstanding feature in the *ordo narrandi*. The most common discursive use, perhaps, is to describe a point of law, as "The Knight's Tale" in fact does twice, six and seven lines after the last, longest *occupatio/praeteritio* comes back to the narrative "pointe." The Athenians there are debating what policy to follow toward their allies, and in particular how and whether to demand the "obeisaunce" of Thebes. The polity of the poem, in other words, returns to its starting point, the question of whether Theseus should make war against Thebes, as if the intervening events of the tale have had no discernible effect or influence on Athenian rule. Indeed, little apparently happens *after* the events of the tournament for "certeyn yeeres," a span that is filled with mourning in Athens.

This mourning ends not because Athenians have recovered from the loss of Arcite, but because of a definite ritual span, a fixed number of years that are devoted to mourning. That moment is established by the return of Athenian polity, the resumption of "certeyn points": mourning ends when all of the Athenians come to an agreement "by oon general assent"—also the "comune vois" of English polity. Political normalcy returns only when mourning ends (remember that the tale begins with Theseus unable to enter Athens because of the delegation of mourning Theban women). This Athens is very different from the one Gillian Rose describes in *Mourning Becomes the Law*: there, she reads Phocion's wife's defiance of his enemies' order to leave the body of her husband unburied outside the walls of Athens as the establishment of a law that corrects an absolutist, inhumane *nomos*, and that also refuses to tolerate mere despair. For Rose, in other words, mourning is not something to be suspended, but something to be somehow integrated into the normative work of the law. She sums up this very subtle and nuanced vision of a law that specifically accounts for human failure several times in her work with the injunction to "keep your mind in hell, and despair not."[42] In "The Knight's Tale," however, mourning stands outside the law as its exception, yet the exception that establishes the pragmatic functionality of the law. The law need not account for mourning, for there is nothing to be done; and in the interregnum of mourning, the law's impotence against what Theseus himself calls "nedes" or necessity is in fact a recognition of a law that supersedes, and lies at the heart of, the Athenian drive for order and *dominium* (I.3028). It is the law that is always there, even if unrecognized or avoided—the law of Saturn. His orbit, the widest of all the planets', describes a destructive circularity that frames all other actions in the transitory world, just as the return of law halts the outward observance of mourning, not its affective truth. Although he gives it immediately after mourning has ceased, for example, Theseus's speech is fundamentally about the inescapability of finitude and imagines a world suffused with mortality. The First Mover, he says, has given "Certeyne dayes and duracioun / To al that is engendred in this place" (I.2996–97). The qualifier *certeyne* is striking, because it immediately follows the passage we have been discussing, in which the word is used three times in quick succession, to qualify "yeeres," "contrees," and "points" (of law). The span of life, in other words, is constrained by the same limits as time, place, and discourse. Its certainty is the limit of finitude, beyond which it cannot move, any more than we can experience eternity, boundlessness, or the Word in the present.

The narrative point, in other words, is a utopic figure. Its appearance would mean the end of mourning, or, more precisely, an end to its implacability. It is the affect that corresponds to the vast circle of Saturn, the real but unappreciated law of this universe. Our ability to recognize this—our ability to recognize what Theseus so clearly cannot—does not mean that we have glimpsed a world beyond the scope of the one that Boethius and Philosophy discuss in the *Consolation*. It means that *we see it more clearly*: our cosmological perspective tells us that the universe is framed by finitude and destruction, and that the only continuity possible is the law of continual catastrophe. This is more or less the lesson that Boethius learns about the limits he faces at the end of his life, because they are in fact the end of life, or at least the commencement of the finitude that structures the entire created world. Paradoxically, in committing himself to the orderliness of Jupiter's world, Theseus has committed himself to finitude, rather than to the principle of divine transcendence. His faith that it is limits that allow Jupiter to reform the world commits him to a circularity that Philosophy condemns. Theseus's formulation of this, that Jupiter converts "al unto his proper welle / From which it is dirryved," sounds superficially like the Platonic doctrine of procession and recession that Philosophy takes for granted (I.3037–38). In Plato and Boethius, the movement is from the infinite to finitude and back again, not the change of one kind of temporal being into another that might be regarded as good—what Theseus describes as a "welle," both a form of the good and its source. But the good Theseus discovers at the end of the tale is simply the emergence of a temporal good: marriage, which St. Paul treats as a capitulation to sensuality, and an institution whose impermanence and arbitrariness Chaucer's pilgrims, after the Knight is done narrating *le nozze d'Emilia*, will proceed to describe in detail.

The circularity that Theseus describes, in other words, is not the divine circularity of the universe, but the futile circularity of the sublunary world. What permanence there is, as the *Consolation* discusses, is the permanence of the law of finitude. This law is also imagined as a circle, but one in which the attachment to finite goods is represented as the force that constructs a vicious circle. In adducing the evidence of geographical and temporal boundaries to confirm the fact that Jupiter "stable is and eterne," Theseus is actually arguing the opposite (I.3004). The stability that he seeks from Jupiter is precisely that of the outer edge of the circle, where, Boethius says, the "gretter bondes of destine" lie.[43] The law that binds us to mortality is precisely the law that keeps us from the "point," the center where the centrifugal force of continual dying "ceseth to ben schad and to fleten diversely" and where mourning and storytelling die away to nothing.

CHAPTER SEVEN

The "Deth-dyinge" of Will:
Piers Plowman

After the librarian's death,
> The library no more keeps its timings.
—P. P. Ramachandran

It is hard to tell, when you read only the poetry of the late fourteenth century, that the Black Death had ever arrived. I have already examined the
way Chaucer thinks about it obliquely in *The Book of the Duchess* and "The
Knight's Tale." But those poems might be excused, because they are set in
otherworlds—classical Athens and a dream vision—and it may not be surprising that one does not find an abundance of topical references in them.
In a poem such as *Piers Plowman*, which is set explicitly in Worcestershire
and London and concerns exactly the historical moment at which the poem
is being written, it is harder to account for the relative absence of one of the
most devastating events in contemporary memory. At the end of *Piers Plowman* Kynde sends forth "pestilence," but as one part of a very large package of
maladies (B.20.80–99).[1] It is that this point that a personified Death appears,
a Death who is often *the* Death—the plague—in texts from the late fourteenth century on. But it is still just one of the three agents of death, along
with Kynde and Elde, and it acts more or less the way personified Death
acts in many other poems, killing indiscriminately and unexpectedly.[2] Even
the word *morreyn*, which describes one of the weapons Death uses, could refer
equally well to animal deaths or famine. I will argue later that there is more
to this apparently conventional death—but there is also less, especially when
we remember that William Langland is really an Edwardian poet, who, unlike Chaucer, was an adult when the Black Death arrived.[3]

The word *pestilence* appears nine times in the B text of *Piers Plowman*, and each time not as the main topic.[4] In its last occurrence, it is part

of a list of disasters—Death and his catastrophes in passus 20 ("Feueres and Fluxes, / Coughes and Cardiacles, Crampes and tooþaches, / Rewmes and Radegundes and roynouse scales, / Biles and bocches and brennynge Agues, / Frenesies . . . keene sores . . . pokkes and pestilences . . . corrupcions" [B.20.81–99]). In his sermon *ad status*, Reason blames the pestilence (exactly as Jerry Falwell and Pat Robertson did with the arrival of AIDS in the 1980s) on "pure synne." But that single line is dwarfed by his description of the disastrous "southwest wind" of 1362, partly because it offers Langland metaphors like the uprooted tree, which will appear later in the poem. Next to that passage, his silence about the resonances of the plague perhaps indicates how little the disease will figure directly in the composition of the poem. In the Prologue, parsons and parish priests complain that their parishes are poor "sith the pestilence time" and ask leave to flee to London (B.Pr.84). This passing reference to the Black Death has little more discursive importance than a temporal marker, and nothing that follows is *explicitly* connected to its effects—although many of the poem's themes seemingly spring from legislation passed in the wake of the plague.[5]

Langland's treatment of death in the rest of the poem tends to be surprisingly conventional. The poem's first use of the word, in fact, belongs in the bedrock of proverbial sayings. Holy Church says, in passus 1, that faith without works is "as deed as a dore-nail" (B.1.187). It's an expression that also appears in the mid-fourteenth-century English translation of William of Palerne (which Andrew Galloway has speculated is part of *Piers*'s literary matrix) and is the kind of pithy statement about death that Langland harnesses for rhetorical effect. Elsewhere it's useful as part of the generative machine of alliteration: original sin is a "dedly deth," a death that sounds like a truism, reduced to a two-point theological jingle; anyone who fails to love remains in "deth-dyinge"; the end of life is a "deth-day"; martyrs die a "doleful deth" for the sake of faith. This virtual subordination of death to the formal demands of the poem in these micro-instances can be extended to include the macro-instances of its criticism of the friars, who are guilty of converting death into a silver-catching, window-glazing industry (B.11.70ff).

More tellingly, at the very point where Langland introduces his critique of the fraternal death industry, he has become newly aware of his own finitude. Couetise-of-eyes has encouraged him to depend upon the friars to assuage his guilt over, as she puts it, "how þou come to goode" (B.11.53);[6] in this reassuring complacency (in the C text, Couetise-of-eyes momentarily calls the dreamer himself "Rechelesnesse"; C.12.4), salvation is recast from the remnants of ethical work, even perhaps including the dreamer's work of and in the poem, the work of "how þou come to goode." Yet the "wordes" of Couetise-of-eyes are "so swete," as the Dreamer says, that he "foryede youþe and yorn into Elde" (till my young days were done and I'd drifted into age [B.11.59–60]) and only then discovers that the false fraternal economy of salvation will now fail him, or more precisely will fail his body: "rohte ye neuere," he says to his confessor, "Where my bodye were buryed" (you couldn't possibly care less . . . Whose earth covered my corpse; B.11.74). It is when death approaches that the question of finitude is raised most starkly: when the resources of youth, of work, of wealth, are exhausted. This is the moment at which the poem discovers, or rediscovers, the mode of proceeding established by Holy Church's sermon on truth in passus 1. In the C text, what the dreamer says he must now do is make public the transgressions of this fraternal death industry, to, in his words, "seien þat were treuthe; / The sauter sayth hit is no synne for suche men that ben trewe / To segge as they seen" (to say what the truth was; the Psalter says that it is no sin for truthful men to say what they see; C.12.27–28). In a sense, the immanence of death (at least of the dreamer's death) forces truth into the realm of finitude, to bring to light the particular ways in which the economy of the fraternal afterlife, and the ethics that it enables, terminate in nullity and death. So at least part of what the poem does from this point on is to register an archive of transgressions against death—transgressions against, more precisely, a good death, and in terms of the poem, the transgressions that prevent the saying of truth, the making of a good end. As I will discuss in a moment, this does not mean that the poem's treatment of death becomes persistently lucid; in fact the question of "truth" will come up again in the case of the kind of death suffered by just pagans. In what follows I will discuss how *Piers Plowman* moves from a treatment of death that, in the A text, seems little more significant than the yoking together of sonic doublets to a more elaborated awareness of it in the B text and finally its announced presence from the very beginning of the poem in the C text.[7]

Anne Middleton's article on John But's continuation of the A text shows how thoroughly he incorporates in an ending of the poem figures of death and finitude, pressed into the service of making a good end with the knowledge that the death of the poem's author prevented him from making a good end himself.[8] One response to that interference in the ending of the poem, addressed by Middleton and others, is that its concern with ending is not forced on it, imposed by an historically contingent actor, but implicit in the poem from early on. Yet that does not seem to be the case. The fullest expressions of death come at the end of the B text, with death's army, which dashes "kynges and knightes, kayseres and popes" to dust, to the more personal death that Will says "drough neigh me" and makes him quake with dread. These extended encounters with death, and others such as those of physicians who try to help Lif stave it off with drugs, in the poem's last passus suggest that in a very literal sense death is a late acquisition for the poem. As the B text draws to a close, death comes increasingly into the field of view. But first it comes as the adversary of the poem's adversary, the scourge that will correct the crowds who follow the Antichrist after he has "Torned . . . vp so doune . . . þe crop of truþe" (B.20.54–55); indeed, it comes out of what is most proper and natural to our existence, from Kynde itself, who brings about death by catastrophic illness (catastrophic in both senses—massive and horrible, and brought "out of þe planetes" [B.20.80], the astrological genesis of earthly illness). At this point Kynde and Death are closely allied, not just as campaigners in the battle against "gyle," "untreuth," and "Lif," who represents a kind of solicitude for aristocratic pleasure and privilege, but as aspects of the Aristotelian spectrum of generation and corruption: it is Kynde who "þoruȝ corrupcions kilde ful manye" (99), complicit in death's work if not closely identified with it.

Why does death appear in this catastrophe only at this point, after widescale death has already entered the world? I think part of the answer is in the specific targets of death—indeed, in the manifest difference that Death, unlike Kynde, *has* targets, whereas Kynde just has modes of killing ("Feueres and Fluxes, / Coughes and Cardiacles, Crampes and tooþaches, / Rewmes and Radegundes and roynouse scales, / Biles and bocches and brennyng Agues; / Frenesies and foule yueles" [B.20.81–85]). Death, on the other hand, works *after* Kynde, and on particular groups: "Death came driving after him and dashed all to dust / Companies of kings and knights, Kaisers and popes. / Learned or unlearned, he let no man stand / That he hit squarely who ever stirred afterward. / Many a lovely lady and their lover-knights / Sank down swooning for sorrow of Death's blows" (Deeþ cam dryuynge after and al to duste passhed / Kynges and knyghtes, kaysers and popes; / Lered ne lewed he leet no man stonde, / That he hitte euene, þat euere stired after. / Manye a louely lady and hir lemmans knȝtes / Swowned and swelted for sorwe of deþes dyntes [B.20.100–105]). The response to death here, filtered through the medium of the romance, with its swooning and swelting ladies hearing of the death of men on the field, suggests that Death works in a different register than does Kynde. If Kynde's work unfolds in the domain of medicine, death's is more overtly literary, acting on and in the field of romance tropes. Death shows up, in other words, after death has already afflicted the world—after the death that is implicit in Kynde has emerged—and it goes to work on the "lered and lewed" with a thoroughness that recalls the comprehensiveness of the poem's opening vision of a "fair feld ful of folk."

What, then, should we make of the ending of *Piers Plowman*, where death comes to the dreamer in such an apparently idiosyncratic fashion? Death in passus 20 moves from the general to particular; from death as life—in its finitude as its essential characteristic (Kynde sends diseases and other manners of death to all the states and conditions of the living)—to death as what doesn't arrive for the individual (Langland growing old, death drawing nigh). There death arrives with Kynde ("kynde passede / And deeþ drogh neigh me" [B.20.199–200]), and Elde is in the company of Death. But does this mean that Kynde passed by, or that Kynde passed on, passed away—that it began to ebb, as if it were a Scholastic form susceptible of intension and remission? When death gets personal in passus 20, it seems to become idiosyncratic; Langland no longer uses the tropes he deploys so fully in passus 18, a rejection that his own presence signals. This moment may be not an interlude, as Pearsall describes it, but a moment in which Langland allows himself to think about how to end it all, about how even a long will diminishes and loses power, which is not the same as coming to a good end. As A. C. Spearing said, the end of the poem makes the connection more explicit, which "Langland had half-seen at the end of the A-Text" between the "last Days of the world" and "the last days of the Dreamer's life."[9]

But despite the approach of idiosyncratic death and a personal dread of it—the "care" that Will asks Kynde to bring him out of—this confrontation with death is informed not only by the poet's awareness of the twofold ending, but also of the staging of encroaching death in previous texts. In literary texts, Elde and Infirmity attack the dreamer in both Guillaume de Deguileville's *Pèlerinage de la vie humaine* and *The Parlement of the Thre Ages*, both of which Langland may have known.[10] The transformation of Will by Elde also turns him into the *facies hippocratica* of medical and admonitory texts, first making him bald (although hilariously, it has to be said):

. . . ouer myn heed [Elde] yede,
And made me balled bifore and bar on þe croune;
So harde he yede ouer myn heed it wole be sene euere.
"Sire yuele ytauȝt Elde!" quod I, "vnhende go wiþ þe!
Siþe whanne was þe wey ouer mennes heddes?" (B.20.183–87)[11]

[Old Age . . . went over my head,
And made me both bald in front and bare on the crown;

So hard he went over my head it will always be evident.
"Mister bad-mannered Age," I said, "may mischief go with you!
Since when was the highway over men's heads?"]

But Elde can't take a joke and pummels Will with the textbook symptoms of imminent death, beating out his teeth, crippling him with gout, making him impotent. All Will can do is watch "deeþ drogh neiȝ me" and pray for deliverance—although the deliverance he prays for is nothing less than death. He cries "to kynde: out of care me brynge!" (B.10.200–201).

Will's complaint about encroaching death, its oppression of his faculties and the dread it brings with it: who will "out of care me brynge," he asks Kynde plaintively, sounding like Suso's *discipulus* in that dialogue worrying that such "cares oppress [his] mind that he can hardly see what to do."[12] Without dwelling on all of the verbal echoes of Suso at this point in the poem (for instance, poisons that hinder on page 250, and Langland's discussion of poison at Christ's crucifixion and passus 20 of the C text), I will just note that Kynde tells Will to go to the Barn of Unity, which he reaches by "roaming" through "Contricion" and "Confession" (B.20.212–13); in Suso Death tells the *discipulus* to "gather into the heavenly barn . . . the treasures of heaven" and to do this by "true contrition and pure and complete confession while you are healthy and young."[13] In other words, one of *Piers Plowman*'s more idiosyncratic moments is actually a version of one of the most conventional treatises and treatments of dying. "Kynde" takes Will through contrition and confession to Unity in a movement that turns us to the penitential manual in general, and to the literary archive in particular, to Suso's famous chapter, the source of most of the tropes of death in the late fourteenth century.

That is the archive from which the A and the B texts draw their representations of death. But not the C text. It places the "fair feld ful of folk" not between a tower and a dungeon, but between the tower where Truth dwells and the "dale" where death is situated (C.Pr.17). Death appears as one of the boundaries of the poem's domain—in other words, late in the history of the poem's revisions. That death takes this long to appear in the history of the poem is a little surprising, because the two lines that describe the dale or the ditches beneath the dungeon were always constructed entirely around the alliteration of "d": "A depe dale byneþe, a dongeon þerInne / Wiþ depe diches and derke and dredfulle of siȝte" (A deep dale beneath, a dungeon tower in it, / With ditches deep and dark and dreadful to look at [B.Pr.15–16]). And the word "dredful" appears again in the poem only in conjunction with the alliterative double "death": passus 7, "To purchace pardon and þe popes bulles. / At þe dredful dome, whan dede shulle rise / And comen alle bifore crist acountes to yelde" (To purchase pardon and the Pope's bulls, / At the dreadful doom when dead men sall arise / And all come before Christ and account to him [B.7.192–94]); and passus 20, "There was 'harrow!' and 'help! Here comeþ kynde, / Wiþ Deeþ þat is dredful to vndo us alle!'" (There were howls of "Help! Here comes Kind / With Death that is dreadful to undo us all! [B.20.88–89]). Obversely, when the word *death* appears in the poem it is in lines where it overwhelmingly determines the alliteration (forty-nine out of fifty-four times), even where it is not the principal noun. In some cases its aural presence almost seem to dictate its inevitable pairings—death and the devil, or the poem's confrontation with death, almost a confrontation with death's ownmost sonic destiny: death "fordone" (a phrase that shows up six or seven times). In a number of lines, death faces itself across the caesura: "þat deeþ down brouʒte, deeþ shal releue" (B.18.141; a variant of this line is used four times). It is clear that death is a part of Langland's art, as if death were the final artist (*ars ut artem falleret*): "So shal þis deeþ fordo, I dar my lif legge, / Al þat deeþ dide first þoruʒ þe deueles entisyng; / And riʒt as þegilour þoruʒ gile bigiled man formest, / So shal grace that bigan al make a good ende / And bigile þe gilour, and þat is good sleighte: / *Ars vt artem falleret*" (So shall this death destroy—I dare bet my life— / All that Death did first through the Devil's tempting. / And just as the beguiler with guile beguiled man first, / So shall grace that began everything make a good end / And beguile the beguiler—and that's a good trick: / *A trick by which to trick treachery* [B.18.157–161a]).

But there's something a little too neat about this confrontation of death with its own immanence, its meeting its own finitude so completely in a poem that is haunted by its unendingness, its lack of finitude. In undoing the neatness of such an art of death, the poem suggests that a discourse of finitude that fails to fully install it, that is, that fails fully to come to an end, to terminate it, has failed to appreciate the extent of its finitude—the extent of its obligation not to invent ends but to discover them. Death lurks at the beginning of the poem, but it does not show up there until the poem's third major version, as if called into being at the beginning of this version by the poem's successive failures to end in the previous versions. A subtle symptom of this problem appears in Trajan's translation of a Latin half line. In arguing for the primacy of the work of love, he not only subordinates learning to it, but annuls the importance of learning altogether: whoever pursues learning without love, he says, "*manet in morte* / . . . lyueþ in deeþ deyinge" (B.11.176). Trajan's translation of the substantive *mors* by a participle calls attention to the difficulty of talking about death in a substantial sense, as a phenomenon that is contained and can fully be designated. It suggests, more pointedly, that death is a problem somehow specific to English, to the language of the poem. That is, it is a metonymic indication of the formal and ethical problem of the poem as a whole: how to make a good end when so much of the poem describes the experience of endings that are failures or collapses of the poem's initiatives—the failure to define meed, the failure to plow the half acre, the failures to define Dowel, the failure to unite in the Barn of Unity.

But if the C text begins with death lurking just past the field of human action, that does not necessarily mean that death is always more present, more obvious, in the C text. In fact, in one crucial instance it is not: in the discussion of whether Trajan's soul will be saved. In the B text, Trajan is both more securely situated within death and offered a more literally cryptic possibility for salvation. The means by which salvation is possible (*vix salvabitur*) is worked out in language that is famously obscure, language that—in the sense that it demands to be unriddled, to be solved, yet offers either a multiplicity of answers or none—is cryptic:

> Ac truþ þat trespased neuere ne trauersed ayeins his lawe,
> But lyueth as his lawe techeþ and leveþ þer be no bettre,
> And if þere were he wolde amende, and in swich wille deieþ—
> Ne wolde neuere trewe god but trewe truþ were allowed.
> And wheiþer it worþ of truþ or noȝt, þe worþ of bileue is gret,
> And an hope hangynge þerInne to haue a mede for his truþe . . .
>   (B.12.287–92)

> [But truth that never trespassed nor transgressed against his law,
> But lives as his law teaches, and believes there is no better,
> And if there were he would adopt it, and in such a will dies—
> Would never true God wish but true truth were allowed.
> And whether it's witness of truth or not, the worth of belief is great,
> And a hope is hanging in it to have reward for his truth.]

Truth itself is a kind of crypt in this passage, a rhetorical enigma, exploiting *ambiguitas*, hiding the truth of salvation from easy access. Indeed, one needs exactly the kind of resources to unlock this truth that the B text says will save (or might, or will barely, save) the just pagan: "wit and wisdom . . . was som tyme tresor / To kepe wiþ a commune; no catel was holde bettre, / And muche murþe and manhod" (wit and wisdom . . . was once a treasure / To keep a community with: no capital was held better, / And much mirth and manhood [B.12.295–97]). In the C text, part of what's left out is the quotation from Psalm 25, "si ambulavero in medio vmbre mortis" (at B.12.291). In the C text, Trajan no longer walks in the valley of the shadow of death. I don't think the omission of that line means that the C text is less concerned with the immanence of death. If anything, a corollary change at the beginning of the poem makes death's immanence a problem not only for the odd virtuous pagan, but for all of us.

In the course of revision, the poem's emphasis moves from an hypothesis of universal salvation for those who die a good death (make a good end) to the recognition of universal death at its very beginning. Where the "fair feld ful of folk" in the B text is bounded by a "depe dale" whose significance is unknown until Holy Church reveals it as the castle of Wrong in the next passus, the field in the C text is bounded by a dale whose significance the dreamer immediately suspects: "deth, as y leue, / Woned in tho wones" (C.Pr.17–18). I think that the predicament of death for a classical pagan is the motive for this substantial revision, which moves the question of salvation for a singularly ethical Roman emperor who dies well to the poem's beginning, where every action is framed by death, its shadow extending into the darkness beyond the poem's deadly limit.

Trajan's quotation of the Gospel of John at the beginning of his speech, "qui non diliget manet in morte," which provides the thema for his discourse, now becomes part of the entire poem's thema. We dwell with death as long as we forget to love; but we dwell with death for the length of the poem because we still don't love, as Kynde's admonition "lerne to loue" in the final passus of the poem implies (B.20.208; C.22.208). Behind this formulation lurks the logical question, familiar from sophismata and syncategorematic treatises, of how we can talk about something that has already ceased, a problem that the oxymoronic English translation only intensifies: how can one be said to live in "deth-dyinge" at all? The C text's omission of the English translation moves this distracting logical problem into the background; it makes this part of Trajan's speech less cryptic. But the resituation of death at the beginning of the poem only moves the scope of a narrow logical problem, a problem of designation, to the scope of the entire poem, its entire field of beings who make the problem of how to live with death always adjacent an ethical, rather than logical, problem, a vernacular rather than a learned one.

Another way in which the revisions to the Trajan passage change the cryptic question of Trajan's salvation to a more universal situation is the omission of the acrostic sentence "Deus dicitur quasi dans eternam vitam suis, hoc est, fidelibus," a sentence that hides the encrypted possibility of eternal life in the name of God (DEVS) (B.12.290); what replaces it in the C text is the ending of the parable of the talents: "Quia super pauca fuisti fidelis" (Because you have been faithful over a little I will set you over much [C.14.214a]). It is a verse that imagines the possibility of salvation not as a riddle, not as something obscured by the very death it seeks to avoid, but as the beginning of a continuity that extends into the infinite: one talent that becomes many, an archive that becomes all truth.

It might be surprising to use the word *archive* to characterize anything to do with Trajan, whose scornful interjection "ȝe? Baw for bokes!" is one of the most memorable moments of the poem, and one of the most forceful rejections of book learning (B.11.140). He might seem to be a figure of willed ignorance, a fourteenth-century Donald Trump. Nicolette Zeeman has argued that Trajan's paganism represents the condition of *kynde*, demonstrated by Rechelesness's appropriations in the C text of parts of Trajan's B text speeches and by Trajan's salvation by "lewte" and "loue."[14] Yet Trajan is, I think, the only classical figure to speak in *Piers Plowman* (with the one-and-a-half-line exception of Plato saying something he didn't actually say: "'*Homo proponit*,' quod a poete, and Plato he hiȝte, / 'And *Deus disponit*,' quod he; 'lat god doon his wille,'" at B.11.37–38), and his first words disparage the very means by which an English subject in the late fourteenth century would come to know about the classical world: "ȝe? Baw for bokes!" At the very least, there's a minor irony in having the grand figure of a Roman emperor using the demotic of fourteenth-century England, speaking like the seller of hot pies in *Piers Plowman*'s prologue.

Trajan is not quite the simple and unlettered opposite of clergy or Scripture, despite his contempt for books. Indeed, he not only finds love and "lewte" in a book, but describes them as a book written by the finger of God (B.11.167–71). And Trajan describes the consequences of refusing to love by quoting from a book, a Gospel: "For Seint Iohan seide it, and soþe are his wordes, / *qui non diligent manet in morte*. / Whoso loueþ noȝt, leue me, he luyeþ in deeþ deyinge" (For Saint John said it, and his sayings are true: / *Who loveth not abideth in death*. / Whoever loves not, believe me, he lives in death-dying [B.11.176–77]). It is true that he disparages law and logic a little later, saying that there is little "alowaunce" made for them in the *Legenda sanctorum*. The *Legenda sanctorum* is, in other words, the standard for a discourse's utility, and it is a book that is deeply instrumental in his extensive literary afterlife. It was both "loue," says Trajan, *and* "lernyng of my lyvyng in treuthe" that saved him and that makes him an exemplum of mercy, as, he says, "clerkes fyndeth in bokes." Without the texts that memorialized his justice, in other words, Trajan's devotion to love and "lewte" would have remained unknown. And he is, of course, at this moment also an object of "lernyng" enfolded in a book, replicating, as Zeeman says, "the unclear boundaries of the exemplum, appearing unannounced and in the text to tell his own story."[15] But Trajan seems always to have been enfolded within texts. Jacob de Voragine's account of Gregory the Great's rescue of Trajan from the pains of hell was circulated and reworked in a number of textual forms, including sermons, distinctions, questiones, summae, and political treatises (Vincent of Beauvais's *Speculum historiale* gave Trajan another career as a figure of the right use of the "science of power").[16]

In a literal and genealogical sense, Trajan's presence in the poem is inconceivable without the medium of the book. Trajan's own reference to the *Legenda* for the continuation of his story impresses on us this obvious and perhaps somewhat banal point. But in many ways the various versions of the Trajan story are also conditioned by a recognition of the instrumental work of books. In all of these, Gregory was moved by the story of Trajan's mercy to a widow who implored him to avenge the death of one of her sons. To requite her loss, Trajan handed over one of his own sons, who may or may not have committed the murder. One of the earliest versions, written in Whitby in the eighth century, makes the explicit point that the reason Gregory reacted so emotionally to the story of Trajan was that it exemplified the admonition of the book of Isaiah ("Iudicate pupillo et defendite uiduam et uenite et arguite me, dicit Dominus" [Is. 1:17–18]): As the *Whitby Life* says, it was "just what we read about in the Bible."[17]

The story of Trajan that Gregory recollected had to have been transmitted by a text. If this part of the story about Gregory is true, the text would have been Dio Cassius's *Roman History*, but Gregory would have been misremembering it, because Dio's story is about Diocletian, not Trajan. In the most literal sense, then, Trajan's salvation is impossible without the presence of books: the first coherent versions of Gregory and Trajan's salvation appear in the *Whitby Life* and a life written by John the Deacon, both in the eighth century.

Subsequent versions mimic the bibliographic genesis of the story of Trajan's postmortem rescue from the pains of hell. Rather than narrate the story of Trajan and the widow at the point in his life of Gregory where Gregory passes through the Forum of Trajan, for instance, Vincent of Beauvais refers the reader back to a previous section of his own text for that account (Trajan's story is in book 11, chapter 46; the story of Gregory in book 23, chapter 22).[18] John of Salisbury's account of the Trajan story is underscored by a remarkable act of textual invention: book 5 of Policraticus, says John, is extracted from a work by Plutarch called the *Institutio Trajani*.[19] But, as

Janet Martin has shown, John almost certainly invented it for the *Policraticus*, both legitimating it by its association with Trajan and underscoring the importance of learned instruction for the wise rule of Trajan. Whether John and others knew more about the specifically literary feats of Trajan isn't known. But the Trajan who says "baw for bokes" in *Piers Plowman* is the bibliophobic evil twin of the historical Trajan. It was under Trajan that the greatest library of the Roman Empire was built—the Bibliotheca Ulpia, named after him (Marcus Ulpius Trajanus). Its two buildings, one devoted to Latin books and the other to Greek books, stood on either side of the column of Trajan, precisely where Gregory the Great recalled Trajan's merciful act. It is not clear whether the library was still standing when Gregory walked through Trajan's forum, but it was the site of regular public readings of the *Aeneid* through the sixth century, and as late as 455 a statue of the poet and French bishop Sidonius Apollinaris was erected at the library; in an epigram, he wishes Trajan could see the statues of the authors in his library. For part of its history, the Ulpian Library was the repository for records of senatorial proceedings and imperial edicts (according to Flavius Vopiscus). In short, unlike the book-scoffing Trajan in *Piers Plowman*, the historical Trajan was one of the greatest archivists of the classical world.[20]

Yet despite the absence of this historical aspect of Trajan in *Piers Plowman*, or perhaps because of it, the Trajan in the poem mounts a powerful argument not for the texts of clergy, logic, or "lawe," but the divine book of the world, or the book that records the acts of saints. His argument is similar to Lady Philosophy's in *The Consolation of Philosophy*, who urges Boethius to meditate not on the books in his library, but on those in his heart. When properly selected and located, in other words, a collection of books becomes an archive, a trace of past events that still make demands on the present and that holds out the promise of the fulfillment of law beyond the violation, or the failure, of the law. Trajan's archive moves him back from the end and the telos of the old law, from its termination in eternal punishment to the beginning offered by the new law (a topic on which he discourses at length). But just what does this mean for the poem? One answer is that Langland is imagining the possibility of universal salvation, as Nicholas Watson has argued.[21] But Trajan's archive also contains the trace of actions that are prior to books, a "pure treuthe" that he exemplified in life (B.11.150). On the one hand, this truth is effective only because of Gregory's postmortem intercession, an intercession made possible, after all, by the archive of Trajan's life. It is an exceptional account of salvation: Gregory is criticized for interceding on behalf of someone whom God has already condemned and is punished with ill health for the rest of his life.

Trajan's assertion of the efficacy of "pure treuthe" is breathtaking in its solipsistic neglect of its real conditions of possibility, and perhaps also in his attempt to extrapolate a universal law of salvation from it. But in one sense, that is precisely what makes Trajan a figure of the archive: he is saved quite apart from books, but he is saved because of them. One purpose of an archive is to make legitimate or possible a certain impossibility, either of presence or of pure action. As Eric Prenowitz says, "An archive is there for those who cannot communicate with such a solipsistic solitude in the presence and the present of its untimely happening. For while an archive may not be an end, it is only a beginning. It is not *the* beginning, and it never contains its own beginning. It can only be a translation of its conception."[22] The exemplary lesson of Trajan is, after all, partly about the singular quality of his relation to death, a relation that is the result of an exceptional purity, indeed the purity of truth, and an exceptional intervention. Yet Trajan is one of the poem's most extensive answers to the problem of universal death, and in what follows I will argue that the ambivalence of Trajan in the B text in relation to death and books is resolved in the C text by converting at least part of the poem itself into an archive.

The two questions of divine justice might not be related specifically to each other in theological discussion. But the connection between a death that is unjust because it happens outside the dispensation of Christianity and the redemption that is an exception to this injustice is precisely what the figure of Trajan in *Piers Plowman* embodies. As a just pagan (although one who lived after the death of Christ), Trajan stands for the multitude of deaths outside the New Law; but in *Piers Plowman*, which attributes to him the knowledge of the Bible and salvation history that a Christian would have, Trajan represents the soteriological obverse of the problem where justice could be found in massive death: not the problem of massive damnation for the unwitting, but the problem of whether a singular observance of justice can possibly, but not necessarily, save the just person. I think, in other words, that Langland uses Trajan as a way to think about our response to the burden of our responsibility to the past, which is precisely the predicament of time. Will what happened then (the damning of the just but ignorant dead) happen to us later? I don't want to take up that large question, which has already been explored by Langland scholars.[23] I want instead to focus on the literal sense of the word *predicament* in the phrase "the predicament of time." I don't mean "predicament" in the modern sense of a difficult situation; I mean "predicament" in the sense in which it is used in medieval logic, as one of ten categories of being—or of the words we use about being—that make up whatever can be said about anything (Aristotle calls these *ta legomena*—things that can be said or predicated of something). I want to focus here on the category of time in particular, which for anyone working in the tradition of Aristotle raised an almost intrinsic problem: if time is a category of being, then what are we doing when we refer to something in the past that no longer exists?

This problem is as much a part of the Trajan episode as theology is, and I will explore this in a little while. But first I would like to point out a further irony in the figure of Trajan: he is a figure who raises the problem of the salvation of just pagans precisely because he embodies, increasingly, in the late Middle Ages, the continuing presence of a classical (pagan) past in medieval Christianity. Because he is actually saved, Trajan represents a better example of the sanctification of the classical past than all of the glossators of Virgil and commentaries such as *L'Ovid moralisé*, which cannot include the literal and historical levels in their allegoresis. The dreamer raises the question of salvation just before Trajan speaks, and he phrases it as an explicitly disputative topic, like a quodlibet in the university: the dreamer says he began "wiþ myself to dispute / Wheiþer I were chosen or noȝt chosen" (B.11.116–17). This disputative language recurs at the end of passus 12, where Imaginatyf discusses the problem of Trajan's salvation: "contra!" and "ergo," he says. The formulation of the binary, unchangeable nature of salvation ("chose or noght chose") raises not just a theological question but a logical one as well, one whose stakes were seen as the possibility of saying anything beyond the immediate instant of being. This passage is also concerned with the infamous problem of how we can talk about being and time together, if the subject to which we're referring no longer has being. The difficulty in designating nonexistent things is that we don't know what the *is* is in sentences such as "Caesar is dead." If he's dead, then we can't say that he "is" anything, because that would imply that he is not dead. One solution was to consider the use of ampliation, extending the temporality of a verb to include past, present, and future. But this was still a matter of great debate.

Imaginatyf claims, somewhat sophistically, that because just pagans such as Trajan will "barely be saved," therefore they *will* be saved (see the Latin quotation of the First Letter of Saint Peter at B.12.278–79). But his claim rests on his apparent assurance that the future tense can designate something that "is" true; that its validity depends not upon the unsettled question of future contingents, but upon the possibility that something that "is" not (because it lies in the future) can even be referenced. And the problem is pushed further in Imaginatyf's attempt to make this a universal statement: "wolde nevere trewe God but trewe truthe were allowed." His statement is riddled with tautology, but the verbs too offer so many possibilities for construing their tenses that it is difficult to know *when* exactly these things happen, or happened, or *might* have happened, or *might still* happen.

The question that seems to be on the margin when Imaginatyf says that the just man "will be" saved is the central problem here. Imaginatyf's conclusion is not, strictly speaking, about salvation directly, but about the conditionality of past or future being: "wheiþer it worþ of truþe or noȝt" (B.12.291). Yet this line is not really about salvation, but about whether the "*bileue* . . . of trueþe" is "gret" under any conditions. To be pedantic, which is to say, to be logical, how is it possible for the "treuth" to be true if it is *not* true—that is, whether it exists ("worþ") or not? It is possible that Langland is just making an observation that belief in something true is, or it can be, strong. But I do not think that that is likely, given the complexity and sophistication of these few lines at the end of passus 12. How, then, is this not an *impossibilia*, a thing that does not appear to be true but can conceivably be resolved? I suppose the easiest reading here is "whether or not it's true/will be true, one's belief in truth is strong (or a true belief is strong)." If it is true that belief is persistent whether or not the object of belief exists, then the line is making a more or less psychological point about the conditions under which we need belief.[24] But in a section where the language is so condensed, so much is at stake, and so much care in reading is demanded, it is not likely that this simple and probably wrong reading is exactly right. In the terms of medieval logic, how is this not nonsensical?

It is actually medieval logic that makes sense of the sentence. Whether something can or will happen ("worþ") or will not happen is a question of being, asked, more particularly, about the category of time. It concerns a verb ("worþ") with a difficult temporal designation: it is, it happens, it will happen. . . . But it is also a statement of what has been true in the past. That is, it is a question of whether Gregory's saving of Trajan was an act that can only happen once or refers to an ongoing possibility—that is, whether Will's salvation can conceivably exist or not. In other words, this is a question primarily of reference: how can we refer to the truth of something that does not exist in *this* present, this moment of utterance? This question is more vital to medieval logic and theology than it might seem. One of the propositions that Richard Kilwardby went to the trouble of condemning in 1277 was that a verb in the present tense could be distributed for all differences of time—in other words, that the present tense could refer to something in the past: for instance, that "Caesar *is* dead" could be the same as "Caesar died."[25] All of this hinged on how much work verbs of being in the present ("is" is the archetypal one) could do in referring to other times, and how they could do it.

One of the influential solutions to the problem is William of Sherwood's, in the first systematic treatment of supposition theory: "It must be known that the word 'is' is sometimes taken equivocally, for sometimes it indicates actual being (*esse actuale*), which is due to (*debetur*) something actually existing, and sometimes conditional being (*esse habituale*), which is due to that which is in itself some nature and is suited (*natus*) to be conditionally in some singular, although it is not actually."[26] This second kind of *is* is an "is" that refers to something that is "neither necessary nor impossible." William calls it a contingent proposition, and it describes this crucial line at the end of passus 12. Neither necessary nor impossible: that is precisely the situation of Trajan in salvation history. Whatever it is we refer to when we talk about Trajan's salvation, we are referring to a past that cannot exist in the present—to an act of special dispensation that cannot become a general dispensation. But how is this fair or just? The answer here is that the sentence is not a statement of a specifically theological principle but of a *logical* one: that the possibility of referring, in the present, to the past *must* be conditional—that is, a possibility that must remain just that, a possibility. Salvation, in other words, might be something that is suitable to be in some singular thing—the just person—but it remains a possibility precisely because it is not necessary. The irony of Trajan, in other words, is that by living within the law (he "lyveþ as his lawe techeþ and leveþ þer be no bettre" (lives as his law teaches, and believes there is no better [B.12.288]), he demonstrates the exception upon which the law is founded:

> Loue and lewtee is a leel science,
> For þat is þe book blissed of blisse and of ioye:
> God wrouȝte it and wroot it wiþ his owene fynger,
> And took it moises vpon þe mount alle men to lere.
> "Lawe wiþouten loue," quod Troianus, "ley ther a bene!" (B.11.167–71)

> [Love with lawfulness is a reliable science,
> For they are the blessed book of bliss and of joy,
> God first fashioned it and with his own finger wrote it,
> And gave it to Moses on the mountain that all men might learn it.
> "Law without love," said Trajan, "that's worth less than a bean!"]

In other words, love, which is precisely something beyond law (something that can't be legislated), is here the law itself—the book "blissed of blisse and of ioye" given to Moses—*and* what the law doesn't include. Law is nothing without love—which means that what the law must leave out is exactly what legitimates the law.

This reading of that one line with the resources of medieval logic rather than theology is perhaps rather intricate, but my primary point is that when we try to come to terms with Langland's "theology," we also have to take account of the *form* that it takes, down to its finest details. Theologians, like analytical philosophers, tend not to appreciate the messy, complex way in which writers often express themselves. They usually deal with abstract propositions that have been extracted or distilled from complex discursive environments. Think about Anselm's ontological argument: most of us think immediately about it as a syllogism, yet it is part of a long and earnest meditation on contemplation. If Langland had framed his problems in terms of abstract theological propositions it would be easier to say what his theology is. But he doesn't, because for him theology is entangled with and in the details of the logos, the word that Anselm says is "true and simple Existence."[27]

Again and again, the poem imagines the problem of justification in terms of the documentary discipline that the archive represents. Indeed, the image that precipitates Trajan's outburst is Will's attempt to think through the problem of predestination by comparing the individual Christian to a serf who wishes to break a contract. Will answers his own worry over whether he is "chosen or nought chosen" with a quick reaffirmation of universal salvation for anyone who wills salvation, "Sarȝens and scismatikes and . . . the Iewes," as well as, indisputably, "alle cristene" (B.11.120–23). Yet, strangely, once this consoling answer is imagined as a documentary relationship, it becomes an image of the restriction placed on Christians by their coming to Christ. One cannot repudiate one's faith, and therefore one's salvation, any more than a serf can make his own contracts. This serf/Christian is controlled and punished by a metaphorical manorial archive: because he will "renne in arerage" from wandering "recchelesly" about (B.11.129–30), he will eventually have to requite the obligations that are being recorded against him: "reson shal reekne wiþ hym . . . And conscience acounte wiþ hym and casten hym in arerage" (reason shall have a reckoning with him and rebuke him in the end, / And Conscience account with him and convict him of debt [B.11.131–32]). The reward for "his arrerages" will be Purgatory, the postmortem archive established by the development of archival and accounting sciences in the twelfth century and maintained by the archives of chantry chapels, necrologies, and trental masses—incidentally, a practice attached to the name of St. Gregory from at least the thirteenth century in

England. As Andrew Galloway says of this passage, it describes an "unliberating, imprisoning, and judicial view of Christianity [and] in particular presents history in general as . . . an inflexible law of legal containments."[28] It is against this archival restraint, and not merely hell, that Trajan breaks loose by repudiating the authority of books. Yet he does not break free of the archive. As I have argued, the revisions to the figure of Trajan require us to think of *Piers Plowman* as an archive in which we discover more fully Trajan's significance: the image of a serf wandering "recchelesly," for instance, becomes more fully thematized in the C text, where a great deal of Trajan's speech (in editions where it is assigned to him) is spoken by Recchelesness himself, a figure whose coincidence with Trajan evacuates or cancels some of the sense of historical and textual responsibility that attaches to Trajan in the B text. Recchelesness becomes an important figure in his own right in the C text. But if "recchelesness," the neglect of the archive, becomes more important, the C text also places all of us on the threshold of death's dwelling, threatened and goaded by the archive that has become the whole poem.

So far I have been tracing, without discussing explicitly, a distinction between the archive and the crypt. Briefly and in general, there are three main differences between those two: the crypt seals out the living from the dead, not necessarily the other way around; it tends to attribute to the dead some vestige of life, or of being, that has not been fully terminated; and it is characterized by secrecy, privacy, and enigma. The archive is public, related to the traces of power, and characterized by lucidity and access. Think of the difference between the unintelligible tomb in *St. Erkenwald*, of which no trace can be found in the archive, and the very public address of some of John Lydgate's poetry. In the fifteenth century Lydgate's writing about the dying and the dead is not only about the demonstration of the social fact of death, its very public nature, but is often expressed in relation to an idea of belatedness—and, more important, a sense of the past as continuous with the present, the kind of situation that Amy Appleford describes for the Dance of Poulys, which adorned the cloister added by Dean More in the 1420s.[29] Painted on the very walls that enclosed a formerly open churchyard, the mural becomes a structure of an enclosure that contains, and indeed enables, the historical representation of social relations, which is precisely that of the archive. A monastic or ecclesiastical cartulary, for instance, served to keep in perpetuity the memory of a benefactor, much as a necrology did, and also to preserve sacred space by recording the social and economic transactions that help to preserve the work of memory itself, in the form of the liturgical commemoration of the dead. In the monastic cartulary, as Constance Bouchard says, the past "was a *collection* of events, each with a very present and ongoing significance."[30]

The emergence of the figure of the archive in the evolution of the poem is tied to the emergence of the figure of literature as a form of work that must be registered in a socially recognizable form, in what must begin to appear in the archive. The relation between the poem's work and its legitimizing archive is the explicit subject of the famous "autobiographical" passage in passus 5 of the C text, perhaps one of the poem's last sections to be revised. Reason and Conscience accuse Will of shirking his proper labor responsibilities by spending his life working on the very poem in which they are now appearing. As Anne Middleton has argued, this passage casts the question of literary being in terms of the problem of registration, that is, the place that this kind of work, this writing, occupies in the array of crafts imagined and registered by legislation aimed at making labor as scriptable as possible.[31] But when the question of writing is directed at death, Langland does not so much frame writing as a kind of *impossibilia* or a gamble, as in C.5, but as a consolatory archive. At the end of the poem, Conscience expresses his wish that the disruptive fraternal death industry, which leads only to cryptic death in hell, "withoute nombre" (C.22.270), be subordinated to archival order: "Y wolde witterly that ye were in register / And youre nombre vnder notarie sygne and notherr mo ne lasse" (C.22.271–72). Yet even hell has its records: the poem's most extended and direct confrontation with death is, of course, in the scene of the harrowing of hell, where death is represented in a surprisingly literary way—at least surprising in a poem whose affiliations with the corpus of English vernacular literature are almost as obscured as Chaucer's own. Death is represented there as a literary trope with its origins pointedly in liturgical drama and sermon exempla. Most famously, death has been tricked by a trickster, "a gyn [engyned]" (B.18.252).[32]

Death is necessary to teach us what finitude is, in order for infinitude to make sense: "Til moreyne [plague/famine] mete with us . . . ne woet [knows] no wyht [no one], as Y wene [believe], what is ynow to mene [what enough means]" (C.20.225–26); what we learn from the "wo" of finitude is what "loue is and lisse withouten ende" (C.20.236). This overcoming of death makes it not only an object of knowledge, but the means by which the knowledge of infinitude becomes possible, the recognition of the "death of kynde" whose record of sorrow and care allows us to identify what true "wele" is. Death, in other words, becomes a kind of archive, containing the knowledge of an entrance into history that, while unpleasant, is necessary, because its clearly articulated presence allows us to understand its contrary more fully. An archive is also a beginning to historiography, after all, an arche. It is precisely at this point in the poem, in the harrowing of hell's overcoming of death, that the clearest image of these two functions of writing emerges—the figure of Boek with its "two brode eyes" witnessing both to what has happened in history, the incarnation, and to what is about to happen: "Y, Boek, wol be brente bote he aryse to lyue" (C.20.264). This last verb (cf. Wittig, who argued that it is "to live" and not "to life") suggests that this archive of death will become a testimony of life, a "legend of lif," a record of the death that is transcended historically and not just epistemologically, and it forms a kind of formal closure in Book's speech itself, which ends four lines later with a warning that those who don't believe in the new law will "be ylost lyf and soule" (C.20.268).[33] There is a pun here that suggests both the failure of the unbeliever to be registered in this "legend of lif" *and* the loss of a part of an archive: the individual soul is also the lost leaf of a book.[34]

As the geographer (not the philosopher) Gillian Rose argues, the meaning we gain from an archive exceeds its classifications. On the one hand, it holds in reserve not simply the past that it enshrines, but a future that will extend its meaning. On the other, an "archive is a space devoted to knowledge and Reason, to art and Culture, and . . . the bodily is thus in itself an intrusion that challenges its founding discourses."[35] The archive is a place where the body does not belong; the crypt is a place where the body does belong. There is something entailed in the very nature, the assumptions, the practice, of the archive that takes us beyond the fate of the body. In one sense, we cannot speak of the fully human without the archive. As the philosopher Gillian Rose puts it in her work on twentieth-century archives and the question of justice, "We cannot speak without spirit, without, that is, taking up a relation to the relation, to the ensouling of things when they become meaning. When we speak of death, which is the demarcation between physical nature and signification, we take up a relation to the relation of body and soul, their salvation or damnation."[36] In a philosophical, rather than a merely historical, sense, all literature, as Maurice Blanchot argued somewhat enigmatically in his landmark 1948 essay *Literature and the Right to Death*, and which influenced Rose greatly, "*begins* with the end."[37] This end is more or less the death that language brings about: when we designate something, or even form an idea about it, it takes on a different order of existence; it is no longer the thing itself, but the word or the concept that names it: "the concept is the murder of the thing." Blanchot's essay imagines that literature deals with both the relation between things and their designation, between their life as existing things and their death in orders of representation. Literature, in other words, looks both back toward the hecatomb of things and ahead toward a kind of freedom from the finitude of names, a death that liberates as opposed to one that constrains and merely cancels possibility: "the language of literature is a search for this moment which precedes literature."[38] It is an analytic of finitude, a means of understanding how the search for terms, for the precise and permanent naming of things, can be such an unending and infinite enterprise, the play of pure and devastating possibility from which we wake, as in *Piers Plowman*, at the interminable end of things.

CHAPTER EIGHT

The Physics of Elegy: *Pearl*

'Tis death, death only, sets a measure.
—Panchatantra

In Old English poetry, I argued in previous chapters, the elusive finality of death is represented by the trope of the grave, which becomes a theater for the soul. The soul, and we as readers, cannot stop at death: as Emily Dickinson memorably said, we ride in a carriage with Immortality. Put more awkwardly, death is not a terminus, an indivisible point, but the continuation of either living or dying. The dream vision *Pearl*, one of four extraordinary works (*Sir Gawain and the Green Knight*, *Cleanness*, and *Patience*) by a single poet who wrote in the late fourteenth century, is about death, yet it contains numerous moments in which the dreamer overshoots death only to go on living.[1] Yet for him, living is also the confining condition of mortality, especially when it is juxtaposed with the poem's sumptuous and overwhelming visions of what it means to live eternally. The more he sees of heaven in his vision, the more he desires it; but that desire for more is precisely what marks him as a transient being who longs for permanence.[2]

Even desire has limits—which is to say that the poem's vision implies that desire is something that can be measured, and that marks and is marked by certain quanta. The dreamer realizes, too late, that yearning too much after what he most yearns for will keep him from attaining it: if he had "yerned no more then was me gyven" (1190), he says, then he might have been able to stay in paradise forever. That moment sums up two important things about the poem: it assumes that affect is something that has degrees of intensity that can be measured, and it demonstrates that this practice is deeply paradoxical. This unsustainable paradox—at least unsustainable for the dreamer—opens the poem itself. The dreamer briefly describes the beauty and value of a pearl that is lost, sliding through the grass into the earth, in an image that is reminiscent of the opening shot of David Lynch's *Blue Velvet*, in which the camera sinks beneath a placid suburban lawn to reveal a grotesque subterranean world.[3] But in *Pearl* the grave that the dreamer regards longingly (in a way specifically characterized as the longing of *fin amor*, or "luf-daungere" [11]) becomes the occasion for a transcendentally beautiful vision of eternity. The dreamer's experience of finitude and loss, in other words, is what enables his vision of heaven and the resurrected Pearl, now appearing as a girl dressed in blazing white robes and numerous pearls. Especially prominent is a large white pearl on her chest, so extraordinary that all the dreamer can say is that his mind would "dryȝly demme / Er mynde moȝt malte in hit mesure" (the man who attempted to imagine its magnitude/ would find himself flummoxed, his mind befuddled [223–24]). It is not entirely clear what *malte* means here, and this difficulty may be a deliberate example of something that cannot be fully comprehended (the only places where the verb *melten* means either "to measure" or "to comprehend" are here and in the same poet's *Cleanness*). Later in the poem *malte* clearly refers to the dissolution of the mind under the onslaught of infinite delight (1154). In this poem, at least, the verb *malten* is a cryptic one that means two contradictory things simultaneously. In the first case, melting indicates comprehension; in the second, it indicates *in*comprehension. Joy and understanding flicker back and forth between positive and negative senses, a semantic condensation of the contradictions that structure affect and intellect in the contemplation of infinitude. Even apparent understanding of the fact of death is called into question by the very sentence that holds out the possibility of understanding: "Althaȝ oure corses in clottez clynge, / And ȝe remen for rauþe wythouten reste, / We þuroutly hauen cnawyng; / Of on dethe ful our hope is drest" (And though our corpses decay in the clay / And you cry with lament unremittingly, / one hope above all stays alive in our hearts, / that our souls are saved by a single death [857–60]). Knowledge, especially thorough knowledge, implies certainty; and a thorough knowledge of something, one would think, precludes the necessity of having to hope that it is actually true.

Four hundred years later Immanuel Kant would describe this strangely pleasurable experience of the inadequacy of determinate judgment in the face of infinitude as the sublime.[4] The mind's continued, and compulsive, attempt to estimate the magnitude of something that is beyond measurement is, he says, precisely aesthetic. This is perhaps why it could be said that the awful finitude of the grave shadows *Pearl*'s compulsive aestheticizing of experience. It might be more accurate to say that the poem's aesthetic is its attempt to express an experience that is otherwise beyond estimation—that is, beyond finitude.

On the one hand, the poem quite clearly recognizes that the nature of at least some beauty is finite. The "concatenation" word of the second section, the word that appears in the first and last lines of each stanza, is *adubbement*, an Old French word that appears in Middle English only here. It is usually glossed as "adornment," but in Old French it most often refers to the act of dubbing—specifically, arming—a knight.[5] It connotes human action, human artifice, human convention. But from the start this "adubbement" seems more than human. The rocks in the visionary landscape gleam so brightly that, says the dreamer, "wern neuer webbez þat wyȝez weuen / Of half so dere adubbemente" (never on this earth did a human hand / weave cloth so exquisite in ornament [71–72]). This is precisely an example of what Kant means by "aesthetic measurement" in the face of the sublime, "an absolute measure, beyond which no greater is subjectively (for the judging subject) possible."[6] The landscape is still an "adubbement," but one that exceeds the faculties. The word *dere*, which appears throughout the section in conjunction with the word *adubbement*, implies two things about that experience: it demands continual efforts to place it in relation to some kind of human experience, to estimate its worth, how "dear" it is. It also implies a more immediate, intuitive, and comforting experience: it connotes something beloved, something experienced without calculation. One of the poem's ultimate lessons, however, is that finitude makes it impossible to separate one experience from the other, to love without limit.

The poem's manifold kinds of "adubbement"—intricate jewelry, the complexity of the natural world, the poem's own interlocking form—invite its readers to luxuriate in and marvel at the poem as an aesthetic and intellectual triumph. We do that as long as we forget that its spectacle is predicated on death, which the poem explicitly encourages us to do. It doesn't take the dreamer long to forget his grief (86) once he arrives in the first *locus amoenus* of the dream. The poem can cause the reader to forget that its images of permanence are in fact as transitory as the dreamer's life (indeed, the final paradox of the poem is that, in the poem's narrative order, it is the dreamer's mortal life that persists, not the maiden's). Yet transience is introduced into the poem by the dreamer himself: as he gazes across the river from his place in the "dere adubbement," he finds that his appreciation of the scene's beauty has been overtaken: "if hit watz fayr þer I con fare, / Wel loueloker watz þe fyrre londe" (though it was wonderful here where I walked / it appeared more wonderful over the water [147–48]). Even aesthetic experience in the poem is compared and measured, intensifying and receding. Rather than the end, the terminus, of all human aspirations as it is presented in stoicism and various Platonisms (*eudaemonia, frui, ataraxia, vita beata* [*bios makarios*], *beatitudo, felicitas*),[7] bliss is merely another quality that intensifies and decreases, and, like other emotional and mental phenomena in the poem, it can be measured. Even in the first, "outer" place in the dream, the dreamer estimates that the human heart cannot experience more than a tenth of the bliss that is encountered in that locus amoenus: "For vrþely herte myȝt not suffyse / To þe tenþe dole of þo gladnez glade" (a human heart could hardly hold / one-tenth of the rapturous gladness it aroused [135–36]).

Along with such efforts to estimate the bliss of infinitude, *Pearl*, especially in the beginning, pours over death an amalgam of metaphors. The second, third, and fourth stanzas compare death to an abandoned arbor, the loss of a pearl or a gem, the absence of an object of *fin amor*, a "swete" song, a muddied color, undying plants, plants that die in order to give life, the sowing of wheat, the harvesting of wheat in August, perhaps the spread of the odor of sanctity (13–48). Similarly, the verbs that accompany death suggest anything but a single moment. The pearl does not simply go away; it "yode": that is, it fell (or poured) like running water onto, or into, the ground (the boundary between eternal and mortal life is represented later in the poem as a running river [10]).[8] Similarly, the "rychez" that are the pearl start to rot, a vaguely demarcated physical process. Death is a becoming, a dynamic action, rather than the single "spot" that the dreamer imagines is the final resting place of the maiden. From the very first stanza, he himself undergoes a gradual declination. He begins to dwindle "(dewyne" [11]) away for the pearl he has lost: *dewyne* means to languish, but more strictly to diminish to the point of nothingness.[9]

The several variants of the word *decline* in the poem also reinforce the impression that death is a motion, not a point. When the dreamer realizes that "Þurȝ drwry deth boz vch man dreue" (323), he invokes something like the lonely exile of the speaker in the Old English poem *The Wanderer*: "Now rech I neuer for to declyne, / Ne how fer of folde þat man me fleme" (I'm indifferent now to how far I might fall / or the distance and depth to which I'm driven [333–34]).[10] Yet this sentence doesn't describe just exile in the stark terms of a poem such as *The Wanderer*, or quite the metaphysical terms of Augustine's *regio dissimilitudinis*. *Decline* isn't a term that is really redolent of Anglo-Saxon exile; it connotes a specifically a Latinate, Anglo-Norman decorum of dying, even of the physics of retrograde motion. The term's connection with measurement and estimation may be underscored by its position in line 333 at precisely a quarter of the way through the poem: multiplied by four, 333 equals 1212, the poem's total number of lines; the multiplication of three by four is also the structure of the poem's stanzas of three quatrains. *Decline* is a term that appears frequently in the central medical text of the fourteenth century, Guy de Chauliac's *Chirurgia magna*, to describe both the weakening of the body and the fading of color.[11] Another variant of the word *decline* appears in one of the most complex and haunting figures of dying in the poem, the coming of the metaphorical night at the end of the parable of workers in the vineyard: "Anon þe day with derk endente / Þe niȝt of deth dotz to enclyne" (Soon their day, edged with darkness, / descends at dusk into deathly nighttime [629–30]). I would like to spend a little time examining this line's complex structure, meaning, and intellectual context because it illuminates the resonances of the poem's treatment of death.

Another way to put the declining of the "niȝt of deth" is that the day (of life) declines. The MED's entries for *endente* and *enclyne* suggest that the metaphor is the setting of a jewel, the chasing around the mount, on the metal. That certainly is likely, given the number of metaphors drawn from jewelry in the poem. Yet that doesn't quite make sense of the metaphorical movement in the line, which describes not a static representation, the jagged boundary between night and day, but the inevitable and ongoing movement into the night. It is a reciprocal movement, both an impetus given to the day by the night of death (night makes the day move toward death) and a description of the passage, the inclination, of the day toward night.

What lies behind this strangely arcane way of describing nightfall? I think the poet uses the terms and concepts of the fourteenth-century Aristotelian physics of motion that the Oxford Calculators disseminated (in treatises such as Heytesbury's elementary *Termini naturales*).[12] Motion, as Walter Burley explained it, should be described from two perspectives, a *penes causam* and a *penes effectum*, velocity in respect of a cause and velocity in respect of an effect.[13] William of Ockham preferred to describe motion as an "inclinatio ad quietem."[14] More precisely, Ockham describes the "inclinatio ad quietem" as the "intensive quality" of the movement toward death, a movement that was imagined in terms of a form that was subject to intension and remission. As we will see, this assumption that everything moves toward *quietus* underlies *Pearl*'s distinctive treatment of death. First, however, I would like to show how the inclination toward quiet informs some of the poem's most basic images that concern death.

In the medieval analytics of motion (whether in logic or in physics), two specific examples recur over and over: how and when an individual (usually Plato or Socrates) moves from or toward complete whiteness, and how every form of being moves from heat to cold.[15] The predominant examples of physical change, indeed, are degrees of heat and cold, beginning with Aristotle's *De longitudine et brevitate vite*, which explains death as the replacement of vital heat with frigidity. This may be why *Pearl* describes burial as the sinking of body into the earth once it becomes colder using the terms of the intension and remission of forms: "Thy corse in clot mot calder keue" (320). That comparative "calder" points out that in life we are subject to an increase of *frigiditas*. Coldness isn't a secondary effect, the result of death, but a quality in whose presence death appears once that quality becomes intense enough. In the framework of Oxford physics, that intensity, indeed the appearance of death itself, must be capable of being analyzed as a term, as both the terminus of a motion and as a particular kind of *suppositum*— a proposition whose analysis discloses the precise terms by which we understand a phenomenon.[16] That is, death is inseparable from its terms, whatever those might be. I would like now to consider how *Pearl* uses the other principal example of a movement toward an end point: the intensification of whiteness, which is also related to death.

Whiteness is the pearl's principal attribute: "Blysnande whyt watz her bleaunt" (wearing a gown of iridescent white [163]); "her vysayge whyt as playn yuore" (her face was . . . fine and ivory-white [178]); "Al blysnande whyt watz hir beau biys" (Her fine linen shone luminously white [197]); "her ble more bla3t þan whallez bon" (her complexion whiter than the bone of a whale [213]); "Her depe colour 3et wonted non / Of precios perle in porfyl py3te" (the almost transparent appearance of her pallor / compared well with those priceless pearls [216]; here whiteness is represented in terms of intensity); "bornyste quyte watz hyr uesture" (everything she wore was wondrously white [220]). This figure of intensified whiteness is also a body of death, the pale corpse of the girl presumably named Pearl whom the dreamer is mourning at the beginning of the poem. One form must die for another, more or less intense, form to appear in its place. Walter Burley called this the destruction of forms, the unfolding of motion, indeed of any change, through a series of terminations. Burley's slightly younger colleague John Dumbleton says that "the recipient is denuded of all form in order that it may receive form."[17] But another way of thinking about physical change in Oxford was to imagine it as a steady decline or increase of a quality inherent in the thing. Much of the poem's representation of death suggests this steady slipping toward death. Rather than a series of destructions or losses, it represents the approach of death as a steady-state experience: "drwry deth" must be sustained ("dreue") before one can cross the stream ("dam" [324])—more literally, before God can "deme" him over the "dam." Characteristic of the poem's emphasis on inhabiting the moment of change is another image of the passing-away of the day, not in terms of relative white and black, or day and night, but in terms of an intermediate color: "þe world bycom wel broun" (537)—night is in a state of becoming, of dying rather than death.

This preference for sustaining the moment of change underpins what the poem's use of the word *enclyne* means: "anon the day with dark endent. . . ." The metaphor of teeth biting into the day suggests a visceral and somewhat terrifying way of imagining the coming of the night. But the "endente" also suggests an endenture, a document whose name comes from the observation that its shape comes from something that looks like a bite. Once two identical texts that describe an agreement—usually a transfer of rights in property—are copied out, one below the other, on a single *folium*, it is ripped or cut in half, leaving a wavy edge on both. Only the matching half of this "endented" edge will authenticate it. In other words, the destruction of the day by encroaching night in *Pearl* also intimates a kind of rupture that will eventually allow us to see the totality of the eschatological day in which universal meaning is restored.

Until that day, knowledge is something subject to degrees of measurement: "Inoghe is knawen that mankyn grete / Fyrste was wroght to blysse parfyt" (637–38). That certitude is something that can be increased or decreased might not seem surprising to us, but it is one of the abstract motions that Dumbleton tries to map out in his *Summa de logicae*.[18] The primary theological problem behind the Calculators' inquiries into the measurement of things began with the huge problem of merited and effective grace. How much did it take to be saved?[19] *Pearl* examines this question, as many other texts do, as the problem of the relation between labor and reward in the parable of the vineyard. Among other things, that parable illustrates both the desire behind the need to calculate (to ensure equity) and the pointlessness of doing so. The poem's answer is canny, sensible, and somewhat jocular: "the grace of God is gret inoghe" (612), a reiterated phrase that links together the five stanzas of the section. This central section of the poem, in other words, affirms six times (the sixth is the phrase repeated in the first line of the next section) at precise intervals that there is no need at all for precisely the speculative calculations that pervaded English Scholastic theology.

No matter what kind of quality the Calculators tried to measure, it could be expressed in terms of quantity by its degree of intensity, which followed the arc of any created thing toward its *finis* (as Aristotle called it), its *locus* (as commentators on Aristotle called it), or its point of rest or

quiescence. Just as earth naturally inclined downward to its natural resting place, so did heat incline toward cold, or life to death. It is important
to remember, however, that the *finis* was not the same thing as annihilation; qualities and quantities merely ceased to change once they reached
quiescence. This movement is not entropy, but something very close to
what Freud described as the natural tendency of organic instincts to regress
to their "primitive" condition.[20] Freud identifies this as inanimate matter,
and death as the means by which animated organisms return to it. Just a bit
later, however, he has changed the goal to death itself, referring instead to
the *Erreichung des Todeszieles*, the attainment of the goal of death, toward
which living things are impelled.[21]

   Which of these is the ultimate end, then—inanimate matter or death?
I would argue that it is precisely this subtle distinction that is the target of
much of the poem's speculation and imagination. This distinction makes
all the difference to the dreamer, because it provides the structure of his
experience. He experiences his loss at first as merely the return of the pearl
to the inanimate matter of earth, the necessary and inevitable termination
of its natural movement, its "color" now "clad in clot," lying in the "moul"
(22–23). What is striking about the dreamer's lament is how precisely he
observes the sensual particulars of the loss of the pearl while maintaining
its status as a metaphor. That is, the pearl is contaminated by its fall to
earth, yet its nature as a pearl, its substance, is fundamentally unchanged.
At the same time, however, its nature as a *metaphorical* pearl means that it
never had such a substantial being in the first place. It is inanimate matter
standing for the creation of inanimate matter, its marring by earth an insubstantial change that represents the substantial change from being to nonbeing. As with so many aspects of the poem, the metaphorics and metaphysics
of the pearl are doubled back on themselves. What is tangible is ultimately
intangible, although that intangibility stands for a real change to preexist-
ing matter: the loss of the pearl becomes—and is all along—mourning for
a dead girl, and the substantial density of the pearl turns out to have been
metaphorical from the beginning. Another way of understanding this is that
the subject of mortality in *Pearl*—the change of animate to inanimate matter—is inextricable from poetic language and form.

   The poem inscribes one of the most elaborate and gorgeous debts to
finitude in all medieval literature. Its first and final lines link together a
poem made up of 101 stanzas of twelve lines each, a circle made up of precisely 1,212 lines altogether. The poem's form, in other words, is a vast
calculatory project, attempting to contain and measure the tendency toward death or nonbeing. Its circularity is another way in which the poem

imitates the formal perfection of the pearl's roundness and offers itself as a way in which the mind can finally grasp the complex relation between loss and beauty. But the poem also incorporates imperfection in its invitation to try to glimpse something beyond finitude. As David Coley has argued, *Pearl*'s second stanza is rife with words that allude to the bodily signs of pestilence—*spot, clot, moul, bolne, bele*—and the poem's emphasis on the spotless nature of the heavenly Jerusalem and its occupants offers a form of redemption profoundly motivated by the contemporary moment's circumstances of dying.[22]

One of the attributes of this language of dying, in *Pearl* at least, is its constant slippage between a kind of hyperspecificity and abstraction. The dreamer describes particular kinds of flowers that grow on the spot where he lost the pearl—"Gilofre, gyngure, and gromylyoun, / And pyonys powdered ay bytwene" (43–44). But these are flowers that are more signs than botanical quiddities. They echo the kind of spice garden described in such widely read and imitated texts as *The Romance of the Rose*.[23] The peonies are "powdered" between them, as if they are heraldic devices. The gillyflower, one of the most prized flowers in northern medieval gardens, was frequently used as a symbolic rent payment at Christmas.[24] The gromwell (*granum solis*) embodies the very logic of generation and corruption that this early passage in *Pearl* concerns: the seed of the flower is also known as the "margery perl."[25] The equation of seed and pearl recapitulates, although in a cryptic and somewhat obscure manner, the previous stanza's description of how the original pearl's fall into the earth is like the death of a "grayn" or seed that produces life.

In that stanza the dreamer notices the flowers growing on the grave, "blomes blayke and blwe and rede" shining "ful schyr agayn the sunne" (27–28). These flowers evoke the springtime garden of the *reverdie*, a trope that begins so many medieval poems. But, as with *Sir Gawain and the Green Knight*, where the *descriptio* of springtime is bracketed by descriptions of wintertime, the trope here suggests much more about endings than beginnings. These blooming flowers represent not the irrepressible force of life, but the dialectical insistence of death:

> Flor and fryt may not be fede
> Þer hit doun drof in moldez dunne;
> For vch gresse mot grow of graynez dede;
> No whete were ellez to wonez wonne.
> Of goud vche goude is ay bygonne. (29–32)

[Flower and fruit could never fade
where my pearl entered the dark earth;
grasses must grow from lifeless grains
or wheat would never be brought to the barn.
For goodness out of goodness is born.]

Neither flowers nor fruit will fade here; they represent a kind of blossoming that lasts beyond the ephemeral moment of springtime. Their paradoxical quality is begotten, as the poem might say, of another paradox: they represent life only because they are made possible by death. These flowers and fruit grow out of "graynez dede," an image that fundamentally rewires the medieval trope of poetic opening: the principle of generation is not the grain but its death. The "goud" that the next line refers to, in other words, is also death, which enables further good to be "bygonne." These five short lines not only develop an allegorical reading of the flowers on the "spot," they do so by reversing the meaning that flowers conventionally bear at the beginning of a poem. These flowers are permanent not because they exist in some kind of dreamlike, otherworldly *locus amoenus*, but because they also represent the nonexistence of flowers, the necessity of the death that makes their existence possible. The sensual immediacy of these flowers—their colors and smells—is sustained by the unseen, unheard abstraction of death. They will not fade or decay as long as they can die—an apparently nonsensical statement. And it might be, except that the poem actually means, as one recognizes in this instant, that the *kind*, the *nature*, of flowers and fruit will not die because it is sustained by the process of generation and corruption.

These lines also echo earlier discourses on what makes such writing possible in the first place. The springtime analogy for a poem's beginning seems to develop out of such medieval treatises on how to develop a piece of writing as Geoffrey of Vinsauf's *Poetria nova* or Matthew of Vêndome's *Ars versificatoria*. In explaining how to use *amplificatio* to construct a work, Geoffrey recommends digression. The sample he gives is really a kind of analogy, in which love is like spring: "A flower, earth's child, bursts forth into the breeze and smiles at its mother. Their first foliage adorns the tips of the trees; seeds that were dead spring up into life."[26] This brief excerpt expresses the conventional logic of the springtime topos, which makes the lines from *Pearl* seem like a movie run backward. But Geoffrey's passage is also haunted by mourning. The rationale for the analogy, indeed, describes exactly the kind of loss that the dreamer is experiencing at that moment: a love that "is a spur to grief, and grief a witness to the strength of love."[27] Geoffrey's analogy ends by implying that this grief may actually be the inevitable end of love: "the promise of harvest lives in the first tender blade."[28] In Geoffrey's work, however, this harvest is what we see in front of us, the rhetorical result of the work of amplification: from a small seed grows this much larger discourse. The section on *amplificatio* as a whole ends by restating its fundamental principle in terms taken from this passage: "plentiful harvest [*permulta seges*] springs from a little seed [*semine pauco*]."[29] This image of *amplificatio* represents what the poem has just done—created a harvest of *exempla* out of brief principles—and spells out how planting and harvesting are fundamental tropes. In one sense, *Pearl* demonstrates these tropes in a literal and extensive way, developing an entire section out of the Gospel of Matthew's parable of the workers who are paid the same amount, regardless of how long they worked, to bring in the harvest. But in another, *Pearl* envisages harvest as a death that simply repeats originary death. When the dreamer returns to the "erber grene" where the pearl is entombed, it is harvest time ("Quen corne is coruen wyth crokez kene" [when corn succumbs to the sharpened scythe; 40]). This harvest is, in a sense, what will be gathered in for the rest of the poem, the visionary experience that follows from the dreamer's loss. The word *corne* as a metonym for the harvest might be explained by Geoffrey of Vinsauf's use of the word *seges*, which, while it is usually translated as "harvest," literally means "cornfield." This bravura passage, in other words, writes about death by using texts that show how to write by digressing into topics that happen to be the setting of the poem (the garden) and its primary topic (the arrival of grief).

Although the poem opens with a lament about a lost pearl, the maiden explains that the dreamer has lost not a pearl, but a rose, which becomes the pearl. But the dreamer fails to grasp the transformation of rose into pearl, and so a more literal kind of exegesis begins in the sixth section of the poem: art doesn't terminate the failure to apprehend death. As Spearing describes it, at this point of the poem "doctrinal exposition replaces symbolic development and more straightforward homiletic methods of instruction are used."[30] The emergence of the rose through the nature of mortal termination is a metonymy for what happens in the entire poem: because the symbol does not redeem our knowledge of the phenomenon of death, it is put to death, rendered literal, and reemerges as the more "discursive" (Spearing's term, though not applied to the pearl) pearl of great price (732). Art can't be apprehended in life; it will destroy us, or we have to be destroyed in order to inhabit its place (our mind will melt). So didacticism, more literal discursiveness, is what keeps our knowledge alive. More precisely, it is what keeps *us* alive; the earlier implicit reference to the pearl of great price must be apprehended more literally and materially. The dreamer, once compared to a jeweler, now is compared to a merchant, a mere enumerator of prices (the poem compares him to the merchant of Matt. 13:45–46). The "great price" of the pearl is both a metonym of its pricelessness in the (metaphorical) economy of salvation and the provocation for the exercise of more practical quantification: precisely *how* great is the price of the pearl?

At times this slippage of reference and designation calls attention to the necessity, or the impossibility, of attaching the term *pearl* to any suppositum whatsoever. The dreamer's address late in the poem to the maiden collapses in a dizzying nested collage of container, contained, part, and whole: "'O maskelez *perle* in *perlʒ* pure, / Þat berez,' quoþ I, 'þe *perle* of prys'" ("Oh pure and incomparable pearl, / bearer of the priceless pearl," I said [745–56]). The term wavers on the edge of intelligibility, and only the hard work of delineating what is predicated of the pearl in each case offers some help in understanding the basic structure of the image. But the primary effect, of a nonsensical repetition of the word that is purportedly the most important in the poem, still lingers.

In one sense, that is how we speak of the dead. The only way in which we can talk about Aristotle "doing" something or "being white" is to assume, says supposition theory, that Aristotle's being is *in the understanding* of anyone uttering, reading, or hearing that phrase. In many ways the appearance, the designation, of the pearl in the poem works just like this. She exists, has being, in the discourse of mourning and dreaming, but not in the active, deliberate, waking designation of things. The dreamer finds himself, as he tells us at the beginning of the poem, an observer of a grief system: the poem substitutes an appeal to sensuous knowing for the unknown and unknowing extremes of both his own dwindling away and the elusiveness of the lost pearl itself: "I dewyne, fordolked of luf-daungere / Of þat pryuy perle withouten spot" (I mourn now, with a broken heart, / for that priceless pearl without a spot [11]). The body of the pearl, like that of the dreamer, which is left behind on the mound at the start of the dream, suffers the adequation of his body to a loss around which it seems to be organized. The pearl, for example, is described as having no "spot" precisely because it transcends materiality—that is, extension—altogether. But so does the dreamer, whose spirit springs from the "spot" at which he begins the narrative.

An explicit statement of this contradiction underlies an earlier invitation to understand what the pearl's supposition is. By a kind of negative dialectic, the pearl's substantiality is confirmed by what it is not, or by what contains it. Through "kynde of þe kyste þat hyt con close / To a perle of prys hit is put in *pref*" (through the nature of the chest where it lies, / its worth as a precious pearl is proven [271–72]). Notice the language of demonstration (i.e., logic) here; it is possible that the word *kynde* in this case refers to the Aristotelian categories of being, which the *Pearl* poet describes explicitly as the "kynde of Aristotle" later in the poem ("Arystotel nawþer by hys lettrure / Of carped þe kynde þese propertéz" (not for all his letters and lectures / could Aristotle tell of your attributes [751–52]). The form of the pearl emerges only because of the "kynde" of chest in which it is enclosed: a coffin and a receptacle that publishes its contents rather than concealing and guarding them.[31]

In many ways, *Pearl*'s source of invention is the pearl itself. It becomes the poem's fetish, appearing over and over in various manifestations, including the circular form of the poem itself. The word is excessively polyvalent, designating a multitude of phenomena: it is a jewel, a daughter, the object of a parable (the pearl of great price), Mary, the pure soul, virginity, a particular virgin, a more abstract figure of perfection, and even another name, Margaret, the English name derived from the Latin *margarita*. The extent to which the name Margaret can be the synonym of "pearl," and in which the play between them can structure a text, can be seen most clearly in Thomas Usk's *Testament of Love*, which acrostically encodes (or encrypts) the name Margaret in its proemium.[32] The pearl itself seems bound, or determined, by something like this complex relationship, described via negative predication. The tag reiterated at the end of each stanza of this first section, "perle without spot," reminds us over and over that names involve negation (as Spinoza said in a famous letter, every determination is a negation). The naming of the pearl is not exactly an apophatic act, a naming of the unnamable. In fact, the poem traces the opposite problem: the excessive, saturated term. But at the same time it is repeatedly described in the first section in terms of its negation of an attribute, the absence of any spot. Its particular being is determined, at least in part, by the negation of attributes that might normally belong to it. Although *perle* is the poem's keyword, it also enfolds a kind of emptiness and lack. Like the keystone of an arch, it holds a structure in place by sustaining the tension of opposite and opposing forces. The pearl, which embodies a circular completeness that also hides its interior (again, encrypts it), is the symptom of the poem's recurrent preoccupation with appearance and nonappearance, and with the boundaries between life and death.

But the pearl is only the most obvious of the terms that the poem unpacks as it labors to represent the impossibility of death. Even the word *spot*, the most minimal of designations, is subjected to this philosophical work. We do not leave behind the spot where the dreamer's body lies; it is, in fact, the very spot, as the dreamer says, "that I in speche expoun" (37). The spot is, in the strict sense of the word, an "exponible," something about which something can be said. It is also something that makes speech possible—indeed (at least at this point) the very *materia* of the poem: it is also the section's concatenation word. But its repetition, its expounding, also undoes it: it is no longer a singularity. It appears over and over, and in different places, turning a single spot into a discursive domain that spans five stanzas. Many of the concatenation words in the poem unfold similar paradoxes. Eight of the ten times that the word *date* appears as a concatenation, it refers to either a point in or a span of time: the season (504), the time of year (505), the time of day (515, 529), the beginning of the day (517), the ending of the day (528, 540, 541). But the other two occurrences of the word have nothing to do with time. First, the maiden's status as a queen is "to dere a date" (492), too high a social position or too great a reward (in the sense of *datum*, gift) for her. She exceeds a certain position or degree of merit: the term *date* is used in a severely literal, etymological way. Secondly, the maiden responds that the goodnesse of God "has no date," which uses the term in a sense attested only here (according to the *Middle English Dictionary*), as a nontemporal limit or boundary.[33] The play among the three distinct senses of the word in this section, then, is a symptom of the dreamscape's underlying indistinction between limits in time, space, and qualities.

The second stanza in that section uses the word *terme* as a synonym for *date*: "Of tyme of yere the terme was tyght" (503). The peculiar syntax of the sentence, in which the subject is the third noun, suggests, on the contrary, a more rigorous way of reading the section. The term *terme* itself—*terminus* in Latin—means a number of things, from a span of time, a point in time, a beginning or an end, to the word analyzed in a proposition—the *suppositum* of terminist logic (hence the adjective *terminist*). This sentence, indeed, makes the suppositum clearer than the subject: what this proposition ultimately refers to is the use of the word *terme* to supposit for "time of year." In that sense, the section is, among other things, an exercise in determining the suppositions of the word *terme* itself, and the word *date*.

The various suppositions of the words *terme* and *date* point out the way in which one of the recurrent interests of the poem is the interrogation of its own terms, and in particular the way in which the work of measurement, or calculation, lies at the heart of understanding the essential movement of the poem. The concatenation word *more* in the tenth section, which follows the stanza linked around the word *date*, pushes the problem of the relation between quantity of time and space further. In the final stanza of the section the dreamer objects to the implication of the parable of the vineyard by citing a verse from the Psalms against that interpretation, describing it as a "point determinable" that God disposes according to merit. The last line of this section seems to be a kind of sophism that plunges us deep into the perplexities of the calculation of movements: "Euer the lenger the lasse the more" is a seemingly nonsensical or contradictory assertion that nevertheless, like the classic sophism, invites us to resolve its meaning (600). Andrews and Waldron read this line as being more "emphatic than logical," but surely the point is that this line is precisely logical. It describes not a mathematical or economic calculation, not a relation between quantities, but a relation between qualities. The pair "less" and "more" is placed precisely within the analytic of quality by Peter of Spain, which means that the relation is not determined by simple addition and subtraction, but by intension and remission.[34] That is, it is regulated by the greater or lesser intensity of the quality, by the degree of latitude, by what the poem calls "the lenger," which is to say the greater presence of "less," a completely meaningful utterance precisely because "less" is a quality. What's used here is not the discourse of economic reciprocity, in other words, but the discourse of proportionality—not simple cause and effect, but a more complex interrogation of causation. It is a kind of syncategorematic problem, with a double, proportionable signification.

A common sophism on the syncategorematic word *quanto*, for instance, asserts that "the more you learn [or know], the less you know" (*quanto magis addiscis, tanto minus scis*).[35] In his discussion of the word in his foundational treatise on syncategoremata, Peter of Spain suggests that such problems concern the Aristotelian causes implicit in the actions they describe. His example of a final cause concerns the relation between labor and satisfaction: "the greater the reward, the more easily the labor is borne" (*quanto premium maius, tanto labor facilius toleratur*).[36] This example just happens to emphasize the implicit point that the dreamer is making in *Pearl*: that labor can't be considered apart from its affect, that the proportion due to the subject can't be worked out unless one takes into account the individual perspective of the laborer. This seems to be what the dreamer means when he refers to the "point determinable" of the Psalm, which says that workers are paid according to their merit. In the theory of supposition, a determinable is the scope of a particular proposition, that is, the terms that are included in deciding how it makes sense, refers to, most fundamentally, substance. So, as Walter Burley says, in the sentence "Socrates is a white man," " 'white' is a determination that posits its determinable"; in the sentence "Socrates is a dead man," however, the determination "takes away," as he puts it, and refers to the opposite of its determinable. In other words, Socrates can't be a man, because he is dead.[37] In *Pearl*, however, the work of termination begins to falter, and perhaps for the same reason: terms aren't very good at describing nonbeing. It's difficult to determine, as the dreamer comes to realize, how something so obviously substantial in its whiteness as the pearl, and yet dead, can also be calculated, reckoned, in terms of economic or judicial proportion. Even within the horizon of terminist constraint, the dreamer acknowledges, in the same stanza, that God is outside boundaries of such kind, that he moves beyond terms in the physical, temporal, and linguistic senses, that he is, in the dreamer's words, "pertermynable" (596).

Again and again the poem discovers the limits of its own horizon, the extent of its terms, and yet attempts to put the interminable into its own terms. As early as the first glimpse of a pearl on the pearl's breast (itself a kind of dizzying effect, almost an evacuation of the term *pearl* itself, when you think about it), the dreamer posits both the interminable and the terms in which it can be placed: "A mannez dom moȝt dryȝly demme / Er mynde moȝt malte in hit mesure. / I hope no tong moȝt endure / No sauerly saghe of þat syȝt" (The man who attempted to imagine its magnitude / would find himself flummoxed, his mind befuddled. / In truth, no tongue could ever tell / a sensible syllable about that stone [223–26]). But the poem goes on to try to do just that, to put the pearl into terms; and more than that, to put into measures what it says here can't be measured, what can't be subjected to the calculus of motion.

This is an eschatological perspective, a perspective from beyond life, and it seems to abolish some of the most fundamental categories of being themselves, including time: "Now is þer noȝt in þe worlde rounde / Bytwene vus and blysse bot þat He withdroȝ, / And þat is restored in sely stounde" (In a blessed hour He restored our bliss, / and now there is nothing in this wide world / that stands between us and ecstasy [659]). A "sely stounde" is literally an innocent time, a time of innocence, but also a time innocent of demarcation or termination, a time that can't be ended or indeed named. This eschatological perspective destroys more than the calculus of time, which is, after all, not part of the ground on which we base our existence: all we have of time, as Dumbleton says, is the limit, the term, of the time that is past (Augustine makes that point, too, more poetically, in the *Confessions*).[38] This perspective also abolishes quite literally the ten fundamental categories into which Aristotle divided all properties of being. As the dreamer puts it in a passage I have already mentioned, "Arystotel nawþer by hys lettrure / Of carped þe kynde þese propertéz" (751–52). What the language of the poem analyzes is not, finally, the terms of being, but the terms

of dying, the terms in which motion and time, the province of physics, the
secondary effects of substance, are ultimately as inadequate as the terms by
which they are understood. Dying, that is, living, is a state of inquietude,
the state of restless motion and of speech, the state of physics. Yet death,
the *quies* that is beyond the senses, beyond the analytic of motion, is the
knowing of plenitude, a knowing that explains how the complete privation
that is death is also the principle of totality, a "dethe ful," as the pearl calls
it, that saturates the poem (860).[39]

The section in which the phrase *dethe ful* appears happens to be the section of the poem that contains an extra stanza, for a total of six where every
other section has five. That extra stanza spoils the poem's architectonic
regularity just as extra space between two columns would spoil the façade
of the Parthenon. But because of that stanza, the poem has a total of 101
stanzas—the same as *Sir Gawain and the Green Knight*—and 1212 lines, a
number that underlines the twelve in each stanza. The stanzaic superfluity
that wrecks the formal end of the poem also expresses a certain perfection
of form in its own right, outside the immanent terms of the poem. This is,
after all, a poem about dying, about the appearance of what follows the form
of life, the end of the movement that we call living. What follows the end
can only be appearance, but an appearance that conceals what it stands for.
As Hegel puts it, "Appearance is the arising and passing away that does not
itself arise and pass away, but is 'in itself' [i.e., subsists intrinsically], and
constitutes the actuality and the movement of the life of truth."[40]

Perhaps a simpler way of putting this is that dying is the same as being caught in representation, caught in the body whose death is caused by
representation: "Hade bodyly burne abiden þat bone, / Þaȝ alle clerkez hym
hade in cure, / His lyf were loste anvnder mone" (Any mortal man, having
seen such a miracle, / despite the craft and cures of his doctor, / would go
to his grave beneath the moon [1090–92]). Humans cannot bear infinitude,
and we can only contemplate it through metaphor and analogy. We can only
apprehend it directly in death. Yet the formal principle of the body, that is,
its end, is not itself the "dethe ful" that leads to what the poem calls true
"cnawying," the anagogical revelation of the answers to all mysteries. No
motion, no matter how intense or comprehensive, traces the real form of
that death.

The poem suggests the two brightest heavenly bodies as possibilities,
but even they fail. The inhabitants of the heavenly Jerusalem "nedde nawþer
sunne ne mone" (1044). The moon comes close, though: the concatenation
word in the eighteenth section actually is "mone," and in that section the
moon plays an active role in the regular course of events in the heavenly

city. There are twelve "fruits of life" on the trees there, and each of them "renowles nwe" with every new moon—just as the next stanza of twelve lines renews itself, so to speak, as the word "moon" appears in its first line. The word *moon* also appears in the first line of the next section—as is the poem's practice with a section's concatenation word—and there it plays an important final role. The procession of 144,000 virgins outshines the heavenly city: they are as bright, the poem says, as a moon that rises just as the sun is setting. More precisely, the metaphor describes the narrator's perception of the brightness of the 144,00 virgins: as suddenly as the moon rises at sunset, "So sodanly on a wonder wyse / I watz war of a prosessyoun" (I became aware in a wonderful way / of the sudden presence of a long procession [1096]). This moment slips by so quickly that it is easy to overlook how complex its dynamics are. First, there's the movement in the metaphor: as the sun sets, the moon rises; secondly, there's the movement from vehicle to tenor: the rising moon is like the narrator's awareness; but thirdly, there seems, belatedly, to be a movement from vehicle to another tenor: the rising moon is like a procession. The rising moon replaces the setting sun, a process that surely cannot happen instantaneously. Yet the reciprocal movement of the two somehow describes the instant of the narrator's awareness. The complexity, and perhaps the unsolvable puzzle, of the metaphor's movement recalls the recurrent problem of motion and change in fourteenth-century philosophy. But there is still another metaphor lurking behind this already complex one. The setting sun echoes the earlier metaphor of the ending of day "with derk endent," a process that occurs gradually, and according to the protocol of fourteenth-century physical dynamics: "anon,"[41] "enclyne." The ending of the day in that earlier passage is unmistakably a metaphor for dying: "Anon þe day with derk endent / The niȝt of deth dotz to enclyne" (629–30). Indeed, neither day nor death seems fully to arrive in the poem. When the sun sets at the end of the day in the vineyard, the light merely "bycom wel broun" (537); it is not darkness that arrives, but a transitional state.

The significance of this difficult metaphor for the poem's meditation on the life beyond death is, quite literally, hard to endure. The metaphor, as I have pointed out, appears at the beginning of a section, in which the word *moon* recalls the linking word of the previous section. Its position, in other words, is the formal equivalent of a final statement about how the moon figures dying and death, or a statement beyond or outside the moon's organization of the experience of contemplating life beyond death. The linking word *moon* reiterates, throughout that previous section, the insurmountable difference between the brilliance of the maiden's heavenly city and the "grym," "spotty" moon. The section's last lines make it clear, in fact, that the difference is not only insurmountable, it is literally intolerable: "Hade bodyly burne abiden that bone, / Þagh alle clerkez hym hade in cure, / His lyf wer loste anvnder mone" (1090–92). This sounds like apophasis, the acknowledgment that we can't truly say what God is, but it carries with it a mortal penalty that sounds more like the Deuteronomic God of Mount Sinai whose face we cannot see and live. As is characteristic of the poem, there is something slyer going on. Indeed, we cannot see the heavenly city fully without losing our lives. But that is not some kind of mortal penalty paid for a particularly ambitious visionary experience in a dream. It is the condition that makes it even possible to see the heavenly city at all, the condition of universal mortality. We cannot experience this "bone" until our lives are lost—until we pass beyond a limit that we cannot experience and cannot know. That limit is demarcated by the moon, the boundary in medieval cosmology between change and permanence itself. But because we are on this side of that boundary, we can only experience the limit as change, caught as we are "anvnder mone," knowing nothing but change. We cannot know, nor can we understand (yet), the pearl's transformative and transcendent change beyond limit. We know only the ceaseless dying without death.

CHAPTER NINE

Death, Terminable and Interminable:
St. Erkenwald

Constituisti terminos eius, qui praeteriri non poterunt.
—Fifth Lesson, Second Nocturne of the Office of the Dead

The late fourteenth-century poem *St. Erkenwald* is about a death that has not completed the work of dying, yet holds out hope that a final, good death is possible.[1] It describes the uncorrupted body of an ancient and just pagan judge, discovered in the foundations of St. Paul's Cathedral during a substantial building program. The strange *miraculum* is not documented among the many miracles of St. Erkenwald, which are recorded in accounts of his life written from several different perspectives and at different times. As I will argue in this chapter, the poem uses this mysterious event to examine the difficulty of saying anything about the dead. The judge lies outside human and institutional memory and, most crucially for the poem's theology, outside—before—the dispensation of Christianity. Not only can no one understand the information on the dead judge's tomb, but the judge himself exists (if that is the word for it) in a theologically indeterminate zone, although one that was heavily trafficked by theologians in the fourteenth century. The salvation of a just pagan is really just a test case for the larger theological question about how salvation works (as we have already seen with *Piers Plowman* and *Pearl*): is it a matter of grace, works, a combination of the two, efficacious prayer, the administration of the sacraments, or none of these? And if there is no systematic answer to the problem, what does it say about the limits and disposition of divine power if death is not fully and definitively final, even if only in rare cases?[2]

The answer to this question is an important one for systematic theology but not, as I will argue, for the literary conception of the poem. Precisely because it is a poem it does not need, or does not need to express, a systematically coherent answer. Unlike systematic theology, a poem can suspend or ignore the kind of conclusion that medieval theology demands of its practitioners. But that is not what I think is the most important work of *St. Erkenwald* as a poem: it is built around obscurity; it does not produce obscurity as an effect. The obscurity of the poem's answer is the privilege of literature, which not only can suspend a resolution, but can also explore other connotations of such theological problems. In a striking metonymy, the poem suggests that this is its *modus procedendi*: the inscription on the judge's tomb is never interpreted, the only occasion in medieval litera- ture on which the inscription accompanying the body of a just pagan is not decoded.

In an earlier article I argued that this is because the poem presents death as an unfathomable mystery that can never be solved.[3] This is partially true, but in this chapter I will explore the ways in which the poem is concerned with the difference between the radical alterity of the state of death and the present and ongoing work of dying. The provocative mystery of the un- corrupted body of a pagan in the foundations of St. Paul's is a spectacular invitation to imagine a state beyond the finitude of a single life, and even of the civic life of a cathedral such as St. Paul's.[4] But it also demonstrates how the aesthetic lure of death distracts and covers over the orientation toward death that is the real work of dying. The poem's narrative is fixed on the many ways in which the deep history of cathedral and civic records fails to preserve the identity of the judge, a void that lies at the deepest of the archaeological layers of the cathedral's history. But this overt interest calls attention away from the layered history of the narrative itself, and the body that lies at its origin: the body of St. Erkenwald himself.

The just pagan's body provokes reactions that are remarkably similar to the accounts of the hue and cry that attended St. Erkenwald's body imme- diately after his death. After Erkenwald died at Barking Abbey, the convent he founded for his sister, the nuns there began to argue with the monks of Chertsey (which Erkenwald also founded) and with a group of Londoners (both lay and clerical) over the right to inter the body. The dispute was re- solved only when a crowd of Londoners claimed the body for St. Paul's, and the body was conveyed to London (with the intervention of Erkenwald's first postmortem miracle, the parting of the River Hyde so that the Lon- doners could cross).[5] The Londoners argue that Erkenwald should be buried where he was ordained and appointed prelate: this is the "mos antiquus," they say, quoting handily from Gregory of Tours's account of the argument over the bodies of St. Martin and Lipicinus.[6] The Londoners "accurit" to the body and are accused by the monks of bursting in and seizing it as wolves seize lambs. The Londoners counter by replacing the metaphor of wolves with that of soldiers who will "batter, undermine, and overturn [*subruere atque subuertere*] cities" before they give up the body, anticipating the workers in the poem who "makyd and *mynyd*" underneath St. Paul's.[7] The Middle English poem strikingly echoes the actions of the Londoners in the *Vita* who rush to Barking to see the body of Erkenwald. When the body is discovered in the poem, "Mony hundrid hende men highide [ran] þider sone . . . Laddes laften hor werke and lepen [leapt] þiderwardes, / Ronnen radly in route [quickly in a crowd] with ryngand [ringing] noyce" (58–62). The "ryngand noyce" anticipates the ringing of bells at the end of the poem and echoes the "innumerable co-rejoicers" (*inenarrabiliter colletantes*) who accompany Erkenwald's body with hymns and songs back to London.[8] In *St. Erkenwald*, however, the Londoners raise a clamor in rushing to the body *that they already possess*. Their problem is the inverse of the problem that faces the Londoners of the *Vita*, who already know precisely what Erkenwald's body means: they have a body, but do not know what it means.

But they do know that it means something. It has been buried in an extraordinary monument that is unruined by time, whose state of preservation seems as remarkable as the spectacular nature of its work. The preservation of the judge's body is axiomatically a miracle (it is a miracle that can be immediately grasped), whereas the preservation of the tomb is less remarkable but more symbolically complex. The tomb's ornamentation is strikingly close to what the poem's readers might have expected both from their exposure to contemporary architectural styles and from their encounters with the tomb of St. Erkenwald itself, which was a fashionable tour-de-force of Perpendicular style.[9] The poem's description of the just judge's tomb clearly invites its readers to relate its opulence and skill to the sumptuousness of that and other important tombs of the fourteenth century: "Hit was a throghe of thykke ston thryuandly hewen, / Wyt gargeles garnysht aboute alle of gray marbre. / The sperle of þe spelunke þat sparde hit o-lofte / Was metely made of þe marbre and menskefully planede" (It was a tomb of thick stone excellently carved / Garnished all around with gargoyles of gray marble. / The bolt that fastened it shut on top / Was precisely made from the same marble and gracefully finished [47–50]). The adverbs here insist on the high quality of the work on the judge's tomb: "thryuandly," "metely," "menskefully." The participle *garnished* suggests the purely ornamental quality of the tomb's features. Yet there is a considerable tension between the immediate effect the tomb has on its audience and its details. Much of this passage is deliberately obscure, precisely while it describes contemporary styles. The nouns are so exquisitely precise that they almost never appear in other contexts, and indeed almost never appear anywhere: *throghe* for "tomb," a word we have seen used with similar precision in "Erthe toc of erthe";[10] *gargeles*, the first appearance of the word in English, according to the *Middle English Dictionary*; *garnysht*, another first appearance of the word in English (it also shows up in *Cleanness*); *sperle*, usually suggesting a clasp or a bar, but here meaning a raised lid or canopy (and yet another first occurrence of a word in English—indeed, it still needed to be glossed in the fifteenth century—and a word so obscure for Gollancz that he amended it to *speke*).[11] The point is that the tomb poses not just an historical but also an aesthetic problem. It represents spectacular enjoyment, an immersion in the sublimity of superior craftsmanship and ornamentation. But that enjoyment is inseparable from the obscurity that the tomb also represents, and inseparable from the structure of the poem itself. Part of the reason for the obscurity of these words might be the demands that alliteration makes of the entire lexicon—but that, of course, is part of the enjoyment of the poem.

It is not just the alterity of the object itself, or even the body of the judge, that raises the specter of historical obscurity, but the obscure forms of enjoyment that the tomb poses quite apart from its situation in history. That situation is the primary problem that the poem raises, although always within the context of an enjoyment that depends upon some kind of obstruction: it is impossible ("Hit myȝt not be"), say the onlookers with some consternation, that such a person could be forgotten, that he could not have "in mynde stode longe" (97). The enjoyment of the body in the tomb is made possible by the uncoupling of the aesthetic from the historical: the body conveys something, although it means nothing. One could argue that this is always the condition of enjoyment: as Slavoj Žižek summarizes Lacan neatly, "The only possible signifier of enjoyment is the signifier of the lack in the Other, the signifier of its inconstancy."[12] The most obvious, and problematic, signifier in the poem, however, is the inscription on the tomb. It is exquisitely inscribed in gold that has not faded—which itself provokes some kind of aesthetic wonder at the level of the signifier: its "bryȝt golde lettres" are "enbelicit" around the edge of the tomb. But this wonder seems to be inseparable from the knowledge that the inscription is decoupled from its signified. Although no one knows what the inscription says, its letters are still "verray," an adjective that describes their pristine quality but that really ought to describe their function as effective ("verray") signifiers of some truth. The signified truth of the letters, however, is only aesthetic, an object of unfulfilled desire. They represent the persistent problem that the tomb and the body raise: how to orient oneself toward a history that seems vitally present and unchanged, yet is unintelligible because of the work of history.

The poem confronts this historical unintelligibility in the form of these *litterae* themselves. The text remains inscrutable, unknowable, throughout the poem, which recounts a series of failures to decode it, to apprehend what its enigmatic text says about the past from which it emanates. It is this failure, I would like to argue, that lies at the very heart of *St. Erkenwald* and its narrative of a death that is not fully terminated, not yet one that we can come to terms with. The poem describes a history that extends beyond human memory, and in doing so impeaches the ability of history to commemorate, impeaches even commemoration itself. The pagan judge is not an anomaly in the machinery of remembrance; he represents the machine's eventual obsolescence.

The cryptographic text at the foundation of St. Paul's Cathedral is unsettling in ways having to do with the poem's history, its invention in the late fourteenth century, and the history of St. Paul's itself. The cathedral, indeed, produced a highly public historiography of its own, resting on its authority as the central church of London and ratified by its numerous techniques of documentation, regulation, and chronography. Its numerous chantries and chantry priests followed elaborate calendars marked by death, commemorating mortuary anniversaries, marking off times for those beyond its reach in a vast sociological apparatus of mourning and commemoration.[13] By the time William Dugdale wrote his survey of the cathedral in 1663, there were at least fifty-four priests besides the clergy attached to the cathedral who "celebrated daily for the souls of their Founders," and this was after a number of the chantry endowments had become so impoverished that some priests were made responsible for several chantries.[14] The clamor of anniversary masses and these daily chantry masses marking off mortuary times mingled with the regular offices in the cathedral, a noise beneath which could be discerned the music of sacred and secular time, the animation of devotion and memory. Reaching beyond the span of individual life, St Paul's also marked off the receding histories of its dead and of its own history, the time that exceeded human memory but not the institutional, inscribed memory of the cathedral.[15]

According to a marginal notation in a manuscript of the *Brut* written in the mid-fourteenth century, a tablet was installed in St Paul's in 1345 that listed the years that had passed since important events in the history of England, London, and St. Paul's, including the conversion of the English by Augustine of Canterbury 751 years ago.[16] Beginning with the foundation

of London "per Brutum" 2,405 years previously, it lists two more important events of foundation: of Rome, 2,060 years earlier, and of St. Paul's
itself, 741 years before. The calculation of these dates is not necessarily
remarkable, because similar schemata survive, including one in a London
fishmonger's book from 1395, which lists the years between the destruction of Troy, the construction of London (64 years), and the construction
of Rome (390 years).[17] What is remarkable is the commemoration of such
spans of time in such a public place. Even if the tablet is a complete fabrication, it is remarkable that someone imagined that the best location for
such a chronographic fantasy would be St. Paul's. The tablet articulates the
cathedral's role in the symbolic management of London time and its function as the repository of memory. In the same year, 1345, another important
temporal initiative at St. Paul's reinforced its secular primacy—a large mechanical clock was installed on the west exterior wall of the church.[18] By
the mid-fourteenth century, then, St. Paul's ordered and regulated the times
that could be imagined, from the divisions of hours to times at the gate of
eternity.

The bodies of those who contributed to St. Paul's establishment as the
secular center of eternal London were buried in prominent places around
the choir of the cathedral, their lives and works commemorated by inscriptions that reminded the living of the long reach of the dead around them. On
the south side of the choir stood the tomb of Eustace Falconberg, a former
chancellor of the exchequer and bishop of London from 1221 to 1228, serv-
ing, as his epitaph counted decisively, "Annos 7, & Menses 6, Diem obiit
pridie Kalend. Novembris Anno Salutis MCCXXVII."[19] Nearby, in front of
the chantry he founded, was a tablet petitioning prayer for the soul of Henry
de Chattesden, who died "Octavo Maii, MCC."[20] More loquaciously, the
tomb of Michael de Northburgh enumerated not only the length of his ten-
ure as bishop of London—from 1355 to 1356, when he died of the plague
(grassante pestilentia)—but also the terms of his bequest to the cathedral:
"Idem ego dono nummos ad faciendam unam cistam (qui stabit in Thesauro
Divi Pauli) & Mille marcus in eadem includendas, de quibus possit quilibet
pauper Plebius, sub bono, & excedente Pignore, mutuo sibi recipere Decem
Libras."[21] Speaking ecphrastically from beyond death, Northburgh's tomb
extends its terms to the living, sending out into social existence the accumulated wealth deposited in the chest in the treasury, the tomb's pecuniary
other. The explicit, articulate economy of the chest includes the implicit
economy of the tomb, the *cista* that refers to both receptacles—treasure
chest and coffin—that enrich the work of the dead Northburgh. This linguistic enrichment, the copia of language that animates the work of death

itself, is a feature that several of the tombs in St. Paul's Cathedral shared, a feature that structures the work of the poem *St. Erkenwald* itself.[22]

In inescapable ways, the tomb of St. Erkenwald anchored the habits of the cathedral. By the late fourteenth century, when the poem was composed, it was situated directly behind the high altar, visible from all sides. Its inscriptions, like the inscriptions we have discussed, coordinated the significance of the times of Erkenwald, and the way that they overlapped with national and episcopal times. It describes Erkenwald as the third bishop of London "post Anglo-Saxonicum ingressum," the third son of King Offa, converted to Christianity by Melitus, the first bishop of London, in 642.[23] Erkenwald's conversion of Sebba, king of the East Saxons, was reiterated by Sebba's tomb itself, which lay to the north of Erkenwald's, and which gave the year of conversion that Erkenwald's tomb omitted: 677.[24] Just as prominent in this choir-wide calibration of times, however, was the narrative of the several foundations for which Erkenwald was responsible, especially the abbeys at Chertsey and Barking. This last monastery, which the inscription described as being "ad Berching in ditione [*sic*] Orientalium Saxonum," is the one "in Esex" (108; "Orientalium Saxonum") that Erkenwald is visiting when the judge's body is found in *St. Erkenwald*.[25] Much of the poem's information about Erkenwald himself comes, as we will see, as much from the signifying machinery of the cathedral as it does from less accessible chronicles and *vitae*.

Not only would every visitor to the tomb of Erkenwald have been faced with an account of the works of Erkenwald outside London, but he or she would also have believed that the tomb stood in a part of the cathedral that Erkenwald himself had built. This famous temple of St. Paul, Erkenwald's epitaph informed its readers, was augmented with new buildings (*novis aedificiis*) by Erkenwald.[26] But neither of the two main accounts of Erkenwald's work in life and after death, the *Vita Sancti Erkenwaldi* and the *Miracula Erkenwaldi*, mentions any work done on the cathedral in Erkenwald's lifetime. This reference has baffled the poem's editors, since, as Thorlac Turville-Petre points out, "in fact the thirteenth-century rebuilding of St. Paul's was referred to as 'the New Work.'"[27] This extensive work is indeed widely documented, yet the tomb of its principal architect, Roger Niger, doesn't mention his own work on the cathedral. As Clifford Peterson says, "Erkenwald's association with the New Work is . . . difficult to explain."[28] But Erkenwald's epitaph nevertheless asserted his responsibility for *some* kind of "nova aedificia," and it must have been inevitable that fourteenth-century Londoners mistook his "new" work for the New Work of the previous century. If the poet of *St. Erkenwald* is making the same mistake, the poem attests to the archival *auctoritas* of inscriptions in the cathedral, which both record and establish sanctioned histories. But it is also possible that the poet is making a more sophisticated point about the writing of history: that even the most visible and axiomatic kinds of information conceal, or cause, coincidences and contradictions. That is, the profusion of knowledges about the cathedral is ultimately not an archival repository, but a cryptic one.

Even the voice, since time immemorial the sign of immediacy and presence, points to concealed depths. The judge can only speak in Erkenwald's presence. Its body has kept silent since its unearthing; its voice signifies not just the presence of the judge—a presence that is theologically and ontologically obscure—but the witness of the voice, whose presence is the condition for the capacity for speech in the first place.

The judge's voice is not its own in another sense: his speech is essentially ventriloquized by a "Goste" which has "lant [given] lyfe" to the corpse (192). It is worth remembering that the word *ghost* in Middle English could refer both to a revenant and to a divine spirit. The notion that a spirit could inhabit a body and give it language, as we will see, alludes to the Feast of Pentecost, an occasion that has particular significance for Bishop Erkenwald. But, at the same time, the reanimation of the dead is not an obliteration of death. It is simply an extension of the crypt, a disclosure of what is always implicit in the work of the living and the dying. The crypt protects us as much as it does the corpse from the work of death, keeping from us not only the knowledge of what that work is, but also the uncanny fear that this work goes on in us even before we enter the crypt. The judge's corpse is troublesome not just because it is unknowable but because it persists against all odds, reminding us that, from the vantage of the crypt, the living are only present because the work of death is temporarily suspended, their life lent to them just as much and just as exceptionally as is the judge's.

The scene of death depends upon the equivalences of burial and articulation—the installation of a language of commemoration at the point of death—and so exhumation must involve an inarticulate work, the displacement of the language of commemoration. The voice of the crypt assumes the language of the living, the language that no longer commemorates, remembers, or articulates, the language that in its immediacy fails to keep one place and one time apart from another. While the judge speaks, we're told, "þer sprange in þe pepulle / In al þis worlde no worde, ne wakenyd no noice / Bot al as stille as þe ston stoden and listonde" (there arose in the people / No word in the world, nor did any noise awake) (217–19). It is as if the *vox* is a zero-sum game: there cannot be noise somewhere if there is a voice emerging out of noise somewhere else.[29]

The voice can be charged with meaning—like the judge's voice, which answers all of the questions that the tomb provokes—or it can verge on meaninglessness. Unable to interpret the inscription, the onlookers try mouthing the letters that they see: "all muset hit *to mouth* and quat hit mene shulde" (54). Deciphering takes place through the voice, and so the first action of the onlookers is to try to pronounce the words on the casket. But it is not clear whether doing this is a part of the exercise of recovering their meaning, or whether it is simply a puzzle that is corollary to the puzzle of their meaning. Is the voice the intelligible sign, or is the writing? Both possibilities appear in medieval grammatical theory: the voice is either the sign of a sign, or it is the fundamental expression, the instantiation, of meaning itself. But in the poem either possibility is beside the point, for speech collapses into a nonreferential and spiritless movement of musculature: a musing "to mouth." The failure of speech in the presence of the dead, as Robert Pogue Harrison points out, is also a failure of the "work of separation," which is accomplished by the translation of inarticulate ("irrelative") grief into an "objective or socially shared language of lament."[30] The inability to speak of the dead means that we will remain with them, unable to extricate ourselves from their implacable enigma.

This problem of utterance perhaps explains Erkenwald's ritual distance from the corpse after he returns to London from Barking. He returns to a crowd clamoring to tell him about the "meruayle," but rather than piece the story together from their narratives, he asks for quiet and retreats into his palace for the night, barring the door behind him. He spends the night reciting the liturgical hours, praying for some kind of insight to "kenne / þe mysterie of þis meruaile" (to understand the mystery of this marvel [125]). The poem's echo of *Piers Plowman*'s closing line at this point indicates that the bishop is praying for a solution to more than a mere historical mystery: like Conscience, he "grette after grace" (126), but unlike him Erkenwald receives an "ansuare of þe Holy Goste" (127). Yet it is not clear precisely what this answer is, and despite this clear declaration the events that follow are refracted by ambiguity. The answer comes, for instance, "& after-warde hit dawid" (and it dawned afterwards) (127): does this mean that the answer was revealed then, or that day dawned, or that revelation and daybreak are isomorphic? And Erkenwald's decision to go into the cathedral just then to say the mass of "Spiritus Domini" suggests that the mass itself might be the answer to his prayers. Yet it is most likely the mass appointed for the day and would have been said whether or not Erkenwald had prayed all night. This blurring of action and passivity is characteristic of the theological ambiguity of Erkenwald's later baptism of the corpse and helps to situate the conditions for the corpse's speech within liturgical rather than subjective time. Erkenwald's nightlong vigil delays his approach to the silent and exotic corpse until the morning of the Feast of Pentecost: "Spiritus Domini" is most likely named for the introit for the feast ("Spiritus Domini replevit orbem terrarum: et hoc quod continet omnia"), which celebrates the gift of universal language to the apostles.[31] Erkenwald's initial isolation from the corpse, then, enables him to approach it on the most auspicious day on the liturgical calendar to address a body marked with a language from outside Christendom.

Although divine intervention inspires intelligible speech at the tomb, the resolutely enigmatic inscription *on* the tomb reminds us that language in general can remain meaningless even while still recognizable *as* language. In a small way, the poem has already demonstrated this, in part of the opening series of pagan names that were translated when Augustine arrived in England.[32] Most of them are determined by alliteration ("Jubiter & Jono to Jhesu oþer to James" [22]) or by actual, historical conversions ("Þe Synagoge of þe Sonne was sett [dedicated] to oure Lady" [21]). But the poem turns suddenly vague and abstract when it describes the conversion of St. Paul's itself. It merely says that a "maghty deuel" possessed the "mynster," and that the "title of the temple bitan [given] was his name" (28). Elsewhere the poem gives us the specific names of sites, but in the case of London all we get are the names of names: "deuel," "mynster," even just "name" and "title." It may not be accidental that a writer with this poet's virtuosity begins this account of renaming with names that happen to be linked by alliteration. The poem's beginning demonstrates the referential power of alliterative poetry itself, the principle that its language determines the coherence of the larger world. But the non-naming of St. Paul's is also a mirror image of the unintelligibility of the tomb's inscription. All we can see here at the poem's beginning is the process of imposition, not the meaning that is conferred by a name. The judge, the inscription on his tomb, and St. Paul's are, so to speak, coterminous: they refer to something, but the poem shows us only the most general sign of the presence of language. These non-names, the names of something unnamed, are, I will suggest, an analog of the way in which death is and is not present in the poem.

To imagine history, as the English Middle Ages did, as a series of translations from one place to another (Troy to London) or of cultural imperatives (the *translatio studii* and *translatio imperii*) is also to imagine it as a series of emptied receptacles, a series of graves, a London founded "in memoriam Troie prius destructe," as a London fishmonger's book has it.[33] But this mortuary historiography also shapes the form of the narratives that rise out of it. How else are we to understand the reaction of the crowd in St. Paul's to the voice from the crypt, the silence that comes from beyond the grave irrupting in the midst of this noisiest of cities, the language that brings death with it? What is at stake in memorializing history, this poem suggests, is the very work of memory, not its capacity to conserve but its very genesis out of death. The memory itself is a kind of tomb, a receptacle, a crypt: the *conditorium* of classical mnemotechnics and familial burial, the nightlike chasm (*nächtlichen Schacht*) that Hegel describes. Just as in the tomb, a thing in this chasm no longer has existence (*nicht mehr existend*), yet—and because of this—is stored in an interminable night of infinitely (*unendlich*) many images and representations, memories without memorialization, a death without end.[34]

The writing of history emerges out of an archive already formed, a writing that lies beyond our comprehension, or at least beyond our memories. This is what *St. Erkenwald* confronts us with: the provocation of writing that fails precisely because writing, from its origin, lies beyond memory. In Plato's famous account of the invention of writing, the Egyptian God Amun warns its inventor, Thoth, whose other responsibility is the care of the dead, that writing will only impair the memory, encouraging its users to trust in "external characters" that are not "part of themselves."[35] Writing takes the place of memory, inscribing, literally impressing, its registration elsewhere than the waxlike interior tablets of remembrance.[36] This famous story also thematizes the opposition of writing and memory as the very attempt to master life and death: Amun's opposition to writing can also be seen as a resistance to the disclosure, the public scrutiny and objectivity, that writing brings with it. The hiddenness of the self, the mysterious source of life from within, the breath that animates: all of these things associated with "Amon-Min," "the Hidden One" in Egyptian, with *pneuma*, breath, in Greek, are obliterated by Thoth, the technologist of death and writing, the memorialist.[37] The alternative to the voice that speaks from a concealed, inward site, the voice from the crypt, is the impression always made elsewhere, the impression that renders memory inaccessible. *Erkenwald*'s persistent problem, too, hinges on writing made elsewhere, a writing that remains beyond the reach of recollection, and ultimately beyond memory.

St. Paul's itself was something of an archival machine, a role that the frantic searches through cathedral records for the judge's identity at the beginning of the poem captures. Discovered at the very "fundement" of the cathedral that is being rebuilt, the tomb of the judge appears at the point from which the 741 years since the "prima fundacione" of the cathedral is measured in the 1346 sign. Yet at the very point of its historical intelligibility the tomb troubles the very possibility that history and memory can *remain* intelligible. The first activity around the rediscovered tomb involves a massive attempt to recuperate the meaning of the text on the "bordure enbelicit wyt bry3t golde lettres" (51). But the attempt fails utterly:

> . . . roynyshe were þe resones þat þer on row stoden.
> Fulle verray were þe vigures þer auisyde hom mony,
> Bot alle muset hit to mouthe and quat hit mene shulde:
> Mony clerkes in þat clos wyt crounes ful brode
> Þer besiet hom a-boute no3t to brynge hom in wordes. (52–56)

> [Riddling were the words that stood there in rows.
> Very clear were the letters where the people examined them,
> But everyone mused over them and their meaning with their mouths:
> Many clerks in the close with tonsures
> Busied themselves to no end to put them into words.]

Despite the clear, "verray" legibility of the writing, it remains unintelligible, "roynyshe," incapable of bearing the inspiration of the living, an enigma at the point of articulation that can only be "muset," pondered, in the mouth itself, as a living utterance. The inscription can be articulated only as the symptom of a mystery, in words that will simply never equate with the thing itself. Whatever *voces* lie locked in the inscription's mysterious *verbi* will never again become the living utterances it once recorded.

The very signs of sumptuous wealth framing the judge's body provoke the quest to understand who he was, to make sense of both his life and his death. He is both a symbolic surplus, something whose life obviously meant something, but that the people "my3t not come to knowe" (74), and a literal surplus, a conflation seen especially in the inscrutable, "roynyshe," "bright golde lettres" of the inscription and the "rialle wedes," the excessive signs of rule (the crown "ful riche" and scepter), with which the primitive mourners bedeck the body. Indeed, the judge's death is "menyd" (247), lamented, remembered, and signified all at once, by making his body into not just a remnant of life, but a figure of its surplus: "to bounty [honor] my body thai buried in golde" (248), and a life that has become a surplus, achieving precisely nothing, as he says, because the problem of death has not been worked out: "Quat wan we wyt oure wele-dede that wroghtyn ay ri3t, / Quen we are

dampnyd dulfully" (What does it matter what we accomplished with our
good deeds when we always did right / When we are sorrowfully damned
[301–2]). But the sumptuousness of the judge's remains insists that there is
still something to be accounted for, some kind of value that remains uncorrupted by the passage of time and the intervention of death, some kind of
work that goes on despite us.

The signs that surround the judge commemorate his death, and they
are signs of death themselves. They are remnants that continue to do the
work of death, a work that the poem compares insistently to the work of
registration undertaken on a massive scale by the entire enterprise of this
cathedral at the center of civic life. The chamber in which the judge lies
is an archaeological figure of elapsed time, buried at the deepest levels of
the "New Work" that is being done on the cathedral. Yet the tomb, the
body in it, and the clothes in which it is dressed are "wemles," "freshe,"
"unchaungit," untrammeled by time, sumptuous and strange despite their
uncanny provenance (85–95). The public response to this discovery is expressed in terms of a temporal crisis, an acknowledgment that the economy
of time is breaking down: "Hit myȝte not be bot suche a mon in mynde
stode longe" (97). His sumptuous appearance suggests that he should have
persisted in the memory, in, at the very least, the private memorials that are
one form of death work. On the other hand, however, the evident vitality
of the body suggests that it simply has not been dead long enough for it to
have become the subject of the memorial work of death. "He lyes doluen
þus depe hit is a derfe wonder / Bot summe segge couthe say þat he hym
sene hade" (He lies buried so deep it is a great wonder / That no-one can say
that he was seen alive [99–100]). We have seen already, and see elsewhere
in the poem, that memory founders in response to this problem because it
doesn't begin to grasp the time that has elapsed. And we see rapidly the failure of documents of widely varying legibility and authority to register the
time, even to convey the presence of death, especially the illegible words
found from the remote pagan past, that make up the inscription above the
judge's tomb, and which signify nothing other in this poem than the inability of writing itself to conquer time, to make it articulate. The quest
to articulate time, to find out just how long the judge has been there, leads
the entire cathedral chapter to search through virtually every form of documentary legitimation: every title, token, "breuet," "boke," "martilage,"
"librarie," and "cronicle" (154–56). These are all responses to the problem
posed by the presence of this body, and all are seen conspicuously to fail.
This failure indicts the intelligibility of the many times commemorated in
St. Paul's. What is troubling in this poem, however, is not the description of

an archival project that fails miserably—although for historians that does seem alarmingly plausible—but the question of how this remainder of the past will affect the kinds of work that continue in the present, the question of whether any work, in fact, can be terminable.

But it is the very inviolability of the law under the judge that, while indeed saving him, provokes the necessity of interpretation in *St. Erkenwald*. More precisely, it is the inviolability of the body, its interminable condition in the face of death, that makes the writing that accompanies it, and the enigmatic chronographia he utters, a matter of compelling interest. The body is a condensation of what can't be completed or fully accounted for in the earthly economy. This is what St. Paul's vast historiographical resources have failed to do: they have failed to make sense of this body that persists, or to account for the time in which it has done its long work of death. And, needless to say, this is what the economy of the body's own time has failed to do. The body is committed to the grave as a figure of both the significance of death and of surplus: when he died, says the judge, "alle mened my dethe," lamenting it, but also *menyng* it, signifying and remembering it by covering the body in the surplus of the world, using a word that elsewhere in the poem means "remembrance" and "significance."

The body itself answers the question of its history with another literally cryptic registration. It has lain in the crypt for a time beyond calculation: "the lengthe . . . is a lewid date, to meche to any mon to make of a nombre" (206). Although the time cannot be determined, it can, as the judge goes on to prove, literally be made into a number: "After that Brutus þis burghe [town] had buggid on fyrste [first built], / Noȝt bot fife hundred ȝere þer aghtene wontyd / Before þat kynned [was conceived] ȝour Criste by Cristen acounte / A þousande ȝere and þritty mo and yet threnen aght" (207–10). This cryptic figure elicits from us an awareness of the complex forms of time that establish this place as significant, an awareness that the work of both Brutus and Christ is measured here in the place where the living and the dead converge—that is, in this "lewd" poem and in the learned and sacred spaces of the cathedral. That the poet can make a "nombre" of what is incalculable suggests the capacity of writing for commemoration even while it keeps us at an ineffable distance from the scene of death.

At least two of the epitaphs from tombs in the vicinity of Erkenwald's shrine remind us that the commemoration of death, the inscribed memory of what lies hidden from the world, can only take place at a remove. Commemoration is the mirror of our registration of death rather than our incorporation of it in ourselves, our experience of it. The most significant of these tombs belonged to Roger Niger, the bishop who was actually responsible for the building of the New Work in the thirteenth century. The epitaph on his tomb, which stood near the pulpit on the north side of the choir, noted that he was buried in the year "M. bis C, quarter X."[38] And one of Ralph's successors, Henry of Wingham, who died in 1262, occupied a tomb on the other side of the choir, with an epitaph that placed his death in the year "M. sexagint. bis V, quoq. bis C."[39] The cryptic nature of death is mimetically recorded in such enigmatic, riddling chronographies, and in unravelling them the reader inevitably imitates the complexities of the work of times past and times to come, a kind of riddling *contemplatio* that draws together the times of the living and of the dead. More superficially, these epitaphs figuratively conceal, bury, the time to which they refer under their cryptic integuments. Such ingenuity is precisely the mark of rhetorical pedagogy in the late Middle Ages, the *aenigma* that was a species of trope, and which appeared in various forms in the kinds of manuscripts that circulated widely at the clerical level. One such form of *ornate loqui*, of the *vario et extraneo modo loqui*, is precisely the kind that we see demonstrated on these tombs: "aliquando littera dat representare certum signatum ut puta numerum vel huiusmodi. Ut est hec littera *l*, id est 'quinquaginta,' et *v*, id est 'quinque,' et *x*, id est 'decem,' et huiusmodi."[40] One riddle, indeed, concerns exactly the kind of enigma that these epitaphs do, asking us to compute the span of a life and death: "Questio est quot annis vixit puer ille, qui si vixisset quantum vixit et iterum tantum et dimidium tanti et dimidium dimidii C annos complevisset."[41] This rhetoric of occultation helped to produce, as Andrew Galloway argues, "particular intellectual communities" through the improving "pley" that they offer, of the kind, as Galloway points out, *Piers Plowman* describes in the body of clerks that "solacen hym som time . . . þe parfiter to ben."[42] But the function of riddles is precisely to occult, to hide and bury, and the unraveling of them is, in a sense, the social accident that knits together such communities. Indeed, the very function of cryptic writing may be to conceal the arbitrariness, the *cautelae*, of social relations, the enigmatic, interminable soul hidden beneath the sign.

The circumstances in which the judge's tomb is found, the context for the appearance of this enigmatic text, dramatize the very notion that cryptic writing conceals and discloses the social relations immanent in the scene of death. The discovery of the tomb causes the interruption of the very work that groups together the laborers of London, who move together through the streets of the city to the cathedral to see the tomb, like the "Laddes" who "laften hor werke and lepen thiderwardes, / ronnen radly in route wyt ryngande noyce" (61–62). This identification of labor with public utterance ("ryngand noyce") is one that the poem encourages, even insists on, with its unusually concrete description of labor at the beginning of the poem, a passage that announces the discovery by workmen of this liminal body lying at the foundation of their own work.

The ways in which the poem registers and consolidates London social relations have been observed by a number of commentators.[43] But the division into groups by labor happens before the body is discovered and indeed leads directly to its discovery: "Mony a mery mason was made ther to werke, / Harde stones for to hewe wyt eggit toles, / Mony grubber in grete the grounde for to seche / That the fundement on fyrst shuld the fote halde. / And as thai makkyde and mynyde a meruayle thai founden" (39–43). There is a kind of incoherence in their actions in the first place: they are making something yet also creating a void—*mining*, a word that refers primarily to the undermining of walls in a siege. After the discovery of the tomb, the crowd draws out a further incoherence, savoring the strangeness of the inscription on the tongue and lips as they "muset hit with mouth" (54), a secular version of the contemplative injunction to taste and see.

The doctrinal mystery that lurks behind this is how this can have happened: how could someone who had no knowledge of Christ be saved? It is also a question of justice: how is this kind of unwitting salvation fair to those, like everyone clustered around the cathedral, who have labored to observe the twofold law of Christianity? The question is hardly unique to *Erkenwald*. Yet *Erkenwald* is unique (with the possible exception of *Piers Plowman*) in providing an answer that can be read in multiple ways. The point of the salvation of the judge is not that the theological problem can be answered, but that it constitutes a continuing mystery, a problem that one can continue to muse over. Yet it is fundamentally, from the perspective of pastoral theology and the salvation of one's own soul, an unproductive kind of curiosity.

This is perhaps the poem's greatest irony: that it encourages its readers to speculate about almost every detail, yet in doing so distracts them from the fundamental point: that one should work out one's own salvation, not worry about that of others, and how grace may or may not be operative in them. It is the basic lesson of the parable of the vineyard: as long as we are concerned with equity in an economic *and theological* sense, we will not understand it.

The historical layers that the workers plumb to uncover the pagan judge's body encourage us to think about the events of the poem in terms of salvation history, the relation between the deep history of the city and the gradual unfolding of theological revelation. The attribution of episodes of Erkenwald's own life and death to the action of uncovering the pagan judge is another kind of distraction. It serves precisely to distance Erkenwald from actions that ought to emanate uniquely from him. This is not to say that we should think of the judge's salvation as the effect of Erkenwald's intervention; the poem is quite clear that it is a divine work. From a literary standpoint, this gives Erkenwald the character of a cardboard figure, someone to whom and through whom things just happen. Even the tears of Erkenwald seem to be merely instrumental: they are the means by which the judge is baptized without undergoing baptism in its formal and ritual expression. Most readings of the poem treat these tears as the poetic liberty that the poem takes: the metonymy of a teardrop that represents the sacrament of baptism by water.[44]

But this is a misreading on the same order as forgetting that the narrative that surrounds the discovery of the judge is ultimately a layer of Erkenwald's own life and death. We tend to think about how Erkenwald's tears might save the judge, not what the tears might tell us about Erkenwald's own investment in the scene. The underlying account of Gregory's salvation of Trajan emphasizes the desperation of Gregory's tears: "Since Gregory did not know what to do to comfort the soul of this man who brought the words of Christ to his mind, he went to St Peter's Church and wept floods of tears, as was his custom, until he gained at last by divine revelation the assurance this his prayers were answered."[45] But *Erkenwald*'s version of this event recounts instead what is happening to the judge's soul in the "bapteme" that Erkenwald has effected (330).

Yet why is the judge's exposition of his own baptism as detailed as it is, if the reason he had not already been saved was his ignorance of the specifics of Christian salvation? It may help to explain the theological resolution of the poem. But it may also be detailed because the pastoral theology that underlies this event is an historical artifact that is likely to have been largely forgotten by the time the poem was written in the late fourteenth century. Unlike the forgetting of the pagan judge's identity, however, this forgetting does not go back as far as the classical era, just to the late Saxon period. The account of Gregory saving Trajan with his tears was not written until over a hundred years after Gregory supposedly did it, and six hundred years after Trajan lived, by a monk in the monastery at Whitby. The baptism of Trajan by Gregory's tears is an Anglo-Saxon invention: the notion of a baptism by tears is a distinctive part of Anglo-Saxon penitential theology that does not seem to have been otherwise current in the fourteenth century. The poem's inclusion of this archaic feature of contrition—that one's tears in repentance are a kind of second baptism—clearly refers to a moment when repentance was undertaken late in life, and perhaps only once. The baptism by tears, then, clearly precedes the Fourth Lateran Council's encouragement of annual confession in 1215 and constitutes one of the poem's more extraordinary examples of its subtle observance of historical relativism.

The point is not that we're Erkenwald, praying over the apparently insuperable gap between Christianity and paganism, past and present, but that we're praying that the corpse in the crypt not be ours. The crypt does not signify the alterity of a long-dead culture but rather reflects back on the observers their own contemporary moment: they are not dead but dying, and ought to be performing their own contrition before it is too late.

PART III

Archive

CHAPTER TEN

Lydgate's Exquisite Corpus

It was a crime to leave hidden among the dead and useless, what would
keep the living alive.
—Theodoric

In the last several chapters I have been discussing poems that think about
death as a kind of puzzle that cannot really be solved in a poem. In these
next three chapters I will be discussing poems that imagine either that other
poems or an ideal body of poetry might contain the answer to this puzzle.
These poems imagine that the answer to death lies not sealed in a crypt, but
is set out in legible and intelligible orders of knowledge—in an ideal archive.

I will begin with Lydgate and Hoccleve, for whom Chaucer's work is a
vital archive. His art and his death are imagined in terms of the finitude that
he failed to achieve by dying and leaving his poetic project incomplete.[1] To
revert to Adorno's terms, Chaucer is the spirit that haunts the work that
follows him. To a large degree, Hoccleve and Lydgate are responding to the
notion of incompleteness itself in Chaucer's work, not necessarily to the
incompletion of *The Canterbury Tales*, *The House of Fame*, or "The Monk's
Tale"—an incompletion that, as I have argued, is expressed most extensively under the rubric of tragedy. I will turn, therefore, to Lydgate's own
extensive meditations on tragedy both as an extension of Chaucer's work
and as a synecdoche for Lydgate's own poetic project. Lydgate's definition of
tragedy includes one very important difference from Chaucer's: he knows
that it is performed, and is therefore resolved in and by the present.[2] This
difference, I will suggest, illustrates not just a shift in the mode of tragedy,
but a shift in the alignment of literature with the world itself.

Lydgate describes tragedy as a mute performance by actors in front of a
poet, who stands in a pulpit reading to the audience. This information comes

from the *Troy Book* (2.860–72), but Lydgate's description also invokes the famous portrait of Chaucer standing in a pulpit before Richard II's court, reading his great tragedy of *Troilus*.[3] The scene of tragedy for Lydgate is also the scene of an immense founding authority: the tragedies of Troy, he tells us in the *Troy Book*, were enacted at a time of year that obviously echoes the time of year when *The Canterbury Tales* begin: in April and May, when "flouris fresche" come forth and birds sing "with lust supprised of þe somer sonne" (2.919–20). And in case the significance of this scene is not clear, he finishes his description with the non sequitur that Priamus began the "ryyt of tragedies olde" (2.924). The institution of tragedy, for Lydgate, is bound up with the immediacy of declamation before a court (as with Chaucer's portrait), the authorial initiative that Chaucer's greatest work represents for him, the invention of a cultural form in a time and place that is also the primal scene of national and civic historiography for the English Middle Ages, and the inception of one of the "payens corsed olde rites" that Chaucer will seemingly condemn at the end of *Troilus and Criseyde*, that little "tragedie" (V.1849, V.1786).[4]

The complex associations that tragedy triggers for Lydgate highlight its very different memorial function in his work. Rather than a genre that belongs to a quirky and wealthy monk, who apparently needs to define tragedies before he can recite them and who keeps them privately in his "celle," tragedy in Lydgate is both an embodied practice and the ritual that institutes communal memory. The poet reciting a tragedy rehearses the "noble dedis, þat wer historial, / Of kynges, princes for a memorial" (2.868–69) and their catastrophic aftermath while standing in his pulpit "With dedly face al devoide of blood, / Singinge his dites, with muses al to-rent" (2.898–99). As he does in the prologue to *Siege of Thebes*, his continuation of *The Canterbury Tales*, Lydgate places himself in the middle of the narrative performance. The narrator is a part of the medium of the text, a bodily extension of the story. That is, the poet implicates himself in the poem; it is his own story, in part, that is being narrated, his own torment and grief, his own sense of catastrophic loss. This involvement is the most obvious difference between Lydgate's notion of tragedy and the Monk's relatively bloodless, detached version. While "The Monk's Tale" narrates the fall of the great in chronological order, it is the pure didacticism of the recurring trajectory in each portrait that demands the attention of the audience, not history or literary genealogy itself.

The discursive focus of "The Monk's Tale" is the repetition of the same event in history, which paradoxically is intended, in its original Boethian form, to urge detachment from the very particulars that history narrates, the mere stuff of *temporalia*. Lydgate's idea of tragedy, on the other hand, focuses on the work of commemoration, and in a way virtually antithetical to the Monk's lachrymose conception of history. It is "historial," after all, and the first half of his description of it is a list of the great deeds that tragedy appropriately memorializes. Tragedy in Troy is specifically the work of remembrance, even the remembrance of its own corpus: "whilom þus was halwed the memorie / Of tragedies" (2.860–61). This strange glitch, in which the practice of commemorating itself has to be commemorated in order to work, is a clue to the importance of the impulse behind Lydgate's conception of tragedy: it is important because it narrates the necessity of the archive. In one sense, this archive is the treasury of stories from which he draws, as he does with his lengthy work *The Fall of Princes*, a long poem drawn (like part of "The Monk's Tale") from the archive of Boccaccio's *De casibus virorum illustrium*.[5]

Just as he does in the *Troy Book*, Lydgate uses the prologues to each book as a site to consider the larger questions that the book raises. In several of them he speculates that the importance of the *De casibus* material he is translating, the succession of tragedies, is that it is important as material, not necessarily as ethical precept. Yet he recognizes an important principle behind the selections that Boccaccio made: he didn't record just any old chronicle or history—only those that were "notable, / Auctorised, famous and comendable" (1.153–54).[6] Tragedies are selected because they are important for the present, and because they help to shape it. The verb "auctorised" here is significant: it implies both narratives that bear the stamp of historical veridicality and, more pointedly, those that bear the stamp of an *auctor*.

Yet, although Lydgate's poetry is shot through with the hero-worship of the poet Chaucer, Lydgate does not imagine himself exactly as an author. His self-deprecation is almost a structural element of his writing and echoes a clear concern about whether he really can be considered an *auctor*. His envoy to Gloucester at the end of *The Fall of Princes* apologizes for implicitly comparing himself to Chaucer by undertaking a large body of *De casibus* tragedies. But there is a greater underlying difference between Lydgate's and Chaucer's archives. In "The Knight's Tale" Chaucer undermines the authority of the very archive from which the tale is drawn, Boccaccio's *Teseida*. Whereas Boccaccio describes at length the fate of Arcita's soul after he dies, Chaucer conspicuously omits it. His Knight calls attention to the very archive that Chaucer has abridged and compares the archivist's work to the theologian's (and possibly the seer's): he says he is "no divinistre; / Of soules fynde I nat in this register" (I.2811–12). In other words, Chaucer deliberately makes the archive the site of speculation and eschatological mystery—in other words, a crypt.

Lydgate, on the other hand, finds everything in the archive: he not only assigns the impetus for the project to Gloucester, he lapses into the language of the charter to justify his role: he was born in Lydgate, he says, which was "Be old[e] tyme a famous castel toun; / In Danys tyme it was bete doun, / Tyme whan Seynt Edmond, martir, mayde and kyng, / Was slayn at Oxne, be recoord of wrytyng" (9.3432–35). Lydgate frames his career using archival rather than biographical formulae, recording not his own assertion of his privileges but those that accrue to him because of his historical association with a place and time. Yet this place and time is deeply ambiguous: Lydgate's town is important because of something it no longer has, and that is how it is remembered. It is not clear when the castle in the town of Lydgate was destroyed, but Lydgate's placement of it at the time of St. Edmund's murder compares it to a death that began a long commemorative tradition. In short, Lydgate bends the event of death out of the imponderable and mysterious crypt in which the generation before his placed it into a lucid, if not always truthful or accurate, archive. He was, in fact, involved at the same time in a project that moved the archive out of the cryptic register of the past into the more public medium of the vernacular. While Lydgate was writing *The Fall of Princes* at the abbey of Bury St. Edmund's, Abbot Curteys commissioned him to translate some of the abbey's most important charters into English, which were recorded in one of the two great registers that Curteys produced during his abbacy.[7] Curteys's desire to have them translated into English indicates that he believed that the power of the archive derived, in some measure, from its accessibility. But Lydgate's decision to translate them into Chaucerian rhyme royal rather than into ordinary prose (and, ultimately, Curteys's choice of Lydgate for the job) suggests a more nuanced idea of what this accessibility signified: an archive that not only preserved the privileges of the abbey but also conveyed them in a form that was both vulgar (that is, in English) and monumental, in the stanzaic form with which Chaucer wrote most fully about his legacy at the end of *Troilus*.

Lydgate's self-representation, as well as his representation of what being a "poet" means, is more precisely that of an archivist. This is a role that is subordinate to his much more public role as the Lancastrian poet laureate, but one that nevertheless permeates every aspect of his writing. It is also shaped by the politics of Lancastrian England, although less obviously. Curteys's zeal for the archive was anything but anomalous in fifteenth-century England. The number, sophistication, and distribution of archival projects in monasteries and cathedrals throughout England increased sharply in the first half of the century.[8] Part of the reason for this was the increased need to assert ecclesiastical rights against a more and more powerful baronage, and it could be argued that Lydgate's choice of rhyme royal accomplishes this aim precisely by using a language that would have been both intelligible to, and ceremonially heightened for the benefit of, secular, nonclerical powers.[9] On the other hand, there is a great deal of evidence in Lydgate's poetry itself that the archive was the most stable platform for poetic posterity: at the end of *The Fall of Princes*, Fortune tells Boccaccio (who has been presented throughout the poem not just as Lydgate's ultimate source but as a registrar of events) that his name will be "registrid in the Hous off Fame"—a presumably more carefully kept archive than the one Chaucer describes in his *House of Fame*, with its melting writing surfaces and the arbitrary decisions of Fame. Yet the kind of continuity that the archive makes possible has nothing to do with bodily or personal continuity. Boccaccio's name is just a metonym for the work, as Boccaccio himself makes clear: "lest my labour deie nat nor apalle, / Of this book the title for to saue, / Among myn othir litil werkis alle, / With lettres large aboue vpon my graue / This bookis name shal in ston be graue" (6.225–29). The purpose of a tomb is no longer to protect the living from the dead, as with a crypt, but to preserve the only thing that can be kept from death: the writing that challenges finitude.

But the archive is the very index of finitude, of what has already happened and cannot be changed. This is its consolation; it helps to stabilize the meaning of death, fixing its moment in time and space. Two of the most important documentary compilations of the fifteenth century, the *Liber albus* of London and the registers of Abbott Curteys at Bury St. Edmunds, use the same rationale: to secure the future against the vicissitudes of memory by recording vital information.[10] The *Liber albus* says that one of the problems with human memory is that we simply do not live long enough to form useful memories. Finitude is what makes memory necessary, but it is also what makes it impossible as a hedge against finitude, for mortal memories die. Only a memory unobstructed by finitude is useful, but that is to admit that true memory is not mortal, that in becoming memory it transcends the conditions that hinder the usual formation of memories—in other words, death. But the prologue to the *Liber albus* is not simply making the point that inscription defeats time; as it says, even things that are written down will be forgotten. What will make the *Liber* effective is its archival system, arranging what has been unclassified and scattered throughout the city's miscellaneous collections of charters and rolls. At the same time, however, the compilers of this orderly, and therefore memorable, collection of records accomplish their objective by reinscribing the boundaries of finitude in the collection: it is only the "noteworthy" records that will be written down, not the many more that remained unregistered and uncalendared throughout the city.

William Curteys's register also suggests that memorialization in this archival sense is not an infinitely extended process, a mere prosthetic for memory. It depends upon a finitude beyond finitude: where oblivion has overtaken the important records of the past and individual memories have died, it can be overcome by a restriction in the vastness of the archive. The prologue to John Lydgate's charters says not that the original charters will be translated, but that what is being undertaken is "reducing" them to memory (reducens ad memoriam).[11] The word reductio is often used to describe what happens when you remember something, but it also has a particular, restricted sense. It implies a concentration of what is important in witnessing or recalling a past event: meditating on the passion involves "reducens ad memoriam"; John Gower uses the term in his glosses to the Confessio amantis to mean the contemplation of the moral lesson behind a tale—it means, in other words, what you are left with at the end, the termination and the telos, of an event: its distilled outcome. The phrase is used in at least one will in the mid-fifteenth century as a prelude to the postmortem allocation of the testator's goods.[12] What he "reduces" to memory as he executes the will are the temporal goods he was granted, which metaphorically become a treasury from which he "ordains and disposes" them principally for the purpose of endowing a collegiate foundation and chantry to commemorate his soul. Beneath this complex metaphorical transfer of goods that are "collected" (that is, also remembered, "collatis") is the basic concession that the prayer for the eternal soul is dependent upon the finite goods that can be remembered at that point (that is, either at the composition or at the probation of the will). A life amounts to—and in a sense is—this "reduction." What makes this semantic and metaphysical play even more poignant is a meditation on the way lives tend toward "non esse" the more they cling to "visibiliam essenciam" (186). Read strictly, it negates the devout wish that follows for an impressive and magnificent sepulcher. In a sense, the will more closely mirrors the ambivalence of a desire for infinitude than the sepulcher and chantry do, and it more faithfully records the logical and emotional bonds of finitude.

I am not suggesting that the archive offers a way out of finitude, but that it offers a way of imagining it, although a complex one. It appeals to us because it seems to transcend temporal vicissitude, yet it also confronts us with the irresolvable finitude of its presence. It can never be life itself. The fifteenth-century revision of *La morte d'Arthur* brilliantly reimagines this desire for life out of the archive. Since at least the twelfth century, when the phrase "rex quondam rex futurusque" was recorded on his tomb, Arthur's death suggested more than the mere cessation of *bios* or the termination of a kingdom. Yet the paradox of the epitaph does not really become a problem until the fifteenth century, when Malory pulled his *Morte d'Arthur* out of two (quite different) fourteenth-century poems, the *Stanzaic Morte* and the *Alliterative Morte*.[13] Despite their great differences in scope, scale, and history, both poems end with Arthur clearly dead, and with no evident hope of his return. The only hope of transcending finitude in those poems lies in the work of praying for Arthur's soul, an act that the archbishop of Canterbury undertakes in the *Alliterative Morte*, and that a hermit who was once the archbishop of Canterbury does in the *Stanzaic Morte*. The archive itself remains mysterious in the *Stanzaic Morte*: like the inscription on the tomb of Erkenwald, the real meaning of the inscription above Arthur's tomb remains unclear, an enigma that is not resolved. Yet this lack of resolution is very different from the lack of resolution at the end of Malory's *Morte*. In Malory and other fifteenth-century interventions, Arthur's death becomes a registered death.

It was only in the late fifteenth or early sixteenth century that someone added the phrase "rex futurusque" to the end of the manuscript of the *Alliterative Morte*, which Robert Thornton had included in his great mid-fifteenth-century collection. The paradox of Arthur's death arrives by a process of accretion in Thornton's archive of romances, but in Malory's narrative it is the final, interminable problem, and the first time that the problem is not definitively resolved. The story of Arthur's death becomes interminable after Malory, but securely within the domain of the archive.

Acknowledging that his sources suggest two endings for the life of Arthur—one in which he dies and is buried, and one in which he is nursed back to health on the Isle of Avalon—Malory simply concedes that he does not know what really happened. Yet he does that by appealing to the archive of Arthurian literature: "Thus of Arthur I fynde no more written in bokis that bene auctorysed, nothir more of the very sertaynte of hys dethe harde I never rede." The problem of Arthur is instructive; fifteenth-century texts grapple with the problem that on the one hand Arthur's death has not taken place, that the status of his death is enigmatic, but that on the other there is the local physical evidence at Glastonbury of the epitaph, which sounds definitive about the death. Rather than conceptualize the mysteriousness of Arthur's death, fifteenth-century accounts offer as much evidence from other sources as they can and at most express a preference for one of the possibilities.

Lydgate tends to imagine tragedy as an almost archival act, as the registration of significant deeds that end in death. In his prologue to *The Fall of Princes*, he complains that there are no muses to inspire his own work, now that Chaucer (the "cheff poete off Bretayne"; "of making souereyne"; "the "lodesterre" of "oure language" [I.247–52]) is dead. But in this passage Lydgate conflates the work's final cause—its theme of the "dedlie mortal chaunce" that Fortune inflicts on princes (I.238)—with its efficient cause: his own influences and inspiration. The greatest fall in the poem, at least so far, is that its inspiration has itself suffered the "dedlie mortal chaunce" of Fortune. There is even an intimation that to undertake such a work is to fall victim to the repetition compulsion: Chaucer, says Lydgate, the "fall of pryncis . . . dede also compleyne" (I.249). This citation is profoundly ambivalent, coming at this point of Lydgate's poem. It appears to refer to Chaucer's "Monk's Tale" and so would seem to be an appropriate model for this poem. But the citation comes in the midst of Lydgate's reminder that this poem is about the catastrophe that death brings to the agents of both political and poetic works, and so the catastrophe that confronts Lydgate at the outset is not simply that of losing a significant mentor, but that of discovering that the most suitable muse for the poem—at least the only one that survives—is the very catastrophe that seems to make it impossible to write.

And yet catastrophe can still be written: as Lydgate goes on to point out, not only Chaucer but also Boccaccio has written the "fall of pryncis" (I.270). The impossibility of writing about the catastrophe of death is contradicted by the body of evidence that survives it: those two works by Chaucer and Boccaccio. Had Lydgate stopped here, this might have been an elegant meditation on mortality and memory; but memory for Lydgate is rarely neat and tidy, and perhaps that is the real importance of what he does. He spends the next eighty-one lines (275–356) listing Chaucer's other works, a list that become one of the most important in establishing the definitive Chaucer canon. Yet the list begins with a spectacularly inaccurate entry, attributing *Troilus and Criseyde* to Chaucer's youth (it was written when Chaucer was in his forties), and calls it a translation of a seemingly nonexistent Lombard book called "Trophe," an especially strange mistake given that Lydgate was at that moment writing a poem based on a work by the very author of Chaucer's source for *Troilus*—Giovanni Boccaccio.[14] Lydgate's interpretation of the evidence that Chaucer wrote *Troilus* later in his life is revealing: he says that Chaucer renamed the poem before he died. In other words, the apparent anomalies in Lydgate's catalog can be explained away as archival restructuring, the revision of a crucial reference. Much of the catalog, indeed, includes incidental references that situate the works in time and place, rather than summarizing their contents: *A Treatise on the Astrolabe* was written for Chaucer's son "Lowis" (I.293); *The House of Fame* is referred to solely as "Dante in Inglissh" (303); *The Complaint of Mars* is not named but is described by the brooch that appears in it and by Ovid's authorship of the source (I.322–24); "The Tale of Melibee" is written in prose (346); and it refers to "many a fresh dite, / Compleytnis, baladis, rou[n]delis, [and] virelaies" (352–53). It is a list that is not so much concerned with assessing the qualitative contribution that Chaucer made to English—despite its avowed purpose—as it is with enumerating his works and establishing his rights of authorship to them, rights that extend in perpetuity: the list ends with Lydgate's request to pray for Chaucer's soul (I.357). The list is, in other words, the commemorative equivalent of the inscriptions that ran around the edge of brass portraits on tombs that urge onlookers to pray for the soul of the person commemorated, whose date of death and status or occupation are usually listed. Lydgate's model for literary affiliation is the archive rather than the library, celebrating and preserving information about the dead—the presence of other souls—rather than being a repository of information on how to save and preserve one's own soul, the essential function of the monastic library since Augustine's writing about education and Cassiodorus's *Institutiones*.[15]

When Lydgate imagines the place that his own work will occupy in literary history, he puts his thumb firmly on the "modesty" side of the modesty topos. He has inherited nothing from Homer or Seneca, he says, nor was he ever "acqueynted" with Virgil, Darius Phryges, Ovid, or Chaucer. According to the convention, the implication, if he had ended there, would have been that he does nevertheless belong in their company. But Lydgate looks away from literary tradition at just that point and toward the contemporary circumstances of this document's production. He wrote *The Fall of Princes* by "constreynt" (he was commissioned to do it by Humphrey, Duke of Gloucester), and repeatedly responds throughout the text to requests for particular narratives or conclusions that he says Gloucester has made.[16] In one of his *envois* to *The Fall of Princes* Lydgate underscores his tropes of modesty—he never lived on Cythera (Venus's island) or on Mount Parnassus—by citing his modest birth and conflating his Benedictine habit with the drab writing of records: he will "procede forth with whyte and blak" (9.3440) rather than in the rubricated and illuminated letters of true literature. He imagines himself not as a successor in the steps of Chaucer, Dante, and Virgil, but something more like an executed copy of a charter in a cartulary. He was born in the village of Lydgate, "Be old[e] tyme a famous castel toun; / In Danys tyme it was bete doun, / Tyme whan Seynt Edmond, martir, mayde and kyng, / Was slayn at Oxne, be recoord of wrytyng." That last phrase, "recoord of wrytyng," suggests that he places both himself and his own writing within the archive, not the library. He mentions that Boccaccio's book spans history from Adam to King John of France but describes more fully an archival discovery that he had recently made: "nat yoore agoon / I sawh remembryd the date of thylk[e] yeerys" since John had been taken prisoner at Poitiers, "toold and remembryd by the cronycleer."

In the end, Lydgate wrote three *envois* to Gloucester in the *Troy Book*, each worried about Gloucester's readiness for death and the durability of his own writing.[17] The successive *envois* suggest a fretful worry that the poem has not achieved its purpose, which may be purely pecuniary and petition-ary (he recycles the language of his "Letter to Gloucester" in one of the *envois*). Yet the *envois* situate Gloucester's patronage against the record of past deeds. Writing, says Lydgate, provides the authority by which one possesses temporal goods, and it will determine the amount of reward or punishment in the afterlife. Although the witty, abashed, and veiled assertions in these *envois* appear to be echoing conventional literary petitions (even Lydgate's own), they hint at a more important point. If this entire book is a mirror for princes, albeit one with an abyss behind it, it is aimed at establishing an art of rule for Gloucester, or the young Henry VI, to follow.[18] Yet much of what Lydgate suggests in his *envois* is not emulative but descriptive—it is literally writing that determines future action, not the prince: "As men disserve . . . . equite" (9.3573–76). Lydgate's role is not to serve as a *compilator* of various stories, but as an archivist who presides over records that determine the future of the prince: an *arche* in the original sense, a reserve from which one draws rule and from which one's authority begins.

This is a subtle but ultimately more powerful argument for the author-ity of his own work, which, as we have seen, Lydgate uses conventional literary tropes to undermine. The archive, not the library, offers the way for-ward for Lydgate: literature is the record of what is inscribed on the tomb of the dead. When Lydgate ventriloquizes Boccaccio worrying about his legacy near the middle of *The Fall of Princes*, Boccaccio imagines neither the steps of former poets nor the company of illustrious books, but the grave (his own) as the site of literary registration. Hoping that the name of his work will keep it alive, Boccaccio asks for it to be written on his tomb. Whereas in *St. Erkenwald* the grave contains meaning that escapes the inscription, for Boccaccio the grave is a vacancy that is a mere occasion for the inscrip-tion. It is not his body that will make the grave notable, but the record of his literary corpus—especially, perhaps solely, "of princis . . . the fall" (6.231). Literary history's body, for Lydgate, is like a cyborg designed by Escher, its corpse contained by the corpus at whose heart it lies—a corpus that is really, from the start, the only thing that needs to worry about finitude, because the finitude of the body is certain. I am not invoking the figure of the cyborg here casually, for, as we will see in the case of Hector's body, Lydgate imagines literary infinitude as an unsettling fusion of corporeal and mechanical systems. Less disturbing is Lydgate's fascination with the *Nachleben* of Chaucer, although it is perhaps the most important chest in the vast Lydgatian archive. Lydgate both helps to perpetuate Chaucer's literary influence and depends almost entirely on it for the construction of his own poetic enterprise, and some of Lydgate's most extended and original meditations on literary and personal finitude occur when he is thinking about Chaucer. But I do not mean to suggest that there is anything particularly stable or quiescent about the way in which Lydgate imagines Chaucer's finitude.

For one thing, Chaucer's finitude is not precisely what preoccupies Lydgate. Chaucer's death is really a figure of the impoverishment of the world, a singular devastation of its poetic and linguistic possibilities: "the welle is drie, with the lycoure swete / Both of Clye and of Caliopé."[19] Indeed, the world had already been impoverished, because it was Chaucer who invented the world whose loss Lydgate now laments: Chaucer was the "Flour of Poetes thorghout al breteyne . . . Of wel seyinge first in oure language."[20] Lydgate represents Chaucer as the avatar of two cultural extremes: as the inception of an enriched tradition and the termination of it. Chaucer is, in other words, the limit of language itself, the gauge simultaneously of its possibility and its impossibility.

Lydgate's vision of a post-Chaucerian poet's work is strangely passive: in *The Floure of Curtesy*, for example, he worries not that his ineptitude will spoil the poem, but that the words themselves will "asterte," spoiling the meter ("make it seme lame"). The startling non sequitur "Chaucer is deed" in the next line fails to analyze but exposes the reason behind his difficulties.[21] Lydgate's rhetoric of mourning (perhaps more precisely of melancholy, over the impoverishment of the world) laments the larger, and more essential, condition of poetics in general: to be produced out of an archive.

Lydgate's admiration of Chaucer has been compared to filial devotion,[22] yet I would like to argue here that his relationship to predecessor and model is an impersonal one, a relationship begun by and sustained in the Chaucerian archive.[23] As Thomas Prendergast has argued, Lydgate remains fixated throughout his career with the moment of Chaucer's death, and in many ways Lydgate's persistent evocation of it suggests a melancholic inability or unwillingness to leave the phenomenon of death behind.[24] As a result, Lydgate often represents Chaucer not necessarily as an author, but as an archivist himself. In the prologue to *Siege of Thebes*, Lydgate refers to Chaucer as the "Chief registrer of this pilgrimage," a striking imputation of passivity to the writer of the *Canterbury Tales*, and perhaps a deliberate antonym of the presiding figure of the Host in the *Tales*, whom the pilgrims describe not just as a "reportour" and judge, but also as their "governour."[25] Lydgate's reference to a "registrer" makes it clear that he is thinking about two things here: rule and writing. Lydgate is thinking about Chaucer's tales themselves as the contents of an archive rather than a library: the term *registrarius* at Bury St. Edmunds designated the official in charge of documents, as opposed to the *librarius*.[26] Lydgate's choice of *registrer* to describe Chaucer's role is a carefully considered one: the English Benedictine chapter required the assent of the entire abbatial community before the common seal could be used on any document, and it may have been registered in public.[27] Lydgate represents Chaucer, in other words, as a secular equivalent of the only monastic official whose writing was intertwined with the presence, and the consent, of the entire community. This particular association may have been triggered by the moment in the "General Prologue" of *The Canterbury Tales* when the assembly of pilgrims gives their common consent to the tale-telling competition that the Host proposes: "Our conseil was nat longe for to seche. Us . . . graunted hym withouten moore avys" (I.784–86). Lydgate imagines the *Tales*, then, as an archive: a collection of records of various human actions, but not organized, as in Chaucer, by the authority that governs them (i.e., the Host).

However, poetry also had a quite literal manifestation in the archives of Bury St. Edmunds. Lydgate wrote translations of the abbey's founding charters for one of the two great registers that Abbot Curteys had compiled in the 1440s, when Lydgate was writing *The Fall of Princes*. These poems suggest a way to understand what the archive, in turn, meant for Lydgate as an image of poetic succession and authority. His charter poems do not substantially alter the underlying information of the original charters, but they open them to more widespread scrutiny, in a form that updates, and finds a vernacular equivalent for, the formal Latin of the charters. In the *Siege of Thebes* Lydgate stages this accessibility quite literally, imagining himself riding up to Chaucer's pilgrims and joining the pilgrimage—and his tale is partially a further opening of the archive of Chaucerian narrative, giving us a history of Thebes, where the first real action of "The Knight's Tale" takes place.[28] If one is going to broaden the Chaucerian archive, then one does the opposite of "feyne thinges newe": one points out the presence of even older narrative records of secular history than Chaucer draws from directly (at least in *The Canterbury Tales,* though it could be argued that Lydgate's desire to expound so fully upon Theban history is also motivated by the tantalizing hints of it in *Troilus and Criseyde,* as well). Yet Lydgate's famous omission of Chaucer in his redescription of the Canterbury pilgrims also suggests an acknowledgment that the Chaucerian archive is closed to further supplementation by Chaucer's death; if *The Canterbury Tales* continue, they can no longer be a record of Chaucer's involvement with them.

But Chaucer's absence is also the foundational principle of the archive itself, its *arch*-beginning. Lydgate talks about the death of Chaucer in terms of rhetorical and poetic invention, a death that is itself one of the causes of Lydgate's writing. Because Chaucer died too soon, he says, "Gret cause have I and mater to compleyne / On Antropos and upon hir envie" (*Troy Book* 2.4694–95). In asking Saint Edmund to inspire him at the beginning of the lives of Saints Edmund and Fremund, Lydgate uses the rhyme "aureate" and "laureate," usually symptomatic of his "nostalgia for the golden age of the Ricardian court and its patronage of the Petrarchan laureate Chaucer."[29] Here, however, Lydgate prays for the capacity to write about martyrdom: "Send doun of grace thi licour aureate / Which enlumyneth these rethoriciens / To write of martirs ther passiouns laureat."[30] Lydgate's signature aureate style is here suffused with and prompted by death, but in this case the death of saints, whose merited grace will inspire, or at least illuminate, Lydgate's poetry.[31]

The ambivalent genesis of Lydgate's style out of death rests on the paradox that, on the one hand, poetry since Chaucer has become impossible, yet, on the other, Chaucer is the genius who makes English poetry possible. There is "no making to his equipolent" (*Troy Book* 2.4712)—and the best Lydgate can do is ransack the Chaucerian archive for "som goodly worde" that he can place with his own writing, although such a word would outshine his writing as a ruby does a ring of cheap metal. Yet at the same time Lydgate talks about his own writing's aspiring to the condition of art. When "we," he says, "wolde his [Chaucer's] stile counterfet / We may al day oure colour grynde and bete, / Tempere our azour and vermyloun" (*Troy Book* 2.4715–17). For Lydgate, what is most admirable about Chaucer is his style, particularly in the form of rhetorical tropes, or colors. Here he reifies these colors, as we will see he does for aureate style in general, making them the colors used to pick out illuminated capitals in a deluxe manuscript. Writing after the death of Chaucer is most palpably expressed in the poverty of the page, its lack of the colors that made the Chaucerian corpus an object of spectacular display.

Lydgate's animation of the purportedly dead Chaucerian style is symptomatic of the way he treats dead and dying bodies elsewhere. He returns repeatedly to figures that represent a lack of termination or the disruption of natural processes—a movement familiar from his project of keeping Chaucerian style alive while simultaneously acknowledging its death. He writes the lives of two saints, Alban and Edward, whose heads are reattached to their bodies after death; Edmund's head, which calls out all day to the people searching for it, demonstrates the miracle of speech that outlives death.[32] Conversely, as we will see, Lydgate's evocation elsewhere of the undisrupted continuity of the body's existence comes to represent his ambivalence about the very project of Chaucerian style. In broader terms, Lydgate's avoidance of closure becomes one of the signal features of his own style, most famously in the lengthy unfinished sentence that begins the *Siege of Thebes*.[33] These tendencies are interdependent, and they often appear at the same point in Lydgate's work. Perhaps the most spectacular example is his description of the death and archivization of Hector in the *Troy Book*.

At the instant of Hector's death in his long reworking of the thirteenth-century poet Guido delle Colonne's *Historia destructione Troiae*, Lydgate inserts a seventy-nine-line digression about the very narrative disruption he is embarking on, beginning by asking "how shal I procede / In the story . . ." (3.5423–24). Hector's death disrupts Lydgate's writing as much as it disrupts the polity of Troy (which is the only consequence of Hector's death Guido delle Colonne discusses in this scene), and it has consequences for the terms under which Lydgate's writing will continue. The Muses will no longer guide his "troubled pen," and so Niobe's tears will have to "reyne" into his pen to restore the narrative (3.5444 and 3.5460). As with his play on Chaucerian rhetorical color, Lydgate here emphasizes the materiality of what he is suggesting about the conditions of writing, about the medium in which one can resume the work of the story. It is virtually a Boethian moment, signaling the initiation in "wepynge," as Chaucer's *Boece* puts it, of an enterprise in which the writer is "constreyned to bygynnen vers of sorwful matere."[34] When Troilus dies in book 4, Lydgate says that even Boethius would be unable to lament effectively for him, and neither would Statius or Ovid (4.3008–37). In Lydgate's discursive universe, one disruption becomes the inception of another narrative. Yet there is a more fundamental disruption at the point of Hector's death. Lydgate writes as if he were initiating the epic project all over again, speculating about the proper form of invocation for this part of the *Troy Book*: "O who shal now help me to endyte, / Or unto whom shal I clepe or calle?" (3.5428–29). He rules the Muses out, chiefly because it is not suitable for them to "help in wo / Nor with maters that be with mournynge shent, / As tragedies" (3.5438–40). It is possible that, like Chaucer, Lydgate did not know that there was a Muse specifically for tragedy: Melpomene. But he seems to place tragedy outside the domain of the Muses because he imagines it as a fatal, morbid art whose very physicality represents a mortal affront to the body, threatening to cause the very symptoms it laments: he describes tragedies (or tragedians) as "al totore and rent, "compleynynge . . . with a ded visage" (3.5440–42), a term that suggests both the face of a dead person and the frozen mask of tragic spectacle.

He finds the Fates more suitable for the death of Hector, and the degree to which this death implicates his own poetic work is highlighted by his repetition of his earlier complaint about the death of Chaucer: Atropos has cut the thread of Hector's life "thurgh this grete envie" (3.5479). The calamity of Hector's death is like the calamity of the death of a language, or at least of a style. And so the question is what initiative Lydgate must take to restore the narrative, a narrative that begins again with the epic invocation of a host of possible alternatives to the muses: the Furies, Niobe, Ixion, Sisyphus, the Danaides, Tantalus, and the Fates. These are all figures that represent futility and termination: the Furies, responsible for punishing broken oaths; Ixion, the first slayer of a kinsman, punished by being bound to a fiery wheel; Sisyphus, never properly buried and punished by pushing a rock up a hill forever; the Danaides, who kill their husbands on their wedding night and are punished by carrying water for eternity in jugs riddled with holes; Tantalus, for whom food and water are always just out of reach; Niobe, who is punished by being turned to stone and weeping unceasingly for disrupting a Theban ceremony honoring Leto, the father of her children; and the Fates, who begin and end the lives of humans (3.5430–79). Yet the mortal figures here are also notable for what they continue, despite their fates, and their inability to stop desiring, thirsting, working, or crying links them to Lydgate's interrupted, yet interminable, project of mourning Hector. Lydgate uses the death of Hector as the occasion to imagine a project that will be interminable—not exactly his writing, but a project that will free writing from the disruptive and barren conditions of termination, which is to say, free it from the end to which Chaucer's death has brought style in the English language.

This project is embodied in the exquisite corpse of Hector. As a spectacular object in its own right, it shows up first in Guido delle Colonne. In Benoît de Sainte-Maure's twelfth-century *Roman de Troie* it is merely a corpse placed in extravagant surroundings for the Trojan obsequies (some thirteenth-century manuscript illustrations show the bier but not the corpse).[35] Guido, however, describes Hector's corpse being placed in the middle of the temple made for him, seated and clothed as if "in session," "quasi vivum," as if living. The means by which this is accomplished goes well beyond the technique of Soviet embalming, an occasional sprucing up of the waxworks. It requires an exocirculatory system in which "balsam" and "liquor" from a vessel of gold make their way through a hole in Hector's head, where it preserves his eyes, teeth, and hair, down his throat, through his chest, out to the ends of the fingers, and down to his feet, where there was another vessel full of "pure" balsam. Hector might seem lifelike, but it is difficult not to acknowledge the complexity and artificiality of the system that creates the illusion. To be precise, as Guido puts it, it is not Hector that seems alive, but rather his corpse: "cadauer hectoris quasi corpus viue."[36] Indeed, artifice turns a cadaver not merely into a corpse but a corpus, something that is either fully dead nor fully alive.

It is difficult not to see this as a description of the work that Lydgate imagines himself undertaking, so to speak, in the *Troy Book*. Unlike Lydgate's own "ded visage" in writing this tragic phase of the book, Hector's is preserved, or restored, "By sotil crafte, as he were lyvingye, / Of face and chere, & of quyk lokynge" (3.5657–58). The preservation of Hector's corpse here finally collapses the terms of life and death. In a kind of morbid doubling of the medieval theories of the emanation and intromission of light, the dead and the living watch each other, their "quyk lokynge" the property of both corpse and living corpus. Lydgate makes it clear that the appearance of life is a series of reflections of similitudes: "That it in sight be not founde horrible / But that it be lifly and visible, / To the eye, as be apparence, / Like as it were quyk in existence" (3.5595–98). Whereas Guido merely says that the elaborate piping in Hector's body "conserves" it, Lydgate emphasizes the "craft" involved in a series of concatenated adverbs and adjectives that don't appear in Guido: this work proceeds "by grete avys and subtylite"; the "liquor" pours through channels "lyneally," "direct," "by secre poris craftily" (3.6567–71). Perhaps more important, Lydgate is echoing the craft that matters most to him in his career—that of Chaucer, and especially the high craft of the opening sentence of the "General Prologue": this "liquor" that pours "into euery veyne / Of the cours the vertue dide atteyne" (3.5689–90). Hector's body is preserved by the same distillate of Chaucerian tradition that animates Lydgate's poetic corpus, and in that sense Hector's body should be an unproblematic figure for a poetic that animates the past and lives beyond the present. But the Chaucerian language itself is also a relic, a language reanimated precisely by Lydgate's devotion to it, as much a corpse as is the body of Hector.

But it is not Hector's body only that is the object of Priam's preservation initiatives. He has it set in an oratory, where a college of priests prays per-

petually for the safe passage of his soul to the gods. Their prayers might be
seen as another Lydgatian fantasy of the capacity of poetry to preserve and
to redeem from death, and in a sense they are. Their work, indeed, is enabled and guaranteed by Lydgate's attention to the archive: he describes
Priam's endowment of the oratory, "amortised / Perpetually" (3.5755–56)
with land, as if he were quoting from a foundation charter.[37] The oratory is a
metonym, as Robert Meyer-Lee has argued, for the vast work of "memorial"
that is the project of the entire *Troy Book*, and that work is securely rooted
at every point in the archive.[38] Yet at this precise point of the poem, where
Lydgate writes some of his most solidly reified accounts of the infinitude of
poetry, he also writes anxiously about the management of finitude. While
the priests in the oratory "knele, preie, and wake," he says, he is worried
about how to "caste fully an ende for to make, / Finally of my thridde boke"
(3.5758–59). Yet the manuscripts of Guido's text show no break here, and
Lydgate worries about an end that does not need to be there in the first
place. It is as if he recognizes a fundamental disparity between his work, on
the one hand, and the work of both the Trojan priests and of Guido, on the
other. His work is characterized by halting, in every sense of the word (a pun
that he deploys frequently). Its quest for perpetuity is utterly bound by its
own dialectic of finitude. As he says at the end of this third book, he must
now "return" to the Greeks, to "trace" their already-told story with a "dul
style" (3.5762–63): the leaden style that he is cursed with, and a pen/stylus
that is dulled by the bad infinity of its own repetitions.

But there is another discursive source for a sustaining, animated poetic
for Lydgate's fantasy of preserving Hector's body. Its underlying techniques
draw from the art of alchemy, an art that Lydgate imagines as having deep
affinities with his own. Above all, for Lydgate alchemy represents a way of
analyzing, and even arresting, death. Alchemists would argue that their work
is predicated on a profound respect for nature itself: one of the principal aims
of alchemy was to restore a fallen and decaying world to the purity of its
original condition: making gold, in other words, is less important than the
restoration of a golden age. And despite attempts to legislate alchemy out
of existence in the first years of the Lancastrian regime, it proliferated into
a figure of political legitimation and resistance, of humanist recovery, and,
most concretely, of a distinctively poetic idiom—a style—that was the expression of the regime's potential to restore a golden age.[39]

Opponents of alchemy argued that it collapsed the essential terms of
generation and corruption. In one of the many Pseudo-Lullian treatises, the
interlocutor objects that if alchemy were true, "then the nature of the world
would have no end, and the substance of the universe would have no quiet

since transmutation would go on unceasingly."[40] Citing Aristotle's treatise on generation and corruption as his authority, "Lull" argues that alchemy shows only that the world is not eternal. Yet it does so in a way that suggests a mode different from the convertibility, the reciprocity, of terminist logic or the circularity of the de Lisle psalter in which generation and corruption are reciprocally bound to each other. As "Lull" argues, the "nature of the transmutable metal is more at rest in the nature of that into which it is converted than it was in its own nature, for the nobler nature has the greater appetite to which the lesser submits."[41] Alchemy is imagined as a teleological and restorative project, a means of purifying mutable elements by purging their baser qualities to produce a more refined substance. As Nicholas Oresme's commentary on Aristotle's *De caelo* puts it, "the quintessence is more divine and precious because it is higher than the other elements."[42] Alchemists attempt to purge the unsound and impure qualities of things and restore them to an original soundness, just as, says one treatise, alchemical purification will refine even "aurum leprosum."[43] In many ways, as that last passage suggests, alchemy is an occasional adjunct of medicine. Another Pseudo-Lullian treatise concerns the "Art of Converting Mercury and Saturn into gold and of Conserving the Human Body."[44] Albertus Magnus says that "honest alchemists act toward metals just as physicians do toward their patients. The alchemist first cleans and purifies the old metal, just as a doctor employs emetics and diaphoretics to purge his patient."[45] Alchemists themselves made even stronger claims for the restorative powers of their products. Roger Bacon claimed that "alchemical gold, which contains the four elements in a better proportion than natural gold does, could restore the human body to a condition of elemental equality like that of Adam and Eve."[46] John of Rupescissa's *Liber de quintessentie* contains recipes for alchemical pharmaceutics, especially gold in suspension, known as *aurum potabile* (Chaucer's physician, too, knows that "gold in physik is a cordial" [I.445]).[47] A Middle English translation of the *Liber de quintessentie* claims that this *aurum potabile* was capable of "conseruacioun and restorynge of nature lost" and shows principally how to reduce "an oold feble euangelik man to the firste strengthe of yongthe."[48]

Yet the difficulty of describing, much less practicing, an art that undoes corruption (that is to say, time, as Aristotle defines it), by intensifying mutability and transmutability plagues much writing about alchemy. Alchemical discussions of variance and mutation tend to be the site of anxiety over the ability of language to signify both change and permanence adequately. The inability of alchemists to describe their practices calls into question their ability to effect real restorations. As Patterson has shown, "a synonym is offered to identify an unknown term but is then discovered to be itself in need of identification. . . . The explanation is at once confirmatory (it restates the truth again) and disruptive."[49] That is, the problem that structures the discourse of alchemy is precisely that of termination, in every sense of the word.

Lydgate's brilliant poetic innovation is to link the linguistic anxieties of alchemy with the recuperative promise of aureate language, a project that "regilds," renews, "converves," and transmutes the terms of English in the wake of Chaucer.[50] In his short "Letter to Gloucester," both Lydgate and his purse are ailing patients, the one in the last stages of old age, the other consumed by disease. The purse has fallen ill by what is intended to be a remedy: "A laxatif did hym so gret outrage, / Made hym slendre by a consumpcioun" (14–15). The "laxatif" is of course the outward flow of money that was intended to purge the purse of its too-liberal dispensing of money. This allusion to purging also signals the beginning of a trajectory that parallels the trajectory of alchemical treatises. Indeed, alchemical transformation will provide the antidote to the poem's consumptive flux, a flux that, by the poem's envoy, has affected the purse as much as the poem:

> O seely bille, why art thu nat ashamyd,
> So malapertly to shewe out thy constreynt?
> But pouert hath so nyh thy tonne attamyd
> That *nichil habet* is cause of thy compleynt. (49–52)

In a poem largely concerned with the consumption of health and money, this conclusion describes the poverty of the poem's own diction, the consumption and depletion of its linguistic capital. The degenerative flux that grips the poem's own language is stabilized by the same antidote that restores Lydgate and his purse to health: "briht plate enpreentyd with coignage" (56). The stamping of figures in a base metal is one metonymy of the poem's elliptical incorporation of the transmuting power of aureate language, a "holf-chongyd Latyne" that stamps new rhetorical figures in the base metal of English.[51] A clearer articulation of aureate language as an infusion of new linguistic capital is the description of the components of the remedy in the preceding stanza: "Gold is a cordial, gladdest confeccioun, /Ageyn etiques of oold consumpcioun, / Aurum potabile for folk ferre ronne in age, / In quynt-essence best restauracioun" (44–47). The economic properties of gold restore Lydgate's purse to health, and the medicinal properties of gold in suspension—prepared by these alchemical processes—restore Lydgate's health, and perhaps even restore him to what the *Liber de quintessentie* describes as the "firste strengthe of yongthe."

The "restorative" that is *aurum potabile* also provides a recovery from Lydgate's linguistic decrepitude. The stanza in which the description of *aurum potabile* appears is also, as it happens, a site of especially fecund aureate accumulation: "confeccioun," "consumpcioun," and "restauracioun," as well as "coignage," which completes every stanza, all of which are also the "cleer soun" of coinage that the last line tells us is the real "letuarye" (41–48; 63–64). The sound, of course, is primarily the ringing of coins for which Lydgate hopes. But in a sense that is actually truer to the literal meaning of the phrase, "coignage" describes the entire procedure that underlies the "new" poetics that post-Chaucerian writers were developing. It is precisely the coinage of English words based on Latinate precedents that distinguishes the sound of early fifteenth-century writing: the sound of new coinages transmuting the linguistic poverty of English into the golden—aureate—properties of Latinate diction.

Far from remedying the wavering metaphorical manifestations of the purse and its association with the poet, the *aurum potabile* actually marks the disappearance of the purse from the poem, and the poem's primary topic becomes its own sickness and poverty. In the *envoi* the poet chides the poem, the "sely bille," for "so malapertly" demonstrating its very "constraint." Yet "the drye tisyk [that] makith oold men ful feynt" is what warrants this brazenness—the dry tisik of Lydgate's poverty, the dry tisik of his own age, and—all too apertly—the dry tisik of a language grown old and impoverished (53). It's all of these deficiencies that the poem's *aurum potabile* "recurs," the medicinal cordial for "folk ferre ronne in age," the aureation that is itself *aurum potabile*, that reinvigorates the poem (39, 46). More precisely, it cures the poem of "consumption," of exhaustion, depletion, the presence of "nouthir licour nor moisture" (15, 34). It is hard, Lydgate says, to "likke hony out of a marbil ston," and a groat only gets you one drink (33). What is far better, because it not only lasts but is a "restauracioun," a "recure," "a mery soun," is "quynt-essence," the only remedy against the corruption of economy, language, and body.

Lydgate's yoking of writing to alchemy makes writing too a restorative enterprise, a project that claims to reconfigure the past in its original condition or primal nature. In the particular phenomenon of aureate diction, that project itself claims to have intrinsic value, a kind of gold in suspension, an "aureate licour" (*Fall of Princes*, Pr.461). Aureate diction, like alchemical discourse, is a technology of history. It is an instance of the "scriptural" enterprise that Michel de Certeau describes as the fundamental condition of writing history.[52] Like alchemy, aureate practice resists and indeed represses the tendency toward ceaseless mutation that its own power of transmutation provokes. At almost the precise center of the *Troy Book*, Lydgate inserts a précis of Chaucer's *Troilus and Criseyde* that acknowledges his own linguistic variance, his deviation from a source that nevertheless insistently overcodes his own account: "Lo! here the fyn off false felicite, / Lo! here the ende of worldly brotilnes, / of fleshly lust, lo! here thunstabilnes, / Lo! here the double variacioun / Of worldly blisse and transmutacioun!" (3.4224–28). What seems to be an account merely of worldly transmutation is actually a preface to one of Lydgate's many accounts of Chaucer's "gilding" of the English language: "The hoole story Chaucer kan yow telle . . . he owre englishe gilte with his sawes, / Rude and boistous firste be olde dawes, / That was ful far from al perfeccioun" (4234–39). Chaucer's operation of transmutation, of linguistic, alchemical "gilding," comprehends the "whole story" in a discursive and linguistic unity that contains the endless multiplicity and flux which Lydgate himself recognizes that he will not be able to contain.

And, in fact, when Lydgate returns to the narrative, he writes a long digression on the instability of women that ventriloquizes his own instability. Attempting to recover his thread, he apologizes as much for himself as for Criseyde: "I can noon other excusacioun, / But only kyndes transmutacioun" (3.4441–42). Lydgate's erratic digressions themselves exemplify the mutability of the matter that underlies the narrative, and the mutability of the linguistic surface of the narrative itself. Even Chaucer acknowledged both kinds of variance in his own writing: as he says in *Troilus and Criseyde*, "in forme of speche is chaunge within a thousand yeer" (II.22). And what Chaucer calls "this wrecched worldes transmutacioun" in *Fortune* is an adequate gloss for Lydgate's "kyndes transmutacioun." It also describes what Patterson calls the alchemist's "world of endless transmutation," figured in a long tradition of writing about mundane fortune and described in Aristotle's foundational physics texts.[53] In *Of Generation and Corruption*, for instance, Aristotle argues that "since the change caused by motion has been proved to be eternal, it necessarily follows . . . that generation goes on continuously."[54] "Kyndes transmutacioun" is the exclusive property of neither women nor poor and belated writers, as Lydgate claims, nor of alchemists, as Patterson implies. If "kyndes transmutacioun" is a subjective genitive, then it certainly refers to the larger changes of the natural world. But if it is read as an objective genitive, then it may refer to the transmutation of substance, the quintessential alchemical transformation. As I have suggested, alchemists attempt to distinguish their operations of transmutation from natural mutability. The alchemical quintessence, as one Middle English treatise claims, harnesses the natural powers of transmutation: "oure fifthe essencie is the instrument of alle vertues of thing transmutable

if thei be put in it, encressynge an hundred foold her worchingis."⁵⁵ The
Book of Quinte Essence, in fact, uses Lydgate's phrase to refer to the restorative alchemical transformation. Restoring a man to health, the *Book* says,
is "the hiȝeste maistrie that may be in transmutacioun of kynde."⁵⁶ Chaucer's transformative "gilding" of English is a mark of his "maistrie," the
termination of both "kyndes transmutacioun" and the change that is in the
form of speech.

Lydgate's anxieties about change in the world and change in language
are massively inscribed across the form of the *Troy Book*. This vast project
begins, so Lydgate tells us, at the moment Henry commissioned Lydgate to
write it: four o'clock in the afternoon on Monday, October 31, 1412. This
initial fixing of the vicissitude of time is a metonymic assertion of the validity of his project: it will "thoroȝ writing" refresh "newe" the acts of the past
(Pr.166). More precisely, it is the relation of the past, its archive, that writing itself conserves, a project that is a mere extension, an invention only in
the rhetorical sense, of *gesta* imagined already as writing. Without writing,
Lydgate argues, "age elles wolde haue slayn / By lenthe of yeris the noble
worthi fame / Of conquerours, and pleynly of her name / Fordymmed eke
the lettris aureate" (Pr.208–11). Writing preserves the past, but, more literally, writing preserves the past imagined as writing—particularly the kind of
writing that is Lydgate's high aureate style. There is a certain circularity to
this argument: time dims aureate colors, but aureate writing prevents colors
from dimming. However, Lydgate does not necessarily define aureate writing just as Latinate words imported into English. He faults Homer, Ovid,
and Virgil for concealing the truth "by false transumpcioun" (Pr.264) in the
very "sugred words" (Pr.277), the "fresche and gay" "dites" (Pr.276) and the
"traces" of Homer's style (Pr.308) that elsewhere are the marks of high aureate style. One reason for the apparent inconsistency is that Lydgate here is
praising chroniclers, not poets, and his single criterion is truth in history.⁵⁷
But, as Mary Flannery points out, Lydgate is actually saving poetry from
Guido delle Colonne's blanket condemnation of all poets: Lydgate blames
Homer, Ovid, and Virgil for their partiality, not their mode of writing.⁵⁸
Indeed, Lydgate's praise of Guido's truthfulness is really praise of his use of
amplificatio (which is really to say of Lydgate's style): "he enlumyneth . . .
This noble story with many fresche colour / Of rhetorik" (Pr.362–63). To be
precise, Lydgate does not praise Guido's rhetoric because it is better than
Homer's, Ovid's, or Virgil's; he praises it because it fills in what one of Guido's sources (supposedly Cornelius Nepos) leaves out "because he sette al
his entent / For to be brefe" (Pr.324–25). But Guido's account is not better
just because it is more verbally copious. It is better because it corrects Cor-

nelius's omission of references to time. Cornelius does not enumerate the length of the war, its "firste mevyng and cause original" (Pr.327), "who longest dide endure" at the siege (Pr.344), "how often thei metten in bataille" (Pr.346), "how many worthi loste ther his lyf" (Pr.347). Above all, he did not record the moments at which all of these lives were lost: "of her dethe he dateth nat the ȝere" (Pr.349). It is precisely because Cornelius's account fails to be an archive that it fails as poetry. It is "particular"—fragmentary, only part of the story, and therefore without "fruyte" (Pr.350–51).

What would make a poem about the Trojan War fruitful? What would a poem that is truly a mature account look like? It would have fully inhabited its time. Lydgate ends his translation with an enumeration of the cost of the Trojan War, including a precise tally of the numbers of deaths in the war and its duration (ten years, six months, and twelve days). That is the end of the "Latin," says Lydgate, and to add more would be "a maner of presumpcioun" (5.3365). To mark his scrupulous adherence to his sources, he dates the year in which he finishes, using two systems of archival indexing: 1420, the eighth year of Henry V's reign. To underscore the influence of a documentary model at this point, he says he has calculated this date by "just rekenyng and accountis clere" (5.3367). This, he says, is the "time complet of this translacioun." The elegant syntax of that last phrase, however, betrays the condensation of references to termination at this point of the poem. It primarily means "the time at which this translation was completed," but it also suggests "the completion of time," its fullness, its fruition.

The poem does not quite end here, however. The formal signals of the poem's ending do not merely mark or set the final limit of the poem: they also dilate it, pushing it further from the moment that could have been an ending. In other words, as Lydgate's elaborate calendar indicates, the poem's time begins to take over from secular time. The final fall of Troy is the end of Trojan history, but not the end of the poem. Time might be "complet," but the poem is not—especially because it throws itself into the future in two ways. Its recurrent fantasy of an aureate style that will be worthy of the topic, and of the poem's dedicatee, opens onto a final fantasy in which the recovery of a Chaucerian style will be part of a glorious Henrician "tyme fortunat, . . . the olde worlde called aureat" which "Resorte shal" (5.3399–3401).

Lydgate's endings also position themselves with minute calibrations. The last half line of the *Troy Book*—"thus an ende I make"—claims a finality that belies the many concluding lines inviting readers to amend and improve the book wherever they see deficiencies (5.3612). Even the end that Lydgate declares here depends upon the ongoing "supporte" of the poem's readers for this "litel boke lowly" (5.3611–12). This modesty trope both hides and enables the continued work of the poem, animated not just by being read but by being continued or, more precisely, by being improved. The trope is a piece of tape that remains stuck to Lydgate's hand when he tries to throw it away, but it turns out still to be useful for sticking other things together. Yet the gesture goes further than that: in the context of the many ways in which Henry's victory is a recuperation, restoration, and completion of England's political and linguistic past, the ongoing work of the poem's readers is a modest fulfillment of Henry's restoration of a golden age. The poem itself will (eventually) attain the kind of perfection that is now possible: nothing less than the "ful cessyng of deth and pestilence" (5.3438).

CHAPTER ELEVEN

"Dyynge and talking": Hoccleve's Loquacious Archive

My loneliness is not confirmed by death but broken by death.
—Emmanuel Levinas

The ending of a book and the ending of one's life so obviously "mean" each other that some fifteenth-century writers could hardly bear to finish, or to stop ending, their books. Making a "good end" to a book or poem is unavoidably a metonym of "a good death."[1] In this chapter and the next I shall discuss two of these writers, the poets Thomas Hoccleve and John Audelay. Both of them led retiring lives (Hoccleve as a Privy Seal clerk, Audelay as a chantry priest) and in their writing discovered a public communion that may have otherwise eluded them.[2]

The creation of books whose ending resonates almost unbearably with the approaching death of the writer has been regarded as something of a fifteenth-century specialty. In his landmark study of death and dying, Philippe Ariès argues that death in the fifteenth century increasingly became a private affair, in which "each man . . . discovered the secret of his own individuality."[3] At the end of this movement lies Heidegger's definition of death as one's "ownmost nonrelational possibility," an event that includes no other, no one else.[4] Yet the very idea of the individual forms within a matrix of relationality; similarly, death may become something that every person undertakes on his or her own, but as an event it also becomes public, released from the crypt of catastrophic and unthinkable death. Where Ariès suggested that death became represented as catastrophic in the fifteenth century, I am arguing here that death was already catastrophic, difficult to comprehend, before the Black Death. It is true that the massive public mortality of the Black Death did not immediately produce adequate forms of representing the devastating and inescapable nature of that kind of death, and as I have argued, representations of death in the immediate wake of the plague were troubled and enigmatic, posing a mystery that no one person or estate could resolve.

But in the second generation after the Black Death, representations of death began to appear that addressed the implication of a public in the movement of dying. Forms that had appeared in isolated places became widely popular and broadly disseminated, like the trope of three dead kings confronting three live kings, which was painted in a number of parish churches from the late thirteenth century on but became increasingly popular in the late fourteenth century, appearing on churches from Alton in Strattfordshire, to Belchamp Walter in Essex, to Belton in Suffolk, to Wickhampton in Norfolk. In 1424 in Paris the first representation of the *danse macabre* was painted in the charnel house of the Church of the Holy Innocents, based on a text that may have been by Jean Gerson. Its most distinctive feature is its inclusion of the broad distribution of estates, unlike the three living and three dead, which represent either aristocrats or kings, or *transi* tombs, which necessarily belonged to wealthy and prominent people.[5] The famous copy of the *danse macabre* at St. Paul's, with verses by John Lydgate, is deeply involved in the social and political life of fifteenth-century London.[6] Eamon Duffy argues that the propagation of images of death suggested not morbidity but a "practical and pragmatic sense of the continuing value of life and the social relations of the living."[7] In fifteenth-century France, the replacement of lists of former heroes in romances with the lists of tombs of writers marked not an irredeemable nostalgia but the possibility that literary death would become a form of reanimation among a living public. It's precisely when death seems to become "private," as Ariès argues, that its representations develop their most recognizable tropes. While not altogether denying the element of privacy that Ariès describes, I want instead to think about why the tension between this origin of the bourgeois private subject and its so-evident signs—a death that is, as Andrew Marvell will say, "fine and private"—on the one hand, and a death that follows a publicly acknowledged script, is a kind of lover's discourse.[8] The symptom of this discourse's failures is its compulsion to repeat figures of *ordinatio*, the flashing up before us of forms that anticipate conclusion and finitude, but that remain beyond the grasp of both writer and reader—what we could call the open book of death (not that it lies open, but that its promise to inscribe death has not yet been fulfilled and probably never will be).

Far from being a private event, in fifteenth-century England dying was represented as spectacular, an event that could become the focus of the public gaze. The ordinances for Richard Whittington's almshouse open with a frontispiece showing a dying Whittington surrounded by his physician, his priest, thirteen bedesmen, and his three executors.[9] Five manuscripts of Hoccleve's *Series* end with Lydgate's *danse macabre*, which describes the confrontation with death of every social estate.[10] That this might seem a natural conclusion to Hoccleve's intensely personal experience of contemplating one's own death asks modern readers to cross a considerable cultural distance. What we tend to think of a singular experience, something we have to go through alone, is often assumed, in the fifteenth century, to belong to public discourse.[11]

Hoccleve's *Series*, which at first appears to be a loosely connected collection of poems, is held together by an implicit concern with mortality, a concern that becomes increasingly explicit as Hoccleve develops the work. The first two poems, the "Compleinte" and the "Dialoge," describe how Hoccleve comes to write the *Series*, but the remaining three are substantially translations of other texts, like the penultimate poem, the "Ars vtillissima sciendi mori," an excerpt from book 2, chapter 2 of Suso's *Horologium sapientiae*.[12] There are two holograph manuscripts of the "Ars," Huntington Library MS744, where it appears alone, and Durham University Library M Cosin V.iii.9, where it appears as a part of the *Series* and where other parts refer to it.

Hoccleve probably modified the "Ars vtillissima" to fit the unfolding *Series* after he had translated it separately. But the rest of the *Series* anticipates it in its interests in mirrors of mortality and in death and dying. In what is probably the earlier holograph version of the "Ars," HM 744, the "Ars" appears at the end of the manuscript, along with two lines that do not appear in D: "After our song, our mirthe and our gladnesse / Heer folwith a lessoun of heuynesse."[13] In the margin is a gloss from Proverbs 14:12: "Salomon Extrema gaudii luctus occupat etc." The art of dying is formally and ethically the termination of Hoccleve's life and work, the end of the joy, such as it is, of his poetry. Although Hoccleve does not allude to it directly, the turn from joy to sorrow initiates another important work in the Chaucerian imaginary, Boethius's *Consolation of Philosophy*, which begins similarly in Chaucer's translation: "Allas! I wepynge, am constreyned to bringen vers of sorwful matere, that whilom in florysschyng studie made delitable ditees" (I met. 1).[14] Hoccleve's turn to a "lessoun of heuynesse" signals a transition from one kind of poetry to another, indeed from one set of formal and ethical possibilities to another, as well as the possibility that "ditees" might be adequate for, or not detract from, the gravity of the most useful work of dying.

The "Ars" itself signals a Chaucerian turn from mirth at the end of things with a Parsonlike abandonment of poetic form: "Translate wole Y,

nat in rym but prose, / For so it best is, as þat Y suppose" (930–31). As the
Parson says, his prose will "knytte up al this feeste and make an ende" and
show the way to "Jerusalem celestial" (X.46, 51), a movement that Hoccleve
echoes in a short prose passage that describes how the following work will
point the way to "celestial Jerusalem" (934). Yet Hoccleve's pretext for eschewing poetic form differs from the Parson's.

Whereas the Parson associates poetry with "fables" and "wrecchednesse"
(34) and the *Boece* associates it with delight, Hoccleve unexpectedly turns
to prose precisely because the end of the art of dying is "ioieful" and "glad"
(927). The former two exemplary moments of termination, the Parson's in
knitting up the "feeste" of *The Canterbury Tales* and Boethius's in knitting
up his entire life while under sentence of death, cast aspersions on the delight
of poetry and, in the case of the Parson, recommend prose as a sober alternative to the frivolity of alliterating and rhyming verse. And prose is, in a sense,
the form of termination for Hoccleve, the language that appears as things
near their end; which is to say, the form that reveals itself as things come
close to being perfected. Prose is the language that lies beyond the world,
where being is uncontaminated by unperfected forms; it is a reminder of the
desire for form and the hope of its disclosure. Yet prose is where the stuttering
conversation with the earth becomes pure language. This may be why Hoccleve turns here to prose simply as the most suitable form for relaying delight: "syn it ioieful is and glad / For hem þat hens shuln wel departe away /
And to the blisse go þat lasteth ay, Translate wole Y . . . For so it best is, as
þat Y suppose" (927–31). On the one hand, Hoccleve turns to prose at the end
of his work because Chaucer turns to prose at the end of *his* work. On the
other, Hoccleve does not tell us *why* he supposes this is "best," so we must
infer that Hoccleve means that prose is best because of the account of infinitude he is about to write, as if poetry were inextricably bound *by* termination.

The ending gestures of the *Series*, including the wavering between prose
and poetry, are in every sense Hoccleve's "late style": his struggle to come
to terms with his own finitude in the very self-conscious way that many
fifteenth-century writers did, coupling his life with the concern for "making a good end" to the writing.[15] Hoccleve's own "good end" to his *Regement of Princes* turns the book into a figure of finitude, the long shadow
cast by a book about the education of a monarch. Because the book is about
the universal challenges facing rulers, its conclusion points toward perfection, rather than termination. In other words, its ending constitutes the beginning of the pursuit of the good life that will also shape a realm, the public
playing-out of the advice that a ruler follows. Although—or, more properly,
because—it is addressed to one representative man, it constitutes a general

and public set of principles for the public to observe, as well. It puts into practice the abstractions of the *speculum regis*, which are embodied, if the book is read aright, in the public that the work of the book continues. To end the book in one sense—not to go back to it again and again, or to put it behind you after you finish it—is to make the kind of ending that Hoccleve tries to avoid. But in one manuscript, the *Regement* ends with a scribal addition, a colophon: "nunc me penitet si male scripsit."[16] It is a conventional phrase (as is making a "good end"), but here, poised against Hoccleve's own final lines, it turns the poem into its own fulfillment, a kind of magic collapse of *recte scribendi* into *recte vivendi*. It turns the ending into a personalized concern for an ending that has definitively taken place and whose form cannot be corrected. *Recte vivendi*: Hoccleve's ending leaves us with the hope that we can regulate our own lives.

What Hoccleve calls the "ornat endityng" of Chaucer (1973) is for Lydgate, as we have seen, the expression of a finitude that is overcome by form: the "enlumynyng of the land" (1974). But for Hoccleve it represents the very form of finitude. When Hoccleve thinks overtly about his work *as* poetry, he thinks in terms not just of Chaucer, but of the death of Chaucer.[17] Hoccleve's conception of the work he is doing in poetry seems inconceivable without coming to terms, in every sense of the word, with the event he represents as a catastrophe, a "harm irreparable / Unto us" (2083–84).[18] Chaucer's death transcends the singularity of death and becomes universal. Hegel said that in death we all become universal,[19] but the passage from singularity to universality in Hoccleve's lament for Chaucer has a particular form:

> O deeth, thow didest nat harm singuler
> In slaghtre of him, but al this land it smertith.
> But nathelees yit hastow no power
> His name slee; his hy vertu astertith
> Unslayn fro thee, which ay us lyfly hertith
> With bookes of his ornat endytyng
> That is to al this land enlumynyng. (1968–74).

Chaucer's is a death that cannot be private because of the adequation of his work with the language that was at that point being deliberately shaped as a national idiom; the termination of Chaucer's poetic work impinges on the burgeoning importance of the vernacular. It is in the concern for an ongoing poetic and linguistic work that Chaucer's death is not "singuler," precisely because it opens onto a universal diction, a universal, or at least a universal English, literary language. Hoccleve represents Chaucer's death recurrently as an allegorical, public, and apostrophic death: "Deeth by thy deeth hath harm irreparable / Unto us doon" (2082–83) by despoiling the land of rhetoric; yet, in the very apostrophizing of death, Hoccleve demonstrates the survival of Chaucer in terms that are now adequate to address a catastrophe. The work of dying in Hoccleve is bound up with a public and implicates the entire range of the estates: "as wel the poore as is the ryche; / Leered and lewde eek standen alle ylyche" (2099–2100). One index of the deprivation that Chaucer's death has brought is perhaps the adequation of his death with the very communal work of universal death, the assertion of an increasingly public figure, a death Hoccleve refers to as a "combreworld" (2091).

The difference in the relation between death and poetry in Chaucer and in Hoccleve can be glimpsed in a moment in which Hoccleve echoes Chaucer in the lament. Chaucer follows in Virgil's footsteps, says Hoccleve, but he himself is also following in Chaucer's footsteps by echoing what Chaucer says at the end of *Troilus*. Chaucer says goodbye to his book by telling it to "subgit be to alle poesye; / And kis the steppes, wher-as thou seest pace / Virgile, Ovyde, Omer, Lucan, and Stace" (V.1790–92), and Hoccleve says of Chaucer that "the steppes of Virgile in poesie / Thow folwedist eek" (2089–90). Yet as the ending of *Troilus* hauntingly shows, it is not clear what this legacy amounts to, placed at the mathematically insignificant point that is earth; the deliberate ambiguity of Troilus's final destination (the hollowness of the eighth sphere) stands for the cryptic, uncertain state in which Chaucer places his own poetry. In Hoccleve, the "steppes of Virgile in poesie" that Chaucer follows open onto the broad, secular terrain of universal death: "Every man is maistried," he says (2098); death, not Chaucer, is the master whose example Hoccleve must ultimately follow, especially in the *Series*.

Yet dying in Hoccleve is the representation of a representation.[20] The image of a man "dyynge and talking" is not, as in Suso, an image that suddenly appears (86). In the "Ars," Sapience commands the disciple to create the image himself, internally, in a process reminiscent of Hoccleve's Vinsaufian account of composition elsewhere:

> The disciple of þat speeche took good cure
> And in his conceit bysyly soghte he,
> And therwithal considere he gan and see
> In himself put the figure and liknesse
> Of a yong man. (87–91)

This emphasis on interiority is entirely Hoccleve's addition to Suso's text, and it gives death a contingency that it does not have in Suso.[21] The image of dying is *in* the disciple and is dependent upon the power of his "conceit," just as the run-on line at the end of the same stanza calls attention to the conceit of the rhyme royal that Hoccleve uses, by pointing out a formal gap where there is no syntactic one. This run-on stanza may be the formal equivalent of the image of death, which is both *in* the process of dying and already touched by death. By the end of his discourse, the image lists the symptoms of imminent death at surprising length: the pale face, the dim "look," "heuy as leed," the sunken eyes, the stiff hands, the failing breath and pulse (653–64). These conventional *signa mortis* are intended to warn onlookers of the immanence of death, not to allow the dying person to make his or her own diagnosis. From the point of view of the order of discourse, the dying man is already dead, an image that should not be able to read its own signs of termination. It is caught between what Lacan called two deaths, the space between biological death and the death of the symbolic order. It is in the symbolic order that the subject is dead, while not yet suffering biological death, both an image of an image of death and an image not yet dead.[22] As the disciple says, he is uncertain whether this death has occurred "in liknesse / Or in deede" (753–54). The death that Hoccleve wants to trace in the "Ars" is already a symbolic death, but one that anticipates the advent of physical death, which it does not itself symbolize.[23]

On a structural level, Hoccleve's "Ars" itself is caught between two deaths, that of the disciple in the Suso text and that of the symbolic end that represents death. Hoccleve declares that he is not able to translate the rest of Suso's text on dying and can only attach to the end of the "Ars" a prose translation of the ninth lesson from the Feast of All Souls. Yet in doing so he gives the ending of the "Ars" the same shape as the endings of two of the other works in the *Series*, the "Fabula de quadam imperatrice Romana" and the "Fabula de quadam muliere mala," which both end with prose moralizations of the *fabulae*. And Hoccleve's excuse for not continuing the Suso text echoes his representations of his diminutive powers as the successor of Chaucer, only in this case unable to follow the "other iii partes which in this book / Of the tretice of deeth expressid be" (918–19). He says that he does not dare to "touch" the rest of the treatise because it is too great a thing for "swich a fool" to "medle with" (920–23). What amounts to a brief poetic prologue to the prose translation of the lesson from All Souls' begins with this inexpressibility trope, as if Hoccleve admits to being overmastered by death, which, in effect, terminates his poetic engagement with the topic of dying. Yet the silence about dying that begins this prologue ends with a second appeal to the impossibility of treating his topic adequately, except that the topic has now shifted from death to the "celestial Jerusalem," which "to conprehende þat gladnesse / Verraily no wit may, ne tonge, expresse" (937–38). Formally, the prose translation that follows is the equivalent of the *moralitas* in the two *fabulae*: it provides a reading that transcends the ethical horizon of that which precedes it. Both of the other moralizations end at the point where the prose section of the "Ars" begins, with the disclosure of the ultimate goal of the fable: the "ioie of paradys," in the case of the fable about the empress (1068), and the "contre (þat is to seyn, the regne of heuene)" in the case of the fable about the wicked woman (731). The prose ending of the "Ars," then, functions as a kind of meta-moralization, glossing in much greater detail what the final ending of both fables, and of the "Ars" itself, really is: a preparation for what *follows* death.

In a formal sense, too, the ending of the "Ars" completes the work of preparation for the ending throughout the *Series*, an ending that, because of its frequent anticipation, is somewhat overdetermined. Hoccleve first mentions his translation of Suso near the beginning of the *Dialoge*, where he tells his friend that he intends to undertake it in order to help himself and others prepare for death. This preparation is important because it makes time for a necessary accounting of one's life before it is too late to do so. The reader of the treatise will be able to act "While he tyme hath . . . And not abide vnto his deeþis hour" (223–24). Dying involves a work of termination that gives shape to the ending of life:

> . . . it is ful hard
> Delaie acountis til liif bigynne to colde
> Shorte tyme is þanne of hise offensis oolde
> To make a iust and trewe reckenynge. (227–30)

This making of an adequate end is bound up with Hoccleve's concern for form. Only a deliberate end can fully justify the course a life has taken, and in a sense the final form that life takes is determined by its ending. The central image of the "Ars" itself is a man "dyynge and talking" (86), who is to become a mirror by which one directs oneself toward one's own end. The recognition of an ending that gives form to a phenomenon because of the process of contemplating it is what Kant called "purposive form" or *forma finalis*, and Hoccleve translates a famous passage from Geoffrey of Vinsauf that articulates the importance of anticipating the final form of something before it is created.[24] Before work on a house is begun, it must first be imagined fully, "seen, purposed, cast and ment" (641), Hoccleve makes it quite clear that the recognition of the ending of this project and the ending of his life are coterminous, and that his translation will be the end of his poetic career:

"whanne that endid is I neuere þinke / More in Englissh after be occupied"
(239–40). The ending of the "Ars" is also the end, the termination and the
purpose, of a language, and his "lust," he says, is already "ny mortified" (243).
In the long lament about his health that follows, Hoccleve drops the coterminous concern with his work and his life and imagines approaching death
as an unfolding negation of form. He adapts the formal device of the *signa
mortis* to point out that his own senses and body are weakening (246–52)
and that even his "sentement" is "nowe al another" (252). Everything that is
valued, he says, will lose its color like a flower that is beginning to dry, and
in the passage that follows he fuses a list familiar from romances (such as
Sir Orfeo) with the *ubi sunt* trope in which he anticipates the evacuation of
familiar and desirable forms:

> Lond, rente, catel, gold, honour, richesse,
> Þat for a tyme lent been to been ouris,
> Forgo we shole sonner than we gesse.
> Paleises, maners, castels grete and touris
> Shal vs bereft be by deeth þat ful sour is. (281–85)

At this point death is close to becoming the allegorical, universal phenomenon that Hoccleve writes about elsewhere, that before which we are powerless to act. Death, he says, "shal of vs make an ende" (288), turning on its
head the usual anxiety of fifteenth-century poets, which is how to make a
good end themselves. Death is more powerful than the poet, making ends
of its own determination.

All of this is still bound up with his capacity as a poet who will soon
turn to writing about the ends of things. His own powers are disappearing
just as implacably as are the castles and palaces of the rich, and the modesty
topos he uses to begin this lament about the passing away of things seems
more than perfunctory in the light of his indictment of his own emerging incapacity. He is "bare of intellecte and forme" (238), he says, but will
nevertheless attempt to translate Suso because of the urging of "a devoute
man" (235). Even at the point at which he expresses his deeply personal
failings of body, mind, and work, he attributes his motive to another. The
extraordinary array of endings he contemplates at this point, the death of
all things, is prompted by an awareness of death bequeathed to him in the
form of a social relation, his obligation to the "excitinge and mocioun" of
that devout man (234).

But the prose ending of the "Ars" is also prompted by an uncanny formal relation that implicates the state of Hoccleve's intellect, his capacity

to undertake the very poetic work that he is contemplating. A great deal of
the *Dialoge* involves Hoccleve's attempt to convince his friend that his wits
have indeed recovered enough for him to work on the treatise he refers to as
"Lerne for to Die" (206). It has been five years, he says, since his senses were
restored (446), and, besides, reading too much was not the cause of his mal-
ady. Earlier, in his *Compleinte*, Hoccleve spells out the span of these five
years more precisely: writing at the end of November, he says that at the
last Feast of All Saints (November 1), his senses had been restored for five
years. That means he first *lost* his senses on All Saints' Day (or Eve) the first
day of a two-day-long commemoration of the dead in the medieval English
church (All Souls' Day was November 2). As we will see, this date resonates
throughout the *Series*. In the "Compleinte" Hoccleve represents his mental
illness and its aftermath in terms of a failure of memory and commemoration: in his illness, he says, "the substaunce of my memorie / Wente to pleie
as for a certain space" (50–51), using a definition also found in the *Liber
albus*, which talks about support for those "extra memoriam suam."[25] Conversely, the image of death in the "Ars" says that one of the effects of death
is that one has "slipt out of mynde" (508). Even after his recovery, Hoccleve
talks about his life as a purgatory in which he is not being commemorated
in prayer: "Forʒeten I was al oute of mynde awey, / As he þat deed was from
hertis cherte" (80–81). It is not that his friends no longer remember him;
they do, all too well, because they turn away when they see him approach.
They forget him in terms that echo prayers for the dead, condemning him
to a death without the relief of "cherte," which Jacques Le Goff describes
as "the only sacrament whose efficacy is communicable."[26] Hoccleve's living death leaves him beyond, because it is prompted by, the consolation of
community. It is fitting, then, that Hoccleve marks his completion of the
"Ars" by translating a lesson from the Feast of All Saints, a day of communal remembrance—and the day on which he regained his mental health.

Yet the prose text at the end of the "Ars" does not make as neat an ending as its position would structurally suggest. Although Hoccleve says that
he will turn to prose for that ending, the beginning of the ninth lesson is actually the last stanza of the verse section of the "Ars." And in his holograph,
another *fabula* follows the "Ars," prompted by yet another conversation
with his friend. It is a process that could extend infinitely, as Christina von
Nolcken says: "although this book more than once seems on the point of ending, assembling it is not a process Hoccleve ever seems to have completed."[27]
The very ending of the Suso translation calls attention to Hoccleve's failure
to terminate his work, to make a good ending, with his acknowledgment
that he cannot translate the rest of the treatise and must leave the remain-

ing three parts untouched. Although such disjunctures could be instances of what he calls his bareness of form (238), they are also interpositions that call attention to the importance of ending precisely by its failure to appear. The transition between the Suso text and the Ninth Lesson shows how Hoccleve uses an ending to initiate another text. He seems to use an inexpressibility topos to consolidate the apology for discontinuing the translation of Suso with the beginning of the ninth lesson in a coda that becomes a prologue. He cannot finish the "Tretice of deeth" because it exceeds his abilities to go further:

> Touche y nat dar. Þat labour Y forsook,
> For so greet thyng to swich a fool as me
> Ouer chargeable is, by my leautee,
> To medle with. Ynow the first part
> For my small konnynge is and symple art. (920–24)

Yet the meager talent that purportedly ends his work at this point is adequate to tackle the inexpressible topic of eternal enjoyment by the end of this brief interlude: "for to comprehende þat gladnesse / Verraily no wit may, ne tonge, expresse" (937–38). His translation does attempt to express it, however, even when the inexpressibility is ontological rather than the result of a deficiency of poetic power. As I have suggested, the placement of a reading from All Saints' Day echoes Hoccleve's ongoing concern—at least as expressed by his friend—that he will not be mentally adequate to the task of translating Suso's treatise. The reading simultaneously confirms what Hoccleve recovered on All Saints' Day five years before he wrote the "Compleinte" and calls it into doubt: it is a kind of reverse modesty topos coming at the end of things.

It is harder, however, to make sense of his abjuration of the rest of the "tretice of deeth" (919). He repeatedly mentions his long study of it in the "Compleinte" and the "Dialoge" and makes his determination to translate it clear throughout both. He has thought it over for a while, he says: "Vpon my wittes stithie hath it be bete / Many a day" ("Dialoge," 440–41). His precipitate abandonment of the project undermines the tremendous weight of conclusion that this translation has borne throughout the *Series*. If learning to die well is the proper conclusion of all things, including a work of art, then what does it mean for that lesson not to conclude? One possibility is that the work of dying cannot conclude until the arrival of death, so any other conclusion to it would be false. Yet this is not what Hoccleve says: it is simply too much for him to take on, "Ouer chargeable . . . To medle with"

(923–24); the first part of the treatise is "Ynow" (923). Hoccleve actually calls attention to his failure to make the ending one might expect for his translation, yet makes what Melanie Klein might call a "good enough" ending.[28] As it happens, Hoccleve ends his translation just where Suso's treatise "of deeth" ends, anyway; his protestations of inadequacy might not have been necessary for anyone familiar with the version of the treatise excerpted from the *Horologium sapientiae*.[29]

Hoccleve thus disrupts an existing ending in order to extend the ending of his own text, and the eschatological perspective of the Ninth Lesson is appropriate for the text's vision of the ends of things. Yet, as Christina von Nolcken argues, Hoccleve continues the work of learning to die well beyond that point, by extending the *Series* to include the second and final *fabula*.[30] It is possible to think of the *Series* as a miscellany, a collection of texts that could be extended infinitely and whose arrangement is more occasional than thematic or topical. Indeed, the specific dates that Hoccleve gives for the moments at which he sutures the texts together suggest a kind of serial compilation, in which he merely appends new material to what he has already collected. But these contingent acts of compilation are really second-order phenomena, preserved and even cultivated in Hoccleve's later rewriting of parts of the *Series*. When he says he began his complaint because he could not keep his sorrow "cloos," he seems to mean that he began the *writing* of the "Compleinte," despite his assertion that he "braste out" with it (32, 35): in the beginning of the "Dialoge" it is ready to be read to his friend, who arrives immediately after he has finished it. Yet the "Compleinte" is framed by spontaneous, impulsive acts: Hoccleve's sudden loss of restraint that causes him to burst out in the first place and his friend's frantic knocking at the door when he has finished that outburst. Since he remains by himself— "cloos"—during the "Compleinte," Hoccleve must mean by "bursting out" either that the act of writing is an act of unmediated publication (although he asks later whether he should publish it) or that the moment his friend begins reading, Hoccleve is no longer keeping himself and his sorrow enclosed. Those impulsive moments, in other words, are predicated on the a priori existence of the written "Compleinte" and must have been added after the "Compleinte" was already finished. A famous aside in the "Dialoge" about the clipping of coins must have been written much later, for Hoccleve says that "whanne I this wroot, many men dide amis" (134): the problem seems to have been redressed, and in fact Hoccleve alludes to a statute against coin clipping passed in May 1421, already far enough in the past to have altered practices.[31] The staging of surprise entrances and impulsive projects is a deliberate part of the structure—indeed, it provides the structure—of the *Se-*

ries. The impression of hasty and breathless composition is part of its charm, and it is precisely these moments that tempt us to read Hoccleve's work as compulsively confessional.[32] Confession may be a part of its mode of proceeding, and Hoccleve draws on and transmutates some illustrious examples of confession and interrogation throughout the *Series.*[33] These moments of frank admission about the contingency of the events that shape the *Series* are not divagations from the deeply serious work of the *Series* as a whole, but actually points at which the *skopos* of his project on dying well comes into view. The necessity of dying well is both highlighted and obscured by these points of contingent interruption, points at which Hoccleve speculates about what the final end of his project should be, while acknowledging along the way that it is dying well and writing about how to die well. This play of ending and deferral is the explicit subject of the one addition he makes to the translation of the Ninth Lesson, at its end.

Most of that lesson describes the eternal qualities of the celestial Jerusalem, with its forms of "blisse endelees" (995) and its saints shining in "perpetual eternitees" (955). But Hoccleve adds a coda that describes the alternative, the horror of hell, as what Hegel would call a bad infinity, a place where endings are possible—at least conceivable—but are not made:

> if any ende sholde sue or folwe, that wolde yeue the soules right hy comfort and greatly abregge and lesne hir grief, but awayte nat aftir þat, for it wole nat beytde, for right as the seid ioies been eternal and aylastynge, so been tho peynes infynyt and endeles. (1002–7)

Logically speaking, "peynes" are not infinite, because such infinity depends on a negation of an ending, the "ende" that "sholde sue or folwe." Eternal pain is infinite precisely because it is non-finite, but that finitude itself, which defines it, cannot be a part of the series.[34] Another feature of Hoccleve's version of infinitude here is that it is expressed as an antonymic opposition: "eternal and aylastynge" opposed to the "infynyt and endeles," one set of positive terms expressing eternity opposed to a set of terms that merely negate finitude. But more striking is the relation the terms in this passage bear to the work of ending and continuing the *Series:* Hoccleve could also be describing the contingent form of his whole project, "if any ende sholde sue or folwe." It is our "wirkes in this present lyfe" (1009) that determine whether we will choose the "better part" (1011), and the valence of those works is determined precisely by their ending, by the complete assimilation of the lesson of how to die. Hoccleve's own work continues past this point, to the "Fabula de quadam muliere mala," attenuating what would have been an apposite ending to his own work, an ending that carries the quality of self-reflexive narratorial anxiety about making an end that will leave one unable to make an end to one's own infinite suffering. It is the end of writing, not the end of a text, that offers the real consolation of a good ending, an end that comes only with death. In the meantime Hoccleve is pulled onward by other texts and other interests—those of the friend, with his warnings about what not to write (neither something on death nor something that will disparage women), or those of Humphrey of Lancaster, Duke of Gloucester, and Joan Beaufort, Countess of Westmorland, to whom he dedicated sections of the *Series*. More generally, one could see Hoccleve's writing of the *Series* as the image of sanity he wishes to publish to the world, as an instance of the "commvnynge" that "is the beste assay" ("Compleinte," 217).[35]

Yet in the *Series* this "commvnynge" takes place overwhelmingly among texts. Hoccleve's work is started and halted by the presence or the absence of texts; at the end of the "Fabula de quadam imperatrice Romana" he writes an exchange with his friend about the book in which the missing "moralyzynge" at the conclusion might be found. As Ethan Knapp has argued, the shape of the *Series* is determined by the same collations of documents and the transfer of texts back and forth that Hoccleve observed in his professional practice: the *Series* is "a projection of the labor of the Privy Seal into the world of poetic composition."[36] Yet there is one important difference: the agenda of the *Series* is also driven by the availability of documents, and the sudden unavailability of one simply means that the *Series* no longer discusses it, as with the copy of Isidore's *Synonyma* that he must return to its owner.[37] Rather than record everything that lands on his desk, Hoccleve reads a text in a leisurely manner, as when he takes five years to think about the "Ars," sometimes regretting the loss of a text he would have liked to use in his poetry. His compositional practice may be influenced by the habitus of the Privy Seal; but in its disregard of the urgency of making copies, it does not quite conform to the painstaking and regularized nexus of documents in the Privy Seal. Indeed, the manner in which the book is taken from Hoccleve sounds like nothing so much as the arrival of sudden death: "He þat it ouȝte aȝen it to him took, / Me of his hast vnwar" ("Compleinte," 374–75). Unwary haste is one of the Hocclevian signs of death: in the "Ars" itself, the image of death says that he was "unwaar" of the "comynge . . . sodeyn" of death itself (115);[38] in the *Regement of Princes*, "Deeth was to hastyf" to take Chaucer away (2092). More subtly than Isidore's, the shadow of book 2 of Chaucer's *Boece* falls over this moment: Lady Philosophy says that tragedies are only the deeds of Fortune, "that with an unwar strook overturneth the realms of greet nobleye" (II Pr.2, 69–70). The "unwar" king loses his kingdom, while Hoccleve loses a book; yet both have failed to prepare for the end of things. At such moments one can glimpse the importance of texts to Hoccleve's project of preparing for death. A failure to read one to the end is like what Hoccleve in the "Ars" calls an "undisposid deeth" (181), an event that is precipitate precisely because one has not anticipated its eventuality. To look ahead to the end of things is to be prepared.

Yet Hoccleve's extract from the *Synonyma* begins with a man lamenting the inescapable burden of the past: "My wickidnessis euere folowen me, / As men may se the shadwe a body sue" (320–21). Hoccleve tells us that what Reason said to the man "esid" his heart (313), and he seems to identify with the lamenting man. It is not hard to see the lamenting man as a proxy for Hoccleve's own complaint about the inescapability of his own past, whether it is his madness or his misruled life. Despite the startling vividness with which he describes how he uses the texts he acquires, there still remains something obscure and shadowed about both Hoccleve's past and the texts that he cites or echoes.

CHAPTER TWELVE

The Care of the Archive:
John Audelay's *Three Dead Kings*

Dying is grounded in care.
—Martin Heidegger

This book began by discussing poems written more than four hundred
years before the poem I will discuss in this chapter. Those revolve
around a body that cannot speak because it is dead, and a soul that can. The
poem I will examine here presents bodies that can speak even when they
are in advanced states of postmortem decay, and that speak not to souls but
to the living. The poem, *The Three Living and the Three Dead* (sometimes
called *The Three Dead Kings*, which is the title I will use), appears in a
book full of poems most likely composed by a blind chantry chaplain, John
Audelay, who died around 1426.[1] In one sense, the poem is the negative
image of the world with which the chantry priest is usually concerned: the
soul is the subject and the focus of the intercessory prayers of the chantry,
the body is invisible. In *The Three Dead Kings*, the body speaks to the living (in this case, three kings, precisely the kind of people who would have
chantries founded for them), and the soul is absent. It is absent, that is, only
if one does not include the soul of the reader, to whom the poem is really
addressed. It is a hortatory poem, intended to make the reader aware of the
ongoing necessity to take care of the soul while one is alive. We are the soul,
quiet but anticipatory.

The bodies of the three dead kings who speak are increasingly decrepit
and fragmented, as if to demonstrate that the body has nothing to look forward to, just the process of corruption by which it eventually will become
no longer a body. In a sense, the poem records the process of the body entering the archive, diminishing as it has less and less of the quality of the living body. The vanishing point is the loss of all bodily integrity, of the *forma*

that arranges matter to make it a body: dust. The only discernible trace of any singular body is the tomb itself, distinguished by its position within a church and by its commemorative signs: its design, its materials, its writing. Audelay's poem traces this entire process, as I will discuss at the end of this chapter, showing two things: how the body enters the archive, and how the archive is the condition of poetry.

But first the work of the soul. The poem implies the presence of a soul that is supposed to learn to anticipate its own death, and (if the poem has its intended effect) will remember the poem as preparation for an event that is still to come. In the poem, the encounter with death comes as a shock, and the three living kings are described as experiencing great "care," at this point a synonym for terror (34, 53, 81, 89). Yet care also implies a conscious choice to dwell on something, even to take some responsibility for it. That sense of care is what the poem is designed to elicit, and it is also bound up in the nature of this work as a poem. The first use of the word "care" illustrates how deeply care forms part of the poem's structure. The first king's response to seeing the three dead kings is almost incoherent, merely saying that he is terrified: "Much care us is caȝt • for craft that can / Can I mo no cownsel bot care" (34–35).[2] These lines mark the transition from the main part of the stanza, eight lines of approximately fourteen syllables (although the seventh line, "the bob," is quite variable, as in the first line here, which is nine syllables), to the final five lines, "the wheel," which have fewer syllables and sometimes only two alliterating stresses. The bob and wheel are also connected by an echoed, concatenating word. Here it is "care," which appears at the beginning of the bob and at the end of the first line of the wheel. The word *care* makes a chiasmus that suggests care is inescapable. The kings have "caught" care, and this king's suggestion, to take care as their counsel, almost says what he has just said: they are experiencing tremendous care. But there is a slight movement toward the other meaning of care: to suggest that it can be a "cownsel" suggests that it involves an element of choice. At this point of the poem, that choice may be spurious, and all the king can recommend is to carry on having the emotions that they are having. How this chiasmus moves from tautology to a meaningful distinction is, in a sense, the intellectual drama of the poem.

Anyone who has read Heidegger will have recognized one of the central concerns of *Being and Time: Sorge*, which is usually translated as "care." Its modern English cognate is "sorrow," but *Sorge* more precisely means "concern" or "care," but especially, according to Merriam-Webster, "a feeling bordering on anxiety." In other words, it means precisely what "care" initially means for the three kings. Indeed, the context in which the poem discusses care—the panic that the three kings feel in looking directly at the dead—is a precise dramatization of what Heidegger means by *Sorge*. *Sorge* is, he says in a succinct aphorism, *Sein zum Tode*, being-toward-death.[3] This last concept is simultaneously one of the more difficult to grasp in Heidegger—it is arguably the main subject of *Being and Time*—and the most important, most "authentic," mode of being. Being-toward-death hints at its importance in the "primordial" experience of *Sorge*—being anxious— and gradually reveals itself as solicitude, caring about death as the core of one's essential, inalienable being: "one's ownmost," a concept I have discussed elsewhere in this book.[4] In *The Three Dead Kings* death may be imagined as a more universal experience, something to be shared publicly in texts and regimens of prayer, but it still contains that original nucleus of anxiety and terror. That nucleus is not an accidental feature of the poem. It is what motivates the whole *moralitas* of the story: to the degree that one can experience vicariously the terror of looking directly at death one can begin to practice the solicitude that the realization of one's own death demands. In the poem's world, that solicitude takes the form of penance: for the three kings, it also takes the further penitential steps of satisfaction and possibly restitution for the sin of forgetting the dead: that is why they build the minster. But the sin of forgetting the dead is, more important, the sin of forgetting one's own death. That is why the poem ends with the pessimistic recognition that too few will believe it. That may be an accurate recognition, but it is also a trope that transfers the burden to the reader: it is up to you to believe it, and if you do, you know that you must prepare for death.

But let me return to the topic of the poem as a story that records its own writing. That feature intrudes on the awareness of one's own death, reminding one that—at least at this point—the experience of one's own death is the experience of a textual death, the corpses that appear only in the poem and before the three kings, not before the reader. The experience of death is located only in the text: the poem is a kind of archive, storing the fact and the experience of death for those still to come.

I would like to return to an illustration with which this book began, the figure of Death ringing a bell. Death pokes his spear through the margin of the drawing, as if piercing the border between life and death or between the boundaries of representation and life. He rings a bell whose sound is literally "death," but a sound represented with three different graphemes in the nineteen times it is written in the space around the body of Death: "dethe," "deþ," and deþe."[5] The scene embodies the archive, recording the work of death by acknowledging its various shapes yet registering them in an intelligible order of things, an order that includes and undermines the text of the poem itself. The tip of Death's spear is aimed quite literally right at beauty, at the line "Beaute declyneth hys blossom falleth doune."[6] The point of the illustration is not that beauty can do anything on its own: it is always threatened by Death, and a Death whose representation makes it clear that there is no place for beauty. In its displacement of beauty, this image is like the late medieval *transi* tomb, a cadaverous image placed on a tomb instead of, or underneath, the smooth, polished image of the idealized body. The *transi* tomb depends for its effect on the awareness of the idealized body that is being replaced. What Paul Binski calls the "skeleton in the cupboard of funerary art" challenges the conventions of a mortuary representation that denies the bodily process of death, but it does so by appearing within the awareness of an archive of bodily representations; it challenges a certain decorum of death that erases the real of the dead body.[7]

I do not mean to suggest that dead bodies were not represented before the fifteenth century, just that the interest in acknowledging the dead body, placing it in an archive rather than a crypt, stimulates a demand for literal and formal equivalents of the process of mortification. Neither does this mean that art did not respond to the bodily presence of death without an interest in the kinds of dispersal that death brings with it. The illustration of three living and three dead kings in the thirteenth-century de Lisle Psalter, for instance, is framed by text in all three of the languages of medieval England: Latin rubrics for the accompanying Anglo-Norman poem, and Middle English speech tags for each of the kings.[8] It is a succinct acknowledgment of the universality of death, and also of the way it impinges on the representational resources of all language. The heteroglossia of the page is a canny response to the entropy of dying: the sight of the dead body demands a response, but there can be no single answer to the challenge it presents.

Yet on some level a single answer is what art promises. The three languages of medieval England on the page also reveal a formal decorum that is preserved in the face of death: the highest grade of writing appears in the Latin heading of each stanza in rubricated letters; a slightly lower-grade hand appears in the body of the French poem, written in black ink; and the Middle English tags are crowded into and around the available space above the illustration, sprawling into the margin, unlike the French and Latin text, which is constrained within ruled lines. These different hands also represent different levels of abstraction: a Latin title for each stanza, a French poem introducing the speech of each king in the third person, and a Middle English poem representing the direct, unframed speech of each king. Everything about the page indicates an awareness of the appropriate forms in which the proximity to death should be embodied. Even the slightly haphazard, meandering Middle English text exemplifies a formal decorum that is not immediately evident:

Ich am afert
Lo whet ich se
Me þinkeþ hit beþ deueles þre
Ich wes wel fair
Such scheltou be
For godes loue be wer by me.[9]

The partial rhyme -e links together the second, third, fifth, and sixth lines; the first and fourth lines are linked together by a pararhyme, the consonance of "afert" and "fair." What the tenuous connection of a pararhyme shows, in other words, is that the poem is structured not only by the collective speech of the living followed by the collective speech of the dead, but also by interlacing connections: the third and sixth lines are roughly octosyllabic (depending on whether the "e" is sounded or elided in "þinkeþ" and "deueles"), twice the length of the other four lines. The second and fifth lines rhyme with these two long lines, yet are yoked together by having four syllables each, although separated by rhyme from the first and fourth lines. It is a minimal kind of structure, but it is there, just as the dead selves are linked with the living selves by a connection that is at first not apparent to the living. The link between the living and the dead is subtler than it at first appears, and in this sense the experience of reading the poem echoes the experience of discovering that what links oneself to a dead body is nothing more than a minimal and barely observed change: what is fair becomes fear when refracted by death. But however tenuous it is, there is still an echo between these pairs of lines, a consonance that recognizes the body that is no longer one's own.[10]

John Audelay's much longer version of the confrontation of the living by the dead uses consonance as part of a systematic and highly complex formal scheme. There may be only one other poem outside of the Audelay manuscript that uses consonance, alliterative linking, and the concatenation of the body of a stanza with its wheel: The Poet's Repentance in the Harley Lyrics.[11] Alternating lines rhyme with each other, but successive lines follow in uncomfortable sonic proximity, thrown even closer together by the rule that each word in a doubled consonance (the twin alliterating pairs of a consonance) must also alliterate with its double, and that this alliteration must be used in both lines. In other words, the lines with consonances intrude between lines that rhyme strictly, yet form alliterative rhymes with those pararhyming lines.[12] And even within the consonance scheme there is a further complication: odd and even lines form near-couplets with a "close" consonance; yet the entire octave (and the wheel in its own right) is linked with lines that end in less strict consonances, which depend on the final consonant (and sometimes the penultimate consonant as well). The speech of the second living king illustrates this scheme well:

> Then bespeke the medil kyng, • that mekil was of myght,
> Was made as a man schuld • of mayn and of maght:
> "Methenkys, seris, that I se • the selquoth syght,
> That ever segge under sonne • sey and was saght,
> Of thre ledys ful layth • that lorne hath the lyght—
> Both the lip and the lyver • his fro the lyme laght!
> Fore yif we tene to the towne • as we hadyn tyght,
> Ha ful teneful way, I trow, • that us is taght." (66–73)

> [Then the middle king, of much might, spoke;
> He was made as a man should be, of strength and vigor:
> "I think, sirs, that I see the strangest sight
> That anyone under sun saw and was given,
> Of three very loathly men that have lost the light—
> Both the lip and the liver are separated from the limb!
> For if we go to the town as we had intended,
> A very troublesome way, I believe, is set out for us!]

The entire octave is attached by the final two consonants of each line (-gh and -t); alternate lines are linked by rhyme (myght/syght, syght/lyght), and successive pairs of lines are linked by consonance (might/maght, syght/saght). Each pair alliterates on the same letter (again, might/maght, sight/sight). Audelay also experiments with consonance in the poem preceding The Three Dead Kings, but in this poem his deployment of rhyme and consonance makes a thematic point as well.

As with most versions of the three living and three dead, each figure speaks for one stanza. On a formal level, at least, each discourse is weighted equally, like the pro and contra of a Scholastic distinction. The living and the dead each have their moments of moral suasion, and the more compelling each sounds, the more real dialectical force the conclusion will have. Although not exactly a debate poem, The Three Dead Kings stages challenges and responses like one, and it works as a poem partly because it makes each position aesthetically compelling. Consonance is the ghostly echo of this encounter: it underscores not only the lesson that the dead mirror and echo the living, but also that the relative importance of life and death depends on a parallax effect, just as each consonance is also a strict rhyme in its own turn. Like the optical illusion that cannot be seen simultaneously as two faces and as a vase, the scheme in *The Three Dead Kings* flickers between two perspectives from which everything is rearranged: one cannot be in life and death at the same time. As they are represented by rhyme, the boundaries of life and death are permeable, yet not quite enough so to make for unremarkable cohabitation. Life and death are preserved within their own schemes but echo each other with the voice of the uncanny.

The uncanny is one of the poem's major themes, both haunting and animating the poem's deliberate aestheticism.[13] The largest and most obvious discomfort of the poem is in the doubling of live and dead kings, each living one linked to a dead one. The first living king to speak is answered, three stanzas later, for instance, by the first dead king, whose graveclothes the first living king recognizes. Recognition of a doubled, uncanny figure, in other words, works by an objectifying visuality that structures the poem's aestheticism, which itself has something of the quality of the uncanny. Hegelian recognition is a kind of struggle, a refusal to see one's other in death, but that refusal becomes the very boundary between life and death.[14] The poem opens with a scene that is immediately aestheticized, a boar brought to bay in the first four lines: "Methoght hit ful semlé • to se soche a syght," says the narrator in the fifth line (counting this line, the first two stanzas invoke the narrator's sight four times). The hunt is an object of aesthetic contemplation.

The poem designates what is important to notice by holding it in abeyance, suspending it, in the second half of the opening octave, outside the order of time itself. The ensuing noise of the immobilized hunt is described as lasting from noon until night, a time that nevertheless seems to the narrator as short as a "napwile" (8).[15] As Susannah Fein noticed, one of the motifs of the poem is "paralyzing entrapment . . . enacted metrically as well as narratively."[16] The poem seems to imagine aesthetic contemplation as a kind of suspension of action, a kind of correlative of the stasis of death. And death itself, in the figures of the three dead kings, demands precisely that suspension of action. The three living kings cannot move or turn away ("bec nor bewe" [46]) when they see the three skeletons. Even their horses "abyde" (48). Indeed the entire poem represents *itself* as fixed within the order of art, written on the walls of the church that the three kings later build (141).[17]

Yet I do not mean to suggest that the aesthetic is purely a refuge from decay and death. The poem describes the dead body as an object of horror and revulsion, the lip and "lyver" now missing, the bones "blake" and "bare" (71, 106). The ending makes it clear that the encounter is good not merely for art, but for reminding us of the work of commemoration, and of piety toward the dead. The third dead king, in fact, tells the three living ones to turn from their "tryvyls" (130) while they still have time, which presumably include the very trifles of their hunt, which the narrator finds so appealing at the opening—and it is significant that the aesthetic value of the hunt involves the cultivation of an evanescent moment, a metonym of a life spent without due care for its teleological shape.

Another way to think about the poem's equation of art with stasis is as an archivizing impulse, a desire to confront death by arranging as lucidly as possible the traces of the once-living. The passage from life to death becomes exemplary precisely because of who the dead kings once were: living kings like the three now before them. Rather than obliterate the traces of life, death reveals the truth of social relations. The third dead king advises the living ones to make a "mirour" of him, a reflection of their lives become history, stripped of the delusions that now maintain them:

> . . . My myrthus bene mene:
> Wyle I was mon apon mold, • morthis thai were myne;
> Methoght hit a hede thenke • at husbondus to hene—
> Fore that was I hatyd • with heme and with hyne—
> Bot thoght me ever kyng • of coyntons so clene. (120–24)

> [. . . My joys are few:
> While I was on the earth, all harm was mine;
> I thought it an excellent thing to harass farmers—
> For that I was hated by churls and servants—
> Yet I thought myself a king of excellent repute.]

At the level of language, too, the poem works as an archive. One of the difficulties in arguing that Audelay is the poem's author is in explaining the presence of a large number of rare and outdated words. The two stanzas that describe the hunt are replete with words specific to the hunt—"bay," "rachis," "brachus"—and the slightly obscure words of Norse derivation that appear in fourteenth-century alliterative romances—"byrchyn," "barownce," "barsletys," "schokin," "schaw" (1–26). In several places the off-rhyme involves words yoked together by a common etymology: *tolde/telde, coldis/kelddus, foldis/feldis* (18, 19, 81, 82, 85, and 86). Each of these pairs is an etymological doublet, morphologically different words with the same etymon, and for Ella Whiting they represent a failure of inventiveness "in the making of rhymes."[18] But it is exactly where one word is virtually synonymous with another, yet morphologically different, that the formal pressure of the two types of rhyme is most clearly demonstrated: consonance is not an accidental companion to the strict rhyme scheme, but its haunting in language. I would argue that these moments in the poem represent not the flagging of inventive power, but one of the poem's demonstrations of its fundamental lesson that death leaves nothing unchanged, yet that that message itself can be memorialized, kept from dissolving. At such moments the consonanced lines with etymological doublets show how the writing of the poem is partly structured by the decay of language: these doublets no longer rhyme exactly with each other—their etymon has undergone two parallel changes—yet they maintain an aural and formal proximity demanded by the constraints of the poem.

Like the three living and three dead kings brought together by nightfall, these near rhymes are uncanny doubles of each other, similar in origin but divergent in form. As Derrida said of the word *Geist*, are not "etymology and ghosts . . . the same question?"[19] The poem is more than a mirror: it is an archive that records the inextricable if ghostly link of the past and the present: precisely the form of dying as the process of separating the spirit from the letter. The discourse of dying is the discourse of difference, too: doubled words are uncanny because they no longer possess the identity, the sameness, that is revealed by their difference. The dead speak because of, and about, the dissolution of body and spirit, but their language is the uncomfortable consonance of body and decay, the uncanny speech of doubled bodies that retain vestiges of their individual histories, yet that resemble each other because they are no longer fully inhabited by the spirit that resists the common history of corruption. As we will see, the dead in the poem speak not from outside the realm of history, but from within it: the voices of articulate degeneration.

Yet for an archive—even for an exemplum—these links may appear somewhat tendentious. The mistaking of the three dead kings for "warlaws" by the third living king is perhaps the most obvious of the misprisions that the poem records. Other misprisions, like the recognition by the third dead king that he has misunderstood his own reputation in life, are subtler but strike as hard at the dead kings' (former) convictions that life is valued by the extent of dominion—"Fro Loron into Londen" (95)—by beauty (a "caren" that is "cumle"), or by wealth ("well fore to ware" [108]). Misprision is an index of life, or at least of a life that is not lived as a being-unto-death. The three living kings invest the mist that separates them from their retinues with a fear—an "anguis" and a "care" (32, 34)—that seems unfounded, equivalent to the "awnters" of chivalric quest. When the three corpses appear, "care" returns (53) and does seem a more appropriate response, now that we know that the mist is a metaphor for death. Yet the poem does not spell that out, any more than it explains the depth of the living kings' fear at the moment.

At a structural level, the largest such gap is the relation between the poem's opening and its body. Without much ado, the poem describes the frenzied termination of a hunt and then the abrupt isolation of the three living kings. The poem never explains the relation between the two scenes, but the juxtaposition itself is thematically important. The boar brought to bay anticipates the three living kings trapped by the mist, confronting the specter of death in their own turn. The rich description of the hunt does not actually include the death of the boar, any more than the poem describes the death of the three living kings; indeed the noise, also described as a "hew," around the cornered boar lasts from noon until night. The cessation of the hue at nightfall might in fact indicate that the hunt was *not* finished. Of all the words used to describe the noise—the "how" of the huntsmen (12), the barking ("rerde") of the dogs (3), "tonyng" (19), the blowing of bugles (11, 17), even "talis" (19)—"hew" is the word repeated to link the first stanza with the second: "In holtis herde I never soche hew! / Soche a hew in a holt • were hele to behold" (13–14). The duration of the "hew" structures the first link between stanzas in the poem, stretching it out as a structural principle, a metonym for the duration of the poem itself. But the "hew" is also a metonym for the duration of life, stopped only by the falling of night. It echoes, in fact, the phrase "hue and cry" used in the pleas of forest courts to describe the cessation of the foresters' pursuit of poachers at nightfall.[20] The point is that the object of the chase has not been dispatched, and night is only a temporary suspension of the pursuit of life.

The poem's very obscuring of the crucial link between the hunt and the dialogue is part of the poem's movement from obscurity to the revelation of the true extent of care. The care that begins in mist ends with a new commitment to the care of the dead. At the most literal level the poem reveals the true orientation of the senses in the face of the dead, a movement from the obscurity of airy truisms to the material, bodily presence of death. The first living king, for instance, describes his companions and himself as "kings ful clene" who "cometh of rich kin" (33), a phrase that suggests the lack of encumbrance to their titles and the warrant of legitimate descent from other rulers.[21] But the abstract and somewhat legalistic adjective "clene" takes on a concrete and morbid sense when the second dead king describes his bones as "blake" and "bare," clean, that is, from the encumbrance of the flesh, yet no longer as clean as the unblackened bones of a living king.[22] The second half of the first living king's line, which describes the dead kings as coming "of rich kin," is a phrase that undergoes similar restriction and reification once the dead kings speak. After his brief disclaimer that they are not "fendus," the first dead king tells the living ones that they are, in fact, their "faders of fold that fayre • youe have fondon" (fathers on earth that raised you [93]). That last word, "fondon," takes on a double sense of its own here: the dead kings have both found, encountered, the living kings, who are indeed presently "fayre," but they have also established their reigns, and materially provided for the splendor of their lives.[23] However, the corporal destitution of the dead kings makes it apparent that the wealth (or power—another meaning of "riche") of the living kings is founded on something that does not even rise to the level of a minimal life: the voiding of body and wealth in death. This is what the "riche kin" of the living kings amount to: ancestors bare even of life itself.

At times the speech of the living kings is so vacuous that it achieves a kind of enigma. "I hope," says the first living king, "fore honor of erth • that anguis be ous on" (32). The word "hope" is one of an unusually high number of words that need to be glossed in the poem, and at least three articles on the poem are primarily dedicated to decrypting the arcane words and senses that appear in the poem.[24] But solving textual and lexical cruxes does not exactly make the poem's language entirely lucid, because, as I am suggesting, it flickers between and among the general and restricted senses of words. "Hope," as E. G. Stanley glosses it here, means "assume; believe; think," all senses of the word that appear elsewhere in Middle English. But, as Stanley points out, the contemporary sense of hope as a wish or an expectation is also active in Middle English.[25] The living king's "hope," then, could mean either that he assumes that because of the fog they will shortly be in "anguis," or it could mean that he hopes to have all the honor of the earth—secular power and wealth—after they have experienced the coming anguish, or that he would exchange all the honor of the earth for an escape. For that king, though, it is clear that "honor" is an empty word, a Falstaffian abstraction that could mean virtually anything in the world of the living. But with the appearance of the three dead kings, the phrase takes on a more particular and mordant sense: it is *because* of the honor of the earth that they will suffer anguish, not in spite of it. Their neglecting of the care of the dead in not having masses said for the other three kings is either an ethical alternative to "honor" or a crucial part of it that they have forgotten to observe. But most trenchant of all is the recognition that "honor of erth" means exactly what it says: the legacy of the earth to which those living bodies will return.[26] And indeed the kings have neglected the forms of honor—trental masses and the commemoration of the dead—that the earth demands from the living. In the presence of the all-too-earthy bodies of the dead kings, however, the phrase ultimately means that there can be no honor at all in the earth, nothing that survives the transition to death except for the merest earth.

The vacuity of honor is emptied paradoxically by the presence of death, and the very anguish that the living king so fears will be a mode of redemption. "Anguis" and "care" carry a moral and ultimately eschatological weight in the poem's narrative and will characterize the deepest and most appropriate response to the knowledge that the dead kings bring. Indeed, learning the right mode of anguish might be the poem's central ethical lesson. Unlike the static versions of the theme, the poem works by placing the response to the contrast between the living and the dead in narrative terms—that is, in terms that trace how an attitude is inhabited and embodied. The closing words of the last dead king reprise this lesson both formally and semantically. In moving from the octave to the wheel, with its sense of summation and reprisal, the last king complains that, despite his former glory, no one now cares for him: "Now is ther no knave under Crist • to me wil enclyne, / To me wil enclyne, to me come . . ." (125–26). It is a lament shaped by overdetermined continuities: the repeated phrase that links together octave and wheel, which is here a phrase both longer and more exactly reiterated than any other linking phrase in the poem, and the translation of the Latinate downward movement of "enclyne" to a movement never to be terminated in English.[27] No one, despite the haunting lament, will fulfill the desire of the dead for the termination of death. It will never come. The movement from "enclyne" to "come" repeats a movement that occurs at all levels, from general to specific senses: from general anxiety to specific fear of the dead and of death, from the vagaries of the "honor of erth" to the relegation of the body to earth, from the courtly decorum of "enclyne" to the barest approach of the living to the dead, and from the multiplicity of the "awnters" to the self-referential specificity of the reified poem on the minster walls (31–32).

The same movement from general to restricted senses informs the making of the book in which *The Three Dead Kings* appears. As Susanna Fein has shown, Audelay repeatedly attempts to end the book or to signal its ending, a movement coterminous with his statements about his own death.[28] Ending the book well and dying well are part of the same work of termination, a general motive that becomes a specific and concrete ending only when the book is finally ended with Audelay's death. Termination in language, for Audelay, is a clear metaphor for dying, and Audelay at least once points to his own death as something already accomplished in two of the book's colophons. The book sounds at two points as if Audelay has already died, using the phrase "Cuius anime propicietur Deus," which appears customarily on funerary brasses, often along with a request to pray for the soul of the dead they commemorate: "Orate pro anime. . . ."[29] John Audelay's phrase transforms the book into a memorial, but it extends well beyond the parameters of the customary phrase about the welfare of souls:

> *Cuius finis bonum, ipsum totum bonum. Finito libro. Sit laus et gloria*
>   *Christo.*
> No mon this book he take away
> Ny kutt owte noo leef, Y say forwhy,
> For hit ys sacrelege, sirus, Y yow say!
> Beth accursed in the dede truly!
> Yef ye wil have any copi,
> Askus leeve and ye shul have,
> To pray for hym specialy
>   That hyt made your soules to save,
>   The furst prest to the Lord Strange he was,
>   Of thys chauntré, here in this place,
>   That made this bok by Goddis grace,
>   Deeff, sick, blynd, as he lay. ("Conclusion," 40–52)

> [*He whose end is good is entirely good. The book is ended. Let praise*
>   *and glory be to Christ.*
> Let no-one take away this book, or cut out of it any leaf; I will tell you
>   why:
> Because it is sacrilege, I tell you!
> If you do it, let you be truly accursed!
> If you would like a copy,
> Ask permission and you shall have it,
> To pray especially for him
>   Who made it to save your souls.
>   He was the first priest to the Lord Lestrange,
>   Of this chantry, here in this place,
>   Who made this book by God's grace,
>   Deaf, sick, blind as he lay.]

Audelay's life has dwindled to the point where he lies on the edge of death, in the moment of dying but before death itself. Yet he uses the customary language of epitaph to ask for prayers for his soul, as if he were already dead. All that remains is the bare fact of his life, a body without the extension of the senses. Paradoxically, corporal integrity is one of the main concerns of this colophon, which serves as a warning not to violate the book by cutting out leaves as much as it urges prayer for the soul of Audelay. Audelay's work in a sense becomes the extension of Audelay's soul into the body of a sacralized book: sacrilege, which is what cutting out the pages amounts to, is the violation or the theft of a sacred thing.[30] Despite, and because of, all of the attempts that Audelay makes to end the book, it imagines numerous forms of bodily and spiritual continuity that also thwart the work of termination. As Susanna Fein has said, Audelay, as represented in his colophons, remains perpetually in a state of dying.[31] But this state is not imagined as deeply pathological, as it is in Chaucer (in the figures of the Man in Black and the Old Man of "The Pardoner's Tale"). For Audelay it is the possibility of redeeming everything, producing a good end that will make, as the rubric says, everything good. Neither does the making of the book terminate its extension into time and space. Audelay explicitly allows it to be copied as an alternative to despoiling it: his endings are all about continuity. Although sacred, the book is not a crypt protecting its contents from the depredations of the living. Indeed, its very hope for survival is predicated on its accessibility to further readers and copyists. As a memorial, Audelay's book is far closer to an archive than a crypt.

Formally, the book is an anthology, first described as such by Susanna Fein in 2003. More specifically, she describes it as a compilation of three earlier "books," each of which constitutes an anthology in its own right, "concluded with an appended section."[32] The traces of this anthologizing work can be seen at the conclusions of these anthologies, and without the final section would constitute neatly contained and terminated collections. But the final section's impulse to end the book and Audelay's life together is so protracted that one wonders if the entire manuscript is precisely an anthology. I do not mean that the ending is protracted in form, although it is; I mean that it is evident that Audelay composed additional endings after having already concluded the final section, and his entire book, several times.

The Three Dead Kings was originally intended as the conclusion of the appended section, which itself begins with penitential literature that demonstrates how to make a good end: what Fein calls "The Sins of the Heart," extracted from Richard Rolle's *Form of Living* and a prose piece that compares the preparation for death to the making of a bed. "The Paternoster" follows, then the "De tribus," which is the last part of Audelay's book written by his first amanuensis, Scribe A. The book, then, was originally a highly

complex vernacular work whose narrative of an encounter with the dead
ends in the installment of a perpetual memorial to the events it describes,
a metonymy for the book itself in its final form. The final line of *The Three
Dead Kings* even echoes the colophon quoted above: too few will believe
this, says the poem; may "Oure Lord delyver us from losse" (143). "Losse" is
a word Audelay uses elsewhere to refer to perdition or damnation, but also
strikingly like the colophon's prayer for preservation from the loss of leaves.
At such moments the teleology of the book and the eschatology of the author become almost indistinguishable.[33] At this point the book's termination would, in the strict sense of the word, be perfect. It would demonstrate
a continuity between soul and book, without insisting on the infinitude of
the book to make its work efficacious; both life and book would conclude
together, leaving the work of the soul to eternity.

Yet Audelay's job as a chantry priest was to ensure that souls were not
left to face eternity on their own. His duty was to say prayers for the souls
of his employer and family in order to release them sooner from purgatory.
His ongoing work is echoed in the ending of *The Three Dead Kings*, where a
minster is built, a mural created, and masses for the souls of the dead kings
commissioned. It ends precisely with the work with which Audelay's life
ends, in other words: with prayers for the dead.[34] But Audelay's life and the
work of his book extends beyond this moment. The next ending is a poem
in Latin, "Cur mundus militate sub vana gloria," which echoes several moments of *The Three Dead Kings*.[35] It is prefaced by a loosely paraphrased line
from Ovid's *Heroides*: "Non honor set honus assumere nomen honoris,"[36]
which recalls the *Three Dead Kings'* leveling of the concept of honor. The
poem's last line, "Felix qui poterit mundum contempnere" (40), echoes an
earlier Latin *contemptus mundi* poem, *Mundus deciduus*, which itself borrows from and inverts) a line from Virgil's *Georgics*. In effect, it repeats the
second dead king's admonition to "leve lykyng of flesche" (112).[37] And the
first dead king's warning about the transitory nature of life, "ye beth lykyr
to leve • then levys on the lynden" (you are more suited to leave than leaves
on the linden tree) (94), is echoed by the Latin poem's image of the "leve
folium, quod vento rapitur" (a light leaf, which is seized by the wind [35]).
It is still undetermined whether Audelay himself wrote *The Three Dead Kings*,
but even if he found it elsewhere and merely anthologized it, the two poems
complement each other intelligently, and besides amplifying what the three
dead kings say, it concludes Audelay's entire book with a turn to Latin. It
is a doubly authoritative termination because Audelay no longer need end
with an appeal to his own *auctoritas* in an English poem, but can finish with
an allusive Latin poem.

Yet that is not where the book ends, because Audelay writes a further ending in English, one that neatly knits together the themes of the two preceding poems. In what Fein refers to as the "Conclusion," Audelay opens with a *contemptus mundi* trope: "Here may ye here now hwat ye be. / Here may ye cnow hwat ys this worlde" (Here you may now hear what you are. Here you may know what this world is [1–2]). The site of the "here" is a little vague: it probably refers either to the book as a whole or to the final section, which is pervasively concerned with mortality. But it also sounds like a ventriloquized dead king, offering his corpse as an object lesson in the impermanence of things, as what the third dead king explicitly says is a mirror. Indeed, in the third stanza Audelay *does* offer himself as a negative exemplum: "Loke in this book; here may ye se / Hwatt ys my wyl and my wrytyng. All odur be me war for to be!"(Look in this book; hear you may see/ What my will and my writing is. Let all others take warning from me [32–34]). As with the other gestures of termination, this one conflates the life of the author and the state of his book.[38] Are we meant to think of Audelay's deafness, blindness, and ill health as a reminder that all men are mortal? Or does "here" refer to the book and possibly this particular poem, whose second stanza is a virtual condensation of the *contemptus* theme of the preceding poem? In some uncanny ways, the shadow of Audelay's mortality falls over this ending, speaking with the voice of one already dead, using the words of the dead king in the de Lisle Psalter: "be wer by me," perhaps taken from one of the many wall paintings with the theme of the three living and the three dead.[39]

Like a medieval archive, Audelay's book is tied inseparably to its locale and to the work that it memorializes. It cannot be taken away, and its final words situate it within the ethos of the chantry:

> . . . pray for hym specialy
> That hyt made your soules to save,
>   Jon the Blynde Awdelay.
>   The furst prest to the Lord Strange he was,
>   Of thys chauntré, here in this place . . . (46–50)

As Robert Meyer-Lee suggests, the reader becomes a virtual chantry priest, praying for the soul of the one named, implicated in the work and the place that occupied Audelay in life.[40] Audelay's insistent deixis calls our attention to what, precisely, *is* here before us. If his final injunction had been obeyed, the book would still be where Audelay intended for it to remain, and would still be whole, which it is not; its coextensiveness with the chantry would also remain obvious to a reader. Instead, the fate of the book restricts the deictic moments to the book itself, the frame within which we now read Audelay's work. As a body taken from its place, the book embodies the mortality that Audelay feared it would; but even more perniciously, its loss of situatedness and integrity suggests the termination of damnation rather than the ongoing, restorative work of prayer for the dead. Anyone who cuts out a leaf or takes the book away, says Audelay, will be "accursed in the dede." Its rootedness in the site of its production and its audience suggests more an archive than an anthology, a collection of texts that no longer functions as it should when it is separated from its point of origin, its historical matrix.

Even within the manuscript Audelay and his scribes take care that each text be located, at least notionally, in its proper place. In the first *liber*, entitled "The Counsel of Conscience," the first scribe directs the reader to the "xiij leef afore" for "the day of dome . . . Seche hyt þere þou shalt nott mys."[41] The colophon marks what both rubricator and Audelay regarded as "a definable body of work, separate from what was to follow."[42] It is clear from what the first scribe writes that this first *liber* was conceived and executed as a whole, as well, and the miscopied piece betrays the consciousness that there is a correct place for everything. Such a finding aid is also an archival instrument, a directive that helps to locate crucial information within its context when the sequence can no longer be followed. Indeed, both of the manuscript's concluding pieces refer forward to the worry about the loss of leaves and of lives that the colophon articulates. The final word of *The Three Dead Kings*, "losse," refers catachrestically to damnation; but it also immediately follows the account of the story written on the walls of the minster and imagines "losse" as the consequence for not believing the narrative. It may also anticipate the failure of this archive, the loss of the wall painting, which is also the poem itself. The next poem, "Cur mundus militat," metaphorizes the life of the body as the flower of the grass in sacred "literis," or a "leve folium, quod vento rapitur" (35). This comparison of the loss of life to the loss of a leaf echoes Audelay's own worry about his book's loss of leaves after life draws to an end, and this paronomasia underscores Audelay's equation of life and archive.

In *The Three Dead Kings* also the confrontation of life by is represented as an archival encounter. The second dead king points out that the dead kings are their "faders of fold," but he is first recognized because of the "cros of the cloth • that covered the cyst" (54). The word *cyst* here is primarily metonymy, the seat of the heart standing for the rest of the body, or metaphor, the body as a chest containing the soul. But it may also refer to the thing itself, the chest that is either a coffin or an archival depository; *archa* is used interchangeably with *cista* to designate an archival chest. The word, then, was used for both things, and archival chests often were the size and shape of coffins.[43] Archival chests were identified by systems of *signa*, which corresponded to entries in a cartulary or other document.[44] I do not mean that the "cist" here is primarily an archival chest, but the function of the dead king is also to serve as a kind of walking archive of forefathers. As the multiple endings of the book attest, termination is not complete without, or even because of, copious records of its passage.

Above all, in ending with multiple endings, Audelay turns the book itself into a mirror of his own ending. But it is a mirror reflecting itself, receding infinitely in the search for the "good ende" (38) that is asserted in the book's colophon: "Cuius finis bonus ipsum totum bonum. Finito libro." (39a). The final stanza of the "Conclusion" announces, and sets the conditions for, an archive in which Audelay and his writing can perhaps be disentangled by future readers; but what is important in the poem's immediate horizon here is that there is no distinction between the writer and the work—at least in terms of their endings. This may be a fantasy, but it is one that allows both consolation and *relief* from the finitude that crowds the ending of Audelay's book. As long as one can write about ending, one has not yet ended. The mixed quality of deferral and resignation in Audelay's final stanzas is, in other words, a symptom of the desire to frame work by death—to make the work as densely metonymic as possible—in order to turn finitude into something permanent, rather than a helpful category of ethics. Audelay's endings, in other words, betray a belief in the *being* of death, a permanence that we glimpse by imagining that endings we make are endings that endure, and endings that we imagine have arrived; or, more disturbingly, endings that should arrive but never will.

The three kings go back to their lives chastened, changed men: "thai mend ham that myde" (they kept in mind the final reward [137]). It's a little difficult to say what that means in practice: how did they demonstrate their new orientation to the people around them? Tellingly, I think, the most specific sign of reform is a minster that they build precisely in order to commemorate the event. Unfortunately for the second king, the poem doesn't mention whether the masses said in the minster were for the purpose of "mynnyng" the dead kings (104). The purpose of the minster is ultimately to memorialize, quite literally, the story, which the poem's closing lines tell us is written on the walls. It is likely that the minster does indeed demonstrate the kind of care of the dead that the second king mentions. But that mode is, to read the poem precisely, beside the point of the story. A different kind of care altogether comes into the poem along with the minster: not the visceral terror that the living kings feel, nor the ritual, pious care for the souls of the dead, but something akin to pastoral care. The poem ends with the kind of moralizing conclusion one would expect after an *exemplum* in a sermon, and it echoes the kind of pastoral care that Audelay himself would have performed as a chaplain. But *cura pastoralis* is not precisely the final sense that care has in the poem. The poem is not a sermon exemplum, because, as the poem tells us quite carefully, it is written on the walls of the minster. It is a public, highly visible text that reflects on its own textuality in a number of ways that I have discussed. The story of the poem is the story of how the poem came to be written in the form that it takes, which means that it must talk about itself in the past tense: "on the wowe written this was." This might not be a complete aporia or an unbreakable hermeneutical circle, but it does conclude the poem with a reminder of how highly wrought and conscious of its own form it is. But the poem also recognizes that it demands a particular kind of attention. Its second-to-last line is a skeptical prediction of how the poem will be read: "to lyte will leve þis, alas!" (too few will believe this, alas! [143]). This is not just a pastoral declaration of exasperation with readers; it is also an expression of exasperation over the status of the story as a poem. Will few people believe it because it is a poem? Would a prose account have been more believable? Or does the overwhelming intricacy of the poem offer a warrant of its truth?

No matter what the answers to those questions are, the poem's ending invites—almost demands—that some of the attention we expect to give to amending our lives and preparing for death be given to the poem itself. Why should the poem care whether we believe its story or not? I think Audelay suggests that the attention we give to the poem when we take it seriously is itself a kind of care. The reading of the poem on the wall stands, symbolically and structurally, in the place where one would expect the "mynnyng" of the dead. Reading this story is enacting care for the dead, because it recalls to mind souls that have been deserted, showing what happens when care for the dead is forgotten. It is also about the kind of care that the living should have, the wariness that one should cultivate when death could happen at any moment, the *contemptus mundi* that puts one already in a state of dying. But these lessons can't be drawn from the poem unless one pays—and I mean this in the strictest sense possible—careful attention to the insistent entanglements of the poem's extraordinary form. Reading it elicits, and demands, a care that we would recognize as close reading. But that is not, of course, the purpose for which the poem was written. It demonstrates how the kind of care—a constant, scrutinizing vigilance—that it demands from its readers is precisely the kind of care with which one's whole life must be scrutinized. Care is not just the recognition of the presence of death; it is also the recognition that the entanglements of life that inhibit our care in the largest sense need to be examined minutely, and that this is precisely what gives our lives their form.

ACKNOWLEDGMENTS

I would like to thank the Institute for Advanced Study and the Guggenheim Foundation for their generous support at different stages of this project. For valuable conversation, insights, and invitations to give talks at a number of universities I'm grateful to David Aers, Srinivas Aravamudan, Chris Baswell, Sarah Beckwith, Dan Blanton, Katherine Brown, Eduardo Cadava, Andrew Cole, Giles Constable, Rita Copeland, Kathleen Davis, Caroline Dinshaw, John Fleming, Aranye Fradenburg, Diana Fuss, Emma Gorst, Virginie Greene, Ralph Hanna, Anselm Haverkamp, Daniel Heller-Roazen, Bruce Holsinger, Fredric Jameson, Claudia Johnson, Sarah Kay, Ranjana Khanna, Thomas Laqueur, Clare Lees, Peggy McCracken, Mark Miller, R. D. Perry, Jean-Michel Rabaté, Kellie Robertson (who made some very valuable suggestions as a reader for the Press, as did an anonymous second reader), Martha Rust, Larry Scanlon, Emily Steiner, Susan Stewart, Paul Strohm, David Wallace, Elise Wang, and Michael Wood. The brilliant students in three graduate seminars on death and dying at Princeton University helped me greatly in working through this project. I thought about several books a good deal while writing this book, but their importance for me isn't reflected in the final version of the notes: Thomas Laqueur's *The Work of Dying* in particular, Phillipe Ariès's venerable *Western Attitudes Toward Death from the Middle Ages to the Present*, and Paul Binski's *Medieval Death: Ritual and Representation*. Several books on Middle English literature and death were also helpful: Chris Chism's *Alliterative Revivals*; Sarah Novacich's *Shaping the Archive in Late Medieval England: History, Poetry, and Performance*; Randy Schiff's *Revivalist Fantasy: Alliterative Verse and Nationalist Literary History*. I would also like to thank Randy Petilos at the University of Chicago Press for his incisive guidance and Barbara Norton for her careful copyediting.

Earlier, very different versions of portions of this book were published as follows: chapter 4 in *Reading for Form*, ed. Susan J. Wolfson and Marshall Brown (Seattle: University of Washington Press, 2006), 66–79; chapters 5 and 6 in *South Atlantic Quarterly* 98, no. 3 (Summer 1999): 367–414; and chapter 9 in *New Medieval Literatures*, vol. 5, ed. Rita Copeland, David Lawton, and Wendy Scase (Oxford: Oxford University Press, 2002), 59–85. I thank the journal editors and the publishers for the chance to explore the ideas in these chapters first in their pages.

INTRODUCTION

1. Jane Gilbert, *Living Death in Medieval French and English Literature* (Cambridge: Cambridge University Press, 2011), reads the distribution of mourning and melancholy across a range of French and English texts usefully in terms of the death drive and Lacanian anamorphosis.

2. For a similar position, see Melanie Klein, *The Psychoanalysis of Children*, trans. Alix Strachey (New York: Delacorte Press, 1975).

3. See the discussion of this formalist position in Paul de Man, *Blindness and Insight: Essays in the Rhetoric of Contemporary Criticism* (Minneapolis: University of Minnesota Press, 1983), esp. "Criticism and Crisis," 3–19.

4. See Emmanuel LeRoy Ladurie, *Montaillou: The Promised Land of Error*, trans. Barbara Bray (New York: Vintage, 1979), esp. 218–30; and Thomas W. Laqueur, *The Work of the Dead: A Cultural History of Mortal Remains* (Princeton, NJ: Princeton University Press, 2015).

5. Edward Said, *On Late Style: Music and Literature Against the Grain* (New York: Vintage, 2007). Citations from this work will be made parenthetically within the text.

6. Adorno, "Late Style in Beethoven," 566. In *Essays on Music*, ed. Richard Leppert, trans. Susan Gillespie (Berkeley and Los Angeles: University of California Press), 564–68.

7. Adorno, *Aesthetic Theory*, ed. and trans. Robert Hullot-Kentor (Minneapolis: University of Minnesota Press, 1998), 90. Indeed, elsewhere Adorno describes the notion that death is a final termination as unintelligible, unthinkable—although just as unthinkable as the concept of immortality. Yet is it (?) the unthinkability of finitude that authorizes the possibility of thought itself? "If death were that absolute which philosophy tried in vain to conjure positively, everything is nothing; all that we think, too, is thought into the void; none of it is truly thinkable. . . . Without any duration at all there would be no truth, and the last trace of it would be engulfed in death, the absolute." Theodor W. Adorno, *Negative Dialectics*, trans. E. B. Ashton (London: Routledge, 1981), 317.

8. Adorno, *Aesthetic Theory*, 90.

9. For a useful discussion of Adorno's use of *Geist*, see Adrian Marino, *Adorno's Aesthetics of Music* (Cambridge: Cambridge University Press, 1993), 114–16. Andrew

Hewitt, "Stumbling into Modernity: Body and Soma in Adorno," in *Critical Theory: Current State and Future Prospects*, ed. Peter Uwe Hohendahl and Jaimey Fisher (Oxford: Berghahn, 2001), 69–93, at 72, notes the equivalence of spirit and corpse in Adorno.

10. Adorno, *Aesthetic Theory*, 91.

11. Rossell Hope Robbins, "Signs of Death in Middle English," *Mediaeval Studies* 32 (1970): 282–98.

12. Robbins, "Signs of Death in Middle English," 292.

13. Robbins, "Signs of Death in Middle English," 293.

14. See E. G. Cuthbert F. Atchely, "Some Notes on the Beginning and Growth of the Usage of a Second Gospel at Mass," *Transactions of the St. Paul Ecclesiological Society* 4 (1900): 161–76.

CHAPTER ONE

1. Roger Bacon, *Compendium of the Study of Theology*, ed. and trans. Thomas S. Maloney (Leiden: Brill, 1988), 104.

2. Bacon, *Compendium of the Study of Theology*, 92.

3. Paul Binski, *Medieval Death: Ritual and Representation* (London: British Museum Press, 2001); Michael Camille, *Master of Death: The Lifeless Art of Pierre Remiet, Illuminator* (New Haven, CT: Yale University Press, 1996); and Robert Pogue Harrison, *The Dominion of the Dead* (Chicago: University of Chicago Press, 2003).

4. See, for instance, Simon of Faversham: "quid est eius quod significatur per 'Caesarem'" (to say that Caesar is either alive or dead does not signify). Simon of Faversham, *Quaestiones super libro Elenchorum*, ed. Eileen Serene, Eleonore Stump, Francesco del Punta, Sten Ebbesen, and Thomas Izbicki (Toronto: Pontifical Institute of Medieval Studies, 1984), 161–64, qtd. at 24: "Utrum haec sit vera 'Caesar est mortuus.'"

5. For the poem, see John Lydgate, *The Minor Poems of John Lydgate: Edited from All the Available Mss., with an Attempt to Establish the Lydgate Canon*, vol. 2, ed. Henry Noble MacCracken, Early English Text Society, o.s., 192 (London: Oxford University Press, 1934), 655–57. The illustration is in MS Douce 322, Bodleian Library, Oxford University.

6. See Henry Beauchamp Walters, *Church Bells of England* (London: Oxford University Press, 1912), 154 ff. William Durandus of St. Pourçain's influential thirteenth-century handbook on liturgy, *Rationale divinorum officiorum*, makes it quite clear that the bell should be rung in the last stage of dying: "verum, aliquo moriente, campane debent pulsari ut populus hoc audiens oret pro illo." *Guillelmi Duranti Rationale divinorum officiorum*, 4 vols., ed. A. Davril and T. M. Thibodeau (Turnhout : Brepols, 1995), 1:56 (Lib. I, Cap. IV, 13).

7. Camille also misreads the several thorns as *ys*, so his point is not quite right.

8. On the poverty of direct references to the plague in fourteenth-century English literature, see Siegfried Wenzel, "Pestilence and Middle English Literature: Friar Grimestone's Poems on Death," in *The Black Death: The Impact of the Fourteenth-Century Plague*, ed. Daniel Williman (Binghamton: Center for Medieval and Early Renaissance Studies, 1982), 131–59; and Ardis Butterfield, "Pastoral and the Politics of Plague in Machaut and Chaucer," *Studies in the Age of Chaucer* 16 (1994): 3–27.

9. See David K. Coley, "*Pearl* and the Language of Pestilence," *Studies in the Age of Chaucer* 35 (2013): 209–62.

10. See, for instance, the prologues to both Guillaume de Machaut, *Le jugement du roi de Navarre,* in *Guillaume de Machaut: The Complete Poetry and Music,* vol. 1, *The Debate Series,* ed. R. Barton Palmer and Yolanda Plumley, trans. R. Barton Palmer with Domenic Leo and Uri Smilansky (Kalamazoo, MI: Medieval Institute Publications, 2016); and Giovanni Boccaccio, *Decameron,* trans. Wayne A. Rebhorn (New York: Norton, 2013).

11. See, for example, Jonathan Sklar, *Landscapes of the Dark: History, Trauma, Psychoanalysis* (London: Karnac, 2011).

12. All of these can be found in Aristotle, *The Complete Works: The Revised Oxford Translation,* 2 vols., ed. Jonathan Barnes (Princeton, NJ: Princeton University Press, 1985).

13. D. Vance Smith, *Book of the Incipit: Beginnings in the Fourteenth Century* (Minneapolis: University of Minnesota Press, 2001).

14. On this illustration and its connection to the pictorial schemes of the Franciscan John of Metz, see Mary Dove, *The Perfect Age of Man's Life* (Cambridge: Cambridge University Press, 1986), 80–100. See also Lucy Freedman Sandler, *The Psalter of Robert de Lisle in the British Library* (Turnhout: Brepols, 1999).

15. The poem is quoted in Dove, *The Perfect Age of Man's Life,* 90.

16. Albertus Magnus, *De sex principiis,* in *Opera Omnia,* vol. 1, ed. Auguste Borgnet (Paris: Vivès, 1890), tract. V, cap. Iii, 349A.

17. Albertus Magnus, *De morte et vita,* in *Opera Omnia,* vol. 9, ed. Auguste Borgnet (Paris: Vivès, 1890), tract. I, cap. i, 345a.

18. Margaret Jennings, *The "Ars componendi sermons" of Ranulph Higden, O.S.B.,* Davis Medieval Texts and Studies 6 (Leiden: E. J. Brill, 1991), 53.

19. Boethius, *Theological Tractates and the Consolation of Philosophy,* trans. H. F. Stewart, E. K. Rand, and S. J. Tester (Cambridge, MA: Harvard University Press, 1973), book 4, pt. 2: "nam uti cadauer hominem mortuum dixeris, simpliciter uero hominem appellare non possis . . . est enim quod ordinem retinet seruatque naturam; quod uero ab hac deficit esse etiam, quod in sua natura situm est, derelinquit."

20. Aristotle, *Meteorology,* IV.12: 329b31–330a2. The discussion of the hand and its *ergon* appears in *De partibus animalium,* I.1 640b34–641a21. Both of these are in Aristotle, *The Complete Works: The Revised Oxford Translation,* 2 vols., ed. Jonathan Barnes (Princeton, NJ: Princeton University Press, 1985).

21. L. M. de Rijk, *Aristotle: Semantics and Ontology* (Leiden: Brill, 2002), 339.

22. Peter Abelard, *Logica "ingredientibus,"* pt. 3, *Commentary on Aristotle's "De interpretation,"* ed. Klaus Jacobi and Christian Strub, Corpus Christianorum Continuatio Mediaevalis 206 (Turnhout: Brepols, 2010), 479, 18–21. See Allan Bäck, *On Reduplication: Logical Theories of Qualification* (Leiden: Brill, 1996), 129–31.

23. See Thomas Maloney, introduction to Roger Bacon, *Compendium of the Study of Theology,* trans. Thomas Maloney (Leiden: Brill, 1988), 15. On Ockham, see Allan Bäck, "The Ordinary Language Approach in Traditional Logic," in *Argumentationstheorie: Scholastische Forschungen zu den logischen und semantischen Regeln korrekten Folgerns,* ed. Klaus Jacobi (Leiden: Brill, 1993), 507–30, esp. 524–27.

24. See Sten Ebbesen, "A Dead Man Is Alive," *Synthese* 40 (1979): 43–70.

25. Richard Kilvington, *The Sophismata of Richard Kilvington*, ed. Norman Kretzmann and Barbara Kretzmann (Cambridge: Cambridge University Press, 1990), 102.

26. Thomas Aquinas, *Expositio libri Peryermeneias*, trans. Joel T. Oesterle (Milwaukee, MN: Marquette University Press, 1962), Book II, Lesson 7:8.

27. Peter Abelard, *Dialectica*, ed. L. M. de Rijk (Assen: Van Gorcum, 1970), 197. The example of the dead man comes ultimately from Aristotle's *Peri hermeneias*. See *The Organon, or Logical Treatises, of Aristotle*, vol. 1, ed. and trans. Octavius Freire Owen (London: Bell, 1908), chap. 12, p. 69.

28. Augustine, *City of God*, vol 4, *Books 12–15*, trans. Philip Levine (Cambridge, MA: Harvard University Press, 1966), 13.9: "Aut si moriens potius dicendus est, in cuius iam corpore agitur ut moriatur, nec simul quisquam potest esse uiuens et moriens: nescio quando sit uiuens."

29. Augustine, *City of God*, 13.10.

30. Augustine, *City of God*, 13.11: "Quando itaque sit moriens, id est in morte, ubi neque sit uiuens, quod est ante mortem, neque mortuus, quod est post mortem, sed moriens, id est in morte, difficillime definitur."

31. Augustine, *City of God*, 13.11.

32. See S. Knuuttila and A. I. Lehtinen, " 'Plato in Infinitum Remisse Incipit Esse Albus': New Texts on the Late Medieval Discussion on the Concept of Infinity in Sophismata Literature," in *Essays in Honour of Jaako Hintikka: On the Occasion of His Fiftieth Birthday*, ed. Esa Saarinen, Risto Hilpinen, Ilkka Niiniluoto, and Merrill Provence Hintikka (Dordrecht: Reidel, 1979), 309–29; Kaye, *Economy and Nature in the Fourteenth Century: Money, Market Exchange, and the Emergence of Scientific Thought* (Cambridge: Cambridge University Press, 1998), 201.

33. Robert Kilwardby was especially alert to the consequences for logic of more radical understandings of temporality than his. One of his ten condemnations of certain logical propositions, for instance, sought specifically to restrict the distribution of terms to a "common time," rather than to a "confused time," which would be different for every person who read or uttered a proposition containing such a term: "Item quod terminus cum verbo de presenti distribuitur pro omnibus differentiis temporum." *Chartularium Universitatis parisiensis*, vol. 1, ed. Heinrich S. Denifle and Émile L. M. Chatelain (Paris, 1889), 60.

34. Albert the Great, "Questions on Book X of the Ethics," in *The Cambridge Translations of Medieval Philosophical Texts*, vol. 2, *Ethics and Political Philosophy*, ed. and trans. Arthur Stephen McGrade, John Kilcullen, and M. S. Kempshall (Cambridge: Cambridge University Press, 2001), 49 [3b]. As Albert puts it a little enigmatically in his commentary on Aristotle's *Physics*, "terminus semper est alterius quam sit terminus." Albertus Magnus, *Physicorum libri VIII*, in *Opera Omnia*, vol. 3, ed. Auguste Borgnet (Paris: Vivès, 1890), 473.'

35. For a useful summary of the logical development of the question, see Christoph Kann, " 'Incipit'/'desinit' und die Semantik der Dauer in der mittelalterlichen Logik," in *Das Sein der Dauer*, ed. Andreas Speer and David Wirmer, Miscellanea Mediaevalia 34 (Berlin: de Gruyter, 2008), 89–110.

36. The most important work here is Walter Burley, *De primo et ultimo instanti*, in "*De primo et ultimo instanti* des Walter Burley," ed. H. Shapiro and Ch. Shapiro, *Archiv für Geschichte der Philosophie* 47 (1965): 157–73.

37. In his treatise on first and last instants of change, for example, Paul of Venice moves between both disciplines: he uses the standard example from supposition and modistic theory for designating actions that took place in the past, "sors currit," to discuss physical change. See A. di Liscia, "Tractatus de primo et ultimo instanti Pauli Veneti," in *Das Sein der Dauer*, ed. Andreas Speer and David Wirmer, Miscellanea Mediaevalia 34 (Berlin: de Gruyter, 2008), 144–50, at 145.

38. John Wycliffe, *Tractatus de logica*, 3 vols., ed. Michael Henry Dziewicki (London: Trübner, 1893–99), 3:100–101. Translations from this text are mine.

39. For a useful discussion of Wycliffe's philosophy of time, see Stephen Lahey, *John Wyclif* (Oxford: Oxford University Press, 2009), 118–20. I borrow the film metaphor here from Lahey.

40. "Quod corpus moritur vel mortem patitur quando non est, vel quod separatur pro instanti quando non est anima, aut quod mors non potest esse possibilis, terribilis, vel timenda." Wycliffe, *Tractatus de logica*, 3:101.

41. "Si aliquid moritur, vel mors sibi inest altero dictorum modorum, tunc vivit pro eadem mensura temporis." Wycliffe, *Tractatus de logica*, 3:101.

42. Peter Lombard, *Sententiarum quatuor libri*, vol. 2 of *S. Bonaventurae Opera Omnia*, ed. Collegii S. Bonaventura (Florence: Quaracchi, 1885), II, dist. 19, cap. 6. G. W. F. Hegel, *Über die wissenschaftlichen Behandlungsarten des Naturrechts: Auf der Grundlage der Werke von 1832–1845 neu edierte Ausgabe*, ed. Eva Moldenhauer and Karl Markus Michel (Frankfurt: Suhrkamp, 1979), 434.

43. For a brief but informative discussion of the appearance of the term *latitudo* in philosophical discussions of the limits of human life from the middle of the thirteenth century, especially in Arnaldus de Villanova and Thomas Aquinas, see *Arnaldi de Villanova opera medica omnia*, vol. 2, *Aphorismi de gradibus*, ed. M. R. McVaugh (Granada: Seminarium Historiae Medicae Granatensis, 1975), 92–95. The Galenic sources are in *Galeni De temperamentis libri tres*, ed. G. Helmreich (Leipzig: B. G. Teubner, 1904), and *Ars parva*, translated from the Arabic by Gerald of Cremona (in Galen, *Opera omnia Galeni* [Venice: Philippus Pincius, 1490], 10ra–15vb). McVaugh argues that the discussion in Avicenna's *Canon* is the most likely vector of transmission of the term; see *Arnaldi de Villanova*, 93 n. 5.

44. As late as the third decade of the fifteenth century, medical treatises were still citing the work of Mertonian calculators on the intension and remission of forms. See Brian Lawn, *The Rise and Decline of the Scholastic "Quaestio Disputata": With Special Emphasis on Its Use in the Teaching of Medicine and Science* (Leiden: Brill, 1993), 77–78.

45. See David C. Lindberg, *Science in the Middle Ages* (Chicago: University of Chicago Press, 1978), 231–34. A brief discussion of the *latitudo sanitatis* with *mors* at its base is in John E. Murdoch, *Album of Science: Antiquity and the Middle Ages* (New York: Scribner's, 1984), 160. See also P. G. Ottosson, *Scholastic Medicine and Philosophy* (Naples: Bibliopolis, 1984). Rega Wood, "Calculating Grace: The Debate about Latitude of Forms According to Adam De Wodeham," in *Knowledge and the Sciences in Medieval Philosophy: Proceedings of the Eighth International Congress of Medieval Philosophy, Helsinki, 24–29 August 1987*, vol. 2, ed. Simo Knuuttila, Reijo Työrinoja, and Sten Ebbesen (Helsinki: Luther-Agricola Society, 1990), 373–91.

46. The following discussion of Bonaventure is drawn from Bonaventure, *Commentaria in quatuor libros Sententiarum Magistri Petri Lombardi*, 4 vols. (Rome: Ad Claras Aquas, 1934–41), book II, dist. XVII, art. II.

47. Gillian Rose, *Mourning Becomes the Law: Philosophy and Representation* (Cambridge: Cambridge University Press, 1996), 32.

CHAPTER TWO

1. The difference the Norman Conquest makes is the subject of some debate. See, for instance, the essays collected in Mary Swan and Elaine M. Treharne, *Rewriting Old English in the Twelfth Century* (Cambridge: Cambridge University Press, 2000); Elaine Treharne, *Living through Conquest: The Politics of Early English, 1020–1220* (Oxford: Oxford University Press, 2012); and Laura Ashe, *The Oxford English Literary History*, vol. 1, *1000–1350: Conquest and Transformation* (Oxford: Oxford University Press, 2017).

2. See, for instance, Christopher Cannon, *The Grounds of English Literature* (Oxford: Oxford University Press, 2008), esp. 17–49. For a discussion of how the Conquest produced a new sense of English identity, see Laura Ashe, *Fiction and History in England, 1066–1200* (Cambridge: Cambridge University Press, 2008).

3. W. P. Ker, *English Literature: Medieval* (London: Williams & Norgate, 1912), 51; Stanley B. Greenfield, "The Old English Elegies," in *Continuations and Beginnings: Studies in Old English Literature*, ed. E. G. Stanley (London: Thomas Nelson, 1966), 142–75, at 142; and Jeffrey J. Cohen, *Medieval Identity Machines* (Minneapolis: University of Minnesota Press, 2003), 136.

4. The Norman invasion as a manufactured crisis has a long history, beginning with Henry of Huntingdon's description of it as the Almighty's alienation of "favour and rank from the English nation as it deserved, and caused it to cease to be a people." Henry of Huntingdon, *The Chronicle of Henry of Huntingdon*, ed. and trans. Thomas Forester (London: H. G. Bohn, 1853), book 7, 222. It was the last of a series of plagues sent by God to destroy the English for their sins, whereby the English language and the "English nationality," as R. W. Chambers put it in a famous 1932 essay, "were nearly destroyed," and after which the writing of English virtually ended. See the introduction to R. W. Chambers, ed., *On the Continuity of English Prose from Alfred to More and His School*, Early English Text Society, o.s., 191A (London: Oxford University Press, 1932), lxxxii.

5. For a characterization of Old English verse as mourning its own history, see Renée R. Trilling, *The Aesthetics of Nostalgia: Historical Representation in Old English Verse* (Toronto: University of Toronto Press, 2009).

6. Seth Lerer, "The Genre of the Grave and the Origins of the Middle English Lyric," *Modern Language Quarterly* 58 (1997): 127–61, at 138.

7. Geoffrey Shepherd, "Early Middle English Literature," in *The Middle Ages: The Sphere History of Literature*, vol. 1, rev. ed., ed. W. F. Bolton (London: Sphere, 1986), 81–117, at 81. Quoted in Thomas Hahn, "Early Middle English," in *The Cambridge History of Medieval English Literature*, ed. David Wallace (Cambridge: Cambridge University Press, 1999), 61–91, at 61.

8. Hahn, "Early Middle English," 70.

9. Maurice Blanchot, "Literature and the Right to Death," in *The Work of Fire*, trans. Lydia Davis (Stanford, CA: Stanford University Press, 1995), 300–344, at 336; emphasis in original.

10. Blanchot, "Literature and the Right to Death," 327.

11. Blanchot, "Literature and the Right to Death," 341.

12. For the argument that the passage spoken by the redeemed soul is a later addition, see the introduction to Douglas Moffat, ed., *The Old English Soul and Body* (Woodbridge: Boydell, 1990), at 44; and Victoria Thompson, *Dying and Death in Later Anglo-Saxon England* (Woodbridge: Boydell, 2004), 140–43. Allen Frantzen argues that it may have been part of the original composition. Allen J. Frantzen, "The Body in *Soul and Body I*," *Chaucer Review* 17 (1982): 76–88, at 83. All citations of this work refer to Moffat's edition and will be made parenthetically within the text.

13. Masha Raskolnikov argues that the Middle English debate between body and soul in the early fourteenth-century poem *In a Thestri Stude* (found in MS Harley 2253) marks a distinct break with the "mannered and convention-bound world of female 'allegorical goddesses'" and entered a world in which homosociality and murky hierarchies trouble the traditional decorum of soul and body: "either character could end up on top." As Raskolnikov points out, *In a Thestri Stude* differs from later debate poems because the body, as she puts it, "claims repeatedly that it would prefer to remain silent." Masha Raskolnikov, *Body against Soul: Gender and Sowlehele in Middle English Allegory* (Columbus: Ohio State University Press, 2009), 74–75.

14. S.v. "wemman," in Joseph Bosworth and T. Northcote Toller, *An Anglo-Saxon Dictionary* (Oxford: Clarendon Press, 1898).

15. The Middle English poem can be found in Douglas Moffat, ed., *The Soul's Address to the Body (The Worcester Fragments)* (East Lansing, MI: Colleagues Press, 1987).

16. Boethius, *Commentarii in librum Aristotelis Peri hermeneias pars posterior*, ed. C. Meiser (Leipzig: Teubner, 1880), 1.01.

17. The question of which faculties, precisely, continued after death was a one that was debated throughout much of the Middle Ages.

18. "Since the word consists of sound and meaning, and sound pertains to the ears, don't you think that in the word, as in any living creature, the sound is the body and the meaning the soul of the sound, as it were." Augustine, *De quantitate animae: The Measure of the Soul*, ed. and trans. Francis Tourscher (Philadelphia: Peter Reilly, 1933), xxxii.66. Vivien Law quotes a passage from Priscian in which the author argues that it is the understanding of the hearer that animates the lifeless body of the word: "Just as the human body is composed of its members joined in a firm union, and that body is ruled and governed by the rational soul, so too articulate speech is made up of its units, limbs, as were—speech sounds, syllables and words—into a single body, and is brought alive by another's understanding as if with life and soul"; Vivien Law, *Wisdom, Authority and Grammar in the Seventh Century: Decoding Virgilius Maro Grammaticus* (Cambridge: Cambridge University Press, 1995), 58–59.

19. Augustine, *The Immortality of the Soul; The Magnitude of the Soul; On Music; The Advantage of Believing; On Faith in Things Unseen*, ed. and trans. Ludwig Schopf (Washington, DC: Catholic University of America Press, 1947), 133.

20. Cf. Augustine, *De quantitate animae*; for Aelfric, see Aelfric of Eynsham, *Aelfrics Grammatik und Glossar*, ed. Julius Zupitza (Berlin: Weidmannsche Buchhandlung, 1880), 4. All citations of these works will be made parenthetically within the text.

21. See the "Sermon for Shrove Sunday" in Aelfric, *Aelfric's Catholic Homilies, the First Series*, ed. Peter Clemoes, Early English Text Society, s.s., 17 (Oxford: Oxford University Press, 1997), 1.10.

22. Aelfric, *Aelfrics Grammatik und Glossar*. For more information on Dunstan and Aethelwold's reform efforts in relation to Latin learning, see respectively Michael Winterbottom and Michael Lapidge, ed. and trans., *The Early Lives of St Dunstan* (Oxford: Oxford University Press, 2012), and Wulfstan of Winchester, *Vita Sancti Aethelwoldi: The Life of Saint Aethelwold*, ed. Michael Lapidge and Michael Winterbottom (Oxford: Oxford University Press, 1991).

23. Aelfric, *Aelfrics Grammatik und Glossar*, 1.

24. See Gabrielle Spiegel, *The Past as Text: The Theory and Practice of Medieval Historiography* (Baltimore, MD: Johns Hopkins University Press, 1999), 57.

25. Cf. Riddle 19, "þrafaþ on þystrum." For the riddles, see Elliott van Kirk Dobbie and George Philip Krapp, eds., *The Exeter Book*, Anglo-Saxon Poetic Records 3 (New York: Columbia University Press, 1936). Cf. Matthew 22:13 (the parable of the wedding feast): "& se cyning cwæþ to hys þenon gebindað hys handa & hys fet & wurpaþ hyne on þa uttran þystro. þær byþ wop & toþa gristbitung"; Charles Hardwick, ed., *The Gospel According to Saint Matthew in Anglo-Saxon and Northumbrian Versions, Synoptically Arranged with Collations of the Best Manuscripts* (Cambridge: Cambridge University Press, 1858), 168. See also Matthew 25:30 (the parable of the talents, which Aelfric is quoting here): "wurpað þone unnyttan þeowan on þa uttran þystru." Hardwick, *The Gospel According to Saint Matthew*, 196.

26. "Þa geseah ic saemninga beforan unc onginnan ðeostrian ða stowe & miclum ðeostrum all gefylled . . . Mid ðy wit ða in ða þeostro ineodon, & heo styccemaelum swa micel & swa ðicco waeron, þaet ic noht geseon meahte . . . & mid ðy wit ða forðgongende waeron under ðaem scuan þaere ðeostran nihte." T. A. Miller, ed., *The Old English Version of Bede's "Ecclesiastical History of the English People,"* 2 vols. in 4 parts, Early English Text Society, o.s., 95 and 96 (London: Oxford University Press, 1890–91), 2:426.

27. Seth Lerer, *Literacy and Power in Anglo-Saxon Literature* (Lincoln: University of Nebraska Press, 1991). For a more recent reading of "dyrne" as being essential to Old English literary production, see Benjamin Saltzman, "Secrecy and the Hermeneutic Potential in *Beowulf*," *PMLA* 133 (2018): 36–55.

28. Cf. Fred C. Robinson, "Artful Ambiguities in the Old English 'Book Moth' Riddle," in *Anglo-Saxon Poetry: Essays in Appreciation*, ed. Lewis Nicholson and Dorothy Warwick Frese (Notre Dame, IN: University of Notre Dame Press, 1975), 355–62.

29. Cf. James E. Anderson, "*Deor, Wulf and Eadwacer*, and *The Soul's Address*: How and Where the Old English *Exeter Book Riddles* Begin," in *The Old English Elegies: New Essays in Criticism and Research*, ed. Martin Green (Teaneck, NJ: Fairleigh Dickinson University Press, 1983), 204–30; and James E. Anderson, *Two Literary Riddles in the Exeter Book: Riddle 1 and the Easter Riddle; A Critical Edition with Full Translations* (Norman: University of Oklahoma Press, 1986).

30. Porphyry, *Isagoge*, in *Aristoteles latinus*, I.6–7, in *Categoriarum supplementa:*

Porphyrii Isagoge translatio Boethii et anonymi fragmentum vulgo vocatum "Liber sex principiorum," ed. L. Minio-Paluello, trans. B. G. Dod (Bruges and Paris: Desclée de Brouwer, 1966), *Isagoge* 7.19-23; *Aristoteles latinus* I.6: 13-14.

31. For Aristotle's works, see Aristotle, *The Complete Works: The Revised Oxford Translation,* 2 vols., ed. Jonathan Barnes (Princeton, NJ: Princeton University Press, 1985).

32. Alcuin of York, *De dialectica,* Patrologia Latina 101 (Paris: J. P. Migne, 1863), 949-76; see, at 953B: "quae sensum nostrum per varias divisiones rerum communium ad proprietatem cujuslibet rei introducit."

33. Quoted in D. P. Henry, "Predictables and Categories," in *The Cambridge History of Later Medieval Philosophy,* ed. Norman Kretzmann, Anthony Kenny, and Jan Pinborg (Cambridge: Cambridge University Press, 1988), 128-42, at 132. See also Boethius, "On Division," in *The Cambridge Translation of Medieval Philosophical Texts,* vol. 1, *Logic and the Philosophy of Language,* ed. Norman Kretzmann and Eleonore Stump (Cambridge: Cambridge University Press, 1989), 12-28.

34. "[P]roprie autem terra ad distinctionem <harenae>." Aldhelm, *Through a Gloss Darkly: Aldhelm's Riddles in the British Library MS Royal 12.C.xxiii,* ed. and trans. Nancy Porter Stork (Toronto: PIMS, 1990), 100.

35. Stork amends the Royal MS reading "harenae" to "aquae" because the gloss ends with a citation of the "aridam terram" of Genesis 1:10, but the point would still be the same: that "terra" is to be distinguished from "aqua," and here literally separated from it, as different species of the genus "tellus." Aldhelm, *Through a Gloss Darkly,* 100.

36. Aldhelm, *Through a Gloss Darkly,* 102.

37. Aldhelm, *Through a Gloss Darkly,* 127. There are four other examples of this kind of glossing (55); another kind, which Stork calls the "nomen" gloss, uses a genus term for otherwise unknown or untranslatable terms, such as as "creta: nomen insulae" (55).

38. Boethius, *De divisione liber,* ed. John Magee (Leiden: Brill, 1998), 8; and Boethius, *Opera omnia,* Patrologia Latina 64 (Paris: J. P. Migne, 1847), 877. These three kinds of division belong to what Boethius calls "intrinsic partition"; extrinsic partition, also divided into three branches, concerns accidents: of subject into accidents, of accident into subjects, of accident into accidents.

39. Otto Gerhard Oexle, "Memoria und Memorialüberlieferung im früheren Mittelalter," *Frühmittelalterliche Studien* 10 (1978): 70-95, at 78. See also Léopold Deslisle, ed., *Rouleaux des morts du IXe au XVe siècle* (Paris: Mme. Ve. J. Renouard, 1866); and Jean Dufour, "Les rouleaux des morts," in *Codicologica 3: Essais typologiques,* ed. A. Gruys and J. P. Gurnbert (Leiden: Brill, 1980), 96-102. On the famous roll for Abbess Matilda, the verses from the Abbey of Edwardstowe, Shaftsbury, in quoting a line from Virgil's *Eclogues* ("Your renown, your name, your praise will ever remain"), place the commemoration of Matilda in a specifically literary register (122). Yet the verse additions of several male communities question the suitability of commemorating a woman in this fashion, making the misogynistic claim that because death entered the world through a woman, a woman should not be celebrated in death (101). For Matilda's roll, see Daniel Sheerin, "Sisters in the Literary Agon: Texts from Communities of Women on the Mortuary Roll of the Abbess Matilda of La Trinité, Caen," in *Women Writing Latin,* vol. 2, *Medieval Women Writing Latin,* ed. Laurie J. Churchill, Phyllis R. Brown, and Jane E. Jeffrey (New York: Routledge, 2002), 93-131.

40. London, British Library, MS Egerton 2849.

41. "Die ungeheure Macht des Negativen; es ist die Energie des Denkens, des reinen Ichs. Der Tod, wenn wir jene Unwirklichkeit so nennen wollen." G. W. F. Hegel, *Phänomenologie des Geistes*, vol. 3 of *Hegel: Werke* (Berlin: Hegel-Institut, 1999), 36.

42. See Riddle 43 in Dobbie and Krapp, *The Exeter Book*; for the translation, see Kevin Crossley-Holland, ed., *The Anglo-Saxon World: An Anthology* (Oxford: Oxford University Press, 1999), 246.

43. For a thorough discussion, see Knud Ottosen, *The Responsories and Versicles of the Latin Office of the Dead* (Aarhus: Aarhus University Press, 1993).

44. Quoted in this chapter, n. 30.

45. Aelfric, *Aelfrics Grammatik und Glossar*; further citations of this work will be made parenthetically within the text.

46. Cf. E. J. Christie, "Writing," in *A Handbook of Anglo-Saxon Studies*, ed. Jacqueline Stodnick and Renée Trilling (Oxford: Blackwell, 2012), 281–94, esp. 289–90.

47. Daniel Anlezark, ed. and trans., *The Old English Dialogues of Solomon and Saturn* (Cambridge: D. S. Brewer, 2009), at 99a for "bocstafa brego" and 85a for the injunction to sing. For further discussion, see Katherine O'Brien O'Keeffe, *Visible Song: Transitional Literacy in Old English Verse* (Cambridge: Cambridge University Press, 1990), 54–59; and R. I. Page, "Anglo-Saxon Runes and Magic," in *Runes and Runic Inscriptions: Collected Essays on Anglo-Saxon and Viking Runes*, ed. David Parsons (Woodbridge: Boydell & Brewer, 1995), 105–26.

48. Anlezark, *The Old English Dialogues of Solomon and Saturn*, 161–63a.

49. Martin Heidegger, *Being and Time*, trans. Joan Stambaugh, rev. Dennis J. Schmidt (Albany: State University of New York Press, 2010), esp. 81–87.

50. The heterogeneity of inscription is discussed further in Lerer, *Literacy and Power*.

CHAPTER THREE

1. Derek Pearsall reads it this way in *Old and Middle English Poetry* (London: Routledge & Kegan Paul, 1977) at 76. See also Christopher Cannon, *The Grounds of English Literature* (Oxford: Oxford University Press, 2004), 33–42.

2. On the Tremulous Hand as a link to earlier literature, see Elaine Treharne, "Making Their Presence Felt: Readers of Ælfric, c. 1050–1350," in *A Companion to Ælfric*, ed. Hugh Magennis and Mary Swan (Leiden: Brill, 2010), 399–422.

3. On the Tremulous Hand's language, see Christine Franzen, *The Tremulous Hand of Worcester: A Study of Old English in the Thirteenth Century* (Oxford: Oxford University Press, 1991).

4. Similar points might be made about the poem *Durham* or the linguistic shift in *The Peterborough Chronicle*. For *Durham*, see Elliott van Kirk Dobbie, ed., *The Anglo-Saxon Minor Poems*, Anglo-Saxon Poetic Records 6 (New York: Columbia University Press, 1942), 27. For *The Peterborough Chronicle*, see Susan Irvine, ed., *The Anglo-Saxon Chronicle: A Collaborative Edition*, vol. 7, MSE (Cambridge: D. S. Brewer, 2004).

5. Seth Lerer, "The Genre of the Grave and the Origins of the Middle English Lyric," *Modern Language Quarterly* 58 (1997): 127–61, at 138.

6. Seth Lerer, "Old English and Its Afterlives," in *A Cambridge History of Medieval English Literature*, ed. David Wallace (Cambridge: Cambridge University Press, 1999), 7–34, at 26.

7. Text cited in S. K. Brehe, "Reassembling the First Worcester Fragment," *Speculum* 65 (1990): 521–36, at 530. Further citations of this work will be made parenthetically, by line number, within the text.

8. Aelfric, *Aelfric's Lives of Saints*, ed. W. W. Skeat, Early English Text Society, o.s., 76 (London: N. Trübner, 1881), XXVI.64–69, pp. 128–30.

9. Bede, *Ecclesiastical History, Books I–III* (Cambridge, MA: Harvard University Press, 1930), 2.XII.

10. Bede, *Ecclesiastical History, Books IV–V; Lives of the Abbots; Letter to Egbert*, ed. J. E. King (Cambridge, MA: Harvard University Press, 1930), 5.II.

11. See Sarah Larrat Keefer, "Assessing the Liturgical Canticles from the Old English Hexateuch," in *The Old English Hexateuch: Aspects and Approaches*, ed. Rebecca Barnhouse and Benjamin C. Withers (Kalamazoo, MI: Medieval Institute Publications, 2000), 109–43.

12. Susan Rifkin, "Music at Wulfstan's Cathedral," in *St. Wulfstan and His World*, ed. Julia S. Barrow and N. P. Brooks (Aldershot: Ashgate, 2005), 219–29, at 221.

13. Emma Mason, *St. Wulfstan of Worcester: c. 1008–1095* (Oxford: Blackwell, 1990), at 205.

14. Mason, *St. Wulfstan of Worcester*, 197. See also 209–10.

15. Wulfstan's work had a long afterlife; for the persistence of these saints, see Cynthia Turner Camp, *Anglo-Saxon Saints' Lives as History Writing in Late Medieval England* (Cambridge: D. S. Brewer, 2015).

16. For a survey of Latin and Anglo-Norman twelfth-century hagiographies of English saints, see David Rollason, *Saints and Relics in Anglo-Saxon England* (Oxford: Blackwell, 1989), 215–39.

17. The text of *St. Bede's Lament* is older than the manuscript in which it is copied, and most scholars agree that the Tremulous Hand could not have been its author; see Brehe, "Reassembling the First Worcester Fragment," 533.

18. The litany in the *Portiforium* is actually a twelfth-century revision, which shows how extensive the interest in the compilation of English saints remained. See the texts edited in Michael Lapidge, ed., *Anglo-Saxon Litanies of the Saints* (London: Henry Bradshaw Society, 1991). Fols. 93r–107v of Marston MS 22 (Beinecke Library, Yale University, New Haven, CT), a manuscript of mid-thirteenth-century Penitential Psalms followed by a litany of saints, include at least fourteen English saints.

19. Rollason, *Saints and Relics in Anglo-Saxon England*.

20. Maurice Blanchot, "Literature and the Right to Death," in *The Work of Fire*, trans. Lydia Davis (Stanford, CA: Stanford University Press, 1995), 300–344.

21. Douglas Moffat, ed., *The Soul's Address to the Body (The Worcester Fragments)* (East Lansing, MI: Colleagues Press, 1987). All citations of this work refer to this edition and will be made parenthetically, by line number, within the text.

22. G. W. F. Hegel, *Phenomenology of Spirit*, trans. A. V. Miller (Oxford: Clarendon Press, 1977), 488.

23. Heidegger has to say of this issue, "The unifying that rests in λέγειν is neither a mere comprehensive collecting nor a mere coupling of opposites which equalizes all contraries. The ἐν πάντα lets lie together before us in one presencing things which are usually separated from, and opposed to, one another, such as day and night, winter and summer, peace and war, waking and sleep, Dionysus and Hades." Martin Heidegger, "Logos (Heraclitus, Fragment B 50)," in *Early Greek Thinking* (New York: Harper & Row, 1984), 59–78, at 71.

24. G. W. F. Hegel, *Jenenser Realphilosophie*, vol. 2, *Vorlesungen von 1805–1806*, ed. J. Hoffmeister, 2nd ed. (Leipzig: F. Meiner, 1931); and Hegel, *Jenaer Realphilosophie*, ed. J. Hoffmeister (Hamburg: F. Meiner, 1967). Quoted and translated in Giorgio Agamben, *Language and Death: The Place of Negativity*, trans. Karen E. Pinkus and Michael Hardt (Minneapolis: University of Minnesota Press, 1991), 44.

25. G. W. F. Hegel, *The Philosophy of Nature*, trans. A. V. Miller (Oxford: Clarendon Press, 1970), 384.

26. For a different discussion of the complex negotiations of agency one finds in Anglo-Saxon monastic contexts, see Katherine O'Brien O'Keeffe, *Stealing Obedience: Narratives of Agency and Identity in Later Anglo-Saxon England* (Toronto: University of Toronto Press, 2012).

27. The most recent edition is by Douglas Moffat. Moffat's and Ernst Jaufe's editions read here: "þ<u ma>kien lufe"; the editions of S. W. Singer, Joseph Hall, and Gail D. D. Ricciardi have "þ<u ma>kien." It's possible that the scribe meant "lofe" (praise) for "lufe," although Moffat disputes this emendation and discusses these other editions on p. 88.

28. These examples are listed in Moffat, *The Soul's Address*, 36.

29. Augustine, *The City of God*, trans. Marcus Dods (Edinburgh: T. & T. Clark, 1913), 11.18.

30. Hegel, *Phenomenology of Spirit*, para. 188.

CHAPTER FOUR

1. Hilda M. R. Murray, ed., *Erthe upon Erthe*, Early English Text Society, o.s., 141 (London: Oxford University Press, 1911). The poem will be drawn from this edition.

2. Susanna Fein, David Raybin, and Jan Ziolkowski, eds. and trans., *The Complete Harley 2253 Manuscript*, 3 vols. (Kalamazoo, MI: Medieval Institute Publications, 2015).

3. Mary Douglas, *Purity and Danger: An Analysis of Concepts of Corruption and Taboo* (London: Routledge, 2002). Julia Kristeva, *Powers of Horror: An Essay on Abjection*, trans. Leon S. Roudiez (New York: Columbia University Press, 1982).

4. For a transcript of the speech containing this famous definition, see Evelyn Ashley, *The Life and Correspondence of Henry John Temple, Viscount Palmerston*, vol. 2 (London: Richard Bentley & Sons, 1879), 246.

5. Douglas Moffat, ed., *The Soul's Address to the Body (The Worcester Fragments)* (East Lansing, MI: Colleagues Press, 1987).

6. For an overview of beliefs, see Caroline Walker Bynum, *The Resurrection of the Body in Western Christianity, 200–1336* (New York: Columbia University Press, 1995).

7. "[T]hat matter could not be described except by babbling [*balbutiendo*] in a

certain manner, because there was not yet even [*necdum*] that which speech perfectly explains, and (which) indeed [*sed*] even the intellect is deficient in imagining [*in imaginatione*]." Bonaventure, Sentence Commentary, II.12.art 1, q.3.2. See Bonaventure, *Commentaria in quatuor libros Sententiarum Magistri Petri Lombardi*, 4 vols. (Rome: Ad Claras Aquas, 1934–41). For a related discussion in William of Auxerre's *Summa aurea*, see Guillelmus Altissiodorensis, *Summa aurea*, 3 vols., ed. Jean Ribaillier (Paris: CNRS, and Grottaferrata: Collegium S. Bonaventurae ad Claras Aquas, 1980–87).

8. See Alcuin of York, "*Disputatio regalis et nobilissimi juvenis Pippini cum Albino scholastico*: Dialogue of Pepin, the Most Noble and Royal Youth, with the Teacher Albinus," in *Altercatio Hadriani Augusti et Epicteti philosophi*, ed. Lloyd W. Daly and Walther Suchier (Urbana: University of Illinois Press, 1939), 134–46.

9. Isidore of Seville, Liber I, XXIX, in *Etymologiae*, ed. W. M. Lindsay (Oxford: Oxford University Press, 1911). For the English translation, see Isidore of Seville, *The Etymologies of Isidore of Seville*, ed. and trans. Stephen A. Barney, W. J. Lewis, J. A. Beach, and Oliver Berghof (Cambridge: Cambridge University Press, 2010). In Book XI, on the parts of the human, he cites the Vulgate version of Genesis 2:7 ("Et creavit Deus hominem de humo terrae") in a longer account of why the human comes from humus.

10. The examples that survive are fragmentary, but some can be found described in Charles Boutell, *The Monumental Brasses of England* (London: George Bell, 1849).

11. John's brass was probably made at the same time as his father's. For an illuminating discussion of the ordering and use of funerary brasses during the fourteenth century in one family, see Nigel Saul, *Death, Art, and Memory in Medieval England: The Cobham Family and their Monuments, 1300–1500* (Oxford: Oxford University Press, 2001).

12. The Middle English version, however, does seem to be inserted in the space left available after the Latin and Anglo-Norman versions were written down.

13. The statute continues on the dorse of the preceding roll; the text on the verso membrane does not match up with the membrane before it, either.

14. Murray, *Erthe upon Erthe*, "A Version," Poem 2, p. 1, line 11. From MS Harley 913.

15. Murrary, *Erthe upon Erthe*, 45.

16. Murray, *Erthe upon Erthe*, 45.

17. These examples are all drawn from the Harley 913 text.

18. The Latin poem is written first, in the left-hand column, the French in the right-hand column, and the English below both of them, split between the two columns. The English version must not have been on hand, or else must not yet have existed, when the scribe (or poet) wrote the first two, or he would have run the French poem down the left-hand column and wrapped the remainder over into the second column. The English version is either copied much more carelessly than the other two or is being composed as it is written down.

19. See especially Carter Revard, "Richard Hurd and MS Harley 2253," *Notes and Queries* 224 (1970): 199–202; "Three More Holographs in the Hand of the Scribe of MS Harley 2253 in Shrewsbury," *Notes and Queries* (1981): 199–200; "*Gilote et Johane*: An Interlude in B.L. Harley 2253," *Studies in Philology* 79 (1982): 122–46; "Annote and Johon, MS Harley 2253, and *The Book of Secrets*," *English Language Notes* (1999): 5–19; "From French 'Fabliau Manuscripts' and MS Harley 2253 to the *Decameron* and the *Canterbury Tales*," *Medium Aevum* 69 (2000): 261–78; and "Oppositional Thematics and

Metanarrative in MS Harley 2253, Quires 1–6," in *Essays in Manuscript Geography: Vernacular Manuscripts of the English West Midlands from the Conquest to the Sixteenth Century*, ed. Wendy Scase (Turnhout: Brepols, 2007), 95–112.

20. The prose is named "de dissolutione sui corporis." See Marilyn Corrie, "Kings and Kingship in British Library MS Harley 2253," *Yearbook of English Studies* (2003): 64–79, at 67.

21. The most recent edition is by John Conlee, in *Middle English Debate Poetry* (East Lansing, MI: Colleagues Press, 1991), 10–17. It is the central poem of Masha Raskalnikov's *Body against Soul: Gender and Sowlehele in Middle English Allegory* (Columbus: Ohio State University Press, 2009).

22. Geoffrey of Vinsauf, *Poetria nova*, rev. ed., trans. Margaret Nims (Turnhout: Brepols, 2010). For the Latin text, see Edmond Faral, *Les arts poétique du xiie et du xiiie siècle: Recherches et documents sur la technique littéraire du moyen âge* (Paris: Champion, 1962).

23. See Fein's introduction to the poem in Fein, Raybin, and Ziolkowski, *The Complete Harley 2253 Manuscript*, 96. Marjorie Harrington suggests that the scribe laid out the three poems as if they were a single trilingual poem; see her "Of Earth You Were Made: Constructing the Bilingual Poem 'Erþ' in British Library, MS Harley 913," *Florilegium* 31 (2014): 105–37.

24. See Fein's notes to the poem.

25. See Chaucer, *House of Fame*, 734, in *The Riverside Chaucer*, ed. Larry Benson, Robert Pratt, and F. N. Robinson, 3rd ed. (Boston: Houghton Mifflin, 1986).

26. See Roger Bacon, *On Signs*, trans. Thomas S. Maloney (Toronto: Pontifical Institute of Medieval Studies, 2013). For a discussion, see Allan Bäck, "The Ordinary Language Approach," in *Argumentations Theorie: scholastische Forschungen zu den logischen und semantischen Regeln korrecten Folgerns*, ed. Klaus Jacobi (Leiden: Brill, 1993), 519–24.

27. In his Middle Commentary on Aristotle's *Peri hermeneias*: "eadem vox non possit bis proferri" (the same utterance cannot be pronounced twice). Walter Burley, "Walter Burley's Middle Commentary on Aristotle's *Perihermeneias*," ed. Stephen Brown, *Franciscan Studies* 33 (1973): 45–134, at 105. For this discussion of Burley I am greatly indebted to Jordan Kirk's work on nonsense words. See Kirk, "Theories of the Nonsense Word in Medieval England" (Ph.D. diss., Princeton University, 2013); part of this has been published as Jordan Kirk, "The Hideous Noise of Prayer: *The Cloud of Unknowing* and the Syllable-Word," *Exemplaria* 28 (2016): 97–117.

28. Bertrand Russell describes the logical predicament of identity in similar terms: "Identity, an objector may urge, cannot be anything at all: two terms plainly are not identical, and one term cannot be, for what is it identical with?" See Russell, *The Principles of Mathematics*, vol. 1 (Cambridge: Cambridge University Press, 1903), sec. 64, p. 63.

29. See Daniel Heller-Roazen, *De voce*, in *Du bruit à l'oeuvre: Vers un esthétique du désordure*, ed. Juan Rigoli and Christopher Lucken (Geneva: Métis Presses, 2013), 37–48.

30. Sigmund Freud, "The Antithetical Meaning of Primal Words," in *The Standard Edition of the Complete Psychological Works of Sigmund Freud*, vol. 11, trans. James Strachey (London: Hogarth Press, 1957), 155–61.

31. Murray, *Erthe upon Erthe*, 1.

32. Lincoln Cathedral Library MS 91, fol. 279; and Murray, *Erthe upon Erthe*, 6.

33. See Galloway, "The Rhetoric of Riddling in Late-Medieval England: The 'Oxford' Riddles, the *Secretum philosophorum*, and the Riddles in *Piers Plowman*," *Speculum* 70 (1995): 68–105, at 76; and Neil Cartlidge, "The Composition of BL MS Harley 913," *Yearbook of English Studies* 33 (2003): 33–52, at 51.

34. See BL MS Additional 32622; quoted in Andrew Galloway, "The Rhetoric of Riddling," at 76.

35. Galloway, "The Rhetoric of Riddling," 81.

36. Thomas Wright, ed., *Political Songs and Poems Relating to English History*, 2 vols., Rolls Series 14 (London: Her Majesty's Stationary Office, 1859), 1:127.

37. Found in L. M. de Rijk, *Logica modernorum: A Contribution to the History of Early Terminist Logic*, 2 vols. (Assen: Van Gorcum, 1962–67), 1:333.

38. Anne Laskaya and Eve Salisbury, eds., *Sir Orfeo*, in *The Middle English Breton Lays* (Kalamazoo, MI: Medieval Institute Publications, 1995). For Freud's original line, see Sigmund Freud, *New Introductory Lectures on Psycho-Analysis*, in *The Standard Edition of the Complete Psychological Works of Sigmund Freud*, vol. 22, trans. James Strachey (London: Hogarth Press, 1964), 7–182, at 80.

39. Martin Heidegger, *Parmenides*, trans. André Schuwer and Richard Rojcewicz (Bloomington: Indiana University Press, 1992).

40. Sigmund Freud, "Findings, Ideas, Problems," in *The Standard Edition of the Complete Psychological Works of Sigmund Freud*, vol. 23, trans. James Strachey (London: Hogarth Press, 1964), 299–300, at 299.

41. Martin Heidegger, "The Origin of the Work of Art," in *Poetry, Language, Thought* (New York: Harper Perennial, 1971), 15–86, at 47.

42. See Edmund Husserl, "Grundlegende Untersuchungen zum phänomenologischen Ursprung der Räumlichkeit der Natur," in *Philosophical Essays in Memory of Edmund Husserl*, ed. Marvin Farber (Cambridge, MA: Harvard University Press, 1940), 307–25, note detailed in footnote at 307. For a revised English translation of this essay, see Edmund Husserl, "Foundational Investigations of the Phenomenological Origin of the Spatiality of Nature," trans. Leonard Lawler, in Maurice Merleau-Ponty, *Husserl at the Limits of Phenomenology*, ed. and trans. Leonard Lawler and Bettina Bergo (Stanford, CA: Stanford University Press, 2001), 117–31.

CHAPTER FIVE

1. For many of the precise echoes, see James I. Wimsatt, *Chaucer and His French Contemporaries: Natural Music in the Fourteenth Century* (Toronto: University of Toronto Press, 1991).

2. Geoffrey Chaucer, *The Riverside Chaucer*, ed. Larry Benson (Oxford: Oxford University Press, 1986). All citations of Chaucer refer to this edition and will be made parenthetically within the text.

3. Peter W. Travis explores the full implications of the word in his "White," *Studies in the Age of Chaucer* 22 (2000): 1–66.

4. Roger Sherman Loomis dismissed all such speculations almost seventy-five years ago, pointing out another hidden French reference in the details; see Loomis, "Chaucer's Eight Years' Sickness," *Modern Language Notes* 59 (1944): 178–81.

5. For more on Blanche's "nay," see Maud Ellmann, "Blanche," in *Criticism and Critical Theory*, ed. Jeremy Hawthorn (London: Edward Arnold, 1984), 99–110.

6. Ardis Butterfield, *The Familiar Enemy: Chaucer, Language, and Nation in the Hundred Years War* (Oxford: Oxford University Press, 2009), at 291.

7. For the sources, see the translations in Geoffrey Chaucer, *Geoffrey Chaucer's "The Book of the Duchess": A Hypertext Edition*, ed. Murray McGillivrey (Calgary, Canada: University of Calgary Press, 1997).

8. A. C. Spearing, *Medieval Dream-Poetry* (Cambridge: Cambridge University Press, 1976), at 115.

9. Sarah Kay, *The Place of Thought* (Philadelphia: University of Pennsylvania Press, 2007), 101.

10. Gayle Margherita has commented interestingly on the poem's "obsession with the word 'hool'" and its fetishistic relation to the "illusion of plenitude" in *The Romance of Origins: Language and Sexual Difference in Middle English Literature* (Philadelphia: University of Pennsylvania Press, 1994), 93, 97.

11. Kathryn L. Lynch, *Chaucer's Philosophical Visions* (Cambridge: D. S. Brewer, 2000), 57.

12. Guillaume de Machaut, *Le remède de Fortune*, ed. Ernest Hoepffner, vol. 11, *Oeuvres de Guillaume de Machaut* (Paris: Firmin-Didot, 1911), 2:27–28.

13. The extent is most clear in Wimsatt, *Chaucer and His French Contemporaries*.

14. See the poem in Machaut, *Guillaume de Machaut: The Complete Poetry and Music*.

15. See Anne Rooney, *Hunting in Medieval English Literature* (Cambridge: D. S. Brewer, 1993), 143.

16. Susan Schibanoff makes this point in *Chaucer's Queer Poetics: Rereading the Dream Trio* (Toronto: University of Toronto Press, 2006), 81–82.

17. See his commentary on Aristotle's *On Memory and Recollection*, qud. in Mary Carruthers, *The Book of Memory: A Study of Memory in Medieval Culture*, 2nd ed. (Cambridge: Cambridge University Press, 2008), 175.

18. Quoted in Jamie C. Fumo's excellent survey of the poem's reception history, *Making Chaucer's "Book of the Duchess": Textuality and Reception* (Chicago: University of Chicago Press, 2015), 8.

19. William Shakespeare, *The Norton Shakespeare*, ed. Stephen Greenblatt, 3rd ed. (New York: Norton, 2015); all citations of Shakespeare refer to this edition and will be made parenthetically within the text.

20. Jane Gilbert's reading of the poem as a demonstration of the consequences of interminable mourning in psychoanalytic and sociological terms differs from mine, but is enlightening. Gilbert, *Living Death in Medieval French and English Literature* (Cambridge: Cambridge University Press, 2011) 191–200.

21. Guido of Monte Rochen, *Handbook for Curates: A Late Medieval Manual on Pastoral Ministry*, trans. Anne T. Thayer (Washington, DC: Catholic University of America Press, 2011), 69.

22. Cecilia Gaposchkin, *The Making of Saint Louis: Kingship, Sanctity, and Crusade in the Later Middle Ages* (Ithaca, NY: Cornell University Press, 2008), 14–16.

23. Honorius of Autun, *Gemma animae*, vol. 172 of *Patrologia latina*, ed. J.-P. Migne (Paris: J.-P. Migne, 1854), col. 633.

24. Adriano Oliva, *Les débuts de l'enseignement de Thomas d'Aquin et sa conception de la Sacra Doctrina, avec l'édition du prologue de son commentaire des Sentences* (Paris: J. Vrin, 2006), 304; Averroes, *In metaphysicam*, vol. 5, cited in Oliva, *Les débuts*, 304 n. 15.

25. Chaucer has the same verse of *Te ante lucis* in mind, according to Joseph Wittig, when Aleyn and Nicholas joke about the Miller's family's "complyne" of snoring in "The Reeve's Tale." Cited in George Kane, *Chaucer and Langland: Historical and Textual Approaches* (Berkeley and Los Angeles: University of California Press, 1989), 291 n. 21.

26. D. W. Robertson, Jr., *A Preface to Chaucer* (Princeton, NJ: Princeton University Press, 1962).

27. Lotario dei Segni, *De miseria condicionis humane*, ed. Robert E. Lewis (Athens: University of Georgia Press, 1978), 215. The last sentence is from Revelation 9:6.

28. Job 4:12–17.

29. Lotario dei Signi, *De miseria condicionis humane*, 131.

30. Lotario dei Signi, *De miseria condicionis humane*, 131.

31. Lotario dei Signi, *De miseria condicionis humane*, 133.

32. Lotario dei Signi, *De miseria condicionis humane*, 133.

33. For this identification, see Martin Stevens and Kathleen Falvey, "Substance, Accident, and Transformations: A Reading of the 'Pardoner's Tale,'" *Chaucer Review* 17 (1982): 142–58, at 151.

34. *Brev.* I.dcclxxxii; cited in Stephen A. Barney, *The Penn Commentary on Piers Plowman*, vol. 5, *C Passus 20–22; B Passus 18–20* (Philadelphia: University of Pennsylvania Press, 2006), 34 (B.18.35).

35. H. Marshall Leicester, *The Disenchanted Self: Representing the Subject in the Canterbury Tales* (Berkeley and Los Angeles: University of California Press, 1990), 52.

CHAPTER SIX

1. Geoffrey Chaucer, *The Riverside Chaucer*, ed. Larry Benson (Oxford: Oxford University Press, 1986), 1:2750; all citations of Chaucer refer to this edition and will be made parenthetically within the text. As Glending Olson has argued, Arcite's is a good death in medieval terms, accompanied by reconciliation and attended by witnesses. *Canterbury Tales: Fifteen Tales and the General Prologue*, ed. V. A. Kolve and Glending Olson (New York: Norton, 2005), 68–69.

2. Rita Copeland, "Insinuating Authors," in *Taking Liberties with the Author: Selected Essays from the English Institute*, ed. Meredith McGill (ACLS Humanities E-Book, 2013), https://quod.lib.umich.edu/cgi/t/text/text-idx?c=acls;cc=acls;rgn=div2;view=toc;id no=heb90058.0001.001;node=heb90058.0001.001%3A5.1.

3. Giovanni Boccaccio, *Teseida della nozze d'Emilia*, ed. Edvige Agostinelli and William Coleman (Florence: Edizioni del Galluzzo, 2015), XI.

4. Gillian Rose, *Mourning Becomes the Law: Philosophy and Representation* (Cambridge: Cambridge University Press, 1996), 132.

5. On the interruption as a critique of tragedy, see Henry Ansgar Kelly, *Chaucerian Tragedy* (Woodbridge: D. S. Brewer, 1997), 86–88.

6. As Phillippe de Mézières says, a tragedy moves the soul to compunction and tears (anima mea, alecta hac tragedia multipharie ventillata ad compunctionem et lacrimas),

Oracio tragedica 5.11. Quoted in Henry Ansgar Kelly, *Ideas and Forms of Tragedy from Aristotle to the Middle Ages* (Cambridge: Cambridge University Press, 1993), 182.

7. Quoted in *The Riverside Chaucer*, 2987–3089.

8. For Boethius, see *Theological Tractates and the Consolation of Philosophy*, trans. H. F. Stewart, E. K. Rand, and S. J. Tester (Cambridge, MA: Harvard University Press, 1973). Chaucer, of course, makes a translation of Boethius in the *Boece*.

9. Statius, *Thebaid: Books 1–7*, ed. and trans. D. R. Shackleton (Cambridge, MA: Harvard University Press, 2004); and Statius, *Thebaid: Books 8–12; Achilleid*, ed. and trans. D. R. Shackleton (Cambridge, MA: Harvard University Press, 2004). All citations of Statius refer to these editions and will be made parenthetically in the text.

10. Dante, *Inferno*, trans. Jean Hollander and Robert Hollander (New York: Anchor, 2000), 12.11–27.

11. *Boece*, III, prosa 12.4–8.

12. On love as dying, see John Livingston Lowes, "The Loveres Maladye of Hereos," *Modern Philology* 11 (1914): 491–546; "Hereos Again," *Modern Language Notes* 31 (1916) 185–87; Massimo Ciavolella, "Mediaeval Medicine and Arcite's Love Sickness," *Florilegium* 1 (1979): 222–41; Mary Wack, *Lovesickness in the Middle Ages: The Viaticum and Its Commentaries* (Philadelphia: University of Pennsylvania Press, 1990); and Marion A. Wells, *The Secret Wound: Love-Melancholy and Early Modern Romance* (Stanford, CA: Stanford University Press, 2007), esp. 22–44.

13. For a discussion of prison writing as a genre, see Joanna Summers, *Late-Medieval Prison Writing and the Politics of Autobiography* (Oxford: Oxford University Press, 2004)

14. Aristotle argues that the inability to recollect (especially among melancholics) is like, if not the same thing as, physical wandering that they are powerless to terminate. *On Memory and Recollection, Parva naturalia*, trans. W. S. Hett (Cambridge, MA: Harvard University Press, 1957), 453a.

15. *Middle English Dictionary*, "taas," 1.

16. Lee Patterson, *Chaucer and the Subject of History* (Madison: University of Wisconsin Press, 1991), 201.

17. Sigmund Freud, "A Note upon the 'Mystic Writing-Pad,'" in *The Standard Edition of the Complete Psychological Works of Sigmund Freud*, vol. 19, trans. James Strachey (London: Hogarth Press, 1961), 227–32.

18. As Paul Strohm notes, the legitimacy of the gods is "traceable mainly to the respective breadths of their arcs." *Social Chaucer* (Cambridge, MA: Harvard University Press, 1989), 158.

19. See John of Reading, *Chronica Johannis de Reading et anonymi Cantuariensis, 1346–1367*, ed. James Tait (Manchester: Manchester University Press, 1914), 166.

20. Translated in Rosemary Horrox, ed., *The Black Death* (Manchester: Manchester University Press, 1994), 159.

21. Horrox, *The Black Death*, 164.

22. Horrox, *The Black Death*, 166 and 169.

23. Horrox, *The Black Death*, 170–71.

24. Richard Kaeuper, *Chivalry, the State, and Public Order* (Oxford: Clarendon, 1988), 199–208.

25. Horrox, *The Black Death*, 130.

26. Horrox, *The Black Death,* 69.

27. John of Reading, *Chronica Johannis de Reading,* 149.

28. Ovid, *Metamorphoses,* vol. 2, *Books 9–15,* ed. Frank Justus Miller, rev. ed. G. P. Goold (Cambridge, MA: Harvard University Press, 1916), XIII.167–68.

29. The invention of writing is widely compared to the technique of plowing, which gives "verses" their name—from the turning of the instrument back on its own tracks. See, for example, Isidore of Seville, *Etymologiae,* ed. W. M. Lindsay (Oxford: Oxford University Press, 1911), VI.xii.7.

30. Plato, *Cratylus,* trans. C. D. C. Reeve, in Plato, *Complete Works,* ed. John M. Cooper (New York: Hackett, 1997), 101–56.

31. Plato, *Cratylus,* 408C.

32. *The Riverside Chaucer* 840, nn. 2919–24. The term *religio* is James Nohrnberg's, referring to the "backward bent knees" of the satyrs in book 1 of *The Faerie Queene: The Analogy of the Faerie Queene* (Princeton, NJ: Princeton University Press, 1976), 222.

33. Lucan, *The Civil War,* ed. J. D. Duff (Cambridge, MA: Harvard University Press, 1928), III.402–5. I am not sure that this passage has been noticed as a source of the passage in Chaucer.

34. On the inadequacy of Theseus's speech, see H. Marshall Leicester, *The Disenchanted Self: Representing the Subject in the Canterbury Tales* (Berkeley and Los Angeles: University of California Press, 1990), 367–69. V. A. Kolve says of it that as "an instance of human reason attempting to understand on its own the nature and purpose of human existence, it shows reason confounded, not reason triumphant"; *Chaucer and the Imagery of Narrative: The First Five Canterbury Tales* (Palo Alto, CA: Stanford University Press, 1984), 148. See also Joerg Fichte, "Man's Free Will and the Poet's Choice: The Creation of Artistic Order in Chaucer's 'Knight's Tale,'" *Anglia* 93 (1975): 335–60.

35. *Boece,* V pr. 6; line 180.

36. Chaucer's threefold naming of the "love" between Theseus and Perotheus in the space of three lines (I.1196–98) belies the Knight's abrupt dismissal of it ("But of that storie list me nat to telle" [(I.1200)]) and "The Knight's Tale"'s deliberate curtailing of the consolatory possibility of love.

37. Rose, *Mourning Becomes the Law,* 122; emphasis in original.

38. Most readings of Theseus have argued that he is a normative avatar of Lady Philosophy, that his speech at the end of "The Knight's Tale" is a noncritical endorsement of the cosmological principle of the fair chain of love, and that his argument for making a virtue of necessity expresses Philosophy's ultimate advice that he accept the contingency of finite life as necessary. Where Theseus differs from Philosophy, however, is in omitting the *response* to necessity.

39. See, most famously, D. W. Robertson, Jr., *A Preface to Chaucer* (Princeton, NJ: Princeton University Press, 1962), 260–66; and P. M. Kean, *Chaucer and the Making of English Poetry,* vol. 2, *The Art of Narrative* (London: Routledge and Kegan Paul, 1972), 1–52.

40. See Philip Hardie, *The Epic Successors of Virgil: A Study in the Dynamics of a Tradition* (Cambridge: Cambridge University Press, 1993).

41. Cassandra's retelling of the *Roman de Thebes* in *Troilus and Criseyde* mentions this episode: "Of Archimoris buryinge and the pleyes."

42. Rose, *Mourning Becomes the Law*, 23–26.

43. *Boece* IV, pr. 6, 133–34.

CHAPTER SEVEN

1. William Langland, *Piers Plowman: The B Version*, rev. ed., ed. George Kane and E. Talbot Donaldson (London: Athlone Press, 1988). The B text is the default unless otherwise specified. All citations of this work refer to this edition and will be made parenthetically within the text. All translations of the B text are from E. Talbot Donaldson, *Will's Vision of Piers Plowman: An Alliterative Verse Translation* (New York and London: Norton, 1990).

2. For the generic and political resonances of this leveling in Lydgate's work, see R. D. Perry, "Lydgate's *danse macabre* and the Trauma of the Hundred Years War," *Literature and Medicine* 33 (2015): 303–24.

3. See Ralph Hanna, *London Literature, 1300–1380* (Cambridge: Cambridge University Press, 2005), 247–52.

4. Apart from those discussed in this paragraph, B. IX 167 (unhappy and unfruitful marriages have increased since the pestilence); X 72, 77 (Dame Studie pillories theologians whose abstract work after the plague has rendered their prayers ineffective); XII 11 (Imaginatyf names pestilence as one of the three rods with which God corrects his children (the others are poverty and "angers"); XIII 248 (Activa Vita wishes for a bull that would cure the pestilence, so that the market for his pastries would return).

5. On the relationship of the poem to labor, and to these and the later Statute of Laborers of 1388, see Anne Middleton, "Acts of Vagrancy: The C Version 'Autobiography' and the Statute of 1388," in *Written Work: Langland, Labor, and Authorship*, ed. Steven Justice and Kathryn Kerby-Fulton (Philadelphia: University of Pennsylvania Press, 1998), 208–317.

6. For the C text, see William Langland, *Piers Plowman: The C Version*, ed. George Kane and George Russell (London: Athlone, 1997).

7. If arguments that these versions were composed in a different order are right, then my argument, of course, works in reverse: the poet simplifies an initially complex philosophy of death as he reworks the poem.

8. Anne Middleton, "Making a Good End: John But as a Reader of *Piers Plowman*," in *Medieval English Studies Presented to George Kane*, ed. Edward D. Kennedy, R. Waldron, and J. S. Wittig (Woodbridge: D. S. Brewer, 1988), 243–66.

9. A. C. Spearing, *Medieval Dream-Poetry* (Cambridge: Cambridge University Press, 1976), 159.

10. See the references throughout Andrew Galloway, *The Penn Commentary on "Piers Plowman,"* vol. 1, *C Prologue—Passus 4; B Prologue—Passus 4; A Prologue—Passus 4* (Philadelphia: University of Pennslvania Press, 2006); and Stephen A. Barney, *The Penn Commentary on "Piers Plowman,"* vol. 5, *C Passus 20–22; B Passus 18–20* (Philadelphia: University of Pennsylvania Press, 2006).

11. See the discussion and citations in chapter 5.

12. Henry Suso, *Wisdom's Watch Upon the Hours*, trans. Edmund Colledge (Washington, DC: Catholic University of America Press, 1994), 248.

13. Suso, *Wisdom's Watch*, 250. For more on Suso's fifteenth-century influence,

see Ashby Kinch, *Imago mortis: Mediating Images of Death in Late Medieval Culture* (Leiden: Brill, 2013), 36–68.

14. Nicolette Zeeman, *Piers Plowman and the Medieval Discourse of Desire* (Cambridge: Cambridge University Press, 2006), 227–35.

15. Nicolette Zeeman, "The Condition of Kynde," in *Medieval Literature and Historical Inquiry: Essays in Honor of Derek Pearsall*, ed. David Aers (Cambridge: D. S. Brewer, 2000), 1–30, at 11.

16. For the account of Gregory, including his salvation of Trajan, see Jacobus de Voragine, *The Golden Legend: Readings on the Saints*, 2 vols., trans. William Granger Ryan (Princeton, NJ: Princeton University Press, 1993), 1:171–83.

17. Bertram Colgrave, ed., *The Earliest Life of Gregory the Great by an Anonymous Monk of Whitby* (Cambridge: Cambridge University Press, 1985), 129.

18. Vincent of Beauvais, *Speculum historiale* (Douai: Balthazar Bellère, 1624).

19. John of Salisbury, *Ioannis Saresberiensis episcopi Carnotensis Policratici*, ed. Clemens C. I. Webb (Oxford: Typographeo Clarendoniano, 1909).

20. Some of the books were relocated by the fourth century; writing sometime after 378 CE, Ammianus Marcellinus laments, "the libraries are like tombs, permanently shut"; *The Later Roman Empire (A.D. 354–378)*, trans. Walter Hamilton (New York: Penguin, 1986), XIV.6.18. Still, it remained a place associated with books; around 576 CE, Venantius Fortunatus found "Vergil recited in Trajan's forum in the city"; *Personal and Political Poems*, trans. Judith George (Liverpool: University of Liverpool Press, 1995), VI.8. Sidonius agrees: "Cum meis poni statuam perennem / Nerva Trajanus titulus videret / Inter auctores utriusque fixam Bibliothecae," from Digby 172's glosses on Sidonius; see Robinson Ellis, ed. *Anecdota Oxoniensia* (Oxford: Clarendon Press, 1885), vol 1, part 5, ix epigr 16.

21. Nicholas Watson, "Visions of Inclusion: *Universal Salvation* and Vernacular Theology in Pre-Reformation England," *Journal of Medieval and Early Modern Studies* 27 (1997): 145–88.

22. See his translator's note in Jacques Derrida, *Archive Fever: A Freudian Impression* (Chicago: University of Chicago Press, 1995), 109.

23. See, for instance, Frank Grady, "*Piers Plowman*, St. *Erkenwald*, and the Rule of Exceptional Salvations," *Yearbook of Langland Studies* 6 (1992): 63–88; see also, in answer to Nicholas Watson's position on universal salvation, Derek Pearsall, "The Idea of Universal Salvation in *Piers Plowman* B and C," *Journal of Medieval and Early Modern Studies* 39 (2009): 257–81; and Rebecca Davis, "*Piers Plowman*" *and the Books of Nature* (Oxford: Oxford University Press, 2016), 218–39.

24. In that case, it should be read alongside Steven Justice, "Did the Middle Ages Believe in Their Miracles?" *Representations* 103 (2008): 1–29.

25. See David Piché, ed., with Claude Lafleur, "*La condamnation parisienne*" *de 1277: nouvelle édition du texte latin, traduction, introduction et commentaire* (Paris: J. Vrin, 1999).

26. William of Sherwood, *William of Sherwood's Treatise on Syncategorematic Words*, trans. Norman Kretzmann (Minneapolis: University of Minnesota Press, 1968), 92.

27. Anselm of Canterbury, "Monologion 31," in *Complete Philosophical and Theological Treatises*, trans. Jasper Hopkins and Herbert Richardson (Minneapolis: Arthur J. Banning Press, 2000), 48.

28. Andrew Galloway, "Making History Legal: *Piers Plowman* and the Rebels of Fourteenth-Century England," in *William Langland's "Piers Plowman": A Book of Essays*, ed. Kathleen M. Hewett-Smith (New York: Routledge, 2000), 7–40, at 17.

29. Amy Appleford, *Learning to Die in London, 1380–1540* (Philadelphia: University of Pennsylvania Press, 2014), 55–97. See also her earlier article, "The Dance of Death in London: John Lydgate, John Carpenter, and the *Daunce of Paulys*," *Journal of Medieval and Early Modern History* 38 (2008): 285–314.

30. Constance Bouchard, "Monatic Cartularies: Organizing Eternity," in *Charters, Cartularies and Archives: The Preservation and Transmission of Documents in the Medieval West*, ed. Adam J. Kosto and Anders Winroth (Toronto: Ponitifical Institute of Medieval Studies, 2002), 22–32, at 27.

31. Middleton, "Acts of Vagrancy."

32. I follow the reading the reading of the Hm manuscript grouping here.

33. Joseph S. Wittig, "The Middle English 'Absolute Infinitive' and the Speech of Book," in *Magister Regis: Studies in Honor of Robert Earl Kaske*, ed. Arthur Groos and Emerson Brown (New York: Fordham University Press, 1986), 217–40.

34. See Richard Hoffman, "The Burning of 'Boke' in Piers Plowman," *Modern Language Quarterly* 25 (1964): 57–65.

35. Gillian Rose, "Practising Photography: An Archive, Some Photographs and a Researcher," *Journal of Historical Geography* 26 (2000): 555–71, at 570 n. 30.

36. Gillian Rose, *Mourning Becomes the Law: Philosophy and Representation* (Cambridge: Cambridge University Press, 1996), 32.

37. Maurice Blanchot, "Literature and the Right to Death," in *The Work of Fire*, trans. Lydia Davis (Stanford, CA: Stanford University Press, 1995), 300–344, at 336; emphasis in original.

38. Blanchot, "Literature and the Right to Death," 327.

CHAPTER EIGHT

1. The Pearl Poet, *The Complete Works of the Pearl Poet*, ed. Malcolm Andrews, Ronald Waldron, and Clifford Peterson, trans. Casey Finch (Berkeley and Los Angeles: University of California Press, 1993). All citations of the Pearl poet's work refer to this edition and will be made parenthetically within the text. Translations of the text are from Simon Armitage, *Pearl: A New Verse Translation* (New York: Norton, 2016).

2. Jane Gilbert's rich reading of the Lacanian paradoxes of desire in these terms situates the poem against the courtly French tradition of "marguerite" literature. *Living Death in Medieval French and English Literature* (Cambridge: Cambridge University Press, 2011), 151–90.

3. *Blue Velvet*, dir. David Lynch (1986; Los Angeles: MGM Studios, 2006), DVD.

4. Immanuel Kant, *Critique of the Power of Judgment*, ed. Paul Guyer, trans. Paul Guyer and Eric Matthews (Cambridge: Cambridge University Press, 2000).

5. See John W. Baldwin, *Aristocratic Life in Medieval France: The Romances of Jean Renart and Gerbert de Montreuil, 1190–1230* (Baltimore, MD: Johns Hopkins University Press, 2000), 92.

6. Kant, *Critique of the Power of Judgment*, 135.

7. Jessica Rosenfeld relates some of these terms to the wide semantic field of "jouissance," in *Ethics and Enjoyment in Medieval Poetry: Love after Aristotle* (Cambridge: Cambridge University Press, 2010), 5–8.

8. For this definition of "yode" see Andrews, Waldron, and Clifford, *The Complete Works of the Pearl Poet*, n. 10 p. 54m.

9. See *MED*, "dwīnen." The word is often glossed as "vanescere," to vanish, fade, or disappear. See *MED*, *Bosworth-Toller* ("a-dwinan").

10. In Kevin Crossley-Holland, ed., *The Anglo-Saxon World: An Anthology* (Oxford: Oxford University Press, 1999), 50–53.

11. Guy de Chauliac, *The Cyrurgie of Guy de Chauliac*, ed. M. S. Ogden, Early English Text Society, o.s., 265 (London: Oxford Unviersity Press, 1971).

12. See the discussion in J. A. Weisheipl, "Ockham and the Mertonians," in *The History of the University of Oxford*, vol. 1, *The Early Oxford Schools*, ed. T. H. Aston and J. I. Catto (Oxford: Oxford University Press, 1984), 633ff.

13. See J. A. Weisheipl, "The Interpretation of Aristotle's *Physics* and the Science of Motion," in *The Cambridge History of Later Medieval Philosophy*, ed. Norman Kretzmann, Anthony Kenny, and Jan Pinborg (Cambridge: Cambridge University Press, 1988), 521–36, esp. 534.

14. It does not seem to have been used until the fourteenth century. See Anneliese Maier, *Zwischen Philosophie und Mechanik* (Rome: Edizioni di Storia e Letteratura, 1958), 211.

15. William Heytesbury uses only these two examples, for instance, in his introductory work on the terms of physics: "calefaccio, frigifaccio, albifaccio et similia"; see James Weisheipl, in "Early Fourteenth Century Physics of the Merton 'School,' with Special Reference to Dumbleton and Heytesbury" (D.Phil. thesis, Oxford, 1956), 371.

16. Walter Burley's commentary on Aristotle's *On the Length and Brevity of Life*, for instance, dwells on the complexity of the shifting relation between *caliditas* and *frigiditas* in the movement toward death. See Michael Dunne, "The Causes of the Length and Brevity of Life Call for Investigation: Aristotle's *De longitudine et brevitate vitae* in the 13th and 14th Century Commentaries," in *Vita longa: Vecchiaia e durata della vita nella tradizione medica e aristotelica antica e medieval*, ed. Chiari Crisciani, Luciana Repici, and Pietro B. Rossi (Florence: SISMEL, Edizioni del Galluzo, 2009), 121–47.

17. Quoted in Janet Coleman, "Jean de Ripa O.F.M. and the Oxford Calculators," *Mediaeval Studies* 37 (1975): 130–89, at 154.

18. See the edition of Dumbleton's work as part of Weisheipl, "Early Fourteenth Century Physics of the Merton 'School.' "

19. Weisheipl, "Ockham and the Mertonians," 639; see also Heinz Ristory, *Denkmodelle zur französischen Mensuraltheorie des 14. Jahrhunderts*, vol. 1, *Historische Darstellung* (Ottawa: Institute of Mediaeval Music, 2004) 242. See especially Anneliese Maier, "Das Problem der Intensiven Grösse," in *Zwei Grundprobleme der scholastischen Naturphilosophi: das Problem der intensiven Grösse die Impetustheorie* (Rome: Edizioni de Storia e Letteratura, 1951).

20. Sigmund Freud, *Beyond the Pleasure Principle*, in *The Standard Edition of the Complete Psychological Works of Sigmund Freud*, vol. 18, trans. James Strachey (London: Hogarth Press, 1955); see especially the long discussion in chapters 5 and 6.

21. Freud, *Jenseits des Lustprinzips* (Leipzig: Internationaler Psychoanalytischer Verlag, 1923), chapter V.

22. David K. Coley, "*Pearl* and the Narrative of Pestilence," *Studies in the Age of Chaucer* 35 (2013): 209–62, at 244. See also Andrew Breeze, "*Pearl* and the Plague of 1390–1393," *Neophilologus* 98 (2014): 337–41.

23. Milton R. Stern, "An Approach to *The Pearl*," *Journal of English and Germaic Philology* 54 (1955): 684–92.

24. Cf. Vivien Brown, ed., *Eye Priory Cartulary and Charters: Part One* (Woodbridge: Boydell, 1992), 223.

25. See Albert Way, ed., *Promptorium parvolorum* (London: Camden Society, 1843), 213 n. 4.

26. Geoffrey of Vinsauf, *Poetria nova*, rev. ed., trans. Margaret Nims (Turnhout: Brepols, 2010), 35, lines 547–50.

27. Geoffrey of Vinsauf, *Poetria nova* 35, lines 543–44.

28. Geoffrey of Vinsauf, *Poetria nova* 36, line 551.

29. Geoffrey of Vinsauf, *Poetria nova* 40, line 687.

30. Spearing, "Symbolic and Dramatic Development in *Pearl*," *Modern* Philology 60 (1962): 1-12, at 9.

31. The point, as Spearing points out, is not to contrast heaven and earth but to suggest their continuity, "Symbolic and Dramatic Development," 7.

32. See the discussion in the introduction to Thomas Usk, *The Testament of Love*, ed. R. Allen Shoaf (Kalamazoo, MI: Medieval Institute Publications, 1998).

33. S.v. "date."

34. Peter of Spain, *Syncategoreumata*, ed. L. M. de Rijk, trans. Joke Spruyt (Leiden: Brill, 1992), 407.

35. Peter of Spain, *Syncategoreumata*, 405.

36. Peter of Spain, *Syncategoreumata*, 405.

37. Walter Burley, *On the Purity of the Art of Logic: The Shorter and the Longer Treatises*, trans. Paul V. Spade (New Haven, CT: Yale University Press, 2000) Shorter Treatise, Rule 9, page 25.

38. See Peter of Spain, *Syncategoreumata*, 5.24: "of time nothing exists but the *now*, and this is not time nor is it a part of it, but it is something indivisible in time and that is what time owes its being to," at p. 217.

39. "Of on dethe ful oure hope is drest": "ful" can also be an adverb modifying "drest": on one death our hope is fully placed" (Sarah Stanbury claims this in her edition: Pearl Poet, *Pearl*, ed. Sarah Stanbury [Kalamazoo, MI: Medieval Institute Publications, 2001], n. 38). But the "well-defined caesura" of the *Pearl*-line makes "ful" both the metrical companion of "deth" and its syntactical modifier; for the judgment about the caesura, see the Pearl Poet, *Pearl: An English Poem of the Fourteenth Century*, ed. Israel Gollancz (London: David Nutt, 1891), xxiii.

40. G. W. F. Hegel, *The Phenomenology of Spirit*, trans. A. V. Miller (Oxford: Clarendon Press, 1977), 285.

41. The *Middle English Dictionary* does not define "anon" in this line, but it clearly has the sense "soon," "eventually," rather than "immediately." Sarah Stanbury glosses it as "soon," lines 629-31, n. 30.

CHAPTER NINE

1. All quotations from *Saint Erkenwald*, ed. Clifford Peterson (Philadelphia: University of Pennsylvania Press, 1977). For articles placing the composition of the poem in the late 1380s or early 1390s, based on evidence that it reflects the conflicts of royalist and London civic politics or of the Merciless Parliament of 1388, see Ruth Nissé, "'A Coroun Ful Riche': The Rule of History in *St. Erkenwald*," *English Literary History* 65 (1998): 277–95; and Frank Grady, "*St. Erkenwald* and the Merciless Parliament," *Studies in the Age of Chaucer* 22 (2000): 179–211.

2. These issues are discussed under the terms *potentia ordinata, inordinata,* and *absoluta*. For an overview, see William J. Courtenay, *Capacity and Volition: A History of the Distinction of Absolute and Ordained Powers* (Bergamo: Pierluigi Lubarina Editore, 1990); and Frances Oakley, *Omnipotence and Promise: The Legacy of the Scholastic Distinction of Powers* (Toronto: Pontifical Institute of Medieval Studies, 2002).

3. D. Vance Smith, "Crypt and Decrypt: Erkenwald Terminable and Interminable," *New Medieval Literatures* 5 (2002): 59–85.

4. Other versions of the myth include the discovery of the body of Plato or Socrates. For a more general discussion of the role of pagans in the late medieval religious imagination, see Frank Grady, *Representing Righteous Heathens in Late Medieval England* (New York: Palgrave, 2005).

5. See E. Gordon Whatley, "*Vita Erkenwaldi*: An Anglo-Norman's Life of an Anglo-Saxon Saint," *Manuscripta* 27 (1983): 67–81; "Heathens and Saints: Saint Erkenwald in its Legendary Context," *Speculum* 61 (1986): 330–63; and *The Saint of London: The Life and Miracles of Saint Erkenwald* (Binghampton: Center for Medieval and Renaissance Studies, 1989).

6. Whatley, *The Saint of London*, 210 nn. 17–19.

7. Whatley, *The Saint of London*, 92. Another echo is perhaps the description of the judge's tomb as a "crafte," which may have been suggested by the *Vita*'s reference to the burial as an *opus* (Whatley, *The Saint of London*, 94); and perhaps the theme of a dead body that can still act by the *Miracula*'s observation that even death could keep the dead man (*defunctum*) from achieving acts that testified to the certainty of salvation and the glory of God (Whatley, *The Saint of London*, 100).

8. Whatley, *The Saint of London*, 96, my translation (Whatley has "unspeakably happy").

9. As Anne Rafferty Meyer describes it, the 1313 version of the shrine resembled a miniature church, built on Perpendicular principles, whose elaborate ornament echoes that of the tomb in *St. Erkenwald*. The shrine was "supported by miniature flying buttresses and decorated with blind tracery, ogess, and crocketed pinnacles . . . the pronounced vertical lines of the large, central tier are extended by the arcade behind the gable. . . . Ogival figures appear in the tympanum of the gable and in the heads of the trefoil blind tracery," in *Medieval Allegory and the Building of the New Jerusalem* (Cambridge: D. S. Brewer, 2003), 126–28. John Bowers discusses a number of possible echoes of late Ricardian funereal practice; see his *The Politics of Pearl: Court Poetry in the Age of Richard II* (Cambridge: D. S. Brewer, 2001), 18–21.

10. See chapter 4.

11. *IMED*, s.v. "sperel." See *Saint Erkenwald (Bishop of London 675–693): An Alliterative Poem*, ed. Israel Gollancz (London: Oxford University Press, 1922).

12. Slavoj Žižek, *The Sublime Object of Ideology* (New York: Verso, 1989), 122.

13. For surveys of mortuary practices in the late English Middle Ages, see Eamon Duffy, *The Stripping of the Altars: Traditional Religion in England c. 1400–c. 1580* (New Haven, CT: Yale University Press, 1992), 327–37; Clive Burgess, "'Longing To Be Prayed For': Death and Commemoration in the Later Middle Ages," in *The Place of the Dead: Death and Remembrance in Late Medieval and Early Modern Europe*, ed. Bruce Gordon and Peter Marshall (Cambridge: Cambridge University Press, 2000), 44–65; and Ben R. McRee, "Religious Gilds and Civil Order: The Case of Norwich in the Late Middle Ages," *Speculum* 67 (1992): 69–97.

14. William Dugdale, *The History of St. Paul's Cathedral in London* (London: Thomas Warren, 1663), 41.

15. The bishop of London who reinstituted feasts to commemorate the burial and translation of St. Erkenwald was, as it happens, Robert Braybrooke, the instigator in the consolidation of chantries and other measures taken to renovate the spiritual and economic practices of the cathedral. See Dugdale, *The History*, 21–24; and Rosalind Hill, "'A Chaunterie for Soules': London Chantries in the Reign of Richard II," in *The Reign of Richard II: Essays in Honor of May McKisak*, ed. F. R. H. Du Boulay and Caroline M. Barron (London: Athlone, 1971), 242–55, at 250.

16. London, Lincoln's Inn Library, MS Hale 88, fol. 156v. For a discussion of the historiographic implications of this sign, see my "Irregular Histories: Forgetting Ourselves," *New Literary History* 28 (1997): 161–84.

17. London, British Library, MS Egerton 2885, fol. 8v. Higden's *Polychronicon* is one likely source of this calendar, as is one of numerous versions of the *Brut*. The *Polychronicon*'s dates are close but not identical. It cites forty-four years between the destruction of Troy and the settlement of Britain and 432 years before the foundation of Rome. Ranulph Higden, *Polychronicon Ranulphi Higden monachi Cestrensis*, vol. 2, ed. Churchill Babington (London: Longman, 1869), 142.

18. Dugdale, *The History*, 22.

19. Payne Fisher, *The Tombes, Monuments, and Sepulchral Inscriptions Lately Visible in St. Paul's Cathedral* (London: Payne Fisher, 1684), 24–25.

20. Fisher, *The Tombes*, 26.

21. Fisher, *The Tombes*, 23.

22. See, for example, Ranulph Higden's description of the almost literally animated coffin of a girl: "Cista ejusdem puellae vix bipedalis mensurae sed miabilis archicturae ibidem cernitur, in qua confluctus pugilum, gestus animalium, volatus avium, saltus piscium, absque hominis impulsu conspiciuntur"; in *Polychronicon Ranulphi Higden monachi Cestrensis*, vol. 8, ed. J. R. Lumby (London: Longman, 1882), 54.

23. Henry Holland, *Ecclesia Sancti Pauli illustrata: The Monuments, Inscriptions, and Epitaphs of Kings, Nobles, Bishops, and Others Buried at the Cathedrall Church of St. Paul, London* (London: John Norton, 1633), fol. F.

24. Holland, *Ecclesia Sancti Pauli illustrata*, fol. B.

25. Holland, *Ecclesia Sancti Pauli illustrata*, fol. B. The descriptions of the foun-

dations of the two monasteries also appears in the early eleventh-century *Vita Sancti Erkenwaldi* and Bede's *Historia ecclesiastica gentis Anglorum*, ed. Bertram Colgrave and R. A. B. Mynors (Oxford: Clarendon Press, 1969), 354. See Whatley, *The Saint of London*, 88 and 209 n. 9.

26. Fisher, *The Tombes*, 18.

27. Thorlac Turville-Petre, *St. Erkenwald*, in *Alliterative Poetry of the Later Middle Ages* (Washington, DC: Catholic University of America Press, 1989), 106.

28. Peterson, *Saint Erkenwald*, 37.

29. And *Saint Erkenwald* is full of sound; see John Bugbee, "Sight and Sound in *St Erkenwald*: On Theodicy and the Senses," *Medium Aevum* 77 (2008): 202–21.

30. Robert Pogue Harrison, *The Dominion of the Dead* (Chicago: University of Chicago Press, 2003), 59.

31. Christoph Tietze, *Hymn Introits for the Liturgical Year: The Origin and Early Development of the Latin Texts* (Chicago: Liturgy Training Publications, 2005), 72, for the naming and Feast of Pentecost, the day on which all languages are translated effortlessly. The *Life of Erkenwald* begins with the biblical verse that is the introit for the mass that Erkenwald hears, the *Missa Sancti Domini*.

32. For an extensive argument that the poet had in mind the consecration of a church to the Virgin on the site of a temple dedicated to Minerva in Bath, see Gollancz, *Saint Erkenwald*, xvi–xix.

33. London, British Library, MS Egerton 2885, fol. 8v.

34. G. W. F. Hegel, *Psychologie: Der Geist*, in *Enzyklopädie der Philosophischen wissenschaften im Grundrisse*, Gesammelte Werke 20, ed. Wolfgang Bonsiepen and Hans-Christian Lucas (Hamburg: Meiner, 1992), sec. 453, p. 446.

35. Plato, *Phaedrus*, ed. and trans. H. N. Fowler (Cambridge, MA: Harvard University Press, 1916), 275B.

36. Plato's and Aristotle's favorite analogy for memory is the wax tablet. On impression and memory, Derrida has a brief meditation in *Archive Fever* that considers the interanimation of the technology of printing and Freud's metaphors for memory. See Jacques Derrida, *Archive Fever: A Freudian Impression*, trans. Eric Penowitz (Chicago: University of Chicago Press, 1996).

37. On the etymology of Amun and its Hellenic appropriation, see John A. Wilson, *The Burden of Egypt: An Interpretation of Ancient Egyptian Culture* (Chicago: University of Chicago Press, 1951), 130, 170; and Kurt Sethe, *Amun und die acht Ürgotter von Hermopolis* (Berlin: Gruyter, 1929), 18–27, 126.

38. Holland, *Ecclesia Sancti Pauli illustrata*, fol. F3; and Fisher, *The Tombes*, 66.

39. Fisher, *The Tombes*, 26.

40. London, British Library, MS Additional 32622, fol. 15; edited in Andrew Galloway, "The Rhetoric of Riddling in Late-Medieval Engalnd: The 'Oxford' Riddles, the *Secretum philosophorum*, and the Riddles in *Piers Plowman*," *Speculum* 70 (1995): 68–105.

41. Cambridge, Gonville and Caius College, MS 230/116, fol. 171. Qtd. in Galloway, "The Rhetoric of Riddling," 104.

42. Galloway, "The Rhetoric of Riddling," 97.

43. Especially Grady, "*St. Erkenwald* and the Merciless Parliament."

44. Erkenwald's tears may be the tears of contrition, sometimes called a second baptism. See esp. Thomas O'Loughlin and Helen Conrad-O'Briain, "The 'Baptism of Tears' in Early Anglo-Saxon Sources," *Anglo-Saxon England* 22 (1993): 65–83.

45. Colgrave, *The Earliest Life of Gregory the Great*, 126.

CHAPTER TEN

1. See A. C. Spearing, *Medieval to Renaissance in English Poetry* (Cambridge: Cambridge University Press, 1985), 59–109; Seth Lerer, *Chaucer and His Readers: Imagining the Author in the Fifteenth Century* (Princeton, NJ: Princeton University Press, 1993), esp. 57–116; John Bowers, *Chaucer and Langland: The Antagonistic Tradition* (Notre Dame, IN: University of Notre Dame Press, 2007), esp. 202–15; and James Simpson, *Reform and Cultural Revolution: The Oxford English Literary History*, vol. 2, *1350–1547* (Oxford: Oxford University Press, 2004), 34–67. On Lydgate's "morbid" references, see Thomas Prendergast, *Chaucer's Dead Body: From Corpse to Corpus* (New York: Routledge, 2004); and Robert Meyer-Lee, *Poets and Power from Chaucer to Wyatt* (Cambridge: Cambridge University Press, 2007).

2. On tragedy and performance in Lydgate, see Maura Nolan, *John Lydgate and the Making of Public Culture* (Cambridge: University of Cambridge Press, 2005), 120–83. See also her discussion of his understanding of tragedy in "The Art of History Writing: Lydgate's *Serpent of Division*," *Speculum* 78 (2003): 99–127.

3. John Lydgate, *The Troy Book*, 4 vols., ed. Henry Bergen, Early English Text Society, e.s., 97, 103, 106, and 126 (London: Kegan Paul, Trench, and Trübner, 1906–35). All citations of this work refer to this edition and will be made parenthetically in the text. For the Chaucer portrait, see Cambridge, Corpus Christi College, MS 61. On the way in which that portrait creates an image of Chaucer's audience, see Derek Pearsall, "The *Troilus* Frontispiece and Chaucer's Audience," *Yearbook of English Studies* 7 (1977): 68–74.

4. Geoffrey Chaucer, *The Riverside Chaucer*, ed. Larry Benson (Oxford: Oxford University Press, 1986). All citations of Chaucer refer to this edition and will be made parenthetically within the text.

5. For discussions of the various indebtednesses of Chaucer and Lydgate to Boccaccio's *De casibus*, see Mary C. Flannery, *John Lydgate and the Poetics of Fame* (Cambridge: D. S. Brewer, 2012); Nigel Mortimer, *John Lydgate's "Fall of Princes": Narrative Tragedy in Its Literary and Political Contexts* (Oxford: Oxford University Press, 2005); and Maura Nolan, " 'Now Wo, Now Gladnesse': Ovidianism in the *Fall of Princes*," *English Literary History* 71 (2004): 531–58.

6. John Lydgate, *Fall of Princes*, 4 vols., ed. Henry Bergen, Early English Text Society, e.s., 121–24 (London: Oxford University Press, 1924–27). All citations of this work refer to this edition and will be made parenthetically within the text.

7. See Lydgate's *Cartae versificata* in "Cronica Buriensis, 1020–1346," in *Memorials of St Edmund's Abbey*, edited by Thomas Arnold (London: HMSO, 1896), 3:215–37.

8. Rodney Thomson, ed., *The Archives of Bury St. Edmunds* (Woodbridge: Boydell, 1980), 40. For examples of the many important developments in archives in the fifteenth century, see Trevor Aston, "Muniment Rooms and Their Fittings in Medieval and Early

Modern England," in *Lordship and Learning: Studies in Memory of Trevor Aston*, ed. Ralph Evans (Woodbridge: Boydell, 2004), 235–48.

9. Kathryn Lowe suggests that Curteys may have chosen Lydgate to forestall some of Gloucester's potential antipathy toward the abbey, given Lydgate's status as public poet and sometime protégé of Gloucester; "The Poetry of Privilege: Lydgate's *Cartae versificatae*," *Nottingham Medieval Studies* 50 (2006): 151–65.

10. See the *Liber albus: The White Book of the City of London*, trans. Henry Thomas Riley (London: Richard Griffin, 1861). The registers of Abbott Curteys are London, British Library, MS Additional 14848, and London, British Library, MS Additional 7096. For a useful discussion of the *Liber* and the genre of the archive, see Sarah Elliott Novacich, *Shaping the Archive in Late Medieval England: History, Poetry and Performance* (Cambridge: Cambridge University Press, 2017), 11–15; and on the *Liber albus*'s relation to its compiler's involvement in several London archival projects, including the "Dance of Death" mural in St. Paul's with Lydgate's translation, see Amy Appleford, *Learning to Die in London, 1380–1540* (Philadelphia: University of Pennsylvania Press, 2015), 55–97.

11. John Lydgate's *Cartae versificatae* are printed in Thomas Arnold, ed., *The Memorials of Bury St. Edmunds* (London: Her Majesty's Stationary Office, 1896), 3:215–37.

12. See "Testamentum Domini Radulphi domini de Cromwell," In *Testamenta Eboracensia: A Selection of Wills from the Registry at York*, ed. James Raine, vol. 2 (London: Surtees Society, 1855), 196–200, at 197.

13. Thomas Malory, *Le morte Darthur*, ed. Stephen H. A. Shepherd (New York: Norton, 2003). For the other two works, see Larry D. Benson, ed., *King Arthur's Death: The Middle English Stanzaic Morte Arthur and Alliterative Morte Arthure*, rev. ed., ed. Edward E. Foster (Kalamazoo, MI: Medieval Institute Publications, 1994).

14. For speculation on the origins of the name, see Henry Ansgar Kelly, *Chaucerian Tragedy* (Woodbridge: D. S. Brewer, 1997), 40.

15. See Martin Irvine, *The Making of Textual Culture: "Grammatica" and Literary Theory, 350–1100* (Cambridge: Cambridge University Press, 1994), 195–208.

16. These moments were first discussed in E. P. Hammond, "Poet and Patron in *The Fall of Princes*: Lydgate and Humphrey of Gloucester," *Anglia* 38, n.s., 26 (1914): 121–36. For the intellectual environment of the commission, see Andrew Galloway, "John Lydgate and the Origins of Vernacular Humanism," *JEGP* 107 (2008): 445–71; and Susanne Saygin, *Humphrey, Duke of Gloucester (1390–1447) and the Italian Humanists* (Leiden: Brill, 2002).

17. On Lydgate's use of *envois*, see Jenni Nuttall, "Lydgate and the Lenvoy," *Exemplaria* 30 (2018): 35–48.

18. For this argument, see Saygin, *Humphrey, Duke of Gloucester*, 60–64.

19. John Lydgate, *The Floure of Curteyse*, in *Chaucerian Apocrypha: A Selection*, ed. Kathleen Forni (Kalamazoo, MI: Medieval Institute Publications, 2005), 241–42.

20. John Lydgate, *The Siege of Thebes*, ed. Robert R. Edwards (Kalamazoo, MI: Medieval Institute Publications, 2001), 40, 47.

21. Lydgate, *The Floure of Curteyse*, 234–46.

22. Spearing, *Medieval to Renaissance in English Poetry*, and Lerer, *Chaucer and His Readers*. More recent is Daniel T. Kline, "Father Chaucer and the Siege of Thebes:

Literary Paternity, Aggressive Difference, and the Prologue to Lydgate's Oedipal Canterbury Tale," *Chaucer Review* 34 (1999): 217–35.

23. Lydgate's *Fabula duorum mercatorum* thematizes just this kind of impersonal relationship, between two merchants who are close friends only through the medium of "report and by noon othir mene." See John Lydgate, *Fabula duo mercatorum and Guy of Warwick*, ed. Pamela Farvolden (Kalamazoo, MI: Medieval Institute Publications, 2016), 48.

24. Prendergast, *Chaucer's Dead Body*.

25. Lydgate, *The Siege of Thebes*, 48. Lydgate uses the term "registrer" frequently to indicate the role of a poet: in *The Fall of Princes*, Fortune tells Lydgate that his "name and surname" will be registered in (Chaucer's) *House of Fame*, along with "poetis and notable old auctors" (6.513–14). Earlier in the same book, Lydgate had apostrophized writing as the Chaucerian "registreer" of truth, which causes "thynges dirked, of old that wer begonne, / To be remembred" (6.27–28). In his translation of the *Secretum secretorum*, Lydgate calls the holder of the key to the "treasorye" of the "bawme" drunk at Helicon a "registrer"; see John Lydgate and Benedict Burgh, *Secrees of Old Philisoffres*, ed. Robert Steele, Early English Text Society, e.s., 66 (London: Kegan Paul Trench and Trübner, 1894), 429 and 436.

26. See W. A. Pantin, "English Monastic Letter-Books," in *Historical Essays in Honour of James Tait*, ed. J. G. Edwards, V. H. Galbraith, and E. F. Jacob (Manchester: Manchester University Press, 1933), 201–22. Pantin distinguishes between archive and library as well.

27. See Pantin, "English Monastic Letter-Books," 205.

28. See Spearing, *Medieval to Renaissance in English Poetry*, esp. 66–88.

29. Ruth Nissé, " 'Was It Not Routhe to Se?' Lydgate and the Styles of Martyrdom," in *John Lydgate: Poetry, Culture, and Lancastrian England*, ed. Larry Scanlon and James Simpson (Notre Dame, IN: Notre Dame University Press, 2006), 279–98, at 287–88. Nissé is discussing the judgment of Lerer, *Chaucer and His Readers*.

30. John Lydgate, *John Lydgate's "Lives of Ss Edmund and Fremund" and the "Extra Miracles of St. Edmund,"* ed. Anthony Bale and A. S. G. Edwards (Heidelberg: Universitätsverlag Winter, 2009), 141–43. I am indebted to Nissé's discussion of this passage in " 'Was It Not Routhe to Se'?," 287–88.

31. Robert Meyer-Lee shows how Lydgate conflates the aureate balm of Mary and the aureate aspiration of the poet in *Poets and Power from Chaucer to Wyatt* (Cambridge: Cambridge University Press, 2007), 49–87.

32. Lydgate, *"Lives of Ss Edmund and Fremund,"* 1944–81.

33. For more on this, see my "Lydgate's Refrain: The Open When," in *Lydgate Matters: Poetry and Material Culture in the Fifteenth Century*, ed. Lisa H. Cooper and Andrea Denny-Brown (New York: Palgrave, 2008), 185–96. On a possible solution to that sentence's grammar and reflections about what it means regarding Lydgate's style, see Phillipa Hardman, "Lydgate's Uneasy Syntax," in *John Lydgate: Poetry, Culture, and Lancastrian England*, ed. Larry Scanlon and James Simpson (Notre Dame, IN: University of Notre Dame Press, 2006), 12–35.

34. Chaucer, *Boece*, Met. 1.2.

35. See, for instance, Paris, Bibliothèque nationale de France, MS français 1610.

36. This entire description from Guido can be found in notes to Lydgate, *The Troy Book*, 4:164–65.

37. Priam's direct endowment of it underlines its lack of contingency: many chantry chapels failed because they did not acquire the necessary royal license to amortise rents or property. See Barrie Dobson, "Citizens and Chantries in Late Medieval York," in *Church and City, 1000–1500: Essays in Honour of Christopher Brooke*, ed. David Abulafia, Michael Franklin, and Miri Rubin (Cambridge: Cambridge University Press, 1992) 332.

38. Robert Meyer-Lee, "The Memorial Form of John Lydgate's *Troy Book*," *Exemplaria* 29 (2017): 280–95.

39. On Duke Humphrey's interest in alchemy, see Frank D. Millard, "An Analysis of the *Epitaphium eiusdem Ducis Gloucestrie*," in Linda Clark, *The Fifteenth Century*, vol. 3, *Authority and Subversion* (Woodbridge: Boydell, 2003), 123–24. The "Statute against Multipliers" was passed in 1403 (5 Henry IV cap. 4). Robert Steele suggests that in the 1440s there was an "alchemical revival" with which Lydgate was associated. He quotes a stanza from London, British Library, MS Harley 2251, which is "virtually a Lydgate anthology" (Pearsall, *John Lydgate* (Charlottesville: University Press of Virginia, 1970), 76), that talks about "metalles transmutaciouns"; in 1456 Henry VI appointed royal commissions to investigate the status of "that most precious medicine . . . the Quintessence [by which] all infirmities whatsoever are easily curable, human life is prolonged to its natural limit, and man wonderfully preserved in health and manly strength of body and mind"; see Steele's discussion in Lydgate and Burgh, *Secrees of Old Philisoffres*, 93–94.

40. See the summary of this argument in Lynn Thorndike, *A History of Magic and Experimental Science*, vol. 4 (New York: Columbia University Press, 1934), 43.

41. Thorndike, *A History of Magic*, 44.

42. Nicholas Oresme, *Le livre du ciel et du monde*, ed. Albert D. Menut and Alexander J. Denomy, trans. Albert D. Menut (Madison: University of Wisconsin Press, 1968), 75.

43. See the discussion in J. J. Conybeare, "Some Account of a Scarse and Curious Alchemical Work by M. Meier," *Annals of Philosophy* 6 (1823): 426–36, at 429.

44. Thorndike, *A History of Magic*, 11.

45. See the summary in William Newman, "Technology and Alchemical Debate in the Middle Ages," *Isis* 80 (1989): 423–45, at 432.

46. Newman, "Technology and Alchemical Debate," 437.

47. See Marguerite Ann Halversen, "'The *Consideration of Quintessence*': An Edition of a Middle English Translation of John of Rupescissa's *Liber de consideratione quintae essentiae omnium rerum* with Introduction, Notes, and Commentary" (Ph.D. diss., Michigan State University, 1998). For a sustained discussion of Chaucer's relationship to alchemy, see Alexander N. Gabrovsky, *Chaucer the Alchemist: Physics, Mutability, and the Medieval Imagination* (New York: Palgrave, 2015).

48. *The Book of Quinte Essence*, ed. F. J. Furnivall (London: EETS, 1866), 1.

49. Lee Patterson, "Perpetual Motion: *Alchemy* and the Technology of the Self," *Studies in the Age of Chaucer* 15 (1993): 25–57, at 35.

50. On the metaphorical and real economies surrounding the Letter, see Lisa H. Cooper, "'His guttys wer out shake': Illness and Indigence in Lydgate's *Letter to Gloucester* and *Fabula duorum mercatorum*," in *Studies in the Age of Chaucer* 30 (2008): 303–34. References to the poem will be from John Lydgate, *The Minor Poems of John Lydgate*, 2 vols.,

ed. Henry Noble MacCracken, Early English Text Society, e.s., 107. and o.s., 192 (London: Oxford University Press, 1911 and 1934), 2:665–67, and cited parenthically by line number.

51. John Metham, *Amoryus and Cleopes*, ed. Stephen Page (Kalamazoo, MI: Medieval Institute Publications, 1999), l. 2195.

52. Michel de Certeau, *The Writing of History*, trans. Tom Conley (New York: Columbia University Press, 1988).

53. Patterson, "Perpetual Motion," 46.

54. Aristotle, *Of Generation and Corruption*, in *The Complete Works The Revised Oxford Translation*, 2 vols., ed. Jonathan Barnes (Princeton, NJ: Princeton University Press, 1985), 336a.

55. *The Book of Quinte Essence*, ed. Frederick J. Furnivall, Early English Text Society, o.s., 16 (Bungay, Suffolk: Richard Clay, 1889), 14.

56. Furnivall, *The Book of Quinte Essence*, 15.

57. See Robert R. Edwards, "John Lydgate and the Remaking of Classical Epic," in *The Oxford History of Classical Reception in English Literature I (800–1558)*, ed. Rita Copeland (Oxford: Oxford University Press, 2016), 470–73.

58. Mary Flannery, *John Lydgate and the Poetics of Fame* (Woodbridge: Boydell, 2012), 115–22.

CHAPTER ELEVEN

1. See Paul Binski, *Medieval Death: Ritual and Representation* (London: British Museum Press, 2001), 33 ff.

2. On the importance to his work of Hoccleve's life as a clerk, see Ethan Knapp, *The Bureaucratic Muse: Thomas Hoccleve and the Literature of Late Medieval England* (University Park: Pennsylvania State University Press, 2001).

3. Philippe Ariès, *Western Attitudes toward Death: From the Middle Ages to the Present*, trans. Patricia M. Ranum (Baltimore, MD: Johns Hopkins University Press, 1974), 51–52.

4. Martin Heidegger, *Being and Time*, trans. Joan Stambaugh (Albany: SUNY Press, 1996), 243. On this passage, see Jacques Derrida, *Aporias*, trans. Thomas Dutoit (Stanford, CA: Stanford University Press, 1993), 64–68. Emmanuel Levinas famously countered that death refers to an "interpersonal order." As he says, "Death approaches in the fear of someone, and hopes in someone." *Totality and Infinity: An Essay on Exteriority*, trans. Alphonso Lingis (Pittsburgh, PA: Dusquesne University Press, 1969), 234.

5. For a thorough representation of *danse macabre* imagery, see Elina Gertsman, *The Dance of Death in the Middle Ages: Image, Text, Performance* (Turnhout: Brepols, 2010).

6. Amy Appleford, *Learning to Die in Medieval London, 1380–1540* (Philadelphia: University of Pennsylvania Press, 2015), 89–101; James Simpson discusses its dismantling in *Reform and Cultural Revolution: The Oxford English Literary History*, vol. 2, *1350–1547* (Oxford: Oxford University Press, 2004).

7. Eamon Duffy, *The Stripping of the Altars: Traditional Religion in England, c. 1400–c. 1580* (New Haven, CT: Yale University Press, 1992), 303.

8. Andrew Marvell, "To His Coy Mistress," in *The Poems of Andrew Marvell*, ed. Nigel Smith (New York: Routledge, 2015), 75–84, line 31. "Lover's discourse" refers, of

course, to Roland Barthes, *A Lover's Discourse: Fragments*, trans. Richard Howard (New York: Hill & Wang, 1978).

9. See Appleford, *Learning to Die.*

10. See Christina von Nolcken, "'O, Why Ne Had Y Lerned for to Die?' *Lerne for to Dye* and the Author's Death in Thomas Hoccleve's *Series*," *Essays in Medieval Studies* 10 (1993): 27–51, at 42–43.

11. See John A. Burrow, "Hoccleve's *Series*: Experience and Books," in *Fifteenth-Century Studies: Recent Essays*, ed. Robert F. Yeager (Hamden: Archon Books, 1984), 259–73, at 273 n. 12.

12. This is the title as it appears in Hoccleve's holograph copies of the text and in Thomas Hoccleve, *"My Compleinte" and Other Poems*, ed. Roger Ellis (Exeter: Exeter University Press, 2001). All citations of this work refer to this edition and will be made parenthetically in the text.

13. Ellis, *"My Compleinte,"* 19; on the manuscripts in general, see 19–22. On the manuscripts of the "Ars," see John Bowers, "Hoccleve's Two Copies of 'Lerne to Dye': Implications for Textual Critics," *Papers of the Bibliographical Society of America* 83 (1989): 437–72. For the fullest discussion of the manuscripts of the series, see David Watt, *The Making of Thomas Hoccleve's Series* (Liverpool: Liverpool University Press, 2013).

14. Geoffrey Chaucer, *The Riverside Chaucer*, ed. Larry Benson (Oxford: Oxford University Press, 1986). All citations of Chaucer refer to this edition and will be made parenthetically in the text.

15. For an extended discussion of prosimetra, see Eleanor Johnson, *Practicing Literary Theory in the Late Middle Ages: Ethics and the Mixed Form in Chaucer, Gower, Usk, and Hoccleve* (Chicago: University of Chicago Press, 2012).

16. For a discussion of the *Regiment* manuscripts, see John Bowers, *Thomas Hoccleve* (Aldershot: Variorum, 1994).

17. As Nicholas Perkins puts it, Hoccleve's "absorption of Chaucerian personae and his explicit conjuration of Chaucer's spirit" are a "'dwelling with' the spectral Chaucerian corpus." "Haunted Hoccleve? *The Regiment of Princes*, the Troilean Intertext, and Conversations with the Dead," *Chaucer Review* 43 (2008): 103–39, at 104.

18. Thomas Hoccleve, *The Regiment of Princes*, ed. Charles R. Blyth (Kalamazoo, MI: Medieval Institute Publications, 1999), 2083–84. All citations of this work refer to this edition and will be made parenthetically within the text.

19. Actually, the universal individual, an "empty singular, merely a passive being-for-another." G. W. F. Hegel, *Phenomenology of Spirit*, trans. A. V. Miller (Oxford: Clarendon Press, 1977), sect. 452, p. 271.

20. For a useful discussion of this image in the context of both Hoccleve's work and the fifteenth-century metaphorics of visuality as knowledge, see Shannon Gayk, *Image, Text and Religious Reform in Fifteenth-Century England* (Cambridge: Cambridge University Press, 2010), 77–82.

21. This addition appears in the version of the "Ars" in the *Series* in Durham, Durham University Library MS Cosin V.iii.9. For a comparison of the two versions of the "Ars," see Bowers, "Hoccleve's Two Copies of 'Lerne to Dye.'"

22. See Jacques Lacan, *The Seminar of Jacques Lacan*, book 7, *The Ethics of Psychoanalysis, 1959–60*, ed. Jacques Alain-Miller, trans. Dennis Porter (New York: Norton,

1992), 270–90. For a brilliant reading of the two deaths in Boccaccio's *Il filostrato*, see George Edmondson, *The Neighboring Text: Chaucer, Boccaccio, Henryson* (Notre Dame, IN: Notre Dame University Press, 2011), 99–111.

23. Ashby Kinch's rich reading of the image of death in one manuscript of the *Series*, Oxford, Bodley Arch Selden Supra 53, highlights the function of epistemological mirroring in the work in general, a "deathbed drama whose ultimate force is reciprocal awareness." Ashby Kinch, *Imago Mortis: Mediating Images of Death in Late Medieval Culture* (Leiden: Brill, 2013) 96.

24. Immanuel Kant, *Critique of the Power of Judgment*, ed. Paul Guyer, trans. Paul Guyer and Eric Matthews (Cambridge: Cambridge University Press, 2000), 105. Geoffrey of Vinsauf, *Poetria nova*, rev. ed., trans. Margaret Nims (Turnhout: Brepols, 2010).

25. For a discussion of this phrase, see my "Irregular Histories: Forgetting Ourselves," *New Literary History* 28 (1997): 161–84.

26. Jacques Le Goff, *The Birth of Purgatory*, trans. Arthur Goldhammer (Chicago: University of Chicago Press, 1984), 275–76.

27. von Nolcken, " 'O, Why Ne Had Y Lerned for to Die?,' " 27.

28. On Klein's "good enough" mothering and object-relations theory, see Melanie Klein, *The Psychoanalysis of Children*, trans. Alix Strachey (New York: Delacorte Press, 1975).

29. Only the second chapter of book 2 concerns itself with the art of dying, and the chapter ends just where Hoccleve's translation stops. Book 2 contains six more chapters after this one, not three. Benjamin Kurtz calculated that Hoccleve translated about 79 percent of Suso's chapter. See Benjamin Kurtz, "The Relation of Occleve's Lerne to Dye to Its Source," *PMLA* 40 (1925): 252–75.

30. von Nolcken, " 'O, Why Ne Had Y Lerned for to Die?,' " 42.

31. Information on dating: J. A. Burrow, *Thomas Hoccleve* (Aldershot, UK: Variorum, 1994). On this passage and its relation to the reprobation of the "sect" of Lollardy, see Paul Strohm, *England's Empty Throne: Usurpation and the Language of Legitimacy, 1399–1422* (New Haven, CT: Yale University Press, 1998), 143–46.

32. For a discussion of the self-reflexive career of the *Series*, see Burrow, "Hoccleve's *Series*."

33. He refers to Isidore ("a lamentacioun / Of a wooful man in a book I sy"; *Compleinte*, 309–10) and Job (*Compleinte*, 400), among others. For Hoccleve's use of Isidore here, see A. G. Rigg, "Hoccleve's *Complaint* and Isidore of Seville," *Speculum* 45 (1970): 564–74.

34. G. W. F. Hegel, *The Science of Logic*, ed. and trans. George Di Giovanni (Cambridge: Cambridge University Press, 2010), 192. Earlier in the *Logic* (109) Hegel refers to bad infinity as a "*finitized* infinite"; emphasis in original.

35. For the importance of "commvnynge" in the *Series*, see Knapp, *The Bureaucratic Muse*, 174–83; and James Simpson, "Madness and Texts: Hoccleve's *Series*," in *Chaucer and Fifteenth-Century Poetry*, ed. Julia Boffey and Janet Cowen (London: King's College London, Centre for Late Antique and Medieval Studies, 1991), 15–29.

36. Knapp, *The Bureaucratic Muse*, 181.

37. On the version of the *Synonyma* used by Hoccleve, see J. A. Burrow, "Hoccleve's *Complaint* and Isidore of Seville Again," *Speculum* 73 (1998): 424–28. Rigg first identified

the longer version of the *Synonyma* as the text Hoccleve borrowed in "Hoccleve's *Complaint* and Isidore of Seville."

38. Each line of this stanza is end-stopped, the formal equivalent of sudden death.

CHAPTER TWELVE

1. John the Blind Audelay, *Poems and Carols*, ed. Susanna Fein (Kalamazoo, MI: Medieval Institute Publications, 2009). All citations of Audelay refer to this edition and will be made parenthetically within the text.

2. Fein has "chist" at the end of line 35, which I have emended here to "care." See my discussion of concatenation below.

3. Martin Heidegger, *Sein und Zeit* (Tübingen: Max Niemeyer Verlag, 2006), 329; trans. Joan Stambaugh as *Being and Time*, rev. Dennis J. Schmidt (Albany: State University of New York Press, 2010), 303.

4. See the introduction.

5. Oxford, Bodleian Library, MS Douce 322, fol. 19v.

6. MS Douce 322, fol. 19v, col. b.

7. Paul Binski, *Medieval Death: Ritual and Representation* (Ithaca, NY: Cornell University Press, 1996), 149. The first part of this sentence rewords Binski's comment that *transi* tombs functioned as "commentaries on pre-existing funerary genres," 149.

8. British Library, MS Arundel 83. The Anglo-Norman poem is an abridgement and dialogization of the popular poem *Dit des trois morts et trois vifs*. For editions of five French versions, see Stefan Glixelli, ed., *Les cinq poèmes des trois morts et des trois vifs* (Paris: Champion, 1914). On the theme of mortality in the de Lisle Psalter, see Kathyrn A. Smith, *Art, Identity and Devotion in Fourteenth-Century England: Three Women and their Books of Hours* (London: British Library, 2003), 62–63, 152–55; and Binski, *Medieval Death*, 135–38. The classic studies of the motif in European art are Willy Rotzler, *Die Begegnung der drei Lebenden und der drei Toten: Ein Beitrag zur Forschung über die mittelalterlichen Vergänglichkeitsdarstellungen* (Winterthur: P. G. Keller, 1961); and Johan Huizinga, *The Autumn of the Middle Ages*, trans. Rodney J. Payton and Ulrich Mammitzsch (Chicago: University of Chicago Press, 1996), 156–72. An indispensable account of the structure of memorial intercession in numerous versions of the legend in the context of late medieval, and specifically Lancastrian, culture is Kinch, *Imago Mortis*, 109–81.

9. de Lisle Psalter, fol. 127. It is conventional to say that Audelay's *Three Dead Kings* is the only surviving Middle English poem on the theme, but I argue here that the de Lisle labels are also a poem.

10. Chris Chism also discusses the de Lisle illustration in connection with the *Three Dead Kings* in her excellent account of the poem, *Alliterative Revivals* (Philadelphia: University of Pennsylvania Press, 2002), 244–45.

11. On this point see Ad Putter, "The Language and Metre of *Pater Noster* and *Three Dead Kings*," *Review of English Studies*, n.s., 55 (2004): 498–526, at 513 n. 68. Putter prefers the term "consonance" because, quoting *The Princeton Encyclopedia of Poetics*, pararhyme is "the repetition in accented syllables of the final consonant sound *without correspondence of the preceding vowel- or consonant sounds*" (514–15; emphasis added). Susanna Fein may have first noticed the formal similarities between the two poems; see

Fein, "The Early Thirteen-Line Stanza: Style and Metrics Reconsidered," *Parergon* 18 (2000): 97–126, at 106. Thorlac Turville-Petre says that *Three Dead Kings* "can claim to be the most ornate in the language" but also that the poet "overloads his stanza with more complicating features than any poet could control with entire success"; Turville-Petre, " 'Summer Sunday,' 'De tribus mortuis,' and 'The Awntyrs off Arthure': Three Poems in the Thirteen-Line Stanza," *Review of English Studies* 25 (1974): 1–14, at 6.

12. These observations apply to the octave of each stanza; the wheel complicates this pattern further. A more detailed description of the poem's form can be found in Turville-Petre, "Three Poems in the Thirteen-Line Stanza," 6; and Putter, "Language and Metre," 511–16.

13. The classic discussion is, of course, Sigmund Freud, "The Uncanny," in *The Standard Edition of the Complete Psychological Works of Sigmund Freud*, vol. 27, trans. James Strachey (London: Hogarth Press, 1955), 219–52.

14. See the struggle for life and death during the lord/bondsman's recognition in G. W. F. Hegel, *The Phenomenology of Spirit*, trans. A. V. Miller (Oxford: Clarendon Press, 1977).

15. I prefer the reading "a napwile," which Ella Keats Whiting, Fein, and Turville-Petre use, to the emendation suggested by Ad Putter to "unto napwile," i.e., until bed-time; see Putter, "Language and Meter." *Lectio difficilior* supports "a napwile," which, as Fein nicely says, represents "life seen as a symbolic day, and passing as if in a dream-like flash of noise and excitement" (Fein, nn. 7–8). In addition to Fein's edition, see John Audelay, *The Poems of John Audelay*, ed. Ella Keats Whiting, Early English Text Society, o.s., 184 (London: Oxford University Press, 1931); and Thorlac Turville-Petre, *Alliterative Poetry of the Later Middle Ages: An Anthology* (Washington, DC: Catholic University of America Press, 1989).

16. Fein, "The Early Thirteen-Line Stanza," 117–18.

17. For an extensive discussion of the intersections of the poem's aestheticism, its commemorative purposes, and the context of memorial art in late medieval England, see Ashby Kinch, *Imago Mortis: Mediating Images of Death in Late Medieval Culture* (Leiden: Brill, 2013), 145–81.

18. Whiting, *The Poems of John Audelay*, xxiii.

19. Jacques Derrida, *Of Spirit: Heidegger and the Question*, trans. Geoffrey Bennington and Rachel Bowlby (Chicago: University of Chicago Press, 1989), 99.

20. For instance, "forestarii prosecuti fuerunt malefactors cum hy et cry usque ad noctis obscuritatem." *Select Pleas of the Forest*, ed. G. J. Turner (London: Selden Society, 1901), 80. The calling off of a chase "propter noctis obscuritatem" is something of a term of art. See *Select Pleas of the Forest*, cxcvi, 22, 28, 56.

21. Sense 3(c) for "clene" in the *Middle English Dictionary* is the most apposite here: "clear of encumbrance or restriction, unrestricted."

22. The *MED* cites examples of "clene" as synonymous with both "voyde" and "bare"; 3(b).

23. In the famous "autobiographical" passage of the C text of *Piers Plowman*, Will (or Langland) mentions that his "fader and his frendes fonden me to scole"; see William Langland, *Piers Plowman: The C Version*, ed. George Kane and George Russell (London: Athlone, 1997), 5.36.

24. Putter, "Language and Meter"; Angus McIntosh, "Some Notes on the Text of the Middle English Poem *De tribus regibus Mortuis*," *Review of English Studies*, n.s., 28 (1977): 385–92; and E. G. Stanley, "The Alliterative *Three Dead Kings* in John Audelay's MS Douce 302," in *My Wil and My Wrytyng: Essays on John the Blind Audelay*, ed. Susanna Fein (Kalamazoo, MI: Medieval Institute Publications, 2009), 249–93.

25. Stanley, "The Alliterative *Three Dead Kings*," 265.

26. Another paronomasia involving earth is possibly the second dead king's warning not to believe the "lare" of the "lykyng of flesche" (112), which Turville-Petre (*Alliterative Poetry of the Late Middle Ages*, 156) first suggested could mean both "teaching" and "earth, filth." But see also Stanley, "The Alliterative *Three Dead Kings*," 265–66. If "lykyng" were amended to "lyinge," the concatenation would be chiastic.

27. The concatenations are interesting in their own right: some use repeated words from the B verse of the last line of the octave, some from the A verse, and some from the penultimate line. Two stanzas (and possibly three, if "fare" in line 87 concatenates with "fars" in line 85) use chiasmus in the concatenation as well. Fein's emendation at line 35 of the MS's "care" to "chist" makes it the only octave and wheel that do not use concatenation (although the MS's "care" does not rhyme). Concatenation is not a typical pattern, as Putter suggests ("Language and Metre," 512). But it is interesting that the two (and possibly three) stanzas that use it are the stanzas containing the speech of the living kings.

28. See Susanna Fein, "Death and the Colophon in the Audelay Manuscript," in *My Wyl and My Wryting: Essays on John the Blind Audelay*, ed. Susanna Fein (Kalamazoo, MI: Medieval Institute Publications, 2009), 294–306; and Fein, "Good Ends in the Audelay Manuscript," *Yearbook of English Studies* 33 (2003): 97–119.

29. The phrase was common on memorial brasses through the fifteenth century. Several examples remain in St. Peter Southgate, Norwich. See Francis Blomefield, *An Essay towards a Topographical History of the County of Norfolk*, vol. 4, *The History of the City and County of Norwich, Part II* (London: William Miller, 1806). A fifteenth-century hand uses the same formula at the end *and* on fol. 144v of Cambridge, Gonville and Caius MS 276 [508], a c. fourteenth-century manuscript of Lombard's *Sentences*.

30. For this succinct definition, see Siegfried Wenzel, ed. and trans., *Fasciculus morum: A Fourteenth-Century Preacher's Handbook* (University Park: Pennsylvania State University Press, 1989), 366. It is likely that the horror of sacrilege echoes the infamous episode in which Audelay's employer killed a parishioner inside a church, and so the crime of sacrilege here is located in the body of the book. See Michael J. Bennett, "John Audelay: Life Records and Heaven's Ladder," in *My Wyl and My Wryting: Essays on John the Blind Audelay*, ed. Susanna Fein (Kalamazoo, MI: Medieval Institute Publications, 2009), 30–37.

31. Fein, "Death and the Colophon in the Audelay Manuscript."

32. Fein, "Good Ends in the Audelay Manuscript," 99. On medieval anthologies in England, see Julia Boffey and J. J. Thompson, "Anthologies and Miscellanies: Production and Choice of Texts," in *Book Production and Publishing in Britain, 1375–1475*, ed. Jeremy Griffiths and Derek Pearsall (Cambridge: Cambridge University Press, 1989), 279–315; and Seth Lerer, "Medieval English Literature and the Idea of the Anthology," *PMLA* 118 (2003): 1251–67.

33. See Fein's comments in her edition at n. 143.

34. Robert Meyer-Lee suggests that the manuscript is the "codicological equivalent of a perpetual chantry chapel" in "The Vatic Penitent: John Audelay's Self-Representation," in *My Wyl and My Wryting: Essays on John the Blind Audelay*, ed. Susanna Fein (Kalamazoo, MI: Medieval Institute Publications, 2009), 54–85, at 67.

35. The poem was widely copied and was translated into Middle English. The Latin poem is edited in Fein's edition; for more on it, see F. J. E. Raby, *A History of Christian-Latin Poetry*, 2nd ed. (Oxford: Clarendon Press, 1953), 434–36. The Middle English poem is edited in Carleton Brown, ed., *Religious Lyrics of the XIVth Century*, rev. G. V. Smithers, 2nd ed. (Oxford: Oxford University Press, 1952), 287 n. 134.

36. See Fein's edition at n. 1.

37. For a discussion of *Mundus deciduus*'s borrowing from Virgil, see Piero Boitani, *Chaucer and the Imaginary World of Fame* (Woodbridge: D. S. Brewer, 1984), 70–71.

38. As Fein says, that Audelay "orchestrated his own departure from the book, *in the manner of a death*, fits perfectly with his conception of the book as being coextensive with his own life and deeds"; "Death and the Colophon in the Audelay Manuscript," 296; emphasis in original.

39. For a survey of these, see Carlton E. Williams, "Mural Paintings of the Three Living and Three Dead in England," *Journal of the British Archaeological Association*, 3rd ser., 7 (1942): 31–40. Fein, "Death and the Colophon," 302 points out that the poem's shift to the past tense leaves Audelay speaking "virtually as if he were one of the Dead in *Three Dead Kings*."

40. Meyer-Lee, "The Vatic Penitent," 68–69.

41. Quoted in Fein, "Good Ends in the Audelay Manuscript," 112.

42. Oliver Pickering, "The Make-Up of *Counsel of Conscience*," in *My Wyl and My Wryting: Essays on John the Blind Audelay*, ed. Susanna Fein (Kalamazoo, MI: Medieval Institute Publications, 2009), 112–37, at 114.

43. See Mariken Teeuwen, *The Vocabulary of Intellectual Life in the Middle Ages* (Turnhout: Brepols, 2003), 32. In *Pearl*, for example, the "kyste" is both a coffin and a chest enclosing the pearl; see the Pearl Poet, *The Complete Works of the Pearl Poet*, ed. Malcolm Andrews, Ronald Waldron, and Clifford Peterson, trans. Casey Finch (Berkeley and Los Angeles: University of California Press, 1993), line 271.

44. See Trevor Aston, "Muniment Rooms and their Fittings in Medieval and Early Modern England," in *Lordship and Learning: Studies in Memory of Trevor Aston*, ed. Ralph Evans (Woodbridge: Boydell, 2004), 235–48, at 240; and Rodney M. Thomson, *The Archives of the Abbey of Bury St. Edmunds* (Woodbridge: Boydell, 1980), 31–32.

INDEX

Page numbers in italics refer to figures.

edy, 108, 114, 191–93, 198; *transi* tomb,
216, 233; wall paintings, 216, 244, 248,
290n39; wills, 196
memory, 116, 148, 171, 174–76, 181, 183–84,
192, 198, 224, 270n14, 279n36; failure
of, 91–92, 116; *memoria* in litanies, 97;
reductio, 196. *See also* forgetting
Merciless Parliament, 277
Meyer, Anne Rafferty, 277n9
Meyer-Lee, Robert, 245, 280n1, 282n31,
290n34
Middleton, Anne, 133, 149, 272n5
minotaur, 111, 115
miracle, 171, 172
Miracula Sancti Erkenwaldi, 173, 177
mirror for princes, 218–19
misrecognition, 84, 86, 93–95, 99, 114, 236,
238, 288n14
mnemotechnics, 181. *See also* memory
modesty topos, 199
Moffat, Douglas, 259n12, 264n27
Montfort, Simon de, execution of, 72–73
moralitas, 78, 105, 128, 222, 228, 232
mortality, 4, 17, 45, 73, 92, 98, 111, 118, 123–
26, 129, 130, 152, 159, 170, 198, 217, 247,
287n8
Morte d'Arthur (Malory), 197
Morte d'Arthur, La (Old French), 197
Mortimer, Nigel, 280n5
mortuary circulation, 91
mortuary rolls, 38–39, 261n39
motion, physics of, 18, 24, 67, 155–59, 166–67,
169
mourning, 4, 29–32, 51, 73, 88, 114, 163, 192,
201, 205
Murray, Hilda, 65, 69

naming: critique of, 69; as division, 38–44, 51;
and place, 50–51, 180; of saints, 49–50;
and soul, 59
necessity, 122–23, 124, 125, 129, 271n38
negation, 59–60, 88–89, 164, 223–24, 227
Newman, William, 283n45
Niger, Roger, 177, 184–85; night, 32, 97–98,
156, 158, 179, 181, 239, 288n20
Nissé, Ruth, 277n1, 282nn29–30
Nohrnberg, James, 271n32
noise, 175, 178–79, 185, 239, 279n29
Nolan, Maura, 280n2, 280n5
Norman Conquest, 29, 49, 258n1, 258n4
Northburgh, Michael de, 176

Novacich, Sarah Elliott, 281n10
Nuttall, Jenni, 281n17

Oakley, Frances, 277n2
occupatio, 107, 124, 127, 128
Ockham, William, 21, 156, 255n23
"Of erþ þou were maked," 69–71
Office of the Dead, 41, 45, 50, 65, 171, 262n43
O'Keeffe, Katherine O'Brien, 264n26
Old English Body and Soul, 36, 41
Old English poetry, 152; and elegy, 29–31; and
ending, 31–34; manuscripts of, 30
Olson, Glending, 269n1
Opheltes, 110
Oresme, Nicholas, 208
Oswald, St., 47, 49
Othello, 96
Ottosen, Knud, 262n43
Ovide moralisé, 144
Oxford Calculators, 18–20, 22, 24, 156–59

pagan, just, 133, 138, 139, 143, 144, 172, 173,
187. *See also* Trajan
Palamon, 111, 115, 116, 120, 125, 128
Palerne, William of, 132
Parlement of the Thre Ages, The, 135
Patterson, Lee, 116, 208–9, 211
Pearl poems, 17; *Cleanness*, 153; *Pearl*, 152–
70, 290n43; *Sir Gawain and the Green
Knight*, 160, 168
Pearsall, Derek, 262n1, 273n23, 280n3
penance, 9, 101, 136, 187, 232, 243
Pentecost, Feast of, 178–80, 279n31
Perkins, Nicholas, 17
Perry, R. D., 272n2
pestilence, 85, 131, 176, 214, 215–16; and
Chaucer 3, 92; and *Pearl*, 160; writing
after, 16–17
Peterborough Chronicle, 30–31, 262n4
Peterson, Clifford, 177
Phillippe de Mézières, 269n6
Piers Plowman. See Langland, William
plague. *See* pestilence
Plato, 181, 279n36
Poet's Repentance, The, 234
Pogue Harrison, Robert, 13
Porphyry, 37–38, 41
prayer, intercessory, 57–58, 142, 171, 196, 199,
206–7, 224, 242, 244, 245
predicamenta, 143–44
Prendergast, Thomas, 201, 280n1

Lightning Source UK Ltd.
Milton Keynes UK
UKHW022128130320
360318UK00003B/6